THE JOHN HARVARD LIBRARY

Bernard Bailyn

Editor-in-Chief

VIEWS OF
SOCIETY AND MANNERS
IN AMERICA

By

FRANCES WRIGHT, D'arusmont

Edited by Paul R. Baker

THE BELKNAP PRESS OF
HARVARD UNIVERSITY PRESS
Cambridge, Massachusetts
1963

CONTENTS

VIEWS OF
SOCIETY AND MANNERS
IN AMERICA

v

INTRODUCTION

Among the passengers debarking in New York on September 3, 1818, from the packet ship *Amity,* just arrived from Liverpool, were two well-dressed, unaccompanied young ladies, who undoubtedly attracted more than an ordinary amount of attention from the many onlookers gathered to watch the excitement of the landing. The sight of these travelers was, in fact, unusual, since unaccompanied females, especially well-dressed and apparently well-to-do young ladies, did not often make the difficult journey to America. Even the local press took notice of their arrival. The older of the two, who was tall, handsome and quite striking in appearance, was, it turned out, a young Scotswoman named Frances Wright, and the other, her sister, Camilla. They had come to make a tour of the United States. And their visit was to have some historical significance, for three years later Frances Wright published an account of her impressions which achieved international popularity and brought her a certain fame. In subsequent years, returning to the United States, which she eventually made her home, she became one of the best-known advocates of radical reform in the country, vigorously urging modification of social institutions and staunchly defending unpopular measures. "So closely, indeed, did she associate herself with the radicalism of the day that for a time 'Fanny Wrightism' and 'radicalism' were very nearly synonymous terms." [1]

Although just twenty-three years old when she arrived in New York, Fanny Wright had already been intensely interested in America for several years. At the age of sixteen or seventeen she had come upon Carlo Botta's history of the American Revolution, and from that moment, she subsequently revealed, her attention had been riveted upon the United States "as on the theatre where man might first awake to the full knowledge and the full exercise of his powers." [2] It was difficult for her at first to discover much about America: in the excitement of the ebb and flow of European events during the Napoleonic era no one around her took much interest in the American scene. For a time, in fact, she could find so little information on the young country across the Atlantic that she feared Botta's history was only a romance; finally an atlas reassured her that the United States actually did exist. This personal discovery of America, she confessed, awoke her to a "new existence," and to visit this country "consecrated to freedom" became "her fixed but secret determination." [3] Later, when she was eighteen, she was given access to the collections of the Glasgow University library, and she then devoted herself wholeheartedly to learn all she could about American history and the character of the American people and to prepare herself for the journey she had resolved to make.

Fanny had been a serious and precocious child. She was born in Dundee, Scotland, on September 6, 1795. Her father, James Wright, the only son of a wealthy Dundee merchant, had attended the University of Dublin. An articulate liberal, he was a member of several learned societies and the correspondent of various well-known men of science and letters, including Adam Smith, but he had fallen under official suspicion when he promoted certain French political and philosophical works and sponsored an inexpensive edition of Paine's *Rights of Man*. Before Fanny was two and one-half years old, both James Wright and his wife died, leaving three children and a substantial inheritance. Fanny was taken to England and raised under the guardianship of a maternal aunt. She disliked the household, however, and, seeking solace in the family library, read voraciously whatever came to hand. Her literary explorations led her especially into history and philosophy and "inspired her with a disgust for frivolous reading, conversation, and occupation" as well as for "every kind of quackery and pretension." [4] In time she developed an acutely sensitive social conscience, as she discovered the plight of the poor and the aged and as she became aware of the sufferings of mankind. An extraordinary vice, she began to feel, had corrupted human relationships.

Upon coming of age, she returned to Scotland to spend her winters in study and writing and her summers in visits to the Scottish Highlands. Her enthusiasm for America was further stimulated when she lodged for a time with Mrs. Rabina Craig Millar, who had spent two years in the United States. By this time Fanny had turned from religious orthodoxy to Epicurean philosophy, and in her nineteenth year she wrote a treatise on Epicurus. When she finally made firm plans for a journey to the United States, she did not reveal her intentions to anyone except Mrs. Millar and Professor James Mylne, her great-uncle, who came to see the two sisters embark on the *Amity* and tried to the very last moment to discourage what he considered a foolhardy adventure. Italy and Greece, Mylne suggested, were far more suitable lands to visit for one who had been given a classical education. But Fanny remained adamant (her sister, Camilla, in this, as in so much else, apparently followed her willingly and unquestioningly), asking in reply if a land inhabited by freemen were not more worthy of time and study than countries now inhabited by slaves. " 'The sight of Italy, dear uncle,' she asserted, 'prostrated under the leaden sceptre of Austria, would break my heart.' "[5]

Fanny Wright had made her decision with characteristic firmness of purpose and could not be deterred. Though still very young, she had prepared herself more thoroughly than the usual Old World visitor by reading everything she could find on America. She was especially stirred by the promise of the principles of the Declaration of Independence. Caught up in the first surge of nineteenth-century reformism, she wanted to see for herself how the new social and political ideas were working out. Quite possibly youthful America might have some significant lessons for elderly Europe.

Her ardor for the young country before she started on her journey was thus considerable—probably too great, as she herself came to realize when she later confessed that her enthusiasm had led her to view America as under a "claud-lorraine tint." Taken as she was by "the great principles laid down in American government," she subsequently admitted that her feelings had been so warmed as to have influenced her perceptions, and that she had in fact sometimes mistaken "the restlessness of commercial enterprise" for "the energy of en-lightened liberty." Only later, on a second visit "and a more minute inspection," was she able "to see things under the sober light of truth, and to estimate both the excellences that are, and those that are yet wanting."[6]

Even so, Fanny Wright's positive response to the United States was not unusual for the time. Most other British travelers coming to America during the first quarter of the nineteenth century, though commonly more sober and taking a somewhat less roseate view, likewise revealed a friendly and sympathetic attitude toward the American people, their customs, and their institutions. Today, when we think of the early nineteenth-century English travelers in America we recall most vividly the acid pages of Dickens, Mrs. Trollope, and Captain Basil Hall; but their responses were in fact more characteristic of a somewhat later period. Only in the second quarter of the century were the British writings on America commonly unfavorable; it is in these later reports of English travelers that ridicule often alternates with disgust and contempt.[7]

Unlike the tours of most travelers of the early years of the century, Fanny Wright's first visit to the United States was not at all hurried. Before returning to England in the middle of May 1820, she and her sister had spent the better part of two years in America and had come to know some parts of the country well. The two women remained in New York City for the winter after their arrival, living with a private family. Through a letter of introduction from

Mrs. Millar, they became acquainted with Charles Wilkes, cashier and later president of the Bank of New York, who took a liking to them, acted as their financial adviser, and introduced them into New York society. The young ladies' days and evenings were filled with activity, and, ever alert, Fanny made the most of her new friends, probing, inquiring, and observing, especially to see how the new principles of free institutions were working out in practice.

During the first winter she became involved, as well, in producing a play which she had written a few years previously. *Altorf* was a tragedy on the theme of the Swiss struggle for liberty against Austria in the early fourteenth century. Although performed in New York for only three evenings, the play was well received, and the authorship, not at first acknowledged, was soon made known. When the play was later published, Thomas Jefferson read it and sent Fanny a note expressing his pleasure in the work and his high respect for the author.[8]

In the spring of 1819, Fanny and Camilla Wright began to tour the northern and eastern states. Fanny's interest in and sympathy for the country opened the hearts of the Americans they met, and they were welcomed everywhere by people from all social levels. In western New York state they had a taste of the frontier wilderness; they saw something of Canada and were impressed by the differences in the character of the Canadian and American people; they stopped to visit several battle sites of the recent war; they enjoyed the open-hearted hospitality of Philadelphia and of the new national capital; and in Virginia they received a brief introduction to the South.

To her old friend Mrs. Millar in Scotland, Fanny sent a steady stream of letters, describing her tour and commenting on society and manners in America. Later, back in England and aroused by "the general and absolute ignorance" concerning America, Fanny felt a need to awaken European reformers "to the great principles laid down in American government." [9] With this end in view, she decided to publish as a book some of the letters she had written to Mrs. Millar from the United States. She slightly revised her original correspondence, and twenty eight of these letters formed the chapters of her work, which she appropriately entitled *Views of Society and Manners in America.*

Published first in 1821 in London and New York, and followed later by other English and American as well as Dutch and French editions, the volume was resoundingly attacked by English conservatives but warmly welcomed by English and Continental liberals, who found in the sympathetic treatment of America confirmation of some of their own political views. These published travel letters, the author later wrote, "changed the tone, and somewhat corrected the views, of the leading British periodicals, while they revived, on the European continent, old reminiscences of the country of Franklin and Washington, and a new ardor in the cause of religious and political liberty." [10]

In this correspondence Fanny Wright was strikingly articulate on the theme that a new society with a new culture had been formed in the United States —that it was not just an unsatisfying reproduction of the Old World. Taken together, the New World environment and the new political and social ideas, especially as set forth in the Declaration of Independence, had brought forth something completely different from what Europeans had known before. Visitors from the Old World had to expect that many of their traditional practices and institutions were irrelevant to this new culture.

The letters revealed, too, a significant interest in national character. Some of the most interesting passages concerned influences forming the American character—the respect accorded to the individual and what this meant for conventional European ideas of class position; the absence of poverty and oppression and the importance of the plenitude of natural resources; the widespread system of education, which made it possible for the citizens to rule themselves wisely; the strong identification of the people with their government. The result was a people perhaps overly proud, yet intelligent, shrewd, enterprising and inventive, hardworking, optimistic, responsible and independent, and blessed with good morals and common sense. These people had established new social and political institutions based on their new political ideas and their new system of government. These institutions would in turn mold character and so shape the future. The course of the future in America, indeed, could not be calculated from the experience of the past, for it was in the hands of the citizens themselves, who were being educated to free and rational action. Here men were able to think and act for themselves and in so doing were able to live fuller lives. America, as she indicated, seemed to her Utopia realized.

For the critical reader today the picture of American society and of American history Fanny Wright drew in her letters is sometimes difficult or impossible to accept, distorted as it frequently was by her prejudices and enthusiasms. Her view, for example, of the unanimity of sentiment during the Revolutionary War certainly is not an interpretation that the historian today could agree with. Nor was all so idyllic in the spotless cities and smiling countryside of the East, which she so often viewed through the distorting lens of classical imagery. Nor can one really accept the idea that the American people were all possessed of the high degree of political intelligence she attributed to them. Her strictures on the Federalist Party were considered inaccurate and unfair by contemporary American reviewers, who also pointed out various mis-statements of fact. The whole book, in truth, stated the *North American Review,* could better serve "as the model, toward which [the citizen] should strive to bring his country, rather than as a tablet of actual perfections."[11] One might criticize the author, further, for devoting too much space to the details of organization of certain governmental bodies rather than to the actual workings of these institutions, something that is often left vague. And finally, many passages in the letters seem false stylistically to the contemporary reader; the historical passages particularly tend to be florid, sentimental, and uncritical.

The publication of *Views of Society and Manners in America* was a central event and turning point in Fanny Wright's life. The book brought her new acquaintances and, through one new friend in particular, led to her return to the United States and saw her established in her life's work as a social reformer. The most interesting and historically most significant aspects of her career, then, came during the years after her first tour of the United States and the publication of this volume. But this book, as much as anything else, elevated her to fame and to a place in the history of her times.

The first important new acquaintance arising from the American letters was Jeremy Bentham, who, after reading the book, sought out the young author and invited her to his London home. Here Fanny spent considerable time during the next few years and through Bentham came to know some of the leading British "philosophical radicals"—James Mill, Francis Place, John Austin, George Grote, and John Cartwright. Though she did not turn to utilitarianism, the outspoken anticlericalism, free thought, and liberal political views of this group helped form her own social thought.[12] At this time, in 1822, she published her Epicurean tract, *A Few Days in Athens,* which she dedicated to Bentham.

The second and more important new friendship was with the Marquis de Lafayette, who was so pleased by the young Scotswoman's ardor for America and its political ideals that he wrote to congratulate her and expressed his desire to make her acquaintance. In September 1821, she journeyed to France to meet the famous general. He welcomed her warmly and revealed that the passages in her published letters on the American Revolution had made him " 'live those days over again.' "[13] Sharing a common enthusiasm for the American people and American institutions, the elderly French widower and the youthful Scotswoman began to see one another frequently, and for the next three years Fanny's life became closely involved with Lafayette's. She made long visits to his estate, La Grange; one of her stays there lasted six months. She commenced a biography of her host, and she closely followed the liberal movements in which the general was involved. The affection of the two was undoubtedly genuine, and Fanny, who had been left an orphan when little more than an infant, even proposed that Lafayette adopt her as his legal daughter. As might have been anticipated, Lafayette's family opposed this suggestion. It seemed to them that the old paterfamilias was taking a somewhat more than fatherly interest in this young woman, a view perhaps supported by his frequent expressions of endearment, such as an epistolary reference to her as *"'ma bien aimée, adorée Fanny, la tendre fille de mon choix.'"* [14]

Defeated in the 1824 election to the Chamber of Deputies, discredited for his role in the *Carbonari* conspiracies, and finding himself in financial straits as well, Lafayette decided at this time to accept an invitation to visit the United States; Fanny immediately suggested that she and her sister join him on his triumphal tour. The family raised objections, and, though they later reversed their stand and urged the sisters to go with him, their opposition kept the two young ladies from procuring passage on the same vessel as Lafayette. And so, following the general back to the New World, they arrived in New York in September 1824. Through her book on the United States, Fanny had already acquired a certain literary fame in America; now on her second visit, she would attain fame and notoriety of other sorts.

Lafayette had arranged to have his public reception in New York postponed so that Fanny and Camilla could be present, and they were with the Frenchman, too, when he made triumphal visits to Albany, Philadelphia, Baltimore, and Washington. They joined Lafayette when he spent several days with Jefferson at Monticello. As spectators in the gallery, they watched Lafayette's formal reception by the Senate of the United States. Later, to meet him in New Orleans, they crossed the Alleghenies, first visiting the Rappite communities at Economy, Pennsylvania, and Harmonie (New Harmony), Indiana, and an English settlement at Albion, Illinois, founded by George Flower and Morris Birkbeck, and then voyaged down the Mississippi River. For many Americans the spectacle of the conspicuous Miss Wright either accompanying or following closely after the world-famous Frenchman seemed most unusual and rather improper; gossipmongers had a splendid time. Eventually, toward the end of the general's tour, the visitors parted company, for the two young ladies had decided to remain in the United States.

Other interests had apparently become more important to Fanny than an elderly Frenchman who shared her love for America. Visiting the deep South on this tour, she had come upon the Negro problem face to face and had begun to develop an interest in programs of gradual emancipation. On this second trip, too, she had discovered communitarianism in the two Rappite towns and saw in this device a means of social reform, though she disliked the anti-intellectualism and the religious basis of the communities. She had, as well, become acquainted with several influential political figures, including Jefferson, Madison, John Quincy Adams, and Jackson, with whom she had discussed American social problems. This second visit, significantly, had led her to moderate considerably her earlier enthusiasm for America, as she became acquainted with some of the social evils and abuses of the new nation. Even so, though far more critical of American life, she still remained convinced that in this country were "enshrined all the liberties and all the hopes of the human race." [15]

The treatment of the Negro, Fanny Wright realized, was the great conspicuous failure of American society. On her tour of the South she visited plantations and talked with slaveowners; she discovered that many Southerners deplored the evil but that no one could suggest a practical solution. She quickly saw that merely freeing and enfranchising the Negroes would not work, for in large part they were in no position to participate in a free society. Only after the Negroes had been given some education and trained to support themselves could their freedom be meaningful. Such a program would be expensive, for not only would there be the costs of education and training, but in addition the slaveowners would have to be compensated for their losses. In the long run, the racial problem, she believed at this time, could only be solved by completely eliminating the colored population through a program of colonization.

She embodied her ideas in a plan she published in 1825. Excited by the thought of gradual emancipation and the idea of cooperative labor, she envisioned an experimental community in the South to which slaves would be brought and where, over a period of years, they would be trained for a vocation while working out the cost of their purchase, their keep, and their eventual colonization abroad. The unit of labor would be the Negro family, so that children would not be separated from their parents.

Later that year, aided by the Englishman George Flower, she purchased some 2,000 acres of land for her new settlement of Nashoba in western Tennessee, along the Wolf River, fourteen miles from Memphis. Two white men—James Richardson, a Scotsman living in Memphis, and Richeson Whitby, a former New Harmony resident—came to help direct the project, and a dozen or so slaves were soon acquired. In a short time two double cabins were erected, and fruit trees, vegetables, grain, and cotton were planted. But setting up such a community in the wilderness was hard work, especially since the land was poor and the climate unhealthful. Fanny Wright shortly became incapacitated from overwork and malarial fever. Obliged to go elsewhere to recover her health, she revisited the New Harmony community, which had by this time passed from the sectarian Rappites to the control of the English manufacturer and philanthropist Robert Owen; here, during the summer of 1826, she investigated the new experiments in communal organization. In the spring of 1827, after another short stay at Nashoba, she returned to Europe with young Robert Dale Owen, leaving Richardson, Whitby, and her sister Camilla in charge.

But in the meantime, by a deed of trust signed in December 1826, she had reorganized Nashoba, conveying the property to a board of ten trustees, including Robert Owen and Lafayette. Although the community still aimed to prepare slaves for their freedom, the emphasis was now placed on cooperative communitarianism for both free Negroes and whites. In the reorganized community, modeled upon New Harmony, all members, except those paying a special fee, shared in the labor. There were to be no connections whatsoever with religion, free schooling was to be provided to all children, and the sick and the aged were to be cared for by the community at large. In this reorganization one can see a move toward Fanny Wright's new interests of general social and moral regeneration. American society now seemed to her far less perfect than it had appeared a decade before. This cooperative community, she hoped, would be a pilot project for the reform of American society.

Soon after her departure, however, Nashoba ran into trouble. Indifferent to contemporary American mores, James Richardson, resident trustee and manager, began to live with one of the colored women, and to make matters worse he chose to publicize his action, indicating that at Nashoba sexual liaisons were to be encouraged in cases where both parties gave their unrestrained and unconstrained approval. Although Fanny Wright herself later declared that virtue did not consist "in crucifying the affections and appetites," [16] she wrote at once from France pleading for circumspection. But caution was thrown to the winds, and the quiet and proper Camilla took this inopportune moment to reveal her own disapproval of the marriage tie as irrational and pernicious, though a few months later she herself was legally married to Whitby. Such an experiment of apparent "free love" in the southwestern wilds was too extreme for the American public, and criticism was loud and heated concerning this "one great brothel," which seemingly had cast aside family ties, eliminated the bonds of religion, and looked to the amalgamation of the two races.[17]

In February 1828, when Fanny Wright returned to Tennessee, Nashoba was in grave difficulty. The land had been badly cultivated and the crops were poor; little had been done for the Negroes. Frances Trollope, who had accompanied Fanny back to the United States, was shocked by what she found there. "Desolation," Mrs. Trollope reported, "was the only feeling—the only word that presented itself." [18] The discomforts and the primitive living arrangements were scarcely what Mrs. Trollope had expected from the enthusiastic descriptions of her traveling companion, and after ten days she left for Cincinnati, where she would spend two years gathering impressions for her bitter portrait of America.

Once again the community was reorganized, and the self-emancipation of slaves and active communitarianism were abandoned. Henceforth, only those persons who had the funds necessary to support themselves were to be allowed to participate, and emphasis was to be placed on training schools which would prepare the children for the cooperative way of living to be instituted sometime in the future. Free Negroes were to be admitted, and miscegenation was to be encouraged. But in the meantime Fanny Wright had acquired new interests to the north, and in June 1828, she again departed for New Harmony leaving a resident manager in charge of Nashoba. Finally, in 1830, she acknowledged the failure of her dream of solving the Negro problem. She returned to Nashoba to take her slaves to Haiti, where they were given freedom and asylum. An unfortunate location, public hostility, and confusion in the aims of the community all contributed to the failure of Nashoba; but perhaps as much as anything else, lack of attention to the practical everyday details of organization and administration was responsible.

In Indiana, Fanny Wright purchased half interest in the *New-Harmony Gazette,* in which she promptly inaugurated an all-out attack on American missionary and tract societies, on the resurgent religious revivalism, and on church activity in politics. Renamed the *New Harmony and Nashoba Gazette or Free Enquirer,* the journal aimed at "free, unbiassed, and universal enquiry" in order "to aid in the diffusion of truth, in the spread of liberal principles, and in the dissipation of those prejudices which observation and experience may designate as obstacles in the progressive march of the world from error and suffering toward wisdom and enjoyment." [19] In 1829, Fanny Wright moved to New York City, to which she transferred the journal. Renamed the *Free Enquirer,* it soon became one of the leading free-thought outlets in the country, bringing to public attention not only questions of theology but also of women's rights, educational reforms, and capital punishment and imprisonment for debt. In New York City, she also purchased a former Baptist church for free-thought activities, calling it the Hall of Science; here, besides attending

lectures and debates, those interested could read and discuss the works of
Paine and Voltaire or even participate in gymnastics classes.

During the same period Fanny Wright took to the public lecture platform,
first at Cincinnati and other towns of the Ohio and Mississippi valleys and
later in the major eastern cities. With a rich, contralto voice, a commanding
presence, and a passionate commitment to her radical ideas, she made a striking
impression. Her lectures were always crowded, though sometimes the audience
included hostile critics who attempted to disrupt the meetings by shouting,
turning off the gas lighting, or setting fires. For a woman to lecture in public
was almost unheard of at this time. The press joined the clergy in attacking
her as "the great Red Harlot of Infidelity" and the "whore of Babylon." All
in all, concluded Mrs. Trollope, she made an impression "unlike any thing
I had ever seen before, or ever expect to see again." [20] Not only in her ideas,
but also in her public conduct, Fanny Wright was clearly rejecting much that
Americans held sacred. At many public appearances she needed the protection
of a bodyguard.

Underlying Fanny Wright's mature social thought as set forth in her lectures
of the late 1820's was a materialist view of knowledge. True happiness, she felt,
could only be based on exact knowledge, and such knowledge, in turn, could
only be derived from accurate sense impressions. Exact knowledge was limited
to the field of nature and natural existence, and had to be distinguished from
belief, which concerned matters that were not ascertainable. Too long had men
suffered from the pronouncements of dubious "authorities"; too long had irrational institutions derived from irrelevant past conditions dominated men's
lives. Verified and verifiable knowledge could only be ascertained by a free
spirit of inquiry and investigation and to develop this attitude all men and
women, regardless of their background to be provided with proper educational opportunities. A democracy only be effective if public opinion
were enlightened.

Fanny Wright's social criticism centered few major problems for which
she suggested reforms that would, she believed, promote rationality and enlightenment in men's dealings with one another. Religion, and more specifically
theology, against which she came to direct her heaviest attack, was the principal
evil. Concentrating on things unseen that men could never truly know, religion,
she concluded, promoted errors and a way of thinking completely antagonistic
to the positive and verifiable type of knowledge she saw as necessary to improve
man's lot. The clergy in the United States, moreover, seemed to be attempting
to expand its power by moving into the political arena as well as by playing on

fear and ignorance through religious revivals. The power and the influence of the clergy had to be curbed.

A second problem concerned the status of women in American society. Although on her first visit, she had considered the position of American women to be particularly fortunate, she eventually came to feel that anachronistic legal precedents and popular prejudices had made it impossible for American women to develop their talents properly. Women ought to have access to greater educational opportunity so that they could cease being at the mercy of superstition and quackery; they should have control over their own property; they must be able to break an unsatisfactory marital tie; and they had to be freed of unnatural restraints and be able to enter into sexual relations with all the freedom of men. Birth control practices must be encouraged so that the family size could be restricted if this were necessary. Until women assumed a place in society equal to that of men, human improvement could come but slowly.

The condition of the workingman presented another major problem. Manual labor was the basic source of all wealth, yet workers seldom received a fair share of their own labor. Too often American businessmen strove solely for their own enrichment without realizing the effects of their actions on others. Men had to be made to see the social consequences of their behavior.

The major hope for social betterment lay in education, and to the philosophy of education and to schemes for educational change Fanny Wright devoted many of her lectures and much of her writing. Basic to her social thought was a plea for a national, "rational," republican, free system of education, under state control and available to all children, a system that would encourage both mental and physical development, and stress practical and scientific training. According to her plan, children of both sexes would be taken from their parents and placed under the guardianship of the state at the age of two years. Not only would the parents of students as well as real property be taxed to support the system, but also the older pupils themselves would work for the benefit of the school. Such education could indeed bring about "the salvation and regeneration of human kind." [21]

Her faith in the power of man to improve his condition seemed almost limitless. "Whenever he hath closely observed, accurately calculated, boldly designed, and obstinately persevered, he hath triumphed—triumphed over every obstacle, executed every project, attained every ambition." [22] But men had to see that cooperative effort was necessary to make over their society. As individuals working by themselves, men were weak; as collective humanity, they were strong: to persuade men to work together became a leading aim of her social thought. The process, she realized, would take many generations, and a great deal remained yet to be discovered as to how men and women could best be taught to work toward setting up a social system based on sound knowledge that reconciled liberty and equality and promoted general prosperity, individual virtue, and universal happiness.

Fanny Wright's lectures of the late 1820's not only brought her to the fore in the free-thought movement but soon involved her as well in the new Working Men's Party. Hard times had led to a bitter sense of grievance among many workers, and the *Free Enquirer* vigorously supported the laborers' demands for humanitarian reforms, greater opportunity, and better education, and attacked the banking system and the professional aristocracy of lawyers, politicians, and clergymen whom it saw preying on the common man. So completely did she become identified with this movement, in fact, that the Working Men's candidates became popularly known as "the Fanny Wright ticket." Apparently believing that this identification would hurt the party in the local elections of 1830, Fanny and Camilla again departed from the United States, arriving in France just as the July Revolution broke out.

The following year Camilla Wright died in Paris, and a few months after her death, in July 1831, Fanny was married in that same city to Guillaume Sylvan Casimir Phiquepal D'Arusmont, a Frenchman sixteen years her senior. D'Arusmont, whom Robert Dale Owen characterized as "an unwise, hasty, fanciful counselor, and ultimately a suspicious and headstrong man," was also a social reformer, though on a much more limited scale than his wife.[23] After training in medicine, he had turned to educational theory and practice and had become a follower of Pestalozzi. In his Paris home he had established an experimental school, financed by William Maclure, a wealthy Philadelphia merchant. When the Bourbon authorities became suspicious and closed the school, D'Arusmont had transferred his experiment to Philadelphia. From there, in 1825, he had followed Maclure to New Harmony, where he had set up his School of Industry, bringing with him three French boys whose education he had been supervising. His educational ideas involved "learning by doing," and his "boys" had actually printed the journal which Fanny Wright edited first in New Harmony and later in New York.

The marriage was not a success. D'Arusmont objected to his wife's return to public lecturing, and they quarreled over Fanny's money and over their daughter's education. Frequent separations drew them further apart. Orestes Brownson, who had come to know Fanny well, felt that her marriage marked a turning point in her life, for afterwards "her charm was broken, and her strength departed." [24] Eventually the marriage was dissolved by divorce.

Fanny Wright spent her last years largely in the United States. Returning to

America in 1835, after an absence of five years, she again took to the lecture platform, a convincing supporter of President Jackson. She attacked the Second Bank of the United States as a public menace which tended to concentrate wealth and power and bound the United States to the money power of England. She supported Jackson's Specie Circular and she later defended the Independent Treasury system. Her suggestions for gradual emancipation and colonization of the slaves and eventual assimilation of the free Negroes continued to arouse considerable opposition, and her public appearances again provoked demonstrations and sometimes violence. In these same years, she formulated a philosophical interpretation of history, envisioning a final change, sometime in the future, to a social organization having communal ownership of all real property. After four more visits to Europe, she spent her remaining years in Cincinnati, very much alone, a figure of the past. A broken hip caused by a fall on the ice incapacitated her for almost a year, and she died in Cincinnati on December 13, 1852.

A strong, commanding person of great conviction, honesty, and passion, often imprudent and sometimes overly inflexible in her beliefs, Fanny Wright stands forth as one of the most important women in American history. But she was also something more. For her pioneering work with the Negro, attempting to solve the slavery problem through gradual emancipation; for her experiment in communitarianism, in establishing a pilot project for general social reform; for her continued advocacy of universal, free, practical education for children of both sexes; for her efforts to help the American workingman better his condition; for her work in women's rights, including her ideas on legal equality for women, protection of their property rights, more liberal marriage laws, and birth control, and for the example of a "liberated woman" that she herself set; for her attacks on imprisonment for debt and capital punishment—for her many writings and her diverse activities, Frances Wright holds a secure position as one of the leading American social reformers of the first half of the nineteenth century.

The *Views of Society and Manners in America* comes early in Fanny Wright's career, some years before her social thought was fully developed or her real career as social reformer had begun. Many of the ideas set forth in these travel letters, nonetheless, clearly foreshadow her later concerns and her more mature social thought. More important, the book is significant for the discussion of the character of the American people, their social institutions, and their political beliefs, and of the interrelations of character, institutions, and ideals, and, in this discussion, for the revelations of a liberal, humanitarian mind, formed in the eighteenth-century Enlightenment and becoming acquainted and attempting to deal with the new nineteenth-century democratic world. The value of this volume, therefore, comes as much in its revelations of Fanny Wright herself and what she represents as in the information it gives concerning American society. Though frequently the starry-eyed enthusiast, young Fanny Wright was able to communicate to her many readers her excitement in the United States as a bold new experiment which could have meaning for all men. As the first major work of this social figure, as a revealing discussion of nineteenth-century American character, manners, institutions, and thought, and as one of the outstanding liberal accounts of the United States in the early national period, this book has a significant place in American social history.

Paul R. Baker, 1963

A Note on the Text

The text of *Views of Society and Manners in America* used in the present
edition is that of the first London edition of 1821. The wording of that edition
has been preserved, but minor changes in punctuation and capitalization have
been made throughout, and varying spellings of proper names and irregulari-
ties in publication titles have been adjusted. The italics of the original prose
have been retained where the author clearly used them for emphasis; where
they were used as typographical mechanics, they have been converted to modern forms.

Quotations and paraphrases present special problems since Fanny Wright's
age had little concern for perfect accuracy in such matters. They are both repro-
duced in the present edition as they appeared in the original despite the deviations from the source they may contain. Significant deviations, however, are
described in the editorial notes. Paraphrases appear in quotation marks rather
than in italics as in the original edition.

The present editor's notes are numbered consecutively within each chapter
and have been placed at the end of the author's text. Fanny Wright's footnotes
remain as in the original publication, indicated by asterisks and daggers.

VIEWS

OF

SOCIETY AND MANNERS

IN

AMERICA;

IN

A SERIES OF LETTERS FROM THAT COUNTRY

TO A FRIEND IN ENGLAND,

DURING THE YEARS 1818, 1819, AND 1820.

By AN ENGLISHWOMAN.

But mark the judgment of experienced Time,
Tutor of Nations!   AKENSIDE.

LONDON:

PRINTED FOR

LONGMAN, HURST, REES, ORME, AND BROWN,

PATERNOSTER-ROW.

1821.

[Transcript of the original title page]

TO

CHARLES WILKES, Esq.[1]

OF NEW YORK.

MY DEAR SIR,

Although I am uncertain how far the sentiments contained in this little volume may be in unison with yours, I cannot resist that impulse of the heart which induces me to inscribe its pages to you.

Viewing, as I did, your adopted country with the eyes of a foreigner, I may have been sometimes hasty, and, therefore, mistaken in my judgments. Though I do not apprehend that my inaccuracies can extend to facts of any importance, it is possible that a citizen of America may detect slight errors which the foreign reader cannot be aware of, and which the author herself could not wholly guard against, however authentic the sources whence she drew her information.

Where, in the following letters, I may have expressed opinions at variance with yours, I am persuaded that you will view them with candor; and that, notwithstanding the defects you may find in this little work, you will pardon my seizing this opportunity of openly expressing the high respect I feel for your character, and my grateful remembrance of the many proofs of friendship with which you have honored me.

Permit me to subscribe myself,
My dear Sir,
Most respectfully and
Affectionately, yours,

THE AUTHOR.

London, 20th April, 1821.

ADVERTISEMENT.

The following letters form only a part of a more extensive and desultory correspondence: occasional allusions will, therefore, be found to letters that have been suppressed, as interesting only to the friend to whom they were written.

LETTER I.

Voyage. Iceberg. Ship's Crew. Bay of New York. Arrival in the City.

New York, September 1818.

My Dear Friend,[1]

The report of our safety, as well as of the kind welcome with which we were greeted on landing, by several families in this city, is now, I trust, far on its way towards you. I wrote too rapidly and with a head too giddy (you know what sort of a head one brings out of a ship) to enter into much detail upon the few and dull events of our voyage. We saw spouting whales, and sharks, and porpoises, and all sea monsters in plenty; for the breezes were mild, and the ocean and heaven so fair and smiling, as might well woo all the hideous tribes of Tethys[2] from their dark caverns. But the only sight worth noticing was a large iceberg, in latitude 43, towards the most southern extremity of the Newfoundland Bank. This, for the month of August, was an unusual object in such a latitude; nor shall I easily forget the moment of singular excitement which it occasioned to the captain of the vessel, myself, and another passenger. Light northeasterly winds had prevailed throughout the day, so light, indeed, that the island, which had first been descried in the direct line of our course an hour after noon, lay but some ten miles astern of us an hour after sunset. We were leaning over one of the hatchways in careless conversation, and the eyes of the captain were cast accidentally upon the iceberg, which now (the short twilight having died away) appeared a black three-pointed rock upon the clear blue of the horizon. A sudden exclamation from Captain Staunton caused me and my fellow passenger to start on our feet and gaze as he directed. A bright flame blazed upon the highest point of the distant rock. None of us spoke; we all held our breath, and each wrought out for himself, after his own manner, some tale of hideous calamity and suffering. "A few beings, or it might be, one solitary wretch, had here survived his companions, and clung to this isle of frost, to expire more slowly under the united horrors of cold, hunger, and despair. A pile had been here collected from the disjointed planks of the foundered vessel, which was now kindled, when the first shades of evening afforded a hope

5

that some eye from the receding vessel would catch the signal." All this passed through our minds at one glance of thought. The captain had turned quickly to give orders for tacking about and lowering a boat that should put off to the rock, when suddenly a bright star peered above the crystal and hung distinct and clear over the distant pinnacle, which still, for a while, quivered beneath its receding rays. It was some minutes before we could smile at this sudden and simple explanation of an appearance, which had a moment before so highly wrought up our interest and curiosity.

It is usual to complain much of the discomforts of a ship, and I grant that they are numerous, but to those who are not disabled by sickness or nervous fears, I think a voyage is not without its pleasures and certainly not without interest. Our fellow passengers, mostly Americans, were cheerful, obliging, and conversable, the ship excellent, her captain a weather-beaten veteran, a kind-hearted as well as experienced sailor, who looked not merely after the safety of his ship but the comfort of every living being on board of her. A moralizer might have apostrophized capricious fortune, when he heard this old seaman recount the many times he had ploughed the Atlantic, and thank God that he had weathered every gale, without ever losing (to use the sailor's phrase) a single spar. I have conversed with sailors not half the age of this good captain of the *Amity,* who had never made a voyage *without* losing a spar, and holding their lives in jeopardy into the bargain. But is it not thus on the varied sea of life? Some adventurers set forth in youth and hope, and brave gales and storms, and scud by rocks and shallows with light and easy hearts, and moor at last peacefully in the haven of old age, wrinkled indeed by time, but unscathed by misfortune; while others, blown about at the mercy of the elements, their helm broken and their rigging torn, run foul of every quicksand and die a thousand deaths ere they die at last.

I observed much and often upon the quietness as well as the matchless activity of the crew. No scolding on the part of the captain, or sulky looks on that of the men. By the former, authority was exercised with kindness, and (a sure consequence of this) obedience was by the latter yielded with good humour and alertness. The ship indeed was well named the *Amity,* for I never heard a dispute on board her, save on one night, when I was the unwilling auditor of a dispute in the adjoining cabin, which gradually waxed to a wrangle, between a young Scotchman, firm in the belief of grace and predestination, an older Englishman, as firm in the nonbelief of both articles, and an American, who, without agreeing with either, seemed to keep the peace between both. In this good office he probably succeeded, as in the middle of a nicely drawn distinction on the part of the Englishman between foreknowing and foredecreeing I fell asleep, and waked to no other noise than the creaking of timber and lashing of the waves.

It is worthy of remark that every man of the crew, from the old veteran to the young sailor boy, could read and write, and, I believe, I might almost say *every* man could converse with you upon the history of his country, its laws, its present condition, and its future prospects. When our ship lay sleeping on the waters in a lazy calm, I often whiled away an hour in conversing with one or other of these sons of Neptune, as he sat piecing a torn sail or mending a rope, and I am sure that I never came from the conversation without having gained some useful information, or without having conceived a higher idea of the country to which the man whom I had conversed with belonged.

To one who has only viewed the great deep in contemplative ease and security from its shores, there is something pleasingly exciting in being borne triumphantly over its bosom, and in witnessing how the wonderful creature man struggles with the elements, holding on his adventurous course for days and weeks without doubt or fear, marking his progress over the trackless waste with unerring certainty, and directing his eye yet more steadily to the far-distant port than points his guiding needle to the pole. Forgive me the idle observation that I never fully appreciated the perseverance as well as the adventure of the daring Columbus, until I found myself watching the sun sink and rise, in and from the eternal waters, day after day, and week after week. How extraordinary was the mind which could calculate with such certainty upon the existence of an unknown world! How daring the spirit which could throw itself upon the mercy of a furious and unexplored ocean, hitherto deemed impassable and interminable! How perfect the self-possession which remained unshaken, not merely amid the strife of the elements, but the warring passions —the alternate rage, and fear, and despair of the ignorant and superstitious crew, who formed an united host to whom he was singly opposed. But what a man! Alone supported by his own powerful mind amidst the perils of the deep, the horrors of a mutiny, and the heartsickness produced by hope delayed, when sun after sun discovered the same watery waste—the same unchanging horizon of sky and sea; when night after night bred thoughts, more and more anxious, and danger still more imminent, the apprehension of which it had been defeat or death to betray! How much the human race is indebted to this great mind is still perhaps unknown. The world which a hero discovered and which bigots and robbers for a season polluted with crimes has also been the refuge of the poor and the persecuted of every tongue and every clime, and now exhibits, in its northern section, a well-organized nation in all the vigor and pride of youth and freedom; in its southern, a spirited people awaking from ignorance and resenting oppression, asserting their rights as men and citizens, and laying the foundation of commonwealths, which the next generation may see established in power, rich in resources, enlightened with knowledge, and fenced by the bulwarks of just laws, wise institutions, and generous patriotisms, against the efforts of foreign enemies or the machinations of domestic traitors.

It was not without emotion that, on the evening of the 30th day from that on which we had cleared out of the Mersey, we heard the cry of "Land," and, straining our eyes in the direction of the setting sun, saw the heights of Neversink slowly rise from the waters opposing a black screen to the crimson glories of the evening sky.

You will but too well remember the striking position of New York to require that I should describe it. The magnificent bay, whose broad and silver waters, sprinkled with islands, are so finely closed by the heights of the Narrows, which, jutting forward with a fine sweeping bend, gave a circular form to the immense basin which receives the waters of the Hudson—this magnificent bay is grand and beautiful as when you admired it some twenty years since; only that it is perhaps more thickly studded with silver-winged vessels, from the light sharp-keeled boat through all the varieties of shape and size, to the proud three-masted ship, setting and lowering its sails to or from the thousand ports of distant Europe or yet more distant Asia.

Everything in the neighbourhood of this city exhibits the appearance of life and cheerfulness. The purity of the air, the brilliancy of the unspotted heavens, the crowd of moving vessels, shooting in various directions, up and down and across the bay and the far-stretching Hudson, and the forest of masts crowded round the quays and wharfs at the entrance of the East River. There is something in all this—in the very air you breathe, and the fair and moving scene that you rest your eye upon—which exhilarates the spirits and makes you in good humour with life and your fellow creatures. We approached these shores under a fervid sun, but the air, though of a higher temperature than I had ever before experienced, was so entirely free of vapor, that I thought it was for the first time in my life that I had drawn a clear breath. I was no longer sensible of any weakness of the lungs, nor have I as yet been reminded of this infirmity.

Probably a great proportion of the neat white houses that everywhere peep out from clumps of young trees along the picturesque shores of the surrounding waters have started up since you left this country. As we first slowly entered the New York Bay, with a breeze so light as just to save a calm, it was with pleasure that I observed the number of smiling dwellings that studded the shores of Staten and Long Islands. Here was seen no great proprietor, his mighty domains stretching in silent and solitary grandeur for uninterrupted miles, but thousands of little villas or thriving farms, bespeaking the residence of the easy citizen or tiller of the soil. I should not omit another circumstance which I noticed as evincing the easy condition of the people of this young country. While our ship slowly moved through the still waters, pointing her course to the city, which just appeared upon the distant edge of the bright sheet of silver which opened before us as we cleared the Narrows, numberless little boats, well manned with active rowers, darted from the different shores, and, severally mooring alongside of our lazy vessel with the cry of "All well?" a dialogue ensued, commencing with friendly congratulations between the crews of the boats and the various inhabitants of the ship. On one side queries respecting the length of the voyage, the weather, the winds, and the latest news from Europe; on the other, the health of the city, the nature of the season, of the harvest, the arrival and departure of vessels, and a thousand nameless trifles interesting to men returning from a distance to their native shores. At the close of the dialogue, one or other of the boatmen would carelessly ask if any of the passengers wished to be landed, but the request was always made in a manner which expressed a willingness to render a civility rather than a desire to obtain employment. These boats had something picturesque as well as foreign in their appearance. Built unusually long and sharp in the keel, they shot through the bright waters with a celerity that almost startled the eye. Their rowers, tall, slender, but of uncommon nerve and agility, were all cleanly dressed in the light clothing suited to a warm climate, their large white shirt collars unbuttoned and thrown back on their shoulders, and light hats of straw or cane, with broad brims, shading their sunburnt faces. These faces were uncommonly intelligent. Piercing grey eyes glancing from beneath even and projecting brows, features generally regular, and complexions which, burnt to a deep brown, were somewhat strangely contrasted with the delicate whiteness of the clothing. I made yet another observation upon these natives. They all spoke good English with a good voice and accent; I had before observed the same of the crew of the *Amity*.

Approaching the city at sunset, I shall not soon forget the impression which its gay appearance made upon me. Passing slowly round its southern point (formed by the confluence of the Hudson with what is called the East River, though it seems more properly an arm of the sea), we admired at our leisure the striking panorama which encircled us. Immediately in our front the Battery, with its little fort and its public walks, diversified with trees impending over the water, numberless well-dressed figures gliding through the foliage or standing to admire our nearing vessel. In the background, the neatly painted houses receding into distance, the spiry tops of poplars peering above the roofs and marking the line of the streets. The city, gradually enlarging from the Battery as from the apex of a triangle, the eye followed on one side the broad channel of the Hudson and the picturesque coast of Jersey, at first sprinkled with villages and little villas, whose white walls just glanced in the distance through thick beds of trees, and afterwards rising into abrupt precipices, now crowned with wood and now jutting forward in bare walls of rock. To the right, the more winding waters of the East River, bounded on one side by the wooded heights of Brooklyn and the varied shores of Long Island, and on the other by quays and warehouses, scarce discernible through the forest of masts that were crowded as far as the eye could reach. Behind us stretched the broad expanse of the bay, whose islets, crowned with turreted forts, their colours streaming from their flagstaffs, seemed to slumber on the still and glowing waters in dark or sunny spots as they variously caught or shunned the gaze of the sinking sun. It was a glorious scene; and we almost caught the enthusiasm of our companions, who, as they hailed their native city, pronounced it the fairest in the world.

When our ship neared the quays, there was some bustle, occasioned by the moving crowd of vessels that intervened between us and the shore, and many active tars sprang from the yards and rigging of the surrounding ships to assist in clearing our passage. But neither then nor when we finally touched the land were we boarded by any needy supplicants imploring work for the love of charity, or charity for the love of Heaven. There was, however, no lack of good offices from the busy citizens on the quay. One laid planks to assist the passengers in their descent from the vessel, another lent a hand to stay their unsteady feet, while some busied themselves in taking charge of their bundles and portmanteaus, and many strange tongues and faces spoke and smiled a good welcome to the city. There was in the look and air of these men, though clad in working jackets, something which told that they were rendering civilities, not services, and that a kind "thank ye" was all that should be tendered in return.

Arriving at a boardinghouse which had been recommended to us, we were very kindly welcomed by a sprightly intelligent young woman, the sister of the more staid and elderly matron of the house. The heat continued with little abatement after sunset, and every window and door of the house was open. While seated, refreshing ourselves with tea and fruit and conversing with our lively hostess, a sound, which had filled our ears from the first moment that we left behind us the bustle of the wharfs, now completely fixed our attention. I remembered your account of the din of the frogs, and of your consequent surprise thereat, in ascending the Delaware. But the sound we heard did not at all answer to our preconceived notions of a frog concert. *Tic-a-te-tic, tic-a-te-tac* was cried as it were by a thousand unseen voices. At first we half suspected the sound had its existence in our fancy—a kind memorial, perhaps, bestowed at parting by the giddy ship. Gradually, however, I began to esteem these chatterers breathing realities, and, losing the thread of our gay-hearted entertainer's discourse, I found myself repeating *tic-a-te-tic, tic-a-te-tac.* "I suppose they must be frogs." The word caught the lady's ear. "Frogs! Where?" "Nay; indeed I know not, but somewhere assuredly." "Not here," said the lady. "No!" said I. "Pray then what is the noise?" "Noise! I hear none." If my companion had not here come to my assistance, I should have had serious apprehensions for the sanity of my organs. Backed, however, by her support, I insisted that there certainly was a noise, and to my ears a most uncommon one. Our good-humoured hostess listened again, "I hear nothing, unless it be the catty-dids." "The catty-dids! And who or what are they?" You will probably recognize them for old acquaintances, though I do not remember your mentioning them among the thousand-tongued insects of this land.* This whimsical cry, with the shorter note of the little tree frog, the chirp of crickets, and the whiz and boom of a thousand other flying creatures, creates, at this season, to the ear of a stranger, a noise truly astounding. We are now, however, tolerably familiarized to the sound, and I doubt not may soon be able to say to a wondering stranger, like the young American, "I hear nothing."

* I have since had one of these insects in my hand. In size it is larger than the ordinary grasshopper, and in colour of a much more vivid green. It is perfectly harmless and is altogether a most "delicate creature."

LETTER II.

Boardinghouse in New York. General Appearance of the City and Its Environs.

New York, October 1818.

My Dear Friend,

We have removed from our former residence to a more private boardinghouse at the head of Broadway, a gay street that you will remember, though it has now stretched itself over twice the length of earth that it occupied when you traversed it. This house has been filled with a rapid succession of inmates since we first entered it, and whenever we are not engaged abroad, we find a very pleasing society at the public table. The social mode of living here adopted in the hotels and boardinghouses offers great advantages to foreigners, who may be desirous of mixing easily with the natives and of observing the tone of the national manners. During the few days that we have lived in this house, we have met with a greater variety of individuals from all parts of the Union than we could have done in as many months by visiting in half the private houses of the city. Families from the eastern states and gentlemen from the South and West have successively appeared, and departed, and left with us many invitations to their various dwellings—so warmly uttered that the heart could not doubt their sincerity. We were peculiarly struck by the polished manners of one or two natives of Carolina, and by the independent air, softened by republican simplicity, of some of the adventurous settlers from the infant West. We gleaned from these intelligent strangers many curious facts, tending to illustrate the amazing advance of this country, which imparts to it the character of a player's stage, where both the actors and the scenery are shifted as fast as you can turn your eye. One gentleman, in the prime of manhood, told me that he knew the vast tract which now forms the flourishing state of Ohio when it contained no inhabitant save the wild hunter and his prey. Making lately the same journey, through which he had toiled 20 years ago through one vast, unbroken forest, he found smiling landscapes, sprinkled with thriving settlements, villages, and even towns, and a people living under an organized government and well-administered laws. "I had heard of all this," said my informer, "and knew

12

that it all was so, but when I saw it with my own eyes, I felt as a man might be supposed to feel, who should wake from a sleep of some centuries' duration and find the earth covered with states and empires of which he had never heard the name."

Many changes have taken place in this city and island since you knew them. Streets upon streets have been added to the former, and much draining and levelling (of this last I incline to think too much) has been and is still carrying on in and about it. The citizens of Paris were wont to call the narrow streets of their old capital *rues aristocrates,* and very justly, since pedestrians had to make their way through them at the hazard of their lives. In opposition to this, the streets here might with justice be termed *rues democrates.* Not content with broad pavements, carefully protected from the encroachment of wheels by a sill of considerable elevation, the little inequalities of the ground are being removed with much trouble and expense. I have frequently admired the ingenuity with which a new, or rather an *additional* foundation is introduced beneath a brick house of very tolerable solidity so as to preserve to it the superiority it had hitherto asserted over the passing causeway. But I have not yet had the opportunity of observing a house upon its travels. I am told, however, that the curiosity is still to be seen, though probably very rarely, as the now universal use of brick in almost all the chief cities of the states, as well as the improved style of architecture in the wooden tenements, still prevalent in the country, must have rendered the method of travelling *in domo* and shifting the neighbourhood without disturbing the household gods considerably less feasible. My confidence in the veracity of a friend has been occasionally put to the proof, when he has pointed out to me, in the outskirts of the city, a house that had undergone a transportation of a quarter of a mile to arrange itself in the line of the street, and which stood a very secure looking tenement of two floors, with brick chimneys and walls of very substantial framework.

Notwithstanding the pleasant, opulent, and airy appearance of the city, a European might be led to remark that, if nature has done everything for it, art, in the way of ornament, has as yet done little. Except the City Hall, there is not a public building worth noticing; but it presents what is far better—streets of private dwellings, often elegant and always comfortable. Turn where you will, successful industry seems to have fixed her abode. No dark alleys, whose confined and noisome atmosphere marks the presence of a dense and suffering population; no hovels, in whose ruined garrets or dank and gloomy cellars crowd the wretched victims of vice and disease, whom penury drives to despair ere she opens to them the grave.

I shall not fatigue you with particular accounts of the excursions we have made into the surrounding country. We surveyed with pleasure the thriving farms of Long Island and those of the neighbouring state of Jersey. The country is everywhere pleasingly diversified—gentle hills, sinking into extensive valleys, watered by clear rivers, their banks sprinkled with neat white dwellings, usually low and broad roofed, shaded by projecting piazzas and very generally by enormous weeping willows. These exotics seem to take wonderfully to the soil and climate and are much cultivated in the more immediate neighbourhood of houses, as well on account of their rapid growth as from the massiveness of their foliage, and from their being the earliest trees to bud and the latest to cast their leaves. I could not so well approve of the equally universal culture of the Lombardy poplar, a tree that has no one good quality to recommend it, for the rapidity of its growth can hardly be accounted one, since we can only observe upon it, in the words of the old proverb, that "ill weeds grow apace." One is the more disposed to quarrel with this vile stranger from the uncommon beauty of all the native trees. Nor might the neglect of the more noble sons of the forest find apology in the sluggishness of their growth. In this soil and climate vegetation is so powerful that a very few years may find you seated under the oak that your hands have planted.

There are some very lovely, though few very lordly, dwellings scattered along the shores of this island. You will remember how picturesque these shores are: the one washed by the magnificent waters of the Hudson, and the other by that arm of the sea styled the East River, which runs round the head of Long Island. I know not if you ever navigated this curious channel. The whirlpools of Hell Gate are at high water, with good pilotage, passed by sailing vessels without much hazard and by steamboats without any hazard in almost all states of the tide, those huge leviathans pointing their way steadily through the narrow channels which wind among the whirling eddies that boil on either hand, styled respectively the greater and lesser pots. During the Revolutionary War, a large British frigate, richly laden with specie, seeking to attain the city unobserved by the American force, attempted this intricate passage without the guidance of an experienced pilot. Suddenly assailed by one of the many powerful currents which run with irresistible force in all directions, it was sucked into the largest of these caldrons and, in all its pride and gallant trim, engulfed in a moment.

The summer residences of some gentlemen of the city command a fine prospect of these convulsed and resounding waters, and form pleasing objects when seen from the channel. It is singular, in wandering through this island, to reflect that there is scarce a tree in it older than the independence of the country. A friend pointed out to me some half-dozen veterans that, by some strange chance, had escaped the axe of the British soldier and now overlook the land which freedom has regenerated.* When you look on the young thickets and thriving trees and saplings not yet grown to maturity, which shade the neighbouring villas and fringe the shores, and think that, young as they are, they are old as the country—old as the date of its national existence—you find yourself strangely wondering at the wealth and energy that surround you; and, recalling the rapid strides which these states have made in less than half a century from unknown colonies to a vast and powerful empire, you cannot help invoking the name of Liberty, under whose auspices all has been effected.

* The British, hemmed in by the Americans in their last fastness, the city and island of New York, suffered much distress from want of fuel. They had so completely cleared the island from one end to the other that, at the time of its evacuation, there was not a stick to be found upon it, except the few trees mentioned in the text.

LETTER III.

Manners of the Working Classes. Anecdotes.

New York, November 1818.

My Dear Friend,

You will marvel, perhaps, that I have not observed upon the rudeness and incivility of what are termed with us the lower or poorer classes, but which I know not very well how to designate here, since there seem to be neither poor nor uneducated. As yet my experience would dispose me to dissent from those *travellers in the United States* who complain, in our newspapers and journals, of being elbowed in the streets, and scowled at in the houses, and made uncomfortable everywhere. I have not as yet found even the servants, a race of beings peculiarly quarrelled with by our grumbletonians, either morose or impertinent. They do not indeed read your wishes in your eyes, but I have never found them unwilling to answer them, and that in an obliging manner, when expressed by your tongue. The only exception to this which has as yet come, not within my observation, but to my knowledge, is the following: A young British officer, in his way to or from Canada, was lately lodged in a boardinghouse in this city. The first morning after his arrival he came from his apartment with a face considerably discomfited and wrathful, and seeking the lady of the house informed her that her servant was a very insolent fellow. The sum of the story that could be gleaned from the indignant gentleman was that, when roused in the morning, the servant had not brought him warm water. "I called the fellow and asked him how he thought I was to shave myself, upon which he turned on his heel and never afterwards made his appearance." The lady expressed much concern at the intelligence, adding that she had never found the man insolent nor received complaints of him before, but that certainly, if he had changed his manners, she would part with him instantly; and thereupon called the delinquent before her. In the presence of his accuser, she then began the lecture you may suppose. The man listened in solemn silence, and to the lady's final emphatic enquiry, "John, why did you not bring warm water to the gentleman?" replied, "Because I am not accustomed to answer to the name of d—nd rascal"; and then with philosophic composure John left the room. I need not state that it appeared, upon enquiry, that the demand of the military gentleman had been prefaced by this sonorous title, in style thus, "You d—nd rascal! how do you think I am to shave myself?"

A few days after my arrival in the city I had recourse to rather a whimsical mode of trying the temper of the citizens. I was bound alone and on foot to the house of a friend in a distant part of the city, and I must confess that I was in no difficulty as to the line of my route. Meeting however a man whom, from his appearance, I judged to be a mason, I accosted him with "Friend! can you direct me to such a street?" He paused, and facing about, patiently explained the advance in the straight line that I was to make, with all the turnings that I was to follow afterwards. "But I *guess* you are strange to the city. I have nothing very pressing on hand, and can see you on your way." With all due acknowledgements, I declined the offer as unnecessary. Pursuing my walk a little further, I overtook a woman who was about to cross the street. She had the air, I thought, of a servant, and the apparently well-stocked basket of provisions that she carried seemed to say that she was returning from the market. I addressed her with the same query I had before put to the mason, and she, turning round, with words and signs, replied as he had done; then checking herself, "But perhaps you are a stranger!" "And a foreigner too," said I. "Why then—wait a moment." And crossing the pavement and placing her basket upon the broad stone step leading into a shop, "I will walk with you to the head of the next street, where I can better point your way." "But the basket?" said I, eyeing it over my shoulder where it stood on the step. "What harm should come to it? It will stand there." "Will it?" said I, "'tis an honest city then." "Honest enough for that," said she. I suffered the good woman to accompany me to the spot she proposed, for I own that I was curious to prove whether the basket *would* stand as quietly as its owner reckoned upon. We proceeded accordingly, and, reaching the angle of the street, my kind informer repeated her directions and exchanged with me a "good morning." I waited to trace her back with my eye through the crowd of moving passengers and soon saw her in the distance crossing the street with her basket on her arm. You will think that I had practised sufficiently on the good nature of the public, but I made yet another trial of it. I stept into a small but decent-looking shop. A man, the only person in it, was seated at his ease behind the counter, reading the newspaper. To my query of "Can you direct me? &c." he rose, and coming to the door, ran through the necessary instructions. "But, stop! I have somewhere a map of the city." He sought and found it, and spreading it on the counter traced upon it my route. I thanked him and departed, and was disposed, from the experiments of the morning, to pronounce the city quite as civil as any city in England, and perhaps a little more honest; for, pondering upon the basket, I could not but suspect that it would scarcely have stood as quietly upon an English pavement, or, what I judged was undoubted, a woman with her five senses would never have thought of placing it there.

It is truly interesting to listen to an intelligent American when he speaks of the condition and resources of his country, and this, not merely when you find him in the more polished circles of society, but when toiling for his subsistence with the saw or spade in his hand. I have never yet conversed with the man who could not inform you upon any fact regarding the past history and existing institutions of his nation, with all the readiness and accuracy with which a schoolboy, fresh from his studies, might reply to your queries upon the laws of Lycurgus or the twenty-seven years' war of the Peloponnesus.

Putting some questions a few days since to a farmer whom I met in a steamboat, I could not help remarking to him, when, in reply to my questions, he had run through the geography, soil, climate, &c. of his vast country, just as if its map had been stretched before him with the catalogue of all its exports and imports, that he seemed as intimately acquainted with the produce and practicabilities of the United States as he could be with those of his own farm.

The manner in which an American husbandman or mechanic connects himself with his chief magistrates and legislators, and seems in his discourse to take part in all their measures and decide on their wisdom or error, is apt at first to make a stranger smile. He soon, however, learns to smile at his own ignorance, which could see any presumption in a man's pronouncing upon the fitness of legislators whose character he has studied, or in taking to himself the credit or discredit of their measures, when he has exercised a free voice in their election, or in judging of a question which he perfectly understands or, at least, which he has leisurely considered. I have observed that it is usual for an American in speaking of political matters to say *our* President does so and so; *we* passed, or shall bring forward, such a bill in Congress; *we* took such and such measures with a view, &c. To speak in short from my present confined observations, I should say that it were impossible for a people to be more completely identified with their government than are the Americans. In considering it, they seem to feel, "It is ours: we created it, and we support it; it exists for our protection and service; it lives by the breath of our mouths; and, while it answers the ends for which we decreed it, so long shall it stand, and nought shall prevail against it." If I may trust the report of all my American friends and acquaintances, confirmed by my own limited observation, there appear to be few remains of those party animosities which divided the community at the close of the Revolutionary struggle and the effects of which you found so unpleasing during your short residence in this country. It says much for the good sense of the people and the wisdom of their institutions that one generation should have outlived all the tempest of passion and bitterness of party, occasioned by the clash of interests and opinions in a great national revolution.[1]

Some weeks since, crossing the North River in one of the fast-sailing sloops which crowd in such multitudes upon these waters, I observed a man at one end of the little vessel who first attracted my attention by his interesting appearance. He was well dressed in the plain garb of a working farmer. His silvered hairs and deeply lined countenance told that he was approaching the last resting place of all human travellers, while his unbent figure and mild aspect told, also, that he was approaching it without anxiety. Entering into conversation with him, I learnt that he was a Jersey farmer, who remembered the Declaration of Independence and had drawn a sword in its support. He recollected the first appearance of *Common Sense,* and the electric shock that it produced throughout the country. He could recall the various circumstances of the war and all the hopes, and fears, and rejoicings of the people—"All," to use his own words, "as if it were yesterday." "I have lived," he continued, "to see my country established in her rights, to see her trebled in population, and quit of party jealousies and factions, and I think," said the old man smiling, "that I have now lived enough." I felt somewhat affected by his parting salutation. His discourse had very naturally fixed my attention, which he, perhaps as naturally, had observed with pleasure. When the boat touched the shore, "You seem," he said, "to be a foreigner. I wish you may soon become a citizen, for I think that you are worthy to be a citizen of our country." The old patriot meant this for a compliment; as such I received it, and as such, I assure you, *I felt it.*

It was with much interest that I visited, some evenings since, the little villa of which you once were an inmate. We turned down the little lane, wild and rocky as when you traversed it, and reached the gate just as the sun was sinking behind the heights of the Jersey shore. I thought that you had gazed on the same object from the same spot—I cannot describe how dreary and sad—how fraught with painful recollections the scene was to me, and had I been alone I could have sat down, notwithstanding the keen searching air of a November evening, and moralized with Jacques for good an hour and a quarter. You know the spot; but it doubtless lives in your memory as inhabited by kind friends, and breathing, within and without, warmth, comfort, beauty, and hospitality. We found it desolate and deserted; the house, without a tenant, gradually falling into disrepair, the fences broken down, the trees and shrubs all growing wild, while the thick-falling leaves that strewed the ground and rustled beneath our feet—the season and even the hour—all wooed one on to sickly thoughts, and pressed on the heart the conviction of the slenderness of that link which holds us to this changing world, to its good or ill, its joys or sorrows.

I would finish this letter with a more cheerful paragraph were not the ship that is to bear it to you about to sail. Autumn still lingers with us, or rather we are at present thrown back into July by the Indian summer. Farewell.

LETTER IV.

Appearance and Manners of the Young Women. Style of Society. Reception of Foreigners. General Bernard. Foreign Writers. Mr. Fearon.

New York, February 1819.

My Dear Friend,

My letters have as yet chiefly spoken of our more intimate friends, and have said little of the general style of society in this city. I feel that a stranger ought to be slow in pronouncing an opinion upon these matters, and indeed the rigors of the winter (though unusually mild this year) have for some time past made me rather a close prisoner.

Though the objects around me have now lost the freshness of novelty, they have by no means lost that air of cheerfulness and gaiety which I noticed in my first letters. The skies, though they have exchanged their fervors for biting frosts, have not lost their splendours, nor are the pavements trod by figures less airy now that they are glittering with snows. Broadway, the chosen resort of the young and the gay, in these cold bright mornings seems one moving crowd of painted butterflies. I sometimes tremble for the pretty creatures (and very pretty they are) as they flutter along through the biting air in dress more suited to an Italian winter than to one which, notwithstanding the favourable season, approaches nearer to that of Norway. In spite of this thoughtlessness, the "catch-cold" does not seem to be the same national disease that the Frenchman found it in England. This is the more remarkable as consumption is very frequent, and may be generally traced to some foolish frolic, such as returning from a ball in an open sleigh or walking upon snow in thin slippers.

I believe I have before remarked upon the beauty of the young women; I might almost say *girls,* for their beauty is commonly on the wane at five and twenty. Before that age their complexions are generally lovely, the red and white so delicately tempered on their cheeks, as if no rude wind had ever fanned them, their features small and regular, as if moulded by fairy fingers, and countenances so gay and smiling, as if no anxious thoughts had ever clouded the young soul within. It is a pity that the envious sun should so soon steal the rose and lily from their cheeks, and perhaps it is also a pity that the cares of a family should so soon check the thoughtless gaiety of their hearts and teach them that mortal life is no dream of changing pleasures but one of anxieties and cheating hopes. The advantages attending early marriages are so substantial and the country in which they are practicable is in a condition of such enviable prosperity, whether we regard its morals or its happiness, that I almost blush to notice the objections which, as an idle observer, one might find in a circumstance resulting from so happy an order of things. The American youth of both sexes are, for the most part, married ere they are two and twenty, and indeed it is usual to see a girl of eighteen a wife and a mother. It might doubtless, ere this, be possible, if not to fix them in habits of study, at least to store their minds with useful and general knowledge, and to fit them to be not merely the parents but the judicious guides of their children. Men have necessarily, in all countries, greater facilities than women for the acquirement of knowledge, and particularly for its acquirement in that best of all schools, the world. I mean not the world of fashion, but the world of varied society, where youth loses its presumption, and prejudice its obstinacy, and where self-knowledge is best obtained from the mind being forced to measure itself with other minds, and thus to discover the shallowness of its knowledge and the groundlessness of its opinions. In this country where every man is called to study the national institutions and to examine, not merely into the measures but the principles of government, the very laws become his teachers, and in the exercise of his rights and duties as a citizen he becomes more or less a politician and a philosopher. His education, therefore, goes on through life, and though he should never become familiar with abstract science or ornamental literature, his stock of useful knowledge increases daily, his judgment is continually exercised, and his mind gradually fixed in habits of observation and reflection. Hitherto the education of women has been but slightly attended to. Married without knowing anything of life but its amusements, and then quickly immersed in household affairs and the rearing of children, they command but few of those opportunities by which their husbands are daily improving in sound sense and varied information. The wonderful advance which this nation has made, not only in wealth and strength but in mental cultivation, within the last twenty years, may yet be doubly accelerated when the education of the women shall be equally a national concern with that of the other sex, and when they shall thus learn not merely to enjoy but to *appreciate* those peculiar blessings which seem already to mark their country for the happiest in the world.[1] The number of the schools and colleges established throughout the Union for the education of boys is truly surprising.

Your late distinguished friend, Dr. Rush of Philadelphia, remarks in his paper "On the Mode of Education Proper in a Republic," "I am sensible that our women must concur in all our plans of education for young men, or no laws will ever render them effectual. To qualify our women for this purpose, they should not only be instructed in the usual branches of female education, but should be taught the principles of government and liberty; and the obligations of patriotism should be inculcated upon them." [2] At present it appears to me that the American women are as deficient upon some of these heads as the men are practised. They love their country and are proud of it because it *is* their country; their husbands love and are proud of it because it is free and well-governed. Perhaps when the patriotism of both shall rest on motives equally enlightened, the national character will be yet more marked than it is at present. A new race, nurtured under the watchful eye of judicious mothers and from them imbibing in tender youth the feelings of generous liberty and ardent patriotism, may evince in their maturity an elevation of sentiment which now to prognosticate of any nation on the earth might be accounted the dream of an idle theorist or vain believer in the perfectibility of his species. I ought to apologize for this digression, but before I leave the subject into which I have wandered, I should observe that much attention is now paid to advance the education of women to that of the men, and for this end public schools are rapidly establishing in various parts of the Union on the most liberal terms.

The manners of the women strike me as peculiarly marked by sweetness, artlessness, and liveliness: there is about them, at least in my eyes, a certain untaught grace and gaiety of the heart, equally removed from the studied English coldness and indifference and the no less studied French vivacity and mannerism. They enter very early into society—far too early, indeed, to be consistent with a becoming attention to the cultivation of their minds. I am, however, acquainted with striking exceptions to this general practice. There are some mothers in this city who anxiously preside over the education of their daughters, and are yet more desirous of storing their minds with solid information than of decking them with personal accomplishments. I hope, and am induced to believe, that in the next generation such individuals will be no longer conspicuous among the mass of their fellow citizens. This might be too much to hope in old, slow-moving Europe, but one generation here sees marvellous revolutions. The society—I mean by this, that which is collected into large evening assemblies—is almost exclusively composed of the unmarried young. A crowded room is in this way a pretty scene for a quiet observer to look into for half an hour; but if he have survived the buoyant spirits of first youth, he will then find it better to walk home again. I ought not to omit a remark not merely upon the elegance of the dress of these young gay creatures, but what is far better, on its modesty. It may be sometimes more showy and costly than is wise or befitting in the daughters of a republic, but it never mocks at decency, as does that of our English ladies, who truly have often put me to the blush for their sex and their nation. The fashions here are copied from the French, but I am told by those that are knowing in such matters that they are not very changeable, and that it is judged if not more wise (for this, I fear, seldom sways with youth) at least more becoming to wear the waist and shoulders where nature placed them, than to raise them this month to the ears and sink them the next to the length of our grandmothers. The dances, too (and these young women, as far as my judgment may go with you for anything, dance with much lightness, grace, and gay-heartedness), the dances are also French, chiefly quadrilles, certainly prettier to look at than the interminable country-dance, whose appalling column seems to picture out some vague image of space and time which the imagination cannot see the end of. The young men do not, in general, appear to me to equal in grace their fair companions, nor, indeed, in general ease of manner and address. In accosting a stranger they often assume a solemnity of countenance that is at first rather appalling. They seem to look as if waiting until you should "open your mouth in wisdom," or as if gathering their strength to open theirs in the same manner. I have more than once, upon such an occasion, hastened to collect my startled wits, expecting to be posed and shamed by some profound enquiry into the history of the past or the probable events of the future. I could ill convey to you the sudden relief I have then experienced on hearing some query upon the news of the day, or as to my general opinion of Lord Byron's poetry. It is not from the young men in an idle drawing room that a stranger should draw his picture of an American. He must look at these youths when stamped with manhood, when they have been called upon to exercise their rights as citizens, and have not merely studied the history and condition of their country but are thoroughly imbued with the principles of its government and with that philosophy which their liberal institutions are so well calculated to inspire.

The youth of both sexes here enjoy a freedom of intercourse unknown in the older and more formal nations of Europe. They dance, sing, walk, and "run in sleighs" together, by sunshine and moonshine, without the occurrence or even the apprehension of any impropriety. In this bountiful country, marriages are seldom dreaded as imprudent, and therefore no care is taken to prevent the contracting of early engagements. It is curious to see how soon these laughing maidens are metamorphosed into fond wives and attentive mothers, and these giddy youths into industrious citizens and thinking politicians.

Marriages are usually solemnized in the paternal mansion of the bride, in which the young couple continue to reside for six or twelve months. It is seldom that the young woman brings with her any dowry, or that the husband has much to begin the world with save a gay heart and good hopes, which even should he fail in his profession as lawyer, or physician, or merchant, are not extinguished, for he has still the wide field of bounteous nature open before him and can set forth with the wife of his bosom and the children of his love to seek treasures in the wilderness!

It is very customary in this, and I am told in other cities, to breed up young men to the bar, not always with an idea of their following the profession for a livelihood, but because if they discover talents and ambition it is considered as the best introduction to political life.

Mr. Wells and Mr. Emmet, whose history is in his name, are considered at the head of the New York bar.[3] In the mild manners, in the urbanity and benevolence of Mr. Emmet's character, one might be at a loss to conceive where oppression found its victim. Is it in his powerful talents and generous sentiments that we must seek the explanation? There are other well-known Irish names in this city.

Were it worth while to vindicate this nation from a charge, the absurdity of which I am almost tempted to think must be apparent to those who have advanced it, that there is an illiberal prejudice against the employment of foreign talent, I could from my own observation positively attest the contrary. The well-employed hours of Mr. Emmet, and his highly respected abilities and character, might alone set the charge at defiance. The success of Dr. MacNeven as a physician, and his situation as professor in the College, and the eagerness with which his society is sought by travellers from all parts of the Union, might be quoted as another refutation.[4] But, indeed, it were idle to run through the various instances in which a naturalized citizen has risen to eminence in his profession and commanded consideration from the people of his adopted country. Perhaps where this complaint has been made it has originated in disappointed vanity. It is true that this people have a provoking soundness of judgment and rate men and things according to their net value. They have a straightforward common sense about them that will set nothing down to name or condition: they weigh the man against the trappings of his vanity, and, if they find him wanting, will leave him to walk on his way. I am proud to rank among my friends and acquaintances many individuals who generously ascribe to the liberality of their adopted country the honorable success which has here followed the exercise of their talents. Many of these I have named to you in my earlier letters, and you know how much I am indebted to their friendship and how warmly I return it.

There is yet another foreigner that I am tempted to introduce to you—General Bernard, a native of France and one of the earliest and most distinguished scholars of the Polytechnic School.[5] His manners, simple and modest as those of a sage, frank and independent as those of a soldier; his principles, talents, varied knowledge, and profound science, such as do honor to his school and his nation. After the battle of Waterloo (in which he received six wounds at Napoleon's side) and the return of Louis, he resigned his commission and retired to private life with his family. The king twice solicited his service, but he replied that having been aide-de-camp to the ex-emperor and honored with his intimacy, he could not enter into the service of the reigning family without drawing upon himself the suspicion that, in conduct as well as opinion, he was guided by interest. His conduct as an officer and skill as an engineer were so well known and acknowledged throughout Europe that he received invitations from two other courts, Bavaria and Holland, both of which he successively declined, urging the same reasons that he had pleaded to the French monarch. He remained retired in his chateau and would have remained there still but for the vexation and inconvenience which the underlings of the court knew how to bring to the firesides of the suspected foes of legitimacy. "If they would have let me sit in my chimney corner *sans me dire mot,* I should have been content to sit there still." *"Voilà, mes amis; vous êtes les maîtres; c'est votre tour. Eh bien! jouez, dansez, triomphez, et laissez moi dormir; mais ils ne voulaient pas."* Even England will occasionally afford us examples of petty knaves and busybodies, who, to attract the attention of those in power, will inform themselves of the actions, or, if there be nothing tangible there, of the opinions of their neighbours, and evince their own zeal by denouncing the supposed disaffection of others. General Bernard could not submit to the official visits of the petty magistrates and *curés* of a village, or to those of the undergentlemen of the police of Paris; and though, upon application, the high authorities disavowed any "art or part" in such vexatious proceedings, a disciple of Carnot and aide-de-camp of the *ci-devant* emperor was too fair game to receive the shield of their protection. He was teased and teased till his patience became exhausted, when he addressed himself to the government of the United States and made a tender of his services. They were accepted with every expression of respect and satisfaction, and he was placed immediately in the corps of engineers, with the same rank that he held in the army of France. The United States are believed to have received in him an inestimable treasure. Since the last war it has been a great object with the Congress to fortify the American coasts and lines, to be prepared, in the event of any future hostilities with foreign powers, against such surprises as once lost the infant capital and threatened the destruction of New Orleans. General Bernard has received instructions to take a survey of the country and draw up a report of what he shall consider requisite to complete the plan of precautionary defence, either on the coasts, or on the Canadian, Indian, and Spanish frontiers. He has already examined the southern lines, and proceeds this year to the lakes. The cheerfulness with which this soldier, broken down as he is by military service, undergoes the fatigues of such hard duty—travelling in all ways and in all climates, through all the varieties of forest, swamp, or savanna—and the pleasure and pride which he expresses in being permitted to employ his time and talents in the service of the republic, is truly gratifying to contemplate. It is not from General Bernard that you will hear complaints of the illiberality of this government or the inhospitality of this people; nor is it of such foreigners as this soldier and gentleman that the Americans will express themselves with coldness or disrespect. I often hear them name him with admiration, and acknowledge themselves as proud that their country should be the chosen abode of such a character, as he on his part acknowledges himself in being devoted to its service.

Considering the spleen that for the most part besets men in foreign countries, not merely his own nation, but mankind at large is indebted to the individual who has curiosity and good humour enough to travel among strangers with his eyes in his head and his heart in his hand. But how much more highly are they indebted to him who, to curiosity and good humour, unites every gift of the understanding, possesses all the wide range of knowledge, and inspires a foreign nation not only with respect for his own high merits but for the country which gave him birth. Would a few more such individuals as General Bernard visit this republic, more would be done towards setting the seal of amity between the two hemispheres than was effected by the Treaty of Ghent, or than could be effected by any treaty by official authorities. It is governments that make war, and the same governments that make peace; but the peace they make is only a cessation of hostilities by fleets and armies. They do not *make friends,* and I know not how it is that they contrive that the people under them shall never *make friends* either. In this country, however, you will remember that the government is identified with the people—it is their free voice and their efficient will, and to offend the one is to outrage the other. In the minds of no European people, therefore, can the abuses of malignity or the misrepresentations of ignorance rankle more deeply than in those of the Americans. They cannot say the misrepresentations made of our character and our laws have been drawn upon us by the acts of a government in which we had no share. On the contrary, they are ready to exclaim, "The vast Atlantic separates us from Europe—from its clashing interests, its strifes, and its ambitions. In peace we have established our laws; in the spirit of liberty and good will to man, we have framed our Constitution. The arms of our country have been open to the unfortunate of every nation on the earth. The stranger comes to us, and we receive him, not as a stranger, but a brother. He sits down among us a fellow citizen, and in peace and security gathers the fruits of his industry, professes his opinions, and leaves a free inheritance to his children." If the American thus speaks, who shall gainsay him? If he thus speaks, where is the generous European, the fair, the honorable man that will not acknowledge that he speaks justly, and that will not blush if any of his countrymen have been found among the traducers of his nation?

These observations have been drawn from me by a passage in your last letter. Had you not alluded to the little volume that lately found its way hither, neither should I. The credit that your letter and the letters of other transatlantic friends lead me to think that Mr. Fearon has found in England could alone have induced me to advert to him.[6]

When a friend put this little book in my hand and told me with a smile to study his nation, I glanced at a few pages here and there and smiled too. "It is to be regretted," said my friend, "that our country is visited by so many travellers of this description and so few of any other kind. We are a young people, and therefore perhaps despised; we are a people fast growing in strength and prosperity, and therefore perhaps envied. We have doubtless errors; I never yet saw the nation that had them not. But it is equally certain that we have many virtues. An enemy will see only the former; the friend who would wisely point out both, 'nothing extenuating, nor setting down ought in malice,' would do as kindly by us, as honorably by himself. Will no such man ever come from your country?" "I often lament," he again observed, "that we should be visited only by the poor or the busy, the prejudiced or the illiterate of the English nation. Their reports are received for lack of better and form the texts from which the European journalists draw their reports of our character and our institutions.

"All this were very ridiculous, if it were not very mischievous. Cutting words cut deep, and I fear that we are human enough to feel ourselves gradually estranged from a nation that was once our own, and for which we so long cherished an affection, that I am sure would have grown with our growth and strengthened with our strength had not the *pen* yet more than the sword destroyed it."

I have given you my friend's observations rather more in the form of an harangue than they were delivered, but I saw no reason for breaking them to introduce my own, which were not half so well worded, or so much to the purpose.

LETTER V.

Philadelphia, May 1819.

My Dear Friend,

The rapidity of our motions since our arrival in this city, and the kind attentions of those families to whom our New York and Jersey friends had supplied us with letters, and of others who, without the receipt of such credentials, sought us in our character of strangers and foreigners, has left me little leisure—not for *remembering* my friends in the Old World, but for affording them written proofs of remembrance.

I had been led to expect that the citizens of Philadelphia were less practised in courtesy to strangers than those of New York. Our experience does not confirm the remark. We have only to bear testimony to their civility. There is at first something cold and precise in the general air and manner of the people, particularly so when compared to the cheerfulness and openheartedness of the natives of New York; perhaps too we unfairly contrasted them with those of the amiable circle we had left on the shores of the Raritan or at —— Pennsylvania. This coldness of exterior, however, wears off in a great measure upon further acquaintance, and what may still remain you set down to the ruling spirit and philanthropic father of the city and respect it accordingly.

Though we have found some *quietism* in the society, we have found less absolute *Quakerism* than we expected, and I own that I at first felt something like disappointment, when, on looking round a room, I saw not one drab-coloured son o' Penn in it. It is very true that a man is none the better for wearing a brown coat, but I have a notion that he is sometimes the better for being a *Friend*. There is no ridicule that has ever given more offence to my better feelings than that which is often so thoughtlessly directed against the

30

Society of the Friends. I object to the term "Quakers," a name which they do not acknowledge themselves, and which was affixed to them in derision by those who could perceive their peculiarities of phrase and demeanor, but were unable to appreciate the unpresuming virtues which distinguished them yet more from every Christian sect and society of men on the face of the earth.

The children of the peaceful and benignant William Penn have not only inherited the fashion of their patriarch's garments, but his simple manners, his active philanthropy, his mild forbearance, his pure and persevering charity, thinking no evil and taking no praise.

The annals of the human race present us with no name more dear, at once to humanity and to liberty, than that of Penn. He united every great and every gentle virtue. His intrepidity withstood the frowns of power, his Christian philosophy was superior to the lures of ambition, and while his fortitude resisted persecution, his candor and gentle benevolence never sentenced the opinions of others. His religion was without dogmatism, his virtue without austerity. He was tolerant among bigots, inflexible before tyrants, patient with the factious, humane towards the criminal, fair and just with the savage as with the civilized man. Proud indeed may the republic be which had such a man for its founder and whose history has so generally done honor to his name; and justly venerable, justly entitled to the respect and love of mankind, is the fraternity of which that man was a member (one may almost say the founder) and which has followed up his deeds of mercy by others not less beautiful, tempering the rigors of justice to the offender, relieving the sick and the destitute, and even the criminal in the prisonhouse, teaching virtue to the profligate, practising humanity to the hardhearted, cherishing the unconscious lunatic, bearing with his impatience, soothing his despair, and calming his frenzy.

We may idly speculate indeed upon the silence and quietism that might pervade this now bustling world were all its varied tribes and sects resolved into one society of Friends. The pulse of human life might then, it is true, beat feebly, and we might all live and die without greatly sinning or suffering but without exercising half those energies, bodily and mental, which the conflict of human passions now calls into existence. Whether this were well or ill for us, it matters not to dream upon; there is as little chance of our all turning Friends, as of our all turning angels. But filled as this earth is with noise and contention, it is sweet to contemplate those sons and daughters of peace walking unruffled through the "maddened crowd," their thoughts turned to mercy and unostentatious charity.

It was with much pleasure that I found upon enquiry that many whose dress and phraseology are unmarked by any peculiarity are yet attached to the society, and are proud to rank themselves among its members and to trace back their short line of ancestry to the first peaceful settlers of the soil.

The society has here very wisely relaxed some of its rules. It is no longer necessary for its members to forego innocent amusements or any honest profession, nor considered as an important form to use the second person singular rather than the plural, or to prefer drab cloth or pearl-coloured silk. The same regard to their morals and fair dealings is still preserved; they must be honest members of the community, and then may wear what garments they please. There is, however, much indulgence practised towards the follies and even the errors of youth. A wild young man is privately reprimanded and much time allowed him to gain wisdom and reclaim his habits before he is expelled the society. Expulsion, therefore, is regarded as a serious blot upon a man's character, even by those of other persuasions, as it is known to be resorted to in cases of obstinate vice or convicted fraudulency. It is no doubt wise that, as the community advances in wealth and in that refinement which follows wealth, this truly virtuous society should dispense with some of its less important regulations, which, in a simple age, without being unsuited to the condition of its members, tended to confirm them in sober habits and to keep their thoughts estranged from ostentatious display and idle diversions. Did it not in some degree shape itself to the times, its sons would gradually cease to shape themselves to it, and this school of genuine Christian philosophy would be forsaken, as was that of the unbending Stoics when increasing knowledge rendered its rules irksome and even ridiculous. Applauding the good sense and liberality of this society, so superior in this to many other religious associations in whose members a jealous attachment to the external forms has too often survived that of the internal principles, I cannot help observing that not only has it secured to itself permanency by this wise temper, but has made a better stand against the advance of luxury than it could have done by a more obstinate resistance. Upon closer inspection, you discover in this moral and well-ordered city a still nicer attention to neatness and simplicity of dress and quietness of demeanor in the members of this congregation than in those of any other. The young girls, indeed, are often in feathers and flowers, and this absolutely in the meetinghouse, but it is not unusual to throw them off, as years kill vanity by killing beauty. And even in spite of them, you somehow or other, by the air of the more *posée* matron of the house or the more reserved address of the whole family, and sometimes by the additional help of portraits on the walls, in round-eared caps and starched handkerchiefs, can distinguish the abode of the children of peace and good works from those of other men.

I have no peculiar fancy for the fashions of our ancestors; absurd indeed as our own often are, they are on the whole in better taste. I should not wish to see a whole people in the garb of the Friends, but I have sometimes thought that I should like to see the daughters of these republics clad in that simplicity which is so appropriate a beauty in all that meets the eye and the ear in a young democracy. Let me, however, observe of the young women here, as I before observed of those of New York, that, though they may be decked in the flaunting silks of France and the Indies, their dress is always arranged with womanly modesty; *the bosom never forgets its screen, nor are the ankles and arms exposed to court every idle gaze and bring into discredit the morals of the nation.* You will think me perhaps old-fashioned before my time, but I cannot help judging in part of national as well as of individual character by the general fashion of the garments. It is difficult to take cold manners and haughty reserve as sureties for pure minds, but when the dress is arranged with decency and simplicity we feel disposed to give women credit for modesty and good sense. I cannot as yet accord the latter quality to the young Americans, but I do give them full credit for native innocence of heart, which prevents their gaiety from ever overstepping decency, and, though we should sometimes smile at their vanity, leaves us no room to blush for their immodesty.

It were needless to recount to you the many wise laws and humane institutions for which this country is indebted to the Friends. Penn was one of those rare spirits who learned mercy in the courts of oppression. At a time when the Catholic persecuted the Protestant or the Protestant the Catholic, as one or the other party obtained the ascendant—when the reformed church, after having fought the battle for *conscience sake,* denied that conscience to others for which she had bled herself and enforced cruel statutes against every dissenter from her doctrines or her forms—the mild, but intrepid Penn not only asserted his own right to freedom of opinion, but claimed it also for mankind. Having joined himself to an obscure and persecuted sect, who professed peace and followed good works in a world of strife and hard-hearted bigotry, he confronted, with the energy of insulted virtue and outraged freedom, the tribunal of injustice.* Having borne imprisonments, fines, and insults, and endured all that could rouse indignant or revengeful feelings in the breast of man, this benevolent

---

* The spirited address of William Penn to a London jury can never be forgotten by Englishmen. Being brought to trial at the Old Bailey for having spoken in public according to the rules of his sect, the jury, after listening to his own magnanimous defence, gave in a verdict of "Guilty only of speaking in Grace Church Street." This was pronounced to be no verdict, and the jury, with threats from the bench, were commanded to revise the sentence, when Penn cried aloud to them, "Ye are Englishmen! Mind your privileges! Give not away your right!" The jury, equally high-minded with the prisoner, having endured confinement during the night, without food or fire, pronounced in court next morning a verdict of "Not guilty." Upon this they were fined forty marks each and commanded to prison with the accused.

and truly Christian philosopher devoted his time and his fortune to procure a haven of rest, not merely for his persecuted brethren, but for the persecuted of every sect and clime. A colony of these unfortunates were planted by his hand in the wilderness of the New World, and here did he frame a government "for the support of power, that should be in reverence with the people, and to secure the people from the abuse of power," and declare "that none acknowledging one God, and living peaceably in society, should be molested for his opinions, or compelled to frequent or maintain any ministry whatsoever." [1] This doctrine of religious as well as civil liberty was never abjured by the colonists, and formed a striking contrast to the bigotry of the Puritans of New England and the Lutherans of Virginia.[2] Penn had not, it is true, the merit of being the first to establish the right of religious equality. This honor is due to Leonard Calvert, the Roman Catholic who, in 1634, near half a century before the establishment of Penn's settlement on the Delaware, had proclaimed the same principles in his infant province of Maryland. But the wise decree of this father of Maryland was broken down by the authority of the mother country, first, during the triumph of Puritanism under Cromwell, and again, after that of Lutheranism under William, when Protestant episcopacy was established by law in a province whose principal inhabitants were Catholics. Thus, the infant Pennsylvania stood conspicuous among the colonies as the haven of rest for the persecuted for conscience sake. The Calvinist could fly to New England, the Lutheran to Virginia, but to the woods of Pennsylvania men of every sect could fly; and, at the time of the Revolution, this state was one of the few which, in new modelling her code, had not to abrogate former intolerant decrees against religious liberty or to annihilate the privileges of some pre-eminent church.

To William Penn also humanity is indebted for the first enactment of that beautiful penal code which is now the admiration of all enlightened political economists throughout the world. In retaining the punishment of death even for the murderer, his mild spirit seems rather to have issued the sentence of "blood for blood" in conformity to the divine law, as given in the Old Testament, than from the argued conviction of its propriety. The code of this humane legislator was cancelled by the authority of government, as were the tolerant enactments of the liberal-minded Calvert. After the Revolution, by the strenuous exertions of many philanthropic citizens, among whom were chiefly conspicuous the venerable Franklin, William Bradford, Caleb Lownes, and Dr. Rush, the abrogated code of the father of Pennsylvania again superseded the bloody statutes of England.[3] You are doubtless well acquainted with the pamphlets of Dr. Rush upon this subject. I remember to have seen one in which he ably canvasses the justice and policy of punishing even murder by death.[4] He endeavours, I think, to explain away the Scriptural texts, in obedience to which Penn had adopted his sentence; how far this may be possible, I know not, but it does not appear important. The law of Moses is not the law of Christians, nor the law of nations, and if we dispense with it in other cases, we may be allowed to do so in this.

Thus, in her penal code, as before in her religious liberty, the republic of Pennsylvania set an example of humanity and wisdom to her sister states. Nor were they slow in following it. This mild code has now abolished the punishment of death throughout the Union for all crimes, the *highest* degree of murder excepted (that is, where it is proved to have been premeditated and malignantly wilful), and also all public and corporal punishments, otherwise than by imprisonments and labour justly apportioned to the habits and strength of the prisoner.* The wishes of your honored friend, Dr. Rush, and of other philanthropists have not yet been carried into effect as regards the abolition of the punishment of death in this last case of malignant murder. In considering the atrocity of the crime, we feel that no punishment can reach its deserts; but even with this view, it may be questioned whether that of death be wisely chosen. Solitary imprisonment is proved by experience to be a sentence more dreadful and more dreaded than death. In the prisons of these states, it has subdued the most hardened profligates and inflicted mental agonies which they would gladly have exchanged for the transitory horrors of the scaffold. It is not therefore in mercy to the criminal but to the community that the change can be proposed. The chief purpose of judicial punishments is said to be example. I know not how far the legislator should be guided by this principle, but is it not undoubted that he must be careful that the example, that is, the effect produced by the sentence of the judge and suffering of the offender on the mind of the spectator, shall be pure and decided? Must he not be watchful that no pity for the criminal shall be roused to weaken our horror of the crime?— that our moral indignation shall not be turned aside by an appeal to our nervous sensibility? Executions, where they are frequent, have been found to render the mind callous to the last mortal sufferings of the offender, and thus to leave with it no effect but what is decidedly vicious. To familiarize the human eye to blood is to render savage the human heart. An English multitude of men, women, and

---

* This code must be understood as modified in some of the southern states with regard to slaves. Piracy, which comes under the jurisdiction of the *United* States, has hitherto been subjected to the punishment of death. A law of Congress has now remitted the sentence to confinement in the penitentiary, except in cases of peculiar flagrancy. An overt act of treason (for which no man has ever suffered) and the being taken on the high seas in the smuggled traffic of slaves are the other offences capitally penal by law of the United States.

children crowd round the scaffold of the murderer or the thief with gaping curiosity, as did the French, during the bloody tragedies of Robespierre, round that of the innocent citizen or the intrepid sage, eager only to have their sympathy awakened or perhaps eager only to see how the hapless wretch will meet his fate. On the other hand, where executions are rare, they as naturally excite unmixed horror; the atrocity of the crime and of the criminal are lost in this one overpowering sensation; he whom the heart cursed and at whose sight the blood ran cold is changed in a moment to an object of compassion; his deeds of darkness are forgotten when his life's blood is poured at our feet. The murderer in our eyes is no longer the lifeless wretch; it is the hired executioner. Can the law be wise which thus trifles with our moral feelings? And that it does so, we need not look to the speculations of philanthropists. I have the testimony of many citizens of these republics for asserting that when executions, rare and far between as they are in this happy country, occur, they have no other effect than to excite amazement and horror at the suffering and commiseration for the sufferer. Nay, so much is this the case, that the execution of a pirate, convicted of the most atrocious crimes, has, upon one or two occasions, assumed the appearance of a martyrdom, multitudes crowding to gaze upon him, as led from the prison, with all the respect that the citizens of Rome might have seen a victorious general enter their gates under the honors of an ovation. The criminal himself has caught the enthusiasm of the hour and ascended the scaffold with the majesty of Kemble in Coriolanus, seeking the hearth of his enemy, the scene closing with a funeral procession and all the solemnities of Christian interment.[5] A judicial execution, thus transformed into an heroic tragedy, is something like a farce; but can it be otherwise in a country where the human eye is unused to the sight of human suffering? The fault is not in the people, but in the law—I correct myself: the law being here made by the people, the fault *is* with them. It is time it should be corrected.

I must observe that it does not seem to be the terror of example that is here sought by the infliction of this worst sentence of law, and I am led to believe that it is permitted to remain on the statute book from the persuasion that justice, considered in the abstract, demands for the highest degree of malignant murder "blood for blood." But this principle of retribution cannot however demand that an injurious effect should be produced on the feelings of the community, nor can it require that to any human being should be delegated the office of executioner—an office which no human being should ever be called upon, which no man should ever be *allowed*, to exercise. Rarely, indeed, is this officer of death in requisition in these benevolent republics; the importance of human life is here acknowledged, the dignity of man felt and understood. Law may not lightly molest him, nor justice, except for the last outrage, demand the sacrifice of life. It is not for the sake of the criminal, but of the community that I mingle my wishes with those of the American philanthropists who would blot from their code the penalty of death.

To the Society of Friends also is humanity indebted for a continued opposition to the odious traffic in the African race, for unwearying efforts to effect its abolition, which no clamour, no ridicule, no heart-sickening delays and disappointments could relax, until they were crowned with success. It is pleasing to see these simple and unpresuming friends of man raising their voice in either hemisphere against the most atrocious of all the sins that deface the annals of modern history. All the American colonies may lay claim to the honor, not merely of having yielded, with marked unwillingness and tardiness, to the example of Europeans who sought the coasts of wretched Africa for human objects of barter, but to the constraining edicts of the mother country, which made the new hemisphere the mart for the wretched victims of her avarice. The early laws of the New England colonists upon this subject reflect a glory upon those infant people of which their descendants may well be proud. The struggle of their intrepid houses of assembly against the supreme authority of England to prevent, in the very infancy of this odious traffic, the importation of slaves into their provinces, appears with no less honor in their annals than does their subsequent struggle for national independence.

In Pennsylvania, the Society of Friends were united in opposition to the African trade from their first settlement in the province, and, had they constituted the majority of the population (which their own liberal institutions tended to prevent), it is probable that the European traders would have found the implanting black slavery on the banks of the Delaware impracticable. It must be remembered, however, that the will of the mother country was upon this matter imperative, and that a positive prohibitory statute on the part of Pennsylvania would have been treated in like manner with those of Massachusetts. Her restrictive regulations, however, were numerous, nor could the eager cupidity of the foreign traders ever create a certain market for the enslaved Africans to the north of Maryland. It is a striking fact, and one greatly in favour of religious as well as civil liberty (if in this age of the world either needed the support of argument), that in those provinces where the home authority was insufficient to establish one privileged church this traffic was held in odium from its very commencement. Religion, there ingrafted in the heart, instantly bred scruples as to its legality, humanity, and policy, while in the distant European empires, living under proud hierarchies, and in the neighbouring colonies in which the Church of England had been by law established, the human mind was more slow to acknowledge the crime. It is not to be doubted that the difference of climate between the southern and northern provinces of British America contributed yet more than the differing standard of conscientious scruple among the colonists to produce a more marked reluctance to the trade in the one than the other. Yet we cannot peruse the colonial histories of these states without counting for something the varying influence of religion in those districts where its principles were engrafted in *willing minds,* and those where its forms were established by compulsory edicts.

The low and marshy lands stretching along the coasts and great rivers of the South, tainting the warm atmosphere and generating diseases fatal to a white population, held out too alluring a temptation for the employment of the African, to whose constitution the climate was less fatal, for the offers of the trader to be resisted by the young settlers.* But let it not be forgotten that the slaveholding Virginia, while yet a colony, revolted at the crime to which she had been allured. Her energetic appeal to the throne to release her from the inundation of domestic slavery, which was forced upon her, is grateful to the human heart to recall, and the deaf ear which was turned to her prayer is what the friends of that throne will not wish to remember.[6] The history of African slavery is at once the disgrace and honor of America; the disgrace she shares in common with the whole civilized world—the honor is all her own. Surrounded by every temptation which could seduce her to the crime, at first courted and then awed into compliance, she openly reprobated it when all the nations of the earth were silent, and dared, even in her weak infancy, to brave the anger of a powerful empire in behalf of the wretched slave who was thrown upon her shores. She was the first country to abolish the trade; first by the laws of her separate states, among which Virginia led the way, and secondly by the law of her federal government.[7] More than a dozen years before the abolition of the trade by the British Parliament, it was abolished in America by act of Congress.[8] There is surely something to admire—something grand, as well as beautiful, in the effect of liberty on the human heart. This Congress was composed, in great part, of representatives from slaveholding states, *themselves slaveholders*. Had the British abolition waited until the West India planters should have voted for the measure, when would it have passed? I intend no invidious comparison. There were found among the West India planters some few illustrious exceptions to the crowd of opposers to the abolition. If the exceptions among Americans were found in the opposition, and the crowd on the side of mercy and wise policy, we must ascribe it to the more liberal institutions under which they lived.

* It is highly creditable to the infant Georgia that she, for several years, successfully resisted, by an imperative law, the introduction of slaves into her province.

Canvassed as the question of the African trade has now been, until it is not only set at rest forever, but that men wonder how its legality and humanity could ever be a question, it may be difficult for us fully to appreciate the merits of the infant American colonies, who, more than a century before the attention of Europe was seriously turned to the consideration of this crying outrage, were engaged in passing statutes to prohibit it. To obtain the sanction of the government to any law of abolition was, however, found impossible by any of the provinces until the era of the Revolution, when their governments spoke the will of their people. Then, one after another, the assemblies rendered penal a crime which they had so long denounced, and where circumstances permitted the speedy application of the remedy fixed the year of emancipation for their negro bondsmen. Where, as was the case to the north of the Susquehanna, the slave population was inconsiderable, this was effected with little, or at least with temporary, inconvenience. To the south, where it is numerous and as it were engrafted in the soil, the evil yet needs years of patience, the more perfect understanding of the mischief to the master, or the more universal feeling of the injustice to the slave; the more absolute conviction of the necessity of a remedy, or the more clear insight into the mode in which it should be applied, ere this foul blot can be effaced from that portion of this great Union, and the whole of these confederated republics aspire, in their political, and consequently in their moral, character, to a glorious equality.

It is not for a young and inexperienced foreigner to suggest remedies for an evil which has engaged the attention of native philanthropists and statesmen and hitherto baffled their efforts, though not relaxed their exertions.[9] Those who, removed in distant countries, know only of these southern republics that they are disgraced with black slavery, without reflecting upon the manner and the era in which that curse was introduced, without enquiring into the exertions that may have been made towards alleviating the misery of the negro or finally achieving his emancipation, without considering the difficulties that must impede so great a measure in its progress—the doubts and fears that must be endured, the interests that must be sacrificed, the consequences that must be braved—those who do not know and calmly weigh these circumstances are, I apprehend, not impartial judges of the merits or demerits of the American planters; nor, though they should be among the most generous deplorers of the evil, would they perhaps be the wisest devisers of its remedy. There is, indeed, in the history of African slavery something so revolting that we may well pardon any intemperance of feeling, which, in breathing the energy of virtuous indignation, forgets the measure of justice and visits too heavily the crime upon those who may suffer its continuance both with regret and alarm. That this is more peculiarly the case with the majority of the white population of Virginia cannot be doubted by any candid mind. We need not trust to their opinion, as expressed in private conversation; we have but to peruse the history of their country, the various statutes enacted by their colonial legislators, their unavailing petitions to the throne, their enumeration of the forced continuance of the African trade among the list of grievances which warranted their dismemberment from the British empire, and we shall see how very early they deplored the evil and how ardently they sought to crush it in the germ. The first assembly of their independent republic, amid all the distraction of war and revolution, prohibited the traffic forever, and almost every session of their subsequent assemblies affords some proof that the public mind is ever turned towards the calamity with a view to its alleviation or removal. The most enlightened part of the community appear, indeed, to think these terms synonymous, and that no half measures can ameliorate the condition of the slave or of the master. Every publication that I have seen on the subject, and even the very laws, first trying and then repealing as inefficient or mischievous regulations which went not to the root of the evil, seem to point to emancipation as the final and only remedy.

A plan of colonization has for many years been prosecuted with vigor. The friends and supporters of the societies organized for this purpose even carry their views so far as to propose the removal of such a proportion of the slave population as shall render practicable the emancipation of the remainder. It is obvious, however, that before such a system can be productive of any national benefit, it must be made a national concern. The report of the committee appointed by the first Virginia assembly after the Revolution to revise the laws of the commonwealth contains an amendment by which it was proposed to educate the whole black population at the public expense, and then to send them forth in vessels equipped with arms, implements of husbandry, &c., to the coast of Africa or elsewhere, extending to them the protection of the republic until they should be established as a nation. After much discussion this was abandoned, either from want of funds or a deficiency of persevering benevolence. Some at present have devised the scheme of appropriating to this purpose the money arising from the sale of the national lands. From various circumstances, I am led to think that this measure is neither visionary nor impracticable, especially as it finds supporters among the slaveholders of the South.*

I have not as yet replied to your enquiry and that of your friend concerning the appearance of the black population in those districts of these northern

---

* A motion for this purpose was made in Congress, during the last session, by Mr. Meigs of New York.[10] It was proposed to purchase the slaves from their owners at a regulated price, to fit them out for the colony established on the coast of Africa, and to extend to them the protection of the republic in the manner formerly proposed by Virginia.

republics which we have hitherto visited. I hope you did not suspect me of having thrown your questions aside; I have been slow to answer only because I was unwilling to pronounce hastily.

It has appeared to me, so far as my observations and enquiries may authorize an opinion, that in no one particular has the American character been more unfairly represented than as regards the treatment and condition of the negro. The feelings of a European, when he lands in one of these northern cities, are, I have observed, of a mixed and somewhat contradictory nature. When he sees a crowd of black faces assembled at the corner of a street, or descries the sable cheeks and clumsy features of a negro girl under a pink silk bonnet, the sight offends him from its ugliness, and an immediate distaste at the country, defaced by a mixture of so novel and unseemly a population, takes possession of his mind. It is from foreigners, themselves professing an unwillingness or even an absolute disgust at being served by black hands, that I have heard complaints of the prejudice entertained towards them on the part of Americans.* So little of this prejudice have I observed among this people that, recollecting how very lately it was that the black citizens were their slaves, I was for some time absolutely at a loss to understand how there was not more. I believe, however, that the very cause which I had expected to operate in an opposite manner explains the gentleness of their feelings towards these their freed bondsmen. So much had been said and written in favour of the unhappy African, he had been so long held up to their view as the object of compassion, the slave trade had been for so many years carried on in absolute defiance of the laws of their colonial assemblies, that the majority may be supposed to have been gradually disposed to befriend them in the spirit of political opposition, as well as from the gentler dictates of human pity. There is yet another cause which, in the northern republics, interests the public feeling in behalf of the African—it is his condition in the old republics of the South. The compassion felt in England for the degradation of the black population in her islands cannot necessarily equal that which is here felt for those who are kept in bondage within the bosom of their own America. The strict bond of union which unites the interests of the numerous states seems as it were to approximate the most distant inhabitants of this vast empire to each other. The blot which defaces a portion of the Union is felt as reflecting disgrace upon the whole. The shame and the sorrow which the consideration of the southern slavery keeps alive throughout the great northern and free western states, in quickening their desire to hurry forward the day of its termination, awaken often a bitterness of feeling, perhaps unjust

---

* It was with surprise, that I heard this illiberal disgust expressed, by word and gesture, with peculiar vehemence, by foreign *women*, and these often *ladies*.

and unwise, towards the unfortunate masters of more unfortunate slaves. Much do the southern planters merit of their country for their energetic patriotism in the hour of danger. Well have they often fought the battle in the senate and the field, when transatlantic power has threatened the rights and lives of America's citizens! If they are yet cursed with an institution, at once a misfortune and a disgrace, from which their more fortunate brethren are relieved, let these trace it less to superior humanity or justice than to those happier circumstances which encouraged them at first to resist the evil and enabled them afterwards to correct it. The counsel, and perhaps ultimately the assistance, of the great and numerous northern and western states may in time be useful in relieving their sister states from this crime and calamity—if the former be given with temper and the latter yielded with unpretending generosity.

I apprehend that the friend of humanity may consider with much satisfaction the condition of the negro in the great northern portion of this Union. Everywhere are schools open for his instruction. In small towns, he will find him taught by the same master and attending the same church with the white population. Would it not be more wise to rejoice in this visible decay of prejudice, than to dwell on what remains, and which still ranges the black and white children on different forms in the schoolroom or the place of worship? In cities, the Africans have churches as well as preachers of their own, a fact from which we can only draw a satisfactory proof of their rapid advance in situation and knowledge. A European has learned, perhaps before he lands on these shores, that black and white servants sit down to meat at different tables, and should he find the fact substantiated in the first hotel in which he takes up his lodging, he marks it in his memorandum book with a note of admiration, and follows it up with some reflection upon the liberal opinions that prevail under a democracy. Did he reflect upon the history of this country and the history of the African in every country, and did he consult his own feelings, which, I believe, seldom acknowledge—I do not say an *equality,* but a *similarity* of race between the negro and himself, he would perhaps find little in the circumstance to argue the existence of any peculiar illiberality in the sentiments of this people. That wise institutions will do much towards improving both the physical condition and moral feelings of men, I am ready to admit, but I do not believe that they can perfect either. It seems to me, however, that such an expectation must have been formed by those who are surprised to find in this community an unwillingness to associate with the negro as with an equal. Nature has stamped a mark upon the unhappy African which, though the more cultivated and liberal will account an accidental distinction, the vulgar will regard as a symbol of inferiority. Had not the European of a less humane age degraded the

African below the human standard and laid the benumbing hand of oppression on his intellect, it is doubtful whether the least enlightened of us should ever have seen anything in a sable skin but a whim of nature, or attributed the ignorance and slavishness of the African tribes on their own soil to any other causes than those which variously operate on the human race in all the differing climates and countries of the globe. As it is, an invidious comparison has often been drawn between the black man and the white, which, considering the actual condition of the former, is perhaps neither wise nor humane. In these northern republics, where alone such a comparison could be instituted with any seeming plausibility, a thousand hidden causes conspire to retain the African in a lower scale of being than that of the American. The latter looks around him upon a world of his creation, upon a race of men, his brethren and equals, who, like him, acknowledge no superior but the one great Being who blessed the exertions of their heroic ancestors and to whom their hearts rise in grateful adoration for the blessings showered on their country. What great and invigorating thoughts are here which are unknown to the sons of slaves! It was but yesterday that they were "hewers of wood and drawers of water" in the land which yields them their subsistence; for the very rights with which they are now endowed (and of which their minds can, as yet, scarcely feel the value or understand the meaning), for these very rights, for all they know and all that they enjoy, they are indebted to the repenting justice of *masters*. This repentance, however complete, cannot obliterate in a moment the wrongs of years; cannot transform an abject slave into a virtuous citizen; cannot banish from his mind that he lately trembled at the frown of those who are now his equals, nor banish from the minds of these that it was only by the law of their own lips that he ceased to be the tool of their will. It requires no deep insight into the secrets of human nature to read the consequences of this state of things. There must inevitably exist a barrier between the American and the negro, similar to that which separates the higher from the poorer and less polished classes of society in Europe. The black and the white man are a distinct race, and the distinction is, as yet, no less marked in the internal than the external man. How far a nearer approach in thought, feeling, and moral character, in future generations, may tend to remove the barrier, it is not easy to judge. I must observe that, considering the inferior grade in society that the African as yet holds and considering also the fraction that he constitutes in the sum of the population, it speaks honorably for the morals of the American community that the two races continue so distinctly marked.

Notwithstanding the inferior estimation in which the blacks are held, not so much on account of complexion and feature as from the greater laxity of their morals, they may be more properly said to constitute a distinct than a degraded race. They are equally under the protection of mild and impartial laws; possess, in general, the same political rights with the mass of the community; are more peculiarly the objects of humane consideration with the benevolent and the religious; and are enabled, from the very condition of the country, to procure a subsistence, in spite of their indolence and thoughtless forgetfulness of the morrow. Though neither a frugal nor, compared with the American population, a moral people, they are singularly cheerful and good humoured and are bound in close ties of social intercourse with each other. They are everywhere immoderately fond of dancing and, when assembled for that purpose in the room of a country tavern or in the hall or kitchen of some one of their employers, exhibit a show of finery which might amaze Harlequin himself. It is always thus that man, emerging from the savage or the slavish state, seizes on the indulgencies and the tinsel of luxury, before he discovers the value of those higher enjoyments, derived from the acquirement of knowledge and the cultivation of refined and elevated sentiment. In spite of the many disadvantages under which the African has hitherto laboured, instances are not wanting where he has risen to considerable wealth and respectability, particularly, I believe, in the New England states. Nothing indeed is here necessary but his own exertions to raise him in the scale of being. His political rights must in time awaken in him political ambition, in which he has as yet been usually found deficient. In some of the states the blacks now frequently exercise their right of suffrage, and it is a curious fact that in Massachusetts some black votes were given so long back as the election for the general convention appointed to digest the plan of the federal government. In some of the northern states the right of suffrage is still withheld from the negro, and with seeming reason, for he is evidently, as yet, but ill fitted to exercise it.*

I have wandered into more general observations than I had intended at the commencement of this letter, but, as they rose naturally out of a subject upon which you have expressed some curiosity, I hope they will not appear altogether misplaced.

* Where the negro holds the right of suffrage, I do not believe the *law* excludes him from any public office of the state; the qualifications demanded are, of course, such as he is not likely to be found possessed of. This and custom operate sufficiently to ensure his exclusion.

LETTER VI.

Reference to Lieutenant Hall. Advice to Tourists. Appearance of the City of Philadelphia. Style of Architecture. Statehouse. Remarks on the Conduct of the First American Congress. Anecdotes Relating to That Period. Peculiarities in the Political Character of the People of Pennsylvania. Internal Government of the States.

Philadelphia, May 1819.

My Dear Friend,

I shall not fatigue you with the enumeration and description of the public edifices and institutions of this city. Innumerable travellers, however unwilling to see beauty and good order in the moral and political frame of American society, bear ample testimony to the peaceable virtues and active benevolence of the people of Philadelphia.*

I refer you to Lieutenant Hall † for an accurate and interesting description of the state prison, an object which must attract the attention of every foreigner. Let me, by-the-bye, distinguish from the mass of travellers who have disfigured this country that intelligent officer—not that I am always disposed to think or feel with him in his observations upon this nation. I incline to think that he has not always done justice either to their character or their manners. The same objects often appear so differently to two different pair of eyes, though both should be equally intent upon seeing them as they are, that one might readily be tempted to turn Pyrrhonist and call in doubt not only the sanity of one's judgment but the evidence of one's senses. The fact is that though we should even be disburdened of national and individual prejudice, there will yet

---

* Mr. Fearon indeed says, "Although the eyes and ears of a stranger are not insulted in the openness of noon-day with evidence of hardened profligacy, I have nevertheless *reason to believe* in its existence to a very great extent." [1] Whoever this Mr. Fearon may be, or whatever may have been his motive for travelling through the United States, it is not by such vague insinuations that the character of the moral and truly Christian city of Philadelphia can be brought into discredit either in America or Europe. It had been wise, however, if this writer had always kept to these general terms, and not ventured upon false "facts."

† *Travels in Canada and the United States,* by Lieutenant Hall, 14th Light Dragoons. [2]

45

remain in our constitutional temper, or certain fortuitous circumstances of wind or weather, a dull companion, exhausted spirits, wearied limbs, or some one of the thousand nameless accidents to whose influence we frail mortals are so miserably subjected, enough to jaundice our eyesight and pervert our feelings. A traveller is, of all men, most at the mercy of these nameless trifles; it is a pity, however, that nations should be laid at their mercy too, or rather at the mercy of a jaded traveller's distempered mind. Would it not be a good rule that when a tourist sits down with pen and paper before him to pass judgment upon the world around him, he should first ask himself a few questions: "Am I in good health and good humour? in a comfortable room and an easy chair? at peace with myself and all men about me?" I have a notion that some such short catechism would save volumes of misstated facts and misrepresented characters and keep the peace not only between man and man, but nation and nation, in a manner undesired by statesmen and undreamed-of by philosophers. I mean not exactly to apply this to Lieutenant Hall, whose remarks in general do as much honor to his heart as his head; it strikes me only that he has sometimes judged hastily, or perhaps I think so because I incline to judge differently.

I have mentioned with how much pleasure I found your name remembered in some houses of this city; of course, more particularly in that of the family of the late Dr. Rush. I much regret that this venerable philanthropist should have sunk beneath the weight of years before our visit to this country. It makes even the young pause to ruminate on the swift wings of time, when they find the path of life forsaken by those whom the heart has been taught to venerate. There would, indeed, be much in this city to mark the lapse of years, were not this somewhat checked by the reflection that years, in their effects, count for ages in this young and vigorous world. Washington, Hamilton, Gates, and all the older veterans of the Revolution, who yet trod the stage when you surveyed it, are all gathered to their fathers, and though their names are still fresh in men's mouths, could they now look up from their graves, they might scarcely know their own America.[3]

It is curious to picture the Philadelphia into which the young Franklin threw himself, friendless and pennyless, to seek his fortune, and the Philadelphia that now is—we may say, too, the Philadelphia that he left it, when he sunk, full of years and honor, into the grave. From a small provincial town, without public libraries or institutions of any kind, he lived to see it not only the thriving, populous, and well-endowed capital of an independent state, but the seat of a government, the novelty of whose principles fixed the eyes of the whole civilized world. It has now all the appearance of a wealthy and beautiful metropolis, though it has lost the interest which it possessed to you as the seat and centre of political life. Not merely has it ceased to be the seat of the great central government, as it was when you knew it, but even of that of the Pennsylvania republic. The legislature now meets in Lancaster, about 60 miles west from hence, but this also has already grown out of the centre of the fast-spreading circle of population, and, by an act of the assembly, the capital is ordained to travel yet farther west to Harrisburg, on the east branch of the Susquehanna.[4] This town, the definitive seat of the Pennsylvania state government, is, I am informed, laid out with great care, much on the same plan as Philadelphia, and promises in the grandeur of its public buildings to outstrip the parent city.

I never walked through the streets of any city with so much satisfaction as those of Philadelphia. The neatness and cleanliness of all animate and inanimate things, houses, pavements, and citizens, is not to be surpassed. It has not, indeed, the commanding position of New York, which gives to that city an air of beauty and grandeur very imposing to a stranger, but it has more the appearance of a finished and long-established metropolis. I am not sure that the streets have not too many right angles and straight lines to be altogether pleasing to the eye, but they have so much the air of cheerfulness, cleanliness, and comfort, that it would be quite absurd to find fault with them. The side pavements are regularly washed every morning by the domestics of each house, a piece of outdoor housewifery, by the way, which must be somewhat mischievous to the ladies' thin slippers, but which adds much to the fair appearance and, I doubt not, to the good health of the city. The brick walls as well as framework of the houses are painted yearly. The doors are usually white and kept delicately clean, which, together with the broad slabs of white marble spread before them, and the trees, now gay with their first leaves, which, with some intervals, line the pavements, give an air of cheerfulness and elegance to the principal streets quite unknown to the black and crowded cities of Europe. The plan laid out by William Penn, which has been generally followed, was very early swerved from in one important particular. Instead of leaving a sloping bank of verdure rising gradually from the river, which would have left the city open to the view of its magnificent waters as well as to wholesome and refreshing breezes, it is choked up with wharfs and ugly ruinous-looking buildings, the nest of infection during the heats of summer. Fortunately these are of wood and must soon run their time, when, though it should be found impossible to restore the original plan of the beneficent founder, it is to be presumed that some improvements will be effected. To do without wharfs and warehouses Penn himself might, in these days, allow to be out of the question, but I think that he would recommend their being built of a more pure as well as more durable material than wood. Anything which favours the collection of filth and vegetable matter, which the interstices between the rafts and frames of the projecting quays must now certainly do, should carefully be avoided beneath so fervid a sun as here shines during the summer months. The crowd of ugly buildings and altogether the negligence of this confused corner of the city forms a strange contrast to the regular beauty which opens to the eye the moment you emerge from it. The orderly and cleanly citizens of Philadelphia must, indeed, look to it and amend it altogether, or assuredly the demon of yellow fever will occasionally knock at their doors.

The public buildings are all remarkable for neatness and some for pure and classic elegance. Another bank is about to be built on as simple a model as the Pennsylvania.[5] I trust the citizens will never swerve from the pure style of architecture to which they seem at present to have attached themselves; above all, I trust they will never attempt the gothic, a failure in which being a failure in the sublime is of all failures the worst. The Academy of Arts contains a small but well-chosen collection of pictures, among which I have regarded with most pleasure two modern pieces—an exquisite Niobe by Rehberg and a masterly scriptural piece by the American artist Allston.[6] It is truly surprising how prolific this young country has already been in painters. West, Leslie, Copley, Trumbull, and Allston are names known and respected in both hemispheres.[7] The last-mentioned artist seems destined to rise to peculiar eminence. There is a genius in his conception, an ease in his execution, and a truth in his colouring, which stamp him for a master in his art. He is now in Boston, and, it is said, has patriotically pledged himself to try his fortune in his own country.

The Statehouse, statehouse no longer in anything but name, is an interesting object to a stranger and, doubtless, a sacred shrine in the eyes of Americans. I know not but that I was a little offended to find stuffed birds, and beasts, and mammoth skeletons filling the place of senators and sages. It had been in better taste, perhaps, to turn the upper rooms of this empty sanctuary into a library, instead of a museum of natural curiosities or a mausoleum of dead monsters.* [8] I might have judged that the citizens felt less respect for this venerable building than had been pleasing to me had not every friend or acquaintance that ever passed it with me paused before it to make some observation. "Those are the windows of the room in which our first Congress sat." "There was signed the declaration of our independence." "From those steps the Declaration of Independence was read in the ears of the people." Ay!

* The lower rooms are more appropriately occupied by the courts of law.

and deeply must it have thrilled to their hearts. 'Tis a fine moment to recall; one that swells the bosom and makes us proud of our nature.

Who can consider without deep and affecting sympathy that little assembled senate who, in the name of a young and unskilled people, there set at defiance the power of a mighty empire—not rashly and ignorantly, but advisedly and calmly—having weighed their own weakness as well as their adversary's strength —feeling the heavy responsibility that rested on their decision—calculating the consequences of attempt and failure, and then, with a full conviction of all the mighty odds against them, "having counted the cost of the contest, and finding nothing so dreadful as voluntary slavery," [9] solemnly "appealing to the supreme Judge of the world for the rectitude of their intentions," and pledging to each other "their lives, their fortunes, and their sacred honor," ranging themselves and their infant nation under the banners of liberty, denouncing their oppressors "enemies in war, in peace friends." I know not, in the whole page of human history, anything more truly grand and morally sublime than the conduct of the American Congress throughout that unequal contest, upon which hung not the liberties of one people but those of mankind. How admirable was the moderation which marked their earlier deliberations, the calmness which they opposed to ministerial haughtiness, the firmness they opposed to ministerial obstinacy, tempering vigor with prudence and inflexible principle with respectful submission! How admirable their dignity when called upon finally to decide between *unconditional submission* or *resistance by force!* With what stoical composure they made the noble choice, and, having made it, with what unshrinking fortitude they met all the vicissitudes of fortune—the ebb and flow of the tide of war, the discontent of the factious, the fears of the timid, the despondency even of the high-minded, never cast down by repeated misfortunes, nor too much elated by momentary success. When the houseless people were scattered before their invaders, when the army unpaid, unclothed, vainly sought assistance from the commander, and he vainly sought it in the exhausted treasury, when the sword fell from their fainting hands, and the blank of despair seemed falling on their hearts, still did these patriots weather the storm, still did they find confidence in their just cause, and, with their eyes upon the polestar of liberty, did they steady the helm of the reeling vessel of the infant state, ride out triumphantly the storm of war and revolution, and gain the glorious haven from which their thoughts had never swerved.

The annals of every nation can supply us with some brilliant characters who stand superior to the sordid passions which sway the minds of ordinary men and but too often dictate the feelings of national communities. But how seldom is it that, in the most energetic pages of history, we find a *body* of men uniting all the qualities of sages and heroes—cautious in their deliberations, firm and united in their measures, pure in their feelings, beyond suspicion in their conduct.

To the unbending spirit and perfect rectitude of the Congress was mainly owing the salvation of the American people, not merely from foreign conquest but from intestine broils. To their little senate room, amid all the changes of war, did the eyes of the people ever turn in hope and confidence. Were their little armies defeated, were their heroic generals fighting in retreat, were their cities taken, were their houses in flames, was their commerce destroyed, was their gold and their credit gone—they still looked to that high-minded assembly, whose counsels, they were satisfied, were ever framed with good intention, and whose energies were ever employed to relieve the sufferings that they could not prevent.[10]

It is interesting to imagine what must have been the earnest thoughts of those modern Romans throughout that trying contest—what their anxieties and, finally, what the flood of joy that must have poured on their hearts, when the tidings reached them that the last great victory was achieved. There is a little anecdote, recorded in the history of that period, which seems, in a manner, to set this before us. The old doorkeeper of the house of Congress, when the news suddenly reached him of the surrender of Cornwallis, dropt on the instant dead. The feelings of this poor veteran, too intense for his feeble age, seem to image well those of the members of that assembly, upon which he had been so faithful an attendant.

In the history of the American Revolution, I know not which is most admirable—the integrity of the Congress or the confidence of the people in their integrity. The first was so pure that throughout that distracted period, which might so well have furnished temptation to the selfish or the ambitious, we find not one member of that magnanimous assembly even suspected of peculation, or of a desire of personal aggrandizement; and the latter was so entire that, during the worst days of that stormy period, the public suffering was never charged to any wilful mismanagement on the part of the government, not even when its faith was violated by the gradual depreciation and final extinction of a paper currency, which had been issued without funds and which ceased to circulate with scarce the shadow of a prospect being held out for its future redemption. "The demise of one king (says Ramsay, in his succinct but classical history of his country), and the coronation of a lawful successor, have often excited greater commotions in royal governments than took place in the United States on the sudden extinction of the whole current money. The people saw the necessity which compelled their rulers to act in the manner they had done; and being well convinced that the good of their country was their object, quietly submitted to measures, which, under other circumstances, would scarcely have been expiated by the lives and fortunes of their authors." [11]

That a government framed in all the distraction of revolution—a powerful enemy on the very shores, the emissaries of that enemy in the very heart of the country, the Indians on one side their allies, and the ocean on the other possessed by their fleets—that, at such a time, a government so hastily organized, unpractised in those powers it was called upon to exercise, with armies untrained, unfed, unclothed, and without a treasury to meet the demands that assailed them on every side, the commerce of the country suddenly destroyed, the harvests laid waste, not a guinea in the whole country except in the hands of the enemy—that at such a time and under such circumstances the public confidence should have been preserved, argues a degree of moderation on the part of the government and of good sense and devoted feeling on that of the people, as perhaps in the history of ancient or modern times was never equalled, and certainly has never been surpassed.

In the history of the dispute which first involved the liberty and latterly the very existence of the young America, it is worthy of remark that the prudence of her Congress was always equal to their intrepidity, and their intrepidity to their prudence. Like a cautious general, they advanced slowly but never yielded an inch of the ground they had once assumed. At first called together by the voice of their fellow citizens, without consent, or rather in very despite of existing authorities, the legality of whose title remained unquestioned, they calmly took in review the colonial grievances and petitioned their redress upon those constitutional grounds, acknowledged by the distant monarchy of which they professed themselves, as they, in truth, then appear to have been, loyal and affectionate subjects. Without assuming power to enact laws, they passed resolutions to the sacred observance of which, until redress of the enumerated grievances should be obtained, they bound themselves by the ties of honor and patriotism. That these simple ties should have proved sufficient to hold together the people of numerous and distant provinces, who had heretofore been often divided by jealousies and clashing interests, and to give an effect to the recommendations of private individuals as absolute as could have followed upon the fiat of an established despot, affords a beautiful evidence of the readiness with which national obedience is yielded when the hearts of a people are with their rulers. These laws, but too often found imaginary, were then sufficient at once to supersede the authority of existing law and to triumph over the vulgar passions of humanity. They were stronger than man's avarice and woman's vanity, set at nought poverty and suffering, and transformed a nation of industrious citizens into one of patriot soldiers and high-minded heroes. The state of the public feeling is well expressed by the unpretending historian I have before quoted. "From whatever cause it proceeded, it is certain that a disposition to do, to suffer, and to accommodate, spread from breast to breast, and from colony to colony, beyond the reach of human calculation. It seemed as though one mind inspired the whole. The merchants put far behind them the gains of trade, and cheerfully submitted to a total stoppage of business, in obedience to the recommendations of men invested with no legislative powers. The cultivators of the soil with unanimity assented to the determination that the hard-earned produce of their farms should remain unshipped, although, in case of a free exportation, many would have been eager to have purchased it from them at advanced prices. The sons and daughters of ease renounced imported conveniences, and voluntarily engaged to eat, drink, and wear only such articles as their country afforded. These sacrifices were made, not from the pressure of present distress, but on the generous principle of sympathy with an invaded sister colony, and the prudent policy of guarding against a precedent which might, on a future day, operate against their liberties.

"This season of universal distress exhibited a striking proof how practicable it is for mankind to sacrifice ease, pleasure, and interest, when the mind is strongly excited by its passions. In the midst of their sufferings, cheerfulness appeared in the face of all the people. They counted everything cheap in comparison with liberty, and readily gave up whatever tended to endanger it. A noble strain of generosity and mutual support was generally excited. A great and powerful diffusion of public spirit took place. The animation of the times raised the actors in these scenes above themselves, and excited them to deeds of self-denial, which the interested prudence of calmer seasons can scarcely credit." [12]

But though empowered by their fellow citizens to think and to act for them, at a time, too, when the public feeling was wrought to the highest pitch of enthusiasm, the members of this virtuous assembly never exceeded the necessity of the occasion. They kept in view the interests and honor of the community but held their passions in check. So long as the most distant prospect remained to them of obtaining the acknowledgment of their country's rights, they preserved the language and character of British subjects.

In their second meeting, while they issued their counsels to their fellow citizens to persevere in repelling force by force and entered with them into active preparations for defensive war, they respectfully petitioned the distant throne that these preparations might be rendered unnecessary. The manly style in which they apostrophized the mother country was calculated as well to soothe her pride as to convince her reason. Having stated the grievances which provoked their resistance, they declared "that, notwithstanding their sufferings, they retained too high a regard for the kingdom from which they derived their origin, to request such a reconciliation as might be inconsistent with her dignity and welfare." [13] The contempt thrown upon these remonstrances, and, it is said, the contemptuous language addressed to their venerable Franklin, did yet more to turn the minds of the people from their parent country than did even the sword which she pointed at their throats. However this may be, these united griefs rapidly prepared the public mind for the reception of the numerous energetic pamphlets which began to advocate the national disunion of the colonies from the British empire. The circulation and effect of the well-known *Common Sense* were instantaneous as those of the electric fluid. Thousands were convinced by its homely reasoning, but more were carried away by the passion of feeling, which it wrought to the highest pitch of human enthusiasm. Then followed the Declaration of Independence. The wishes of the people had preceded the act of their rulers, and the style of that act affixed yet a new seal of confirmation to their wishes. The simple exposition of moral and political truths with which it opens elevated still higher the already sublimed tone of the public sentiment; the energetic enumeration of the national wrongs, opposed as in contrast to these great laws of nature, kindled anew the national indignation; the solemn appeal to the great Author of Being, and the sacred pledge of "lives," "fortunes," "and honor," with which it closes, roused all the devotion of human hearts and manly minds. And, assuredly, never was it roused in a better or a nobler cause. It was not the cause of Americans only; it was the cause of the very people whose injustice they opposed. It was the cause of every people on the earth, of the whole great family of humankind. Well might that high-minded patriot and statesman, the English Chatham, exclaim in the British Parliament, in the face of the British minister, "I rejoice that America has resisted!" Well might he observe that "three millions of fellow creatures, so lost to every sense of virtue, as tamely to give up their liberties, *would be fit instruments to make slaves of the rest.*" Had America basely submitted to the encroachments of ministerial parliaments, soon would that same parliament have tried encroachments upon the liberties of England; or had the infant America been overwhelmed by the armies poured upon her shores, with the buried liberties of her people, without farther efforts on the part of their rulers, her victors had buried forever their own national virtue, and honor, and character. Then, indeed, had we read this moral upon England's

faded brow,
Nations, like men who others' rights invade,
Shall doubly rue the havoc they have made,
And, in a brother's liberties o'erthrown,
Shall weep to find that they have wreck'd their own.

Thoughts of a Recluse.[14]

Considering the common frailties of human nature, we might well be at a loss to account for the uniform rectitude of the first rulers of these infant republics. But the secret is thus simply explained by Ramsay: "The public voice elevated none to a seat in that august assembly but such as, in addition to considerable abilities, possessed that ascendency over the minds of their fellow citizens which can neither be acquired by birth, nor purchased by wealth." [15]

The occasional weakness of the central government during the Revolutionary struggle was as much owing to the unwillingness of its members to assume too much, as to the difficulty of exacting obedience or of procuring the unanimity of measures (which can alone render the greatest national struggles effective) throughout the extent of the vast and thinly peopled territory which was everywhere assailed by invading legions. The vigilant patriotism of the Congress was as uniformly exerted to protect the civil as the national liberties of their country; for the former they began the struggle, and, when necessity compelled them to prosecute it for the latter, they never for a moment lost sight of the one or the other. They seem to have ever held before them that page of the history of their English ancestors, when having risen against the tyranny of a monarch, the people fell beneath that of a soldiery. These indeed are the Scylla and Charybdis between which it is so difficult for a nation to steer during the storm of political commotions: it was here that the vessel of the state was wrecked in England at the era of the Commonwealth; it was here that it was wrecked in France at that of the Revolution. If it be not impossible, it is at least incalculably difficult to establish the liberties of a country on a solid foundation by means of a vigorous army. It is, indeed, the most efficient weapon wherewith to combat tyranny, but it is a two-edged one; it forces open the temple to liberty, but stabs her as she ascends her throne. The earlier Congress may perhaps be judged to have carried their scrupulous precaution too far, to have exerted, if I may so express myself, too paternal a dominion for a season of such exigency, to have calculated too much upon that moral force which they saw so powerfully exerted around them, to have deemed, in short, the self-impelled energy of the country to have been sufficient to spurn the invaders from her shores. That their first calculation was erroneous is undoubted, and the experience of a second campaign induced them to adopt more vigorous measures. But their vigor was ever so tempered with prudence, their ardor for speedy relief from foreign violence so balanced by the dread of nerving too strongly the hands of internal power, that they have frequently been censured for too excessive a moderation, for dreaming, in short, upon abstract rights, while the very existence of the nation was at stake. The more reflecting, especially among Americans, who may be allowed to be the best judges of a scene in which they or their fathers were the actors, are wont to ascribe to the Revolutionary Congress a wisdom as practical as it was beautiful. They were *not* dreaming upon abstract principles; they were guarding the actual rights and preserving the morals of the community. They judged it a lesser evil that the war should be somewhat protracted than that the seeds of political evil should be engrafted on the soil. They accounted it impossible to make slaves of a people who were determined to be free, and the result proved that they judged wisely. The Fabian shield employed by their wise general in his military conduct was spread by themselves over the civil government. Their aim was to do nothing that might afterwards require to be undone, a rule the steady adherence to which imparts more lasting strength to a government than any which has ever been devised. It must farther be observed that the powers of Congress were at this season by no means clearly defined, and had they incautiously stretched them too far, they might have roused opposition and so divided the community. As it was, they held it united; indeed, the unanimity of sentiment which prevailed throughout this scattered community during that grievous and protracted warfare is perhaps not the least striking feature in the character of the times. No jealousy of the government, none of the commander, ever mingled its leaven with the patriotism of the people; both indeed were so pure, it was impossible to doubt them. And this it was that blunted the swords of the enemy, and before which their experienced and well-provisioned armies fell one after another, as the ripe leaves of the forest before the invisible breezes of heaven.

I must here recall to you that singular evidence of the devotion of the national feeling afforded, I think, in the seventh year of the war, after the revolt of the Pennsylvania line. You will remember the hard sufferings which produced the mutiny. Fainting under the united hardships of military duty and deficient food and clothing, they withdrew from the body of the army, demanding that which their officers had not to give, the immediate supply of their necessities. To awe them into obedience, General Wayne presented his pistols; [16] they pointed their bayonets at his breast. "We love and respect you, but if you fire, you are a dead man. We are not going to the enemy; but are determined on obtaining our just rights." They withdrew in good order, with their arms and fieldpieces, to a neighbouring town, committed no devastations, but obstinately persisted in their demands. Congress dispatched some of its members to the mutineers, but before these arrived, emissaries from the enemy appeared among them. Unconditional terms were offered—gold, preferment, and the immediate cover and assistance of a body of royal troops, already on their march towards them. Their reply was the instant seizure of their evil tempters, whom they sent immediately under a guard from their own body to the same general who had pointed his pistols at their lives. At the appearance of the Congress' commissioners, their grievances were stated and redressed; but when President Reed offered them a hundred guineas from his private purse as a reward for their fidelity in having surrendered the spies, the sturdy patriots refused them. "We have done a duty we owed our country, and neither desire nor will receive any reward, but the approbation of that country for which we have so often bled." * A country peopled by such men might be over-run, but could not be subdued.[17] This conviction supported the Congress in the most trying emergencies; they ever preserved equal hopes and asserted the same claims, whether their fellow citizens were victorious or defeated. They seem to have foreseen this consequence from defeat, a new ardor in the cause of liberty, and most truly were their expectations answered. The national spirit ever rose highest in the moment of adversity; the greater the pressure, the more vigorous the rebound; the longer the blessings of peace and independence were withheld, the fiercer was the desire for their possession.

I shall perhaps weary you with these reflections upon past events. They are so glorious, however, that the mind has pleasure in recurring to them. Such actions inculcate lessons beyond all that the schools can teach, which charm the dull monotony of ordinary life, refute the misanthrope, and encourage the hopes of good men. It is true that great excitement, that is, perhaps, great crimes, are necessary to call into being great virtues. The world is happier, therefore, when these are left in embryo, but it is good to have proof that the seeds are there, lest we should sometimes doubt it. You will say, perhaps, that, according to this calculation, the balance is even, but it is not. As the shadow of a giant will hide the littleness of a multitude of dwarfs, so will the dignity of a hero outweigh the meanness of a host of common men. What child, in reading of the torments of Regulus, does not so triumph in the proud constancy of the Roman, as to forget with him the coward cruelty of his enemies? In reading the answer of the member of Congress, when tempted to betray his country, "Tell the King of England, I am not worth buying; but that, such as I

* Among these soldiers were some naturalized citizens, natives of Ireland, a country which has sent forth many an able hand and head to the American wilderness, many, too, of high birth, but whom political or religious persecution has made aliens and foreigners.

am, he is not rich enough to do it," who does not, in the indignant scorn of the patriot, forget the littleness of those spirits who doubted his virtue? [18] In contemplating the sufferings of those who endured in a noble cause, we have a secret assurance that the magnanimous mind had that within itself which the oppressor never dreamed of. In considering Henry Laurens in his prison, when we hear him spurning the offers of liberty and ministerial favor and braving the last threats of power rather than demand of his son a moment's relaxation from his duty, we forget that we are reading of a man bowed down with infirmities and feel that his spirit rose then yet more proudly in his narrow prison than it did when, in the strange revolution of human affairs, he was called forth to mediate a peace between his enemies and his victorious countrymen. You may not be acquainted with the anecdote to which I allude; it is one among a thousand recorded of the intrepid assertors of American independence.

Henry Laurens, a gentleman of property and high consideration in this his native country, was deputed by Congress, in the latter years of the war, to negotiate a treaty between the United States of America and those of Holland.[19] He was captured on his passage and thrown into a close and grievous imprisonment in the Tower of London. Many propositions were there made to him, which were repelled with indignation. At length, news being received that his eldest son (a youth of such uncommon talents, exalted sentiments, and prepossessing manners and appearance, that a romantic interest is still attached to his name) had been appointed the special minister of Congress to the French court and was there urging the suit of his country with winning eloquence, the father was requested to write to his son and persuade his return to America, it being farther hinted that, as he was held prisoner in the light of a rebel, his life should depend upon compliance. "My son is of age," replied the heroic father of an heroic son, "and has a will of his own. I know him to be a man of honor. He loves me dearly, and would lay down his life to save mine, but I am sure that he would not sacrifice his honor to save my life, and I applaud him." This veteran was not many months after released, with a request from Lord Shelburne that he would pass to the Continent, and assist in negotiating a peace between Great Britain and the free United States of America and France, their ally.*

It is a singular and perhaps a somewhat inexplicable circumstance that the state of Pennsylvania, colonized by the most peaceable set of men that the earth could well furnish, has been the seat of more political contention than any

---

* Colonel Laurens, his interesting son, having executed his commission in France, returned to resume his place in the army. He was killed in the very last days of the war, in an insignificant skirmish, just when the liberties of his country were decided.

other of the Union. It is true that the primitive Society of Friends made but for a short term of years a majority in the province, yet the explanation of the fact cannot well be found in any peculiar turbulence of disposition in the people. Whether it was that their earlier legislators were less skilled in the science of government than those of the other provinces, or whether it was owing to accidental causes not now easy to trace, we find them disputing in the first page of their colonial history with their governors and deputy-governors, even with their friend and parent William Penn himself. A people seldom, perhaps never, complain without good cause, and the candid mind of Penn seems to have admitted this truth. He frequently new-modelled the constitution which the colonists had first received from his hands, and the alterations appear to have been amendments; but whenever he delegated the power he had preserved to himself, as proprietor of the infant province, it appears to have been abused. So true is it that irresponsible authority can never be lodged in the hands of any individual, however good or wise, without risk to the peace of a community. It is possible, indeed, that a people may govern themselves ill (though it is always probable that they will understand their own interests better than others can for them); but the having themselves to blame for the misfortunes that befall them, and possessing the power to work their remedy at pleasure will at least save much public tumult by shortening the term of their ill humour. The political disputants, however, until the era of the Revolution, employed no keener weapons than the tongue and the pen, and, with the exception of occasional wrangles with a neighbouring province touching the boundary line, in which the proprietors were more concerned than the people, their quarrel seems always to have regarded the vital liberties of the community.

I have alluded to the political history of this commonwealth, because there are in it some peculiarities. Its people appear to have been singularly jealous of their liberties, and at the same time to have been slower to discover the best mode of securing them than those of their sister states. Though the intention of their first legislator was to "frame a government for the support of power, that should be in reverence with the people, and to secure the people from the abuse of power," neither he nor his immediate successors could effect this most desirable object.[20] The convention called by the people at the time of the Revolution could not fail of better success, since there was no longer any compromise to make with the interests of any one man, or set of men, or with the enactments of a distant government. As the people were now their own lawgivers, whatever they decreed amiss could be forthwith amended, and from that time we find no political disputes in this or the other republics but those of a day.

Several of the states have called subsequent conventions to amend the constitutions then adopted, and in many these alterations have been important.

The old thirteen states, with the exception of two, acknowledged, in their original constitutions, two branches of legislature, a house of representatives and a senate. Pennsylvania and Georgia decreed but one. It appeared to them that, as no distinction of ranks had existence in the American commonwealths, it would not be easy to create two houses of representatives who should differ in anything the one from the other, and consequently that they would only be parts of the same body legislating in different rooms. I have been informed that Franklin was at first among the advisers of this more simple mode of legislation, but that he was, after a short experiment, convinced that it had its disadvantages. The people were convinced of the same, and, in a few years, Pennsylvania and Georgia adopted a senate in the manner of their sister states.[21] Although the two houses are chosen by the same electors, and may be thus said to be the same body divided into two parts, yet as the discussions on any bill take place successively, more time is allowed for deliberation.* Experience has taught communities that though, upon some rare emergencies, decision and dispatch may further measures important to the public weal, as a general rule it is better to make laws too slowly than too hastily. Pennsylvania seems, indeed, to have been aware of this, and, in order to provide against any precipitancy in her legislative proceedings, she adopted an expedient quite peculiar to herself and which was more in the spirit of the old democracies of Greece than those of modern times. In place of a senate, she first enacted that the opinion of the people at large should be taken upon every question brought forward by their representatives. To effect this, every bill was published after its second reading in the house, and time allowed for the body politic of the state to submit their opinions to their servants in council. One can barely imagine a mode of legislation more troublesome than this. It was, of course, soon abandoned, together with a council of censors, whose duty it had been to sit in periodical judgment upon the whole government of the state, legislative and executive, and to report accordingly. After the Revolution, the lapse of a few years and the trial of a few experiments calmed the spirit of controversy which had so long beset this people. Their rights being now fairly established and guarded beyond the possibility of invasion, party animosities have subsided, and the wheel of government, moved by the united impetus of the whole people, turns noiseless and unimpeded, watched by all and suspected by none.

The constitutions of all these different confederated republics differ in little

---

* An attempt is made in some few of the states to constitute a difference between the two houses by requiring a higher rate of property to qualify a senator than a representative; many also require the senators to be older than the members of the other house.

the one from the other. The legislative power is vested in a general assembly, consisting of a senate and house of representatives; * the executive in a governor, or in a governor with the assistance, or perhaps it were more correct to say, the *impediment* of a council. This impediment, at first adopted by all the original thirteen states, has been abolished by several and has not been adopted by those which have been subsequently added to the Union.† A majority, however, of the old thirteen states retain this check upon the will of their chief magistrate.[22] Considering the short term of his authority and the slender powers with which he is vested, many regard this check as unnecessary, some think it mischievous, as it tends to retard the operations of government, while others think it salutary on that very account. Perhaps the truth is that it is very unimportant. This will more clearly appear if we consider the supreme authority of the legislative branch of the government, which is, in fact, the people speaking and acting distinctly and definitively in the person of their representatives. The governor does, indeed, possess a veto upon the decision of the two houses, but his veto is not decisive. He must, within a given time, return the bill, stating the grounds of his dissent, when the question is debated anew, and two thirds of both houses are then required to give the effect of a law; but as this majority can impart to it that effect without the signature of the governor, it is, of course, rarely refused. I know not, indeed, that the case ever occurs: it is clear that it can only occur where the voices of the legislators are pretty equally divided, and, consequently, when the wisdom of the proposed law may be supposed to be more than usually doubtful. That the door should then be left open for its reconsideration must surely be accounted wise, and we must farther suppose that the executive could never adopt the extraordinary measure of withholding its consent, but on a question of vital importance as well as of doubtful merits. By the English constitution a veto is granted to the monarch, and this without a second appeal to the legislative authority. If this veto is never exerted, it is evidently because the royal influence can previously affect the legislative decision, and thus virtually speak the will of the monarch, without the too apparent and irritating opposition of his voice to that of the nation. Whatever power the executive here possesses, it is direct; its influence is nothing: it must simply approve or dissent. The governor is as powerless to affect the voices of the assembly as any other individual in the commonwealth; they are all powerful on the other hand to affect his, or, as we have seen, can render it nugatory. The powers of the governor vary somewhat in the different states, and it is, perhaps, singu-

---

* With the single exception of Vermont; she has hitherto held to the system first adopted by Pennsylvania and Georgia, and legislates without a senate.

† Also with the exception of Vermont.

lar, that in Pennsylvania, where there has ever existed an excessive jealousy of the executive, its powers are greater than in other states. The governor is un-shackled by a council, holds his office for three years, and is trusted with the disposal of many public offices, which, according to the constitution of most of the other republics, are voted by the joint ballot of both houses of assembly.

One might amuse one's self by imagining that the citizens of this state were so constitutionally disputatious as to be unwilling to forego all opportunity for wrangling. By throwing upon their chief magistrate the choice of judges, mayors, recorders, &c., they reserve to themselves the possibility of quarrelling with him. This seems to be a fashionable amusement, as it is also in the state of New York, where the appointment to some of the chief public offices is also vested in the governor, though with the concurrence of a council. The bickering that this gives rise to in the public prints may be very entertaining to those en-gaged in it, but lookers-on may be allowed to think it very ridiculous and alto-gether unworthy of the dignity of these two important republics.

All public offices, whether in the disposal of the governor, or the legislature, or the people, are held only on good behaviour and are, not excepting the gover-nor, liable to impeachment in the house of assembly. The concurrence of two thirds of the representatives is necessary to pass sentence, which extends only to removal from office and disqualification to hold thereafter "any place of honor, trust, or profit, under the state."

It is always provided that no person holding any office under the state or the United States shall be a member of either house of assembly, a regulation of vital importance and without which it is impossible to rely upon the purity of the representative system. The servant of the people must be in the pay of no other man or set of men, or his interests may be at issue with his duty. *Plurali-ties,* indeed, are prohibited in every branch of American government and all the authorities under it. This, of course, imparts to it a vigor and *clean-handed-ness* which no other regulations could ensure.*

The house of representatives may generally be said to be the more popular branch of the legislature: its members are chosen annually by the whole free male citizens of the state.† This may be said to be the case throughout the Union, except in two or three of the old republics of the South. The mode of

---

* A curious instance of political vigilance occurred lately in New York: A postmaster in that city was removed from office because he was found to be a *mail contractor,* the postmaster general in Washington assigning as a reason for his dismissal that the postmaster was the check over the irregularity of the contractor and that, if the same man held both situations, no security could be considered as given to public for the proper fulfilment of the duties of either.

† Excepting in South Carolina, Tennessee, and Illinois, where the elections occur every *second* year.

election employed in the choice of senators varies a little in the different states; in many the term of service extends but to one year, in others to three, four, or, as in Maryland, to five years. But we cannot exactly calculate the varying popularity of the senatorial elections by the greater or less frequency of their occurrence; this is effected by the greater or less extension of the right of suffrage, greater qualifications by some constitutions being required to entitle a citizen to vote for a senator than a representative; by others these are declared to be equal, though the period of election should occur more frequently in the one case than the other. In Virginia, the governor, representatives, and senators are chosen annually, and yet her constitution is the least democratic of any state in the Union. In the eastern, central, and western states, all the elections are thoroughly popular. In Virginia and the Carolinas the suffrage needs farther extension before they can be said to legislate truly upon American principles.

The most admirable contrivance in the frame of these governments is the provision made in all for their alteration and amendment. The *convention* is at once the foundation and cornerstone in the beautiful structure of American government; by its means the constitution of the state is shaped to the wishes of the people as easily and silently as its laws; it is at once the safeguard of the public rights and the keeper of the public peace. The rights of this community rest not on charters or ancient usages, but on immutable principles, which every head and heart is taught to understand and to feel. There is here no refining upon the meaning of words, no opposing of records to reason, no appealing from the wisdom of the present to that of the past; the wisdom of today is often the ignorance of tomorrow; what in one age is truth, in another is prejudice; what is humanity becomes cruelty; what justice, injustice; what liberty, slavery; and almost what virtue, wickedness, and happiness, misery. All things are by comparison; the man of this generation, with views and feeling adapted to earlier ages, is cramped in a sphere of action which those before him found commensurate to their powers and their ambition. If law oppose barriers, his spirit is checked but not quelled. The flood of knowledge gathers strength, and the mound is swept away with a sudden fury, which shakes the very foundations of society and spreads a momentary ruin over the wide field of civilized life. Power and liberty, existing in the same state, must be at eternal war. It is only where one or other rules singly and undisputed that the public peace can be preserved, in the one case by the free exercise of all the human energies, in the other by their extinction.

It has often been asserted by the advocates of despotism that the elements of liberty are wild and intractable. The position is most true where they are found in an atmosphere uncongenial to their nature, where they have to contend with other elements with which they can never amalgamate and which wage with them unceasing warfare. It is common to point our attention to the republics of ancient time and to tell us that free Rome was split into factions and civil wars: without enumerating the many causes found in the distinction of ranks, the jealousy existing between the various orders of society, the powerful armies with their ambitious leaders, which combined to throw society into chaos, we have only to refer to the ignorance of the doctrine of representation. This doctrine, so simple when once revealed, forms the whole science of a free government; this it is which gives to modern liberty a character foreign to that which she bore in ancient times; this it is which has made freedom and peace shake hands and which renders the reign of the one coeval with that of the other.

The representative system, invented, or rather by a train of fortuitous circumstances brought into practice in England, has been carried to perfection in America: by it the body of the people rule in everything; by it they establish their constitutions; by it they legislate according to the constitutions established; and by it again they amend their constitutions, according to the gradual advance of the public mind in political wisdom. Thus, though the form of government should in some cases be found deficient, yet as the door is ever left open to improvement, in system it may always be pronounced to be perfect. "Quelle republiche che, se le non hanno l'ordine perfetto hanno preso il principio buono e atto a diventare migliore, possono, per la occorrenza delli accidenti diventare perfette." * 23

Considering how greatly the human mind is ennobled by liberty and how rapidly it becomes humanized when the book of knowledge is thrown open to its inspection, there is no calculating the progress of a people in virtue as well as power, whose successive generations shall be bred up under benign laws and liberal institutions. Who does not sympathize with the playful wish of the benign sage and devoted patriot Franklin, who, when he saw a little fly escape from a bottle in which it had been imprisoned, exclaimed, "I wish I could be corked up as you have been, and let out a hundred years hence, just to see how my dear America is going on"? 24

* Machiavelli [*Discorsi*] *sopra la prima Deca di Tito Livio.*

LETTER VII.

Society of Philadelphia. Anecdote of a Prussian Officer. Anecdote of Mr. Jefferson. Chevalier Correa da Serra. Mr. Garnett.

Philadelphia, May 1819.

My Dear Friend,

I must not leave this city without observing somewhat more distinctly than I have as yet done upon the general character of the society.

It is difficult to make observations upon the inhabitants of a particular district that shall not more or less apply to the nation at large. This is the case in all countries, but more particularly in these democracies. The universal spread of useful and practical knowledge, the exercise of great political rights, the ease and, comparatively, the equality of condition give to this people a character peculiar to themselves. The man of leisure, who is usually for the most part the man of *pleasure,* may, indeed, find himself somewhat alone in this country. Every hand is occupied, and every head is thinking, not only of the active business of human life (which usually sits lighter upon this people than many others), but of matters touching the general weal of a vast empire. Each man being one of a sovereign people is not only a politician but a legislator—a partner, in short, in the grand concern of the state, and this not a *sleeping* partner, but one engaged in narrowly inspecting its operations, balancing its accounts, guarding its authority, and judging of its interests. A people so engaged are not those with whom a lounger might find it agreeable to associate: he seeks amusement, and he finds business; careless wit, and he finds sense—plain, straightforward, sober sense. The Americans are very good talkers and *admirable listeners;* understand perfectly the exchange of knowledge, for which they employ conversation and employ it solely. They have a surprising stock of information, but this runs little into the precincts of imagination; facts form the groundwork of their discourse. They are accustomed to rest their opinions on the results of experience rather than on ingenious theories and abstract reasonings, and are always wont to overturn the one by a simple appeal to the other. They have much general knowledge, but are best read in philosophy, history, political economy, and the general science of government. The world, however, is the book which they consider most attentively, and make a general practice of turning over the page of every man's mind that comes across them. They do this very quietly and very civilly, and with the understanding that you are at perfect liberty to do the same by theirs. They are entirely without *mauvaise honte,* and are equally free from effrontery and officiousness. The constant exercise of the reasoning powers gives to their character and manners a mildness, plainness, and unchanging suavity, such as are often remarked in Europe in men devoted to the abstract sciences. Wonderfully patient and candid in argument, close reasoners, acute observers, and original thinkers. They understand little the play of words, or, as the French more distinctly express it, *badinage.* When an American, indeed, is pressed into this by some more trifling European or by some lively woman of his own nation, I have sometimes thought of a Quaker striking into a Highland reel. This people have nothing of the poet in them nor of the *bel esprit,* and I think are apt to be tiresome if they attempt to be either. It is but fair, however, to observe that they very seldom do attempt this, at least after they are five and twenty. On the other hand, they are well-informed and liberal philosophers, who can give you, in half an hour, more solid instruction and enlightened views than you could receive from the first *corps littéraire* or *diplomatique* of Europe by listening to them for a whole evening. It is said that every man has his forte, and so, perhaps, has every nation. That of the American is clearly good sense: this sterling quality is the current coin of the country, and it is curious to see how immediately it tries the metal of other minds. In truth, I know no people who sooner make you sensible of your own ignorance. In conversing even with a plain farmer, it has seemed to me that I had been nothing but a foolish trifler all my life, running after painted butterflies, while he, like the ant, had been laying up winter stores of solid mental food, useful at all times and in all exigencies.

I must also remark of this people that they possess an uninterrupted cheerfulness of mind, and an imperturbable evenness of temper, and, moreover, a great share of dry humour, which is the weapon they usually employ when assailed by impertinence or troublesome folly of any kind. I have witnessed many amusing instances of this, and you will find some true specimens in the writings of Franklin, whose humour was truly of native growth.

A story occurs to me at this moment, which, though it perhaps owed something to the manner in which I heard it, may at least serve as an example of the national trait to which I have here alluded. A Prussian officer, who some while since landed in New York on his way to Venezuela, having taken up his lodgings at an hotel in Broadway, found himself in company with two British officers and an American gentleman, who was quietly seated in the recess of a window reading the Washington *Gazette*. The Prussian understood not a word of English, but observed that the two foreigners, in conversing with each other, eternally used the word "Yankee." As they leaned out of an open window which looked into Broadway, he heard them repeat it again and again and seemingly apply it to every citizen that passed before them. "Yankee! Yankee!" at length exclaimed the Prussian; "Que veut dire ce Yankee?" and turned, wondering, to the gentleman who sat apparently inattentive to what was passing. "Je vous dirai, monsieur," said the American, gravely looking up from his paper; "cela veut dire, un homme d'une sagesse parfaite, d'un talent extrême, jouissant des biens de la fortune, et de la considération publique." "En un mot, un sage et un homme distingué." "Précisément." "Mais, monsieur, que la république est riche en sages et en hommes distingués!" "Ces messieurs nous font l'honneur de le croire," bowing to the officers.[1]

You may smile to hear that the Prussian took the explanation in sober seriousness (though you will readily believe that our two countrymen were too petrified to offer it a contradiction) and failed not in employing the word to comment upon the superabundance of *hommes distingués* to be found in the city, as well as upon the force of the language, which knew how to convey so many ideas in one word. It was long before I could understand the drift of the Prussian's discourse; when at length I had drawn the above story from him, and that the mystery stood explained, the joke seemed almost too good to put an end to. As I saw, however, that it was his fixed intention to apply the word in its new meaning to every citizen to whom he meant to do honor, and that, in case of an interview with the President himself, he would infallibly, in some flourish of politeness, denominate him *Chef des Yankées,* I thought it better to restore the word to its old reading.*

As I have commenced storytelling, I must subjoin an anecdote of Mr., or as he is more simply styled, *Thomas* Jefferson, which I received a few days since from a gentleman of this city, and which struck me as not only characteristic of that philosopher but somewhat also of this nation generally.

It was the object of Mr. Jefferson to preserve, in every trifle, that simplicity which he deemed the most appropriate characteristic of a republic. At his en-

---

* Perhaps the original derivation of the word "Yankee" is not generally known in England. It is the Indian corruption of *English, Yenglees, Yangles, Yankles,* and finally *Yankee.*[2] In the United States, the nickname is only jocularly applied to the citizens of New England, whose early settlers were thus denominated by the savages. The Pennsylvanians are known among the Indians by the name of *Quekels,* being a corruption of "Quaker"; the Virginians by that of *Long Knives,* I believe from the bloody wars in which they were continually engaged with the first adventurous settlers of that mother of the Union.

trance into the presidency, he found himself a little troubled with the trifling etiquette which the foreign ambassadors, and more especially their ladies, were essaying to establish in his own drawing room; and, apprehending that the wives and daughters of his official brethren might catch the contagion, he let pass no opportunity of giving it his discountenance. He wisely judged that in this matter, as in most others, example was better than precept, and set about new-ordering the manners of the city, much in the manner that Franklin might have taken. Did he go to make a morning visit, he rode without a servant, tied his horse to the gate, and walked in as plain Thomas Jefferson. Did all the different legations come to dine with him, he received them with indiscriminating politeness and that simple dignity for which he is eminently distinguished; conversing with and welcoming all, he left the company to arrange themselves at his table, of which he so did the honors, as to spread ease and cheerfulness around it, and to make his guests in good humour with themselves and each other. The wife of the Spanish minister, however, upon returning home, began to ponder upon the events of the evening: she had been seated below the lady of ———, my informant forgot which ambassador, but one whom she judged of inferior importance to her liege lord. His most Catholic Majesty had been insulted, she declared, in her person, for was not an insult offered to the wife always offered to the husband, and as in this case an insult offered to the husband was offered to the king of Spain—Euclid himself must have concluded with Q.E.D. The next morning the don could do no less than summon a council, consisting of his most chosen friends among the diplomatic corps. The case was stated, and their opinions severally taken. One ventured to apologize for the President on the ground of his ignorance as a republican of the rules of etiquette. To this it was replied that the dignity of his most Catholic Majesty was not to be laid at the mercy of every man who might call himself a republican. The lady particularly insisted that satisfaction must be given. It was suggested that the best way would be for Spain's representative to go and ask it. The divan broke up, and one of its members went to advise the President of the matter in agitation. Some hours after, Mr. Jefferson, while occupied in his library, was informed that the Spanish minister was in an adjoining apartment; he called immediately for his boots, and putting one on and holding the other in his hand, proceeded to the room. Having half opened the door, he issued orders to the servant behind him, touching his horse, and then advancing, and drawing on as he did so his remaining boot, welcomed his visitor with his wonted amenity. "Pray be seated; be seated; no ceremony here, my good sir. Very glad to see you"; and then, without regarding the disconcerted air of the astonished representative of Spain and the Indies, entered with his wonted ease into general conversation, opposing the gentleman to the minister and the unaffected majesty of the philosopher to the frozen haughtiness of the diplomatist. The combat was soon decided. The Spaniard departed and reported to his lady and diplomatic friends that when they went to the house of the American President they must leave the dignity of their masters at home.

I have already observed upon the *quietism* still discernible in this city; there is, however, much gaiety among the young people and much social intercourse among those of maturer age. Here, as elsewhere, I observe a distinct line drawn between the young and the old. Nothing, indeed, can be more opposite than their characters: the former all life and animation, carolling like young larks in the spring, the latter mild, composed, and devoted—the women to domestic duties, and the men to affairs domestic and public. Some foreigner has said that in Europe there is pleasure without happiness, and in America happiness without pleasure. Something here is doubtless sacrificed to the point of the sentence. I rather incline to think that pleasure is equally found in the two hemispheres, but that in the one she resides with youth and in the other with mature age. In France, for instance, a woman has scarcely an acknowledged existence until some monsieur has placed a ring on her finger; here, with her, the joy of life is in its spring. Truly it is a pretty sight to see these laughing creatures moving and speaking with a grace that art never taught and might in vain seek to imitate. I know not if pleasure be a divinity that should be greatly worshipped; perhaps her spirit intoxicates for a moment to leave the mind vacant afterwards, and the legislator might do wisely who should leave her out of the national pantheon. But if the goddess is to be sought at all, it seems more in the order of nature that it should be when youth and health are mantling on the cheek. Frolic may then find excuse in the quick blood, and Heraclitus himself be won to laugh at it with good humour. The thoughtless girl throws away precious moments, but the thoughtless woman neglects important duties, and she too pursues only the shadow of a shade—witness the faded cheeks and jaded spirits of a London female rake of thirty or forty. The American girl, evanescent as her joy may be, yet finds joy, pure and heartfelt, which older wisdom might almost envy.

> Bless'd hour of childhood! then, and then alone,
> Dance we the revels close round Pleasure's throne,
> Quaff the bright nectar from her fountain springs,
> And laugh beneath the rainbow of her wings.
> Oh! time of promise, hope and innocence,
> Of trust, and love, and happy ignorance!
> Whose every dream is Heaven, in whose fair joy
> Experience yet has thrown no black alloy;

Whose pain, when fiercest, lacks the venom'd pang
Which to maturer ill doth oft belong,
When, mute and cold, we weep departed bliss,
And Hope expires on broken Happiness.

Thoughts of a Recluse.

This last catastrophe, however, seems seldom to happen here. Love at an early age gives place to domestic affection, and pleasure to domestic comfort; the sober happiness of married life is here found in perfection. Let the idler smile at this; it is assuredly the best of heaven's gifts to man.

But talking of youth and youth's folly, I must not forget to report to you a sight, which I doubt if you will believe I saw; I did, however, and that in broad daylight, and in Chestnut Street, Philadelphia. This is the fashionable promenade, as Broadway is in New York, and the figures are equally gay and elegant in both. Walking one morning with a friend, a knot of young men approached, whose air and dress were so strangely foreign to those of the citizens of the country that I at first doubted if I was not transported by some fairy's incantation into New Bond Street or the boulevards. No lounger there, no gay Parisian beau fresh from the fencing master, could have worn waists more slender or looked more like fashion's nondescripts. "Who are those foreigners?" I asked. "They are natives," replied my companion laughing, "but the fools are rare, and I hope, for the sake of the character of our city, will remain so."

There are here some circles of very choice society. There is one lady particularly who appears to assemble all the talent of the city in her drawing room; and of this, by-the-bye, no inconsiderable portion is in herself. I have seldom met a lady who possessed more high gifts, or employed them more unostentatiously, and yet, while the life of the evening circle, her mornings are exclusively devoted to the education of a numerous family, who cannot fail to grow up under such tuition worthy of their country and their name.

We met yesterday at her house a character well known and highly respected throughout this country, the Portuguese minister, Correa da Serra.[3] Mr. Brackenridge of Baltimore, in dedicating to him his little work on Louisiana, has pronounced him to be "one of the most enlightened foreigners that has ever visited the United States." The observations with which he follows up this compliment are so similar to what I have universally heard applied to this amiable philosopher by the citizens of this country, that I am tempted to quote them: "Your amiable simplicity of manners restore to us our Franklin. In every part of our country which you have visited (and you have nearly seen it all), your society has been as acceptable to the unlettered farmer as to the learned philosopher. The liberal and friendly manner in which you are accustomed to view every thing in these states, the partiality which you feel for their welfare, the profound maxims upon every subject which, like the disciples of Socrates, we treasure up from your lips, entitle us to claim you as one of the fathers of our country." [4] After such testimonies from those who can boast an intimate personal acquaintance with this distinguished European, the observations of a stranger were a very impertinent addition. I can only say, that, *as* a stranger, I was much struck by the unpretending simplicity and modesty of one to whom unvarying report ascribes so many high gifts, vast acquirements, and profound sciences. The kindness with which he spoke of this nation, the admiration that he expressed of its character, and of those institutions which he observed had formed that character and were still forming it, inspired me, in a short conversation, with an equal admiration of the enlightened foreigner who felt so generously. As he walked home with me from the party (for your character is not here fastened to a coach, as Brydone [5] found his was in Sicily), I chanced to observe upon the brilliancy of the skies, which, I said, as a native of a moist and northern climate, had not yet lost to me the charm of novelty. He mildly replied, "And on what country should the sun and stars shine brightly, if not on this? Light is everywhere, and is each day growing brighter and spreading farther." "Are you not afraid," I asked, encouraged by the suavity of the venerable sage to forget the vast distance between his mind and years and my own, "Are you not afraid, as the representative of royalty, of loving these republics too well?" He retorted playfully. "As the courtly Melville [6] adjudged Elizabeth the fairest woman in England, and Mary the fairest in Scotland, so I deem this the fairest republic, and Portugal, of course, the fairest monarchy." It was impossible to hold an hour's conversation with this philosopher and not revert to the condition and future prospects of the country which gave him birth. When I pondered on these, it was with pain that I marked the furrows on his brow. Has such a man been born in vain for his country? Is he there too far before his generation, and must he sleep with his fathers, before the light which has burst in full effulgence upon his mind shall gleam one faint ray upon those of his fellow countrymen.*

It is surely a proud reflection for this people that, in the very infancy of their existence as a nation, they should attract the attention of foreign statesmen and sages, and that their country should not only be the refuge of the persecuted,

---

* When, after my return to Europe, the tidings of the revolution in Portugal first reached me, my thoughts reverted to the Chevalier Correa. Should these insignificant pages ever accidentally attract his eye, he will never recall that he once deigned to throw away an idle hour in conversing with their writer, but she is proud to remember it. Nor was it without deep emotion that at one moment she pictured the thoughts and feelings of that benevolent and enlightened friend of humankind.

but often freely chosen as the abode of the philosopher. America need not complain; if she is condemned by the ignorant and the prejudiced, she is applauded by those whose applause is honor; by those too who have closely considered her character, and whose matured and candid judgment enables them to decide upon its merits. A people who have the voices of a Correa, a Bernard, and a Garnett, may laugh in good humour at an Ashe or a Fearon.[7]

The name of Garnett has often appeared in my letters. I hesitate to depict a character which would defy an abler hand than mine; those who have seen the original would find any transcript of it an unmeaning daub; those who have seen it not would deem that the painter drew from an overwrought imagination. I may have already mentioned that he was a native of England and known in early life in that country, as he has since been known in this, for every gift and every acquirement that can ennoble or adorn the human mind. To the world he is best known as a man of science, but the more deep researches which have engrossed him as a mathematician, astronomer, and mechanic form but a fraction in the sum of his rich and varied knowledge. It were idle to recount the mental powers and accomplishments of this venerable sage; the difficulty would be to imagine one that he does not possess. Never was a mind more rich in treasures, never a heart more overflowing with benevolence, never a soul more ardent in the love of liberty and of all that is great and excellent. Were it possible to enumerate the noble endowments of this philosopher, there would still be that in his manners and appearance which would mock description—a simplicity, and withal, a winning grace, that charms alike childhood, youth, and age, which makes ignorance at ease in his presence and gives him the air of a disciple, while uttering the words of wisdom. The countenance whose beauty in its younger days fixed the eyes of Lavater,[8] and was the image from which he drew the portrait of benevolence, might yet picture the same virtue to the same master. Never, indeed, were jewels shrined in a nobler casket; never did goodness beam more beautifully from the eye, or thought sit in more majesty on the forehead; never did wisdom breathe more mildly and playfully from the lips; never were such transcendent powers, such vast and universal acquirements, worn with such modesty and sweetness. How poor are words to speak the charm that hangs about this son of science and of nature! To tell how each accent sinks from the ear upon the heart; how his knowledge instructs, his fancy charms, his playful, sparkling, careless wit enlivens! The moments passed in his presence are counted by sands of gold and are treasured up in the memory for the mind and the heart to recur to, whenever their better powers and feelings may need refreshing. Should the contemplation of human weakness and wickedness ever make us call in doubt, for a moment, the high destinies of our nature, it is by recalling the image of such a sage as this—of such a philosopher of the world and friend of man—that our confidence in human virtue may be restored, our philanthropy quickened, and every generous hope and aim be revived and exerted with new ardor.*

* This venerable philosopher and philanthropist is now numbered with the dead; but eight and forty hours after the writer of these pages parted from him, and almost before she was out of sight of the American shores, he was a corpse. He suddenly fell asleep, full of years, and in full possession of all his great powers, without a struggle or a groan, on the night of the 11th of May, 1820, at his farm in New Jersey. To have known this amiable sage and to have been honored with some share in his esteem, will ever be among the proudest recollections of my life, though it is now also one of the most painful. I beg to apologize to those in either hemisphere who knew this amiable and highly gifted man for this poor tribute to his memory. In no way am I worthy to be the recorder of his virtues, unless the reverence and almost filial affection that I bore to him may seem to afford me a title.

Lest I should appear, in this instance, to have swerved from the rule which every writer of any delicacy will observe—that of abstaining from any remarks, which may tend to attract the public attention to his private friends—I must observe that the distinguished and acknowledged place that Mr. Garnett held in the world of science had rendered him, in some measure, a public character. He is now, too, lost to that world and to his friends; had it not been so, this humble testimony of one who feels herself better for having known him, and which must prove so insufficient to add anything to his fame, would never have appeared to pain his modesty.

LETTER VIII.

Visit to Joseph Bonaparte. General Observations. American Country Gentleman.

Pennsylvania, June 1819.

My Dear Friend,

I have not much leisure to recount the particulars of our peregrinations, nor perhaps would they greatly interest you. In travelling I find it convenient to bear in mind that the ground has been trodden before and that, in detailing the appearance and population of towns and districts, I should only write what others have already written, to whose journals, should you be curious on these matters, you can refer.

It may amuse you somewhat more to receive the account of our visit to Joseph Bonaparte.[1]

Some days since, joined by the friends in whose house we are now inmates, we filled a carriage and light waggon, called a dearborn,*[2] struck across to the Delaware, and then took boat to Bordentown, on the Jersey shore. A friend of our polite Philadelphia acquaintance *****[3] here joined our party, and we walked forwards to the residence of the ex-king. It is a pretty villa, commanding a fine prospect of the river; the soil around it is unproductive, but a step removed from the *pine barren;* the pines, however, worthless as they may be, clothe the banks pleasantly enough, and, altogether, the place is cheerful and pretty. Entering upon the lawn, we found the choice shrubs of the American forest, magnolias, kalmias, &c., planted tastefully under the higher trees which skirted and here and there shadowed the green carpet upon which the white mansion stood. Advancing, we were now faced at all corners by gods and goddesses in naked—I cannot say *majesty,* for they were, for the most part, clumsy enough. The late General Moreau, a few years since, according to the strange revolutions of war-stricken Europe, a peaceful resident in this very neighbourhood, and who recrossed the Atlantic to seek his death in the same battle which sent here, as an exile, the brother of the French

---

* From the American general of that name, to whom the farmer and country gentleman are under infinite obligations for its invention.

emperor—this general, in the same Parisian taste, left behind him a host of pagan deities of a similar description, with a whole tribe of dogs and lions to boot, some of which I have seen scattered up and down through the surrounding farms.[4] Two of these dumb Cerberuses are sitting at this moment on either side of a neighbouring gentleman's door, and the children of the family use them as hobbyhorses. Truly, the amusement of the child has often less folly in it than that of the man; the child rides the hobby, while the hobby too often rides the man; and then, if ambition be the hobby he chooses, the man rides down his fellow creatures. Happy the country where, without iron laws, all men are a check upon each other! I thought this when I entered the house of the brother of Napoleon.

Until the entrance of the count, who was superintending the additions yet making to the house, we employed ourselves in considering the paintings and Canovas, of which last we found a small but interesting collection.[5] It consists chiefly of busts of the different members of the Bonaparte family. The similar and classic outline prevailing in all is striking and has truly something *imperial* in it. As these were the first works of this Italian Phidias that I had met with, I regarded them with much curiosity. There are two small pieces of most exquisite workmanship—a naked infant (the little King of Rome), lying on a cushion, which yields to the pressure of one of the feet with a truth that mocks the marble. I remember a child in the same attitude in a much-prized Rubens, from which my first thought was that the sculptor had caught his idea. But, studying the same nature, genius is often original when vulgar criticism suspects the contrary; the same thought has been elicited from minds that never had communication, and this not once, but repeated times. There was another yet more lovely figure of a girl caressing a greyhound. What softness and delicacy wrought out of such rude materials! It is presumptuous for one so little skilled to venture upon the remark, yet I have always felt my eye offended by the too glaring whiteness of modern sculpture; perhaps the mellowing hand of time is as necessary for the marble as the canvas. Turning to look at David's portrait of Napoleon crossing the Alps, I was greatly disappointed with the expression of the young soldier; the horse has far more spirit than the rider, who sits carelessly on his steed, a handsome beardless boy, pointing his legions up the beetling crags as though they were some easy steps into a drawing room.[6] Such, at least, was my impression. Count Survilliers (he wears this title, perhaps, to save the awkwardness of "Mr. Bonaparte") soon came to us from his workmen, in an old coat, from which he had barely shaken off the mortar, and—a sign of the true gentleman—made no apologies. His air, figure, and address have the character of the English country gentleman—open, unaffected, and independent, but perhaps combining more mildness and suavity. Were it not that his figure is too thickset, I should perhaps say that he had still more the character of an American, in whom, I think, the last-enumerated qualities of mildness and suavity are oftener found than in our countrymen. His face is fine, and bears so close a resemblance to that of his more distinguished brother that it was difficult at the first glance to decide which of the busts in the apartment were of him and which of Napoleon. The expression of the one, however, is much more benignant; it is indeed exceedingly pleasing and prepares you for the amiable sentiments which appear in his discourse. The plainness and urbanity of his manners for the first few moments suspended pleasure in surprise; and even afterwards, when, smiling at myself, I thought, *And what did I expect to see?* I could not still help ever and anon acknowledging that I had not looked to see exactly the man I saw. I felt most strangely the contrast between the thoughts that were fast travelling through my brain, of battles and chances, ambition and intrigues, crowns and sceptres—the whole great drama of the brother's life passing before me—I felt most strangely the contrast between these thoughts and the man I was conversing with. He discoursed easily on various topics, but always with much quietness and modesty. He did and said little in the French manner, though he always spoke the language, understanding English, he said, but imperfectly and not speaking it at all. He expressed a curiosity to become acquainted with our living poets, but complained that he found them difficult, and enquired if there was not often a greater obscurity of style than in that of our older authors: I found he meant those of Queen Anne's reign. In speaking of the members of his family, he carefully avoided titles: it was *mon frère Napoléon, ma sœur Hortense,* &c. He walked us round his improvements indoors and out. When I observed upon the amusement he seemed to find in beautifying his little villa, he replied that he was happier in it than he had ever found himself in more bustling scenes. He gathered a wild flower and, in presenting it to me, carelessly drew a comparison between its minute beauties and the pleasures of private life, contrasting those of ambition and power with the more gaudy flowers of the parterre, which look better at a distance than upon a nearer approach. He said this so naturally, with a manner so simple and accent so mild, that it was impossible to see in it attempt at display of any kind. Understanding that I was a foreigner, he hoped that I was as much pleased with the country as he was, observed that it was a country for the many, and not for the few, which gave freedom to all and power to none, in which happiness might better be found than any other, and in which he was well pleased that his lot was now cast.

The character of this exile seems to be much marked for humanity and benevolence. He is peculiarly attentive to sufferers of his own nation—I mean of France—is careful to provide work for the poorer emigrants, and to others, affords lodging and often money to a considerable amount. His kindness has, of course, been imposed upon, in some cases so flagrantly that he is now learning circumspection, though he does not suffer his humanity to be chilled. This I learned from his American neighbours. I left Count Survilliers, satisfied that nature had formed him for the character he now wears and that fortune had rather spited him in making him the brother of the ambitious Napoleon.

In reviewing the singular destinies of this family, there is one acknowledgment that is forced from our candor: it is that, considering the power that circumstance threw into their hands, they wrested it to less monstrous purposes than has often been done by similarly spoiled children of fortune. We may indeed exclaim, in considering the mad career of Europe's conqueror,

> Ah! how did'st thou o'erleap the goal of Fame!
> Had'st thou but propp'd expiring Freedom's head,
> And to her feet again the nations led;
> Had'st thou, in lieu of War's blood-dropping sword,
> Seiz'd her white wand, and given forth her word;
> Bid the mad tumult of the nations cease,
> And loud from realm to realm cried *Liberty and Peace!*
>
> *Thoughts of a Recluse.*

But it is easier to be a philosopher in the closet than in the tented field, and, in reality, the real philosopher shrinks even from the trial of his virtue. Had Napoleon been such, the destinies of Europe would never have been laid at his mercy. As a soldier of fortune, he fought his way to distinction. That the young ambition which first fixed on him the eyes of men should have died at the most brilliant moment of his career, had been little less than miraculous. As it was, all was in the common order of vulgar humanity. He dared all things for a throne; he gained it, and then dared all things to throw splendour around it. It was false splendour, you will say. True, but it was false glory that allured him to the throne. The mind that coveted the one must necessarily have desired the other. Instead of quarrelling with successful ambition, it might be more rational, as well as more useful, to upbraid the nations that stoop to its insolence. If despots sometimes make slaves, it is no less true that slaves make despots. If men value not their own liberties, are they to expect that others will for them? They may find those that will fight their battles, but not those that will guard their rights. Heroes are more rare than warriors; thousands are born who can master others, but scarce one in a generation who can master himself. The fallen tyrant has been a good schoolmaster to the nations of Europe; may they profit by the lesson.

You will, perhaps, at first be scarcely disposed to admit the surmise that it is easier to speculate upon the future destinies of Europe in this hemisphere than the other. It is not only that vehement jealousies and vacillating parties distract the attention of the more near observer and prevent him from calmly considering the ultimate tendency of those great principles which, though now more or less everywhere acknowledged, are found to clash with the prevalent interests of the moment; it is not only that the noise of the combatants is lost in the distance, whilst the petty actors in the shifting scene dwindle into air, leaving only apparent the colossal stage itself and the general purport of the great drama which it exhibits; it is not only this, but that the various revolutions which have convulsed the European Continent have thrown into America a motley crowd of statesmen, soldiers, and politicians, who can here repeat the result of their experience without risk, and consequently without reserve. This continent seems at present to be the great side scene into which the chief actors of Europe make their exits, and from which, in the revolutions of human destiny, they may perhaps again be called to make their entrances.

It was observed, I think, in the English House of Commons, by a generous opposer of the Alien Act, that the present league subsisting between the great European potentates had realized the appalling picture drawn by the masterly pen of Gibbon, when the proscribed sought to fly the power of Rome and found her everywhere. The parallel, however, is not perfect, since there are now two hemispheres, while formerly there was but *one*. Beyond the waters of the Atlantic, the proscribed of every nation, whatever be their merits or demerits, now find a *leucé*,[7] wherein, though they should bring that with them which may poison happiness, they may at least enjoy security. Perhaps I am sanguine, but judging from the sentiments of the foreigners with whom I have chanced to engage in conversation, I feel disposed to augur well of many nations which are now little considered. The march of the human mind is rapid as silent, and many circumstances conspire to accelerate its progress. The very existence of this country teaches volumes. Even those who have never considered its history, and who seek it from necessity, merely as a haven of rest or as a field of mercantile speculation, when they look around them upon a cheerful, intelligent, peaceful, well-ordered community, are led to examine the secret spring which impels and regulates its political machinery. Men are here brought to think who never thought before, and who then bear with them to distant climes the result of their observations. A spark dropt from the torch of liberty will always spread, and spread until it bursts into flame.

It is a useful curiosity which impels us to engage in conversation with a foreigner; however circumscribed his mind, however scanty his stock of information, he is sure to know many things which we cannot know. It is curious also to hear his observations upon the men and things that surround him. Even should he see them through the medium of local or national prejudices, his remarks may be at least amusing, if not instructive—though it is probable, indeed, that they will be the latter also—for in detecting the prejudices of others we are often led to detect our own. It is always with peculiar curiosity that I listen to the remarks of Europeans upon the institutions of this country, and the appearance of its population, often so strangely and sometimes so painfully contrasted with those of their native soil. An Irishman exclaims, "Ah! it is a fine country!" and sighs as he thinks of his own island. A Frenchman observes, *"Mais comme tout va doucement et sagement!"* And a Swede, whom I chanced to cross some weeks since, closed some fervent ejaculations with "Ah! we cannot conshieve de vantages of dish peeplishes"; or, as he afterwards more intelligibly expressed it in French, *"Nous autres Européens nous ne saurions concevoir le bonheur de ce peuple sans en être témoins."*

I have already, in a former letter, introduced you to the family, to whose kindness and hospitality we are here so much indebted. I know not that I have as yet met with a more amiable specimen of the American country gentleman than we have found in this house; his children and infant grandchildren look up to him with that respect and affection which ever bear the most beautiful testimony to a parent's character. In his earlier, I can hardly say more *vigorous* years, he carries his accumulating lustres with so much ease and dignity, he took a part in political life. On retiring from the Senate, he was employed in diplomacy on the Continent of Europe, from whence he returned to pass the remainder of his days on his farm in Pennsylvania. I should like those, whose fancy pictures to them the American farmer as a half-civilized savage, to see this veteran's mild aspect, but unbent and majestic carriage, to see him rendering attentions of the kindest and most finished politeness to all around him, in manner and sentiment invariably the gentleman, the kind and considerate father, companion, and friend.

LETTER IX.

Passage Up the River Hudson. Account of the Academy at West Point. Pass of the Highlands. Arnold's Treachery. Albany and Its Environs.

Albany, July 1819.

My Dear Friend,

The hasty letter I addressed to you from Connecticut will have explained to you my unusual silence and relieved you from any apprehension that it might be occasioned by a broken neck, but in truth you are rather unconscionable in epistolary demands. You had no manner of title to look for a letter by the Martha, and yet I thank you that you did look for it. It tells me that your thoughts are as often on this side the ocean as mine are on yours.

We have just made the passage up the magnificent Hudson (160 miles) from New York to this city, which has indeed but one, though that no unimportant, title to so grand a name, in being the capital of the state. It is probable, however, that the government will soon have to travel in search of the centre of the republic in like manner with that of Pennsylvania. Albany indeed seems to stand as in expectation of her falling honors, for though there are some well-finished streets and many commodious and elegant private dwellings, the general appearance of the town is old and shabby.

You will not care to trace with me the beautiful course of this river. The features of nature, so unspeakably lovely to contemplate, are often tiresome in description. A few observations upon the military academy at West Point will perhaps interest you more than a sketch of the rocks and woody precipices upon which it stands. This interesting academy, which flourishes under the eye of the central government, was established in 1802. Its first organization was devolved by Congress upon the late General Williams, whose talents and unremitting industry did honor to himself and to his country which employed them.[1] The average number of youths educated at West Point varies from 230 to 250; 336 dollars are expended yearly upon each cadet, and the support of the establishment is rated by the government at the sum of 115,000 dollars per annum. The branches of education taught at the academy are similar to those taught at Woolwich and the Polytechnic School of Paris.[2] About one thousand youths from all the sections of the Union have here received a liberal and scientific education. A few of these now fill respectable posts in the corps of engineers, artillery, and other branches of the little army, amounting to a few thousands, which, scattered through this vast empire, are actively employed in the erection and conservation of forts, the protection of the Indian frontier, drawing of boundary lines, roads, &c. By far the greater number, however, retire from this little military fortress to the shade of private life, as peaceful cultivators of the soil, from whence some have been called by the voices of their fellow citizens to fill important civil offices, and all would be found ready at the first call of the republic to rush foremost for her defence.

It is judged by this government, ever liberal in all that touches the real welfare and dignity of the nation, that military knowledge can never be idly bestowed upon a citizen, who, whatever be his condition or calling, must always form one of the *civic militia;* and, looking to the event, always possible and therefore always to be provided against, of attack from foreign powers, it is perhaps the wisest of all conceivable precautions to scatter thus the seeds of military science among the peaceful population. It is true that these may never be required to put forth their fruits. These infant soldiers may live and die as peaceful tillers of the soil, but it is well to know that the trump of defensive war could summon skilled heads as well as devoted hearts to the field. This establishment has yet in it the seeds of more good. These youths, natives of different states gathered from the north, south, east, and west of this vast confederacy, and here trained together for the defence of *the great whole* under the fostering and liberal care of *the government of that whole,* necessarily forget all those paltry jealousies and selfish interests which once went nigh to split these great republics and to break down the last and noblest bulwark of freedom erected on this earth. Scattered again to the four winds of heaven, these sons of the republic bear with them the generous principles here imbibed, to breathe them perhaps in the senate, if not to support them in the field, and to hand them down to future generations through the minds of their children. "The most interesting and important consequences"—I quote the words addressed to me by an enlightened American officer, General Swift,[3] to whom I have often been obliged for many particulars regarding the condition of this country and to whose politeness I am chiefly indebted for my information respecting this establishment—"The most interesting and important consequences which I have noticed as resulting from an education at West Point are a zealous attachment to the political institutions of the nation, a devotion to country, an ardent love of liberty." This last, indeed, I have observed in the mind of an American to be synonymous with the love of the other two. In this country the government is the very palladium of liberty. Her throne is at Washington; upheld there by the united force of the whole people, she throws back light and heat upon her children and defenders. Generally speaking, all those connected with or forming a part of the central government, engaged in its service, or in any manner placed under its more immediate direction or protection are peculiarly distinguished for elevated sentiment, a high tone of national feeling, an ardent enthusiasm, not merely for American liberties but for the liberties of mankind.

The officers attached to the establishment, being distinguished both as men of science and ardent patriots and combining also the mildness and frankness of manner peculiar to the American gentleman, are well fitted to tutor the opinions and feelings of youth. Under their tuition they can acquire no sentiments that are not patriotic and generous; their minds in early infancy imbibe simple but sublime truths, invigorating principles, and all the pride and the energy which go to form free men. It is fine to see how soon the boy learns within the walls of this academy a knowledge of his own high destinies as the child of a republic. Our venerable friend * * * * lately procured admission for his little grandson. "I thought myself," said he, "among a crowd of young Spartans, and found my own little fellow, after a few weeks, looking and speaking as proudly as any one of them."

Among the most promising scholars, there are at present two Indians, the sons of chiefs. In the second class, at a late examination, they carried away several of the prizes. There was an instance of the same kind some years since, but, ere the boy reached his sixteenth year, he left his diagrams (as a young geometrician he had been one of great promise), ran to the woods, and forewent all other ambition for that of excelling in the chase. An officer of the establishment, from whom I had this, added that he had little doubt the two now with them would follow the same example. The account that I have received of the unconquerable wildness of the young savages, who, at different times, have been educated in the various colleges of these states, have sometimes brought to my recollection the experiments of a philosophic old housekeeper, in Devonshire, who was bent upon domesticating a brood of partridges. I remember well how she took me, then a child, into her poultry yard and dilated upon the untameable dispositions of these wild fowl, of which she had possessed herself of a brood for the third or fourth time. "I have reared them now from the egg, and yet two ran away yesterday; and if I had not put the other rogues under a hen coop, they would have been off this morning." I know not how the partridges learned, in the old dame's poultry yard, to connect happiness with hedges and cornfields, but it is easy to see how the young Indian should, in all places and under all circumstances, learn to connect it with the wilderness and the wild deer.

You will understand, from what I have said upon this military academy, that the object of the government, under whose eye and at whose expense it is conducted and maintained, is not to rear a band of *regulars*. The youth are in no way under obligations to enter into the service of the republic, nor indeed, supposing them so disposed, would it often be in the power of the government to gratify the desire. The slender force which is maintained at the national expense and which is barely sufficient for the hard duties in which it is engaged (consisting, as I have stated, in the inspection and erection of public works) admits but of few openings to such as might be ambitious of so arduous a service. It is intended, indeed, to provide a body of men, whose education shall fit them ably to fill the chief posts in this little band, and which has thus a surety of being directed by ability, but as I have stated, a further and more important object is kept in view, namely, that of scattering throughout the Union men imbued not merely with liberal principles but attached to scientific pursuits. The course of study in West Point chiefly differs from that of other colleges in so far as it leans rather more to the sciences and follows up those essential to the soldier in command, more particularly the engineer.

There is little fear in these pacific states of any portion of the citizens acquiring a taste for military glory. The strength of the country can never be put forth but in defence. The very institutions make against any other warfare; the sentiments of the people, inspired by these institutions, make against the same. All here breathes of peace, as well as freedom. American freedom, founded upon the broad basis of the rights of man, is friendly to the freedom of all nations; it looks not with jealousy upon the improving condition of foreign states. It will—it never *can*—attack but when attacked, or grossly insulted, but even in the last case, excepting indeed on the ocean, war here must still be defensive.[4] The *army* is the *people,* and the people must be at home. The enemy must invade before it can be engaged, and then no American need fear the issue. A town may be pillaged, a farm may be burnt, a few acres of cultivated land be laid waste, and then the aggressors must find their ships or be overwhelmed by accumulating multitudes. Foreign politicians, who, speculating upon the prospects of this nation, augur for it a career similar to that of other empires—inoffensive, because feeble in infancy, aspiring and violent in maturing strength, and then hurried into ruin by the reaction which ever returns upon aggression—have, I apprehend, but little considered its position and character. No nation in the whole history of the known world ever stood in a situation at all similar to this; none ever started in the career so equipt to run it well. It has no ambitious rulers, no distinguished classes, who might find it their interest to turn aside the public attention, by means of foreign wars, from the too narrow inspection of their aims or privileges, no colonies, no foreign possessions, requiring the guard of armed forces, or nourishing unjust ambition.

What country before was ever rid of so many evils? Without adverting to monarchies, let us consider the old republics. What points of comparison may we find between Rome and the United States? Rome had an arrogant and artful nobility, whose policy it was to foster the military mania of the people, to employ them in conquests abroad, lest they should aspire to dominion at home. The consequence was inevitable: the army gradually became the paramount order in the state, fell back upon their employers, and swallowed the privileges of the nobility, with every right of the people that the nobility had not swallowed before them.

In considering the history of modern Europe, we ever find the rulers rather than the people lighting up the first flame of war and madly prosecuting it beyond what the strength of the nation can support. It may be urged that an unreasonable war has often been a national one. The fact is undoubted, but we must take into the account the arts first employed by the rulers to rouse the popular feeling, or, supposing it roused without their assistance, the arts invariably employed to keep it alive. Pride and passion may hurry a people into momentary error, but, if left to themselves, time will bring reflection, and reflection, reason. The people here *are* left to themselves; they are their own rulers, their own defenders, their own champions. Should they judge hastily, they can retract their decision; should they act unwisely, they can desist from error. But there is yet a more important consideration—*they are their own teachers*. Not only can none shut the book of knowledge against them, but, by an imperative law, is it laid open before them. Every child is as fairly entitled to a plain but efficient education, as is every man to a voice in the choice of his rulers. Knowledge, which is the bugbear of tyranny, is, to liberty, the sustaining staff of life. To enlighten the mind of the American citizen is, therefore, a matter of national importance. In his minority he is, in a manner, the ward of the ruling generation. His education is not left to chance; schools are everywhere open for him at the public expense, where he may learn to study those rights which he is afterwards called upon to exercise. In this union of knowledge with liberty lies the strength of America. The rights that she possesses, she perfectly understands. Her blessings she not only enjoys, but knows to trace to their true sources. To suppose, therefore, that she can ever idly fling them away, is to suppose her smitten with sudden madness. Whatever may be the career of this nation, it must at least be singular; it cannot be calculated by the experience of the past.

It is impossible to enter, for the first time, the romantic pass of the Highlands and to rest the eye upon the interesting academy of West Point, perched upon one of the highest and most rugged pinnacles, without recalling the traditionary and historical remembrances of the place. In earlier ages this was the region of superstitious terror to the Indian, and even the European hunter. The groans of imaginary spirits changed in time into the shrill pipe of war, and now it is only the mimic drum of the academy that rings among the caverns and precipices, through which the Hudson rolls his deep and confined waters.

It was in the fastness of West Point that, in the moment of his country's worst distress, the traitor Arnold planned his scheme of treachery.[5] There is a moral that breathes from the tale, and that is thus pointed out by the historian: "it enforces the policy of conferring high trusts upon men of clean hands, and of withholding all public confidence from those who are subjected to the dominion of pleasure." [6] It is common to separate a man's public from his private character; the distinction is more than dangerous, it is morally atrocious. It is possible, indeed, that a rapacious soldier or an unprincipled minister may display, in domestic life, some pleasing qualities, and it is also possible that a man, notoriously licentious and unprincipled in private, may preserve a tolerably fair and consistent political character; but this is a chance that none have a right to reckon upon, and on the whole it is to be regretted when this chance occurs. It tends to corrupt the public morals, to lead men of weak heads and strong passions to wear their unblushing vices openly, and even to make them a passport to distinction. It is probable that the example of Arnold served as a useful warning to the people of these states and tended to encourage them in the practice of scrutinizing the secret conduct of those citizens whom they promote to offices of public trust.

It is somewhat remarkable that the licentious and unprincipled Arnold should have been a native of Connecticut, a state, as Ramsay observes, "remarkable for the purity of its morals, for its republican principles and patriotism." [7] This might be wrested into an evidence that early education does little towards forming the character of the man. But there is a species of restraint which, if suddenly removed, may leave the passions more untamed than if no bridle at all had been ever laid upon them. It is not unlikely that the young Arnold was bred up by virtuous but narrow-minded puritans, whose doctrines were hammered into the head rather than breathed into the heart, and which, afterwards uprooted during a stormy intercourse with the world, left no moral feelings to stem the flood of temptation. It was well written by a philosopher, *"On ne dispute jamais sur la vertu, parce qu'elle vient de Dieu; on se querelle sur les opinions qui viennent des hommes."* [8] The Americans are, for the most part, aware of this truth; even the citizens of Connecticut and New England are gradually coming round to the opinion.

It is a proud and gratifying reflection that an arduous revolutionary struggle of eight years' duration brought to light but one such character as Arnold. This single exception was, indeed, a most atrocious one. Born and bred among a simple and moral race, embarking the first and the boldest in the noblest cause in which a patriot could engage, pouring his blood for years freely and, to appearance, ungrudgingly, for a country who acknowledged his services with a gratitude and generosity such as might have melted the heart of a savage, and repaid them with a confidence which might have flattered the most selfish ambition; that a man so situated, so held by every tie that might seem calculated not only to induce but to constrain fidelity, should, in the very last years of the war, have sold himself for a bribe and plotted the destruction of the patriotic army which he had so often led to victory; and that, after his treason had been baffled, he should have served under the standard which he had so often and so boldly defied, laying waste the country of his nativity, and plundering and butchering the people who had so often forgiven his offences, and repaid his services with gold, hardly and yet willingly wrung from their exhausted fortunes—truly there is in this a hardened depravity, an atrocious licentiousness, which, to muse upon, makes the blood run cold. The spot on the beach was pointed out to me, where the traitor met the unfortunate young André, so unfit to be a party in the scheme of wickedness. It seems as if fortune had found a pleasure in opposing every contrast that could set off to worst advantage the villainy of Arnold. The very spy, dispatched by the enemy, proved too artless to sustain the character that was thrust upon him. To portray the feelings of these two men, of characters so opposite, met together in treasonous conference in the dead of night upon the wild and desolate shores of this vast river, might furnish a subject for the painter or the dramatist. The little shallop, moored upon the beach, which has landed the young André; the sloop of war, waiting to assist his retreat, sleeping in the distance on the waters; the outposts of the American army just visible on the tops of the frowning precipices, from which, with hasty and unequal steps, listening to every breeze and startling at his own shadow, the traitor steals to his appointment. The soldiers meet, and each looks round as apprehending listeners in

the savage solitude, one trembling with the sense of his own iniquity, fearing
lest the winds should bear to the little band of patriots, then confiding in his
honor, the purpose of their treacherous commander, the other ashamed of the
part in which he is engaged—his honorable feelings as a man revolting against
the obedience he yields as a soldier to the instructions of his general. How
repugnant to a generous nature a conference held in darkness and disguise,
with a cold and calculating villain, who stipulates the price for which he will
sell his unsuspecting countrymen and companions in arms, the voice of whose
sentinels, perhaps, swells at intervals on the ear!

The interview was prolonged until the dawn threatened them with detec-
tion. The young Englishman was forced to remain in concealment until the
shades of another night should favour his escape. Arnold, having secreted his
companion, returned to his post, to face, without a blush, the heroes he had
sold.

The romantic position held by this detachment of the patriot army increases,
if possible, the interest of the moment: it was posted in a fastness, if not
impregnable, yet such as gave to a handful of men a superiority over thousands;
it stretched along the tops of two ridges, broken into abrupt precipices sinking
on one side into woods and morasses and on the other shelving precipitously
into the deep Hudson, whose channel it here securely shut against the enemy.
Perched like an eagle in his eyrie, the little army looked down securely on its
foes. It had many distresses to bear—hunger and nakedness, with all their train
of evils—but these it bore cheerfully, unconscious of the fiend who had found
his way into this little Thermopylæ of America, and who, in marking out to
its assailants its strength and weakness, forgot not the miseries of its defenders,
which, perhaps, in his calculation reduced their number to a cypher. There
is something greatly affecting, if we suffer ourselves to picture the security of
this little band, seeking forgetfulness of their sufferings in sleep, while their
commander was stealing forth to barter them for gold. The confidence reposed
by the pure-minded Washington in the honor of this veteran soldier is not
less affecting. When he solicited the command of this important post (as it
soon appeared, for the express purpose of selling it to the enemy), some
ventured to whisper doubts of his fidelity, probably from the knowledge of
his debts, as well as the strong suspicion of his having embezzled the public
money and entered into disgraceful contracts and speculations. But the American commander, recollecting the long list of services rendered by Arnold to his
country, and feeling in himself all the honor of a soldier and a man,
generously resented the suspicions cast on one whose valour and truth seemed
to have been so tried and frankly accorded the request preferred to him. Had

this treasonable scheme succeeded, it is painful to calculate the consequences to the country and the cause. West Point was, perhaps, the post of most importance throughout the whole of the Union. It commanded the navigation of the Hudson, secured the communication of all the states one with another, and protected the whole interior of the country. The enemy, already in possession of New York, would have commanded this great river from its mouth to its head, have pierced directly to the lakes, and established a line of communication with Canada. The eastern states, thus cut off from the southern, and assailed on one side from the sea and on the other by land, would have been completely surrounded, and must inevitably have been overrun, as the Carolinas had lately been by the army under Cornwallis; not the least calamitous of the effects that would have accrued from the loss of West Point had been the blow given to the public confidence by so nefarious a treachery. The people might have seen in every officer another Arnold, and the soldiers have attributed every subsequent disaster to the treason of their commanders. Nor must we overlook in the account the despair and rage of the little army, unsuspiciously devoted to slaughter by their own leader and mingling with their dying groans the curses of righteous but impotent indignation. From these calamities America was spared, and the traveller, in visiting this romantic pass, recurs to the tale of Arnold as to that of some demoniac hero of a wild drama.

You remember the circumstances of the closing scene. André found his retreat by water cut off and, in disguise, took his way to New York by land. Challenged within a few miles of his own army by three Americans of the New York militia, he, unpractised in deceit, incautiously betrayed himself. Discovering his error, he offered gold, with any terms they might farther insist upon, but he had no longer to treat with an Arnold. He and the papers found upon him detailing all the particulars of the intended treachery were delivered by his captors to their colonel, and the life of this young officer was forfeited to the law. After his seizure, the first object of the disinterested André was to convey a warning to Arnold; this the latter unfortunately received in time to effect his escape. Having joined the British, the traitor well filled up the measure of his iniquity. Intimately acquainted with all the distresses of those he had forsaken, he exposed their weakness to the enemy he had joined, and imagined that he knew how to practise on it by holding out offers, calculated at once to tempt their ambition and cupidity, and to subdue their spirit, already broken down by famine, sickness, and every suffering which can afflict humanity. But there is a strength in man which an Arnold cannot dream of. There is that virtue which the Romans in their language finely made synonymous with force; and, truly, that courage which has its seat only in the nerves and which the man shares but in common with the brutes is no more to be compared in lasting heat and energy with the heroism of mind than is the parhelion to the sun. The promises of Arnold were impotent as his threats. The fainting soldiers, whom he had sought to betray, were nerved by indignation with new valour. The country, everywhere reduced to the lowest ebb of calamity, gathered confidence from the very circumstance which seemed calculated to annihilate it: not a man deserted his post. His very sufferings became a source of pride, and often of jest; to be half naked and half starving were spoken of as marks by which to know a patriot. Thus is it that man inspired by the noble spirit of independence rises above himself, stands superior to fortune, and discovers the divine image beneath all the weakness and pains of mortality.

We linger here from day to day, unwilling to leave the kind and cheerful circle who administer so pleasingly to us the laws of hospitality. It is time, however, to remember that we have yet a long journey to make and must determine to set forward so soon as the skies shall resume their wonted serenity. This has been a season of uncommon heat, and along the whole line of the coast, one of uncommon drought. At ———, in Jersey, during the latter days of July, the mercury twice rose, in a northern exposure, to a hundred, and for many days successively, when the sun was at his meridian, varied from 90 to 96. Some local causes might there have influenced the atmosphere, as I found its temperature had been some degrees lower in other places, but everywhere it had been unusually high. In many parts where the soil was light, the herbage had totally disappeared, and plants of considerable size and strength were drooping and occasionally quite bereft of leaves. In ascending the Hudson, we had no sooner passed the Highlands than our eyes fell upon carpets of massy verdure, and woods whose foliage was fresh as if daily washed by showers. We could have imagined ourselves in a second spring, but for the tropical heat which followed us, and which was only broken two days since by the grandest and longest thunderstorm that I ever witnessed. The sun has not yet pierced the clouds; his doing so will be the signal for our departure. I have found this extreme heat much less oppressive than I could have believed possible; indeed, I will confess, under hazard of your thinking me fit to live with the giants under Mount Ætna, that I have enjoyed it exceedingly. I find a purity and elasticity in the air that exhilarates my spirits, even while I am half melted by its fervor. It may strike you as singular, if you never made or heard the observation, that the constitution is, in general, not immediately sensible to the extremes of climate. It is often remarked here that a stranger from a more southern latitude feels the severity of a first winter less than the natives, though he should feel the second more, and, in like manner, that one from a temperate climate is, for some years, less relaxed by the summer heats than those who have regularly been exposed to them. This last seems to admit of an easy explanation, but I know not how wise physicians will account for the former; if they cannot explain the fact, they will, perhaps, dispute it, and far be it from me to provoke their wrath by insisting upon it.

In this neighbourhood nature presents many beautiful and some grand features; chief among these is the well-known cataract of the Mohawk, whose waters precipitate themselves over a fine wall of rock just before they unite with those of the Hudson. Its height is stated variously; perhaps sixty feet is nearest the mark. Its immense breadth is by some accounted a disadvantage; I imagine this to be the true source of its grandeur, particularly as there is nothing in the surrounding scenery to assist the effect. For us, however, circumstances combined to throw charms around the spot, when, beneath an Italian sky and on a carpet of verdure which fairy feet might have sought to print their magic rings, we stretched ourselves with * * * * under the shade of a spreading tree and cast our eyes upon the foaming Cohoes, whose dash and roar seemed to cool the fervid air. A group of smiling handmaids meantime spread a repast which an epicure might have envied. The scene, the air, the laughing heavens, and the cheerful companions have graven the place on my memory as one of those "sunny spots" which chequer with gold the shadowy path of human life.

There are several very pleasing falls of water to be found in the hills of the surrounding country, and though in grandeur that of the Mohawk stands pre-eminent, in beauty some may do more than rival it. I have frequently been surprised in the small section of this vast country that I have visited to find, upon a more close examination, wild and romantic features in a landscape whose outline wore a character of mild beauty or dull uniformity; rocky glens, clothed with shaggy wood and traversed by brawling streams, broken into cascades, are not unfrequently found in hills, rising gently out of vast and swampy plains, or skirting valleys, watered by placid rivers, whose banks of alluvial soil are rich with golden harvests. The broken course of America's rivulets and rivers has, I believe, among other appearances, led the scientific to suppose this a world of later formation than the other. I was once much startled by the eager refutation which this hypothesis received from an American naturalist, no less remarkable for the simplicity of his character than for his enthusiasm in his chosen pursuits. Chancing to put a modest query to the philosopher upon the results of his researches into the age of his native continent, I quickly perceived that to question her antiquity were as though you should question her excellence, and you will believe that I bowed out of the subject (for I had never presumed to make it an argument) with all possible politeness and deference.

LETTER X.

Canandaigua, August 1819.

My Dear Friend,

What is there in life more pleasing than to set forward on a journey with a light heart, a fine sun in the heavens above you, and the earth breathing freshness and fragrance after summer rain? Let us take into the account the parting good wishes of friendship, recommending you to a kind fortune, and auguring pleasant roads, pleasant skies, and pleasant everything. A *preux chevalier,* in olden time, setting forth in a new suit of armor, buckled on by the hand of a princess, to seek adventure through the wide world, might be a more important personage than the peaceful traveller of these generations, who goes to seek waterfalls instead of giants and to look at men instead of killing them, but I doubt if he was in any way happier or felt one jot more exquisitely the pride and enjoyment of life, health, vigor, and liberty. These are the moments, perhaps, which, in the evening of life, when seated in an easy armchair, we may rouse our drowsy senses by recurring to, and, like old veterans counting their honorable scratches and all their "hair-breadth 'scapes in the imminent deadly breach," pour into the ears of some curly-pated urchin our marvellous adventures upon the back of a mule, or in the heart of a stage waggon, with a summary of all the bruises and the broken bones, either received or that might have been received by riding in or tumbling out of it. Should I live to grow garrulous in this way, our journey hither may afford a tolerable account of bruises, though it is now a subject of congratulation with me, whatever it may be then, that there must remain a total deficit under the head of fractures.

If our journey was rough, it was at least very cheerful, the weather beautiful, and our companions good humoured, intelligent, and accommodating. I know not whether to recommend the stagecoach or waggon (for you are sometimes put into the one and sometimes into the other) as the best mode of travelling. This must depend upon the temper of the traveller. If he want to see people

as well as things—to hear intelligent remarks upon the country and its inhabitants, and to understand the rapid changes that each year brings forth,
and if he be of an easy temper, not incommoded with trifles, nor caring to
take, nor understanding to give offence, liking the interchange of little
civilities with strangers, and pleased to make an acquaintance, though it should
be but one of an hour, with a kind-hearted fellow creature, and if too he can
bear a few jolts (*not* a few), and can suffer to be driven sometimes too quickly
over a rough road and sometimes too slowly over a smooth one—then let him,
by all means, fill a corner in the post coach or stage waggon according to the
varying grade in civilization held by the American diligence. But if the traveller be a lounger, running away from time, or a landscape-painting tourist
with a sketchbook and portable crayons, or anything of a *soi-disant philosophe,*
bringing with him a previous knowledge of the unseen country he is about
to traverse, having itemed in his closet the character, with the sum of its
population, and in his knowledge of how everything ought to be, knowing
exactly how everything is—or, if he be of an unsociable humour, easily put out
of his way, or, as the phrase is, "a very particular gentleman"—then he will
hire or purchase his own dearborn or light waggon, and travel *solus cum solo*
with his own horse, or, as it may be, with some old associate who has no
humours or his own or whose humours are known by repeated experience to be
of the exact same fashion with his companion's. In some countries you may,
as it is called, "travel post," but in these states it is seldom that you have this
at your option, unless you travel with a phalanx capable of peopling a whole
caravan; eight persons will be sufficient for this, the driver always making the
ninth, seated three in a row.

In this journey, as I have often found before, the better half of our enter-
tainment was afforded by the intelligence of our companions. It was our good
fortune on leaving Albany to find ourselves seated immediately by a gentleman
and his lady returning from Washington to this, their residence. He was a
native of Scotland, but came to this country in his early youth, followed the
profession of the law, settled himself many years since in affluence on his
farm (which seems rather to furnish his amusement than his business),
married into a family that had emigrated from New England, and settled
down in the neighbourhood, and lives surrounded not only by all the comforts
but the luxuries of life. We were variously joined and abandoned by citizens
of differing appearance and professions, country gentlemen, lawyers, members
of Congress, naval officers, farmers, mechanics, &c. There were two characteristics in which these our fellow travellers generally, more or less, resembled each
other—good humour and intelligence. Wherever chance has as yet thrown me

into a public conveyance in this country, I have met with more of these, the best articles of exchange that I am acquainted with, than I ever remember to have found elsewhere.

Our second day's journey was long and fatiguing, but withal very interesting, the weather delightful and the scenery pleasing. The road bore everywhere heavy marks of the *flagellations* inflicted by the recent storms. It seemed often as if not only the rain but the lightning had torn up the ground and scooped out the soil, now on this side and now on that, into which holes, first the right wheel of our vehicle, and anon the left making a sudden plump, did all but spill us out on the highway. To do justice to ourselves, we bore the bruises that were in this manner most plentifully inflicted with very tolerable stoicism and unbroken good humour.

Gaining the banks of the Mohawk, we traced its course for sixty miles, which, between the lower cataract of the Cohoes and the Upper Falls, flows placidly through a country finely varied, rich with cultivation, and sprinkled with neat and broad-roofed cottages and villas, shadowed with trees, and backed with an undulating line of hills, now advancing and narrowing the strath, and then receding and leaving vistas into opening glades, down which the tributaries of the Mohawk pour their waters. Massy woods everywhere crown and usually clothe these ridges, but indeed, as yet, there are few districts throughout this vast country where the forest, or some remnants of it, stand not within the horizon.

The valley of the Mohawk is chiefly peopled by old Dutch settlers, a primitive race, who retain for generations the character, customs, and often the language of their ancient country. Of all European emigrants, the Dutch and the German invariably thrive the best, "locate" themselves, as the phrase is here, with wonderful sagacity, and this being once done, is done forever. Great must be the penury from which this harmless people fly, who are thus attached to the ways of their fathers, and who, once removed to a land yielding sustenance to the swart hand of industry, plant so peacefully their penates and root themselves so fixedly in the soil. As a settler next best to the German, thrives the Scot; the Frenchman is given to turn hunter, the Irishman, drunkard, and the Englishman, speculator. Amusement rules the first, pleasure ruins the second, and self-sufficient obstinacy drives headlong the third. There are many exceptions, doubtless, to this rule, and the number of these increases daily—and for this reason it is a higher class that is at present emigrating. I speak now more particularly of England. It is men of substance, possessed in clear property of from five hundred to five thousand pounds, who now attempt the passage of the Atlantic. I know of thirteen families who lately arrived in these states from the Thames, not one of which is possessed of less than the former sum and some of more than the latter. I fear that the policy of England's rulers is cutting away the sinews of the state. Why are her yeomen disappearing from the soil, dwindling into paupers or flying as exiles? Tithes, taxes, and poor-rates—these things must be looked into, or her population will gradually approach to that of Spain, beggars and princes, the shaft of the fair column reft away.

Something less than twenty miles below Utica, the river makes a sharp angle, in the manner of the Hudson at West Point, running into a cleft or "gap," forced in primeval times, with dreadful convulsion, through the ridge along the base of which it afterwards so peacefully winds. The Mohawk assumes here much the character of Loch Katrine at the Trossachs: the beetling crags, and rocks in ruin hurled, and shaggy wood, grooved in the dark crevices, and little coves, where the still clear water stirs not the leaf that has dropped upon its bosom. But there is no Ben Venue and Ben Ann to guard the magic pass, nor lady with her fairy skiff, nor is the fancy here entitled to image her; it may, however, if it be sportively inclined, picture out the wild Indian paddling his canoe, or springing from rock to rock, swift as the deer he pursues. It is evident that the water once occupied the whole breadth of the ravine, when it must have boiled and eddied with somewhat more tumultuous passions than it shows at present. The huge misshapen blocks that now rise peacefully out of the flood beetle over the head of the passenger, or, standing in the line of his rough path, force him variously to wheel to right or left, bear on their sides the marks of the ancient fury of the subdued element, which, now having sunk its channel, leaves room for the road to scramble an intricate way by its side. When about to issue from the chasm, you open upon the Lesser Falls, so called in contrast to the greater cataract at the mouth of the river. It is a wild scene and helps the fancy to image out the uproar that must in former ages have raged in the depths of the pass below. How astounding it is to trace in the vast works of nature the operations of time, so mighty, and yet so slow, silent, and unseen! The whole known history of man reaches not back to the date of some crevice in a mountain; each fathom, worn by a river in his rocky bed, speaks of untold generations, swept from the earth and lost from her records. How grand is the solemn march of nature still advancing without check, or stop, or threat of hindrance! Ages are to her as moments, and all the known course of time a span.

We reached Utica very tolerably fagged, and bruised as I could not wish an enemy. A day's rest well recruited us, however, and gave us time to examine this wonderful little town, scarce twenty years old. An innkeeper here, at whose door fifteen stages stop daily, carried, eighteen years since, the solitary and weekly mail in his coat pocket from hence to Albany. This newborn Utica already aspires to be the capital of the state, and in a few years it probably will be so, though Albany is by no means willing to yield the honor, nor New York the convenience, of having the seat of government in her neighbourhood; but the young western counties are such stout and imperious children that it will soon be found necessary to consult their interests.

The importance of Utica will soon be increased by the opening of the great canal, destined here to join the Mohawk. We swerved the next day from our direct route for the purpose of looking at this work, now in considerable progress, and which, in its consequences, is truly grand, affording a water highway from the heart of this great continent to the ocean. Commencing at Lake Erie, it finds a level, with but little circuit, to the Mohawk; at the Lesser Falls are some considerable locks; others will be required at the mouth of the river, where the Hudson opens his broad way to the Atlantic. It is thought that four or five years will now fully complete this work. The most troublesome opposition it has encountered is in the vast Onondaga Swamp, and not a few of the workmen have fallen a sacrifice to its pestilential atmosphere.[1]

Leaving Utica, the country begins to assume a rough appearance—stumps and *girdled* trees encumbering the inclosures; log houses scattered here and there; the cultivation rarely extending more than half a mile, nor usually so much, on either hand, when the forest, whose face is usually rendered hideous to the eye of the traveller by a skirting line of girdled trees, half standing, half falling, stretches its vast, unbroken shade over plain and hill and dale, disappearing only with the horizon. Frequently, however, gaining a rising ground (and the face of the country is always more or less undulating), you can distinguish gaps, sometimes long and broad, in the deep verdure, which tell that the axe and the plough are waging war with the wilderness. Owing to some disputed claims in the tenure of the lands, cultivation has made less progress here than it has farther west, as we found on approaching the Skaneateles, Cayuga, Seneca, Onondaga, and Canandaigua lakes. Having passed the flourishing town of Auburn, we found the country much more open, well-finished houses and thriving villages appearing continually. The fifth day from that of our departure from Albany brought us to this village, where our kind fellow travellers insisted on becoming our hosts. The villages at the head of the different lakes I have enumerated above are all thriving, cheerful, and generally beautiful, but Canandaigua, I think, bears away the palm. The land has been disposed of in lots of forty acres each, one being the breadth, running in lines diverging on either hand from the main road. The houses are all delicately painted, their windows with green Venetian blinds, peeping gaily through fine young trees, or standing forward more exposed on their little lawns, green and fresh as those of England. Smiling gardens, orchards laden with fruit—quinces, apples, plums, peaches, &c.—and fields, rich in golden grain, stretch behind each of these lovely villas, the church with its white steeple rising in the midst, over-looking this land of enchantment.

The increase of population, the encroachment of cultivation on the wilder-ness, the birth of settlements and their growth into towns surpasses belief, till one has been an eyewitness of the miracle or conversed on the spot with those who have been so. It is wonderfully cheering to find yourself in a country which tells only of improvement. What other land is there that points not the imagina-tion back to better days, contrasting present decay with departed strength, or that, even in its struggles to hold a forward career, is not checked at every step by some physical or political hindrance?

I think it was one of the sons of Constantine, I am sure that it was one of his successors, who, returning from a visit to Rome, said that he had learned one thing there, "that men died in that queen of cities as they did elsewhere." [2] It might require more, perhaps, to remind a stranger of the mortality of his species in these states than it did in old Rome. All here wears so much the gloss of novelty—all around you breathes so much of the life and energy of youth, that a wanderer from the antique habitations of time-worn Europe might look around and deem that man here held a new charter of existence, that time had folded his wings and the sister thrown away the shears.

LETTER XI.

Genesee. Visit to Mr. Wadsworth. American Farmer. Set-
tling of the New Territory. Forest Scenery.

Geneseo, August 1819.

My Dear Friend,

Taking a kind farewell of our hospitable friends in Canandaigua, we struck
into the forest, and by a crossroad, helter-skelter over stumps and logs, rattled
in a clumsy conveyance to this thriving settlement on the banks of the Genesee.
The road, though rough, was not wholly without its interest: at first, opening
prospects of hills and valleys, where sometimes the white walls of a young settlement glanced in the sun, relieving the boundless "continuity of shade"; and
then bordered occasionally with cornfields and young orchards of peach and
apple, groaning beneath their weight of riches. The withered trees of the forest
stood indeed among them, but though these should mar beauty, they give a
character to the scene that speaks to the heart, if not to the eye.

We were received with a warm welcome by Mr. and Mrs. Wadsworth, a
name you are already acquainted with.[1] The American gentleman receives his
guest in the true style of old patriarchal hospitality—with open hand at the gate
—and leads you over the threshold with smiling greetings that say more than a
thousand words. There is about him an urbanity and a politeness, breathing
from the heart, which courts and cities never teach. Nothing seems to be dis-
arranged by your presence, and yet all is ordered for your convenience and
amusement. You find yourself, in a few minutes, one of the family; frankness
and friendliness draw forth the same feelings from you; you are domesticated
at the hearth and the board, and depart at last with heart overflowing, as from
some *home* endeared by habit and sacred association.

This house stands pleasantly on the gentle declivity of a hill, commanding a
fine prospect of the Genesee flats (beautiful prairie land bordering the river)
and the rising grounds, covered with dark forests, bounding them. Some scattered groups of young locust trees spread their chequered shade upon the lawn,
down which, as seated beneath the porch or in the hall, with its wide open
doors, the eye glances first over a champaign country, speckled with flocks and

herds and golden harvests, and then over primeval woods, where the Indian chases the wild deer. To the right stretches a scattered village of neat white houses that have just started into being, from the bosom of which rises the spire of a little chapel, flashing against the sun; behind, barns, stables, and outhouses, and to the right a spacious and well-replenished garden, with orchard after orchard, laden with all the varieties of apple, pear, and peach.

Mr. Wadsworth is the patriarch of the Genesee district. He is a native of New England, in whose earliest history the name appears frequently and honorably. It is scarcely nineteen years since this gentleman, with his brother, Colonel Wadsworth, pierced into these forests, then inhabited only by the savage and his prey. The rich and open lands here stretching along the river fixed their attention, and having purchased a considerable tract of land from the Indian proprietors, they settled themselves down among them. The first six years were years of fearful hardship; every autumn brought fevers, intermitting and bilious, and this too in a wilderness where no comforts or conveniencies could be procured. Their constitutions, however, hardened by early temperance, weathered this trying season. Other settlers gradually joined them, and now a smiling village is at their door, rich farms rising everywhere out of the forest, and a pure and healthy atmosphere ever surrounding them. Mrs. Wadsworth tells me that her numerous family have never been afflicted with sickness of any kind, nor do we hear of any in the surrounding neighbourhood.

I have not yet seen more thriving or beautiful young settlements than those now surrounding me. Mr. Wadsworth is considered as one of the richest proprietors in the state, and well has he acquired his wealth and generously does he employ it. Like one of the patriarchs of old, he looks round upon his flocks and herds, luxurious pastures, and rich fields of grain, bounteous heaven ever adding to his store, and feels that, under its blessing, all is the reward of his own industry, the work, as it were, of his creation. It is truly a grateful sight to see the wilderness thus transformed into beauty, to see the human species absolved from oppression and, with it, absolved from misery, extending their dominion, not unjustly over their fellow creatures, but over the peaceful earth, and leaving to their posterity the well-earned fruits of their industry and, what is better, the pure example of time well employed. In truth it cheers the spirits and does the heart good to see these things.

Sometimes, indeed, I cannot help contrasting the condition of the American with that of the English farmer: no tithes, no grinding taxes, no bribes received or offered by electioneering candidates or their agents, no anxious fears as to the destiny of his children and their future establishment in life. Plenty at the board, good horses in the stable, an open door, a friendly welcome, light spirits, and easy toil—such is what you find with the American farmer. In England—

> There is a tale the traveller can read
> Who, on old Tyber's banks, hath check'd his steed,
> And paus'd, and mus'd, and wept upon the wreck
> Of what *was* Rome.

You will tell me, perhaps, that I now see the Old World in contrast with the New, that this is comparing age to youth, a comparison that is either unfair or childish. But is it with nations as with individuals? Have they no second youth? We have seldom seen that they have, but few in their old age have shewn such vigor as England. Has she not enough to work her own regeneration? I wish it too well not to believe it.

> Oh England! well I love thee; oft recall
> Thy pleasant fields; thy hills' soft sloping fall;
> Thy woods of massy shade and cool retreat;
> Thy rivers in their sedges murmuring sweet,
> Where once, with tender feet, I wont to stray,
> Muttering my childish rhymings by the way;
> And pouring plenteous sighs, I knew not why,
> And dropping soft tears from my musing eye.—
> Yes! much I love thee;—turn not then away
> As tho' thou heard'st a heartless alien's lay.
> Childhood and dreaming youth flew o'er this head
> Ere from thy pleasant lawns the wanderer fled;
> And tho' maturer years have mark'd her brow,
> And somewhat chill'd perchance her feelings now,
> Still does her stricken heart beat warm for thee,
> Much does it wish thee great,—much does it wish thee *free*.
>   *Thoughts of a Recluse.*

Forgive me this quotation. It expresses my feelings at the moment. I need not say *moment,* for they force themselves upon me very often.

It were difficult, perhaps, to conceive man placed in a more enviable position than he is as a cultivator of the soil in these states. Agriculture here assumes her most cheerful aspect, and (some Europeans might smile doubtingly, but it is true) all her ancient classic dignity, as when Rome summoned her consuls from the plough. I have seen those who have raised their voice in the senate of their country, and whose hands have fought her battles, walking beside the team and minutely directing every operation of husbandry, with the soil upon their garments and their countenances bronzed by the meridian sun. And how proudly does such a man tread his paternal fields! his ample domains improving under his hand, his garners full to overflowing, his table replenished with guests, and with a numerous offspring, whose nerves are braced by exercise and their minds invigorated by liberty. It was finely answered by an American citizen to a European who, looking around him, exclaimed, "Yes; this is all well. You have all the vulgar and the substantial, but I look in vain for the *ornamental*. Where are your ruins and your poetry?" "There are our ruins," replied the republican, pointing to a Revolutionary soldier who was turning up the glebe; and then, extending his hand over the plain that stretched before them, smiling with luxuriant farms and little villas, peeping out from beds of trees, "There is our poetry."

It is not always, indeed, that the farmer may aspire to affluence, as some of our more ignorant emigrants suppose. I have seen small proprietors in this country, whose life was one continued scene of unbroken toil and whose exertions procured little more to themselves and their families than common necessaries and indispensable comforts; these, however, they may always procure, and sometimes, by shifting the scene of their industry, may ensure more abundant returns. But here again there are often positive evils that must be placed in the balance against positive good. The hardy citizen who migrates from the more sterile districts of New England to the virgin lands of the West has to encounter fatigues and but too frequently unwholesome vapors to which even his vigorous constitution may fall a sacrifice. It is wonderful to see how cheerfully these physical evils are braved, and often how well and speedily they are surmounted, but still, with many, a hard-earned competence with health will balance against the chance of greater abundance, purchased by years of sickness or perhaps by a broken constitution.

We should, however, but ill appreciate the causes which pour the tide of emigration from the East to the West, if we considered avarice as giving the sole impetus. It is not a mere calculation of dollars and cents, or a thousand bushels of corn placed against a hundred, which alone sways the mind of the adventurous settler.

The position of this country, its boundless territory, its varied soils and climates, its free institutions, and, favoured by these circumstances, the rapid increase of its population—all combine to generate in this people a spirit of daring enterprise as well as of proud independence. They spurn at little hindrances in narrow room, and prefer great difficulties in a wide horizon. In flying to the wilderness, they fly a thousand constraints which society must always impose, even under the fairest laws. They have here no longer to jostle with the crowd;

their war is only with nature; their evils, therefore, are chiefly physical, and the comforts they may forego are amply compensated by the frets and cares from which they may be released. It is curious to consider the effect which this release from moral ills seems to have upon the constitution. Those who safely weather out the first hard seasoning, or who, from choosing their ground more judiciously, escape with but very little, are often found to live to an unusual age. It is a singular fact that the citizens of the new states are often remarkable for uncommon longevity and universally for uncommon stature. This cannot be accounted for by supposing that they are more exposed to air and exercise—the American farmer is this universally—and though universally the average of his stature is above that of Europeans, it were, perhaps, more just to ascribe this varying standard of bodily vigor to the less or greater pressure of mental solicitude.*

Were the human mind less sensible to the charms of novelty and liberty, the settlement of the new country might be left only to the necessitous. As it is, men of property and gentlemen accustomed to all the refinements of society are found among the first occupiers of the wilderness. When Mr. Wadsworth settled in this district, he formed the advanced guard of civilization; a vast tract of forest stretched behind him, through which he cleared a passage for the necessary implements of husbandry, with considerable toil and difficulty. The tide of human life has now flowed up to him and is rapidly sweeping onwards in all directions.

In the deep verdure of the forest, stretching beyond the open lands that border the river, the eye discerns specks of a browner hue, which mark where the new settler has commenced his work of peaceful industry. It was with much surprise that, in a late excursion, we suddenly opened upon a flourishing little village that has started up in a couple of years, or little more, in the bosom of the forest, a few miles higher up the river.

It was towards evening when we reached the settlement, and then, turning again among the trees and making a short ascent by a road roughly paved with logs, suddenly found ourselves on a lawn in front of a spacious and elegant

---

* I perceive that Lieutenant Hall has admitted among the causes to which he ascribes the gigantic stature of the members from the western states, whom he observed in Washington, "the absence of mental irritation." The other causes which he enumerates, "plentiful, but simple food, a healthy climate, constant exercise in the open air," might better account for the differing stature between Europeans and Americans generally, than between the Americans of the old and new territory.[2] The climate of the eastern and central states, though it should not vie in beauty, must, for some years to come, in salubrity, with that of the western districts. The people of these states generally are well but simply fed and continually exercised. The difference, if any, can scarcely be sufficient to affect the bodily organs.

dwelling. We had already made acquaintance with its hospitable owner, who, with his wife and daughter, had during the day joined our cavalcade in the forest.

Mr. Hopkinson followed successfully for many years the profession of law in the city of New York. His enterprise and good taste seem equal to his opulence. The neighbouring village has grown up under his eye; his house, both within and without, wears the character of convenience and elegance. The manner in which he has cleared the forest in the immediate neighbourhood of his dwelling is peculiarly admirable. In general, the settler cuts to right and left with unsparing fury, anxious only to clear the giant weeds which obstruct the light and choke his respiration. It is a natural impulse, perhaps, which leads him thus unthinkingly to lay bare his cabin to the heavens, but some may doubt if it be very wise, and all will agree that it is in very bad taste. I know not if the observation has been made by others, but it has often occurred to me that the gap made by the settler in the dense mass of the forest must serve as a sort of funnel, by which the hot rays of the sun must draw up the noxious vapors from the surrounding shades. Were he to place his cabin under shelter and commence his chief operations at a little distance, I have a notion that his family would both enjoy more comfort and better health. I have sometimes put a query upon this subject to a farmer, who has invariably assured me that any single tree, if deprived of the support of its neighbours, would infallibly be blown down. This seemed probable enough, but as the assurance was generally accompanied by some reflections upon the uselessness of the long weeds, I felt by no means satisfied that they had ever had fair play. I was convinced of this when, in the neighbourhood of Canandaigua, we found a New England farmer, whose house was surrounded by a fine grove of young hickory, which had been cleared out with care and stood in perfect health and security.

Mr. Hopkinson has tried the experiment on a larger scale and cleared the forest around his dwelling in such a manner as to give to it the air of a magnificent park. It is surprising to see how soon these giants have thrown down their branches, rejoicing in the air and light suddenly opened to them. When first exposed, they have the appearance of enormous shipmasts, their smooth, silvery stems, towering to the skies, sustaining on their heads a circular canopy of verdure, like the umbrella of a Brogdingnag. There is one pecularity that characterizes the American forest, which is wonderfully favourable to the "ornamental clearer": it is the general absence of brush, and the fine smooth carpet of verdure spread by the hand of nature over the surface of the soil.* It is doubt-

---

* May not this be the cause, which, by affording facilities to the hunter, served to arrest the aborigines of North America in the savage state? The woods of the southern continent are

less necessary in this operation to proceed with much caution and to consult the nature of the soil as well as of the tree you intend to preserve. A fence from the northwest must usually be indispensable. Everything seems to have favoured Mr. Hopkinson's improvements, and we should have been well pleased had time permitted us to have surveyed them more at leisure.

Entering the house, the shade of its broad piazzas and Venetian blinds, through which the evening breeze played sweetly, refreshed us much after the fatigues and heats of the day. From the windows the eye glanced down the hill, through vistas tastefully opened in the dense shade, upon the rich valley, watered by the river, and the undulating lands which lay beyond. The last rays of the sinking sun flashed upon the white walls of the little town of Geneseo, perched upon the distant horizon, and shed a flood of glory upon the wide world of primeval forest that stretched around.

While refreshing ourselves with a variety of delicious fruit and, for myself, looking round in wondering admiration at this house of enchantment—for truly, containing, as it did, every convenience and luxury that art could afford, and planted down thus in the bosom of the wilderness, it seemed like nothing else than some palace of the genii—while thus gazing and admiring, a pleasing young woman entered, the wife of a neighbouring settler. She prolonged her stay until the sun had bade good night, and then, requesting us to look in upon her in her log house before our departure, remounted her horse, disappeared in the forest, and gained her home, seven miles distant, more by the sagacity of the steed than any twinkling of the stars.

We made her a visit next day. The dwelling, though small and every way inconvenient, as one might have imagined, to those accustomed to all the comforts of a city life (for this gentleman is an emigrant from Boston, Massachusetts), was rather of larger dimensions than the ordinary log house, being divided into a room and kitchen and having a sleeping apartment above. With all these extras, however, the dwelling was comfortless enough for a five years' residence; yet its owners seemed contented in it, putting off from year to year the building of a better, and finding in this narrow and ill-finished tenement in the wilderness that contentment which many live and die without finding in a palace.

Returning from this excursion, we again traversed the open prairie that here stretches along the watercourse and forms the richest portion of Mr. Wadsworth's magnificent property. We often paused to admire the giant trees, scat-

---

represented as impeded by luxuriant and impervious vegetation. Man, thus shut out from the covert and driven to seek the open plains and valleys, was there naturally lured to the pastoral and agricultural life.

tered tastefully here and there by the hand of nature, their enormous trunks rooted in alluvial soil, pointing up their stems into mid-air like the columns of some gothic minster, and then flinging abroad their mighty arms from which the graceful foliage dropping downwards, opposed, in beautiful contrast, the rich verdure with the clean and polished bark. The finest trees that I had ever before seen had been dwarfs, if placed beside these mighty giants.

The art of ornamental planting has, as yet, been little cultivated in these states. The native forest is generally in sight, and, as the human eye is prone to rest with pleasure on what is uncommon, an American usually considers an open plain as nature's most beautiful feature. The settler's first desire is to have a clear view of the heavens; when his patch of ground is completely naked, he tells you that it looks handsome. As the dense shade of the forest recedes, a tree, in his mind, becomes less associated with wolves and bears, swamps and agues, and gradually he conceives the desire that some sheltering boughs were spread between his roof and the scorching rays of July's sun. His object now is to plant the tree that will grow the fastest, and, consequently, the finest sons of the forest are seldom those that he patronizes. In the older districts of the Union that I have visited, especially in Pennsylvania, I have admired trees of a very noble character, surrounding the dwelling of the farmer or dropped through his fields as a shelter for the cattle.

Of the American oak, there are upwards of thirty varieties, almost as many of the walnut, several of the elm, which is a tree of very uncommon majesty. The sycamore of the Ohio, which can receive half a regiment of soldiers within its trunk, seems to realize the wildest fables of marvel-loving travellers. The maple and the hickory are also remarkable, the former for its elegance, and the latter for the rich colour of its foliage. The ash; the white pine, rising in pre-eminent grandeur; the scent-breathing cedar; the graceful acacia; the wild cherry, with its beautiful fruit clustered on the stalk like currants; and, among the flowering trees, the sweet locust, breathing the breath of violets; the catalpa, with its umbrageous leaves, and luxuriant blossoms; the majestic tulip, pointing up his clean and unencumbered shaft, and throwing down his branches heavy with polished foliage and millions of flowers. Indeed the varieties of the native trees are almost endless, and when cultivated with care, and arranged with taste, may even surpass in majesty the woodland tribe of England.

It has struck me that the American trees (I speak of them when reared for ornament, or dropped by the hand of nature with more taste perhaps than art could rival) have a character which might be termed one of simple majesty, while those of England are remarkable for a romantic or even savage grandeur. The gnarled oak, his boughs covered with lichens, thrust forth horizontally but grotesquely, stands beneath the watery skies of England a hardy veteran, nerved to brave the elements and opposing his broad and shaggy forehead to the storm, as reckless of its fury and indifferent alike to the smiles and frowns of heaven. Vegetation here being much more rapid, the American tree puts forth longer shoots, springing upwards to the sun, with a stem straight, smooth, and silvery, and flinging forth his sweeping branches to wave with every gust. This perhaps applies more peculiarly to the elm, a tree of singular grace and beauty, but answers, more or less, to all the nobler sons of the forest. In general the wood of this country is of superior stature to that of our island, but is charged with fewer branches, or, more properly speaking, *twigs*. Under an oak in England, you can barely see the winter's heaven; here, when stripped of its foliage, the most rugged tree would afford no shelter. There is, in short, less wood, or rather it shoots upwards more in straight lines; the foliage is magnificent and wonderfully varied in its shades. You will remember the glories of the autumnal tints: their richness defies the pen or the pencil.

The character of the American forest you are, perhaps, familiar with: springing out of a virgin soil and struggling upwards to catch the sun's glance, the stems are frequently of enormous stature, and, from the dryness of the atmosphere, wholly free from moss and lichen. I have already noticed the absence of brush, and the carpet of verdure that covers the soil; where this is firm and dry, nothing can be more pleasing than to wander among these primeval shades—at least those will think so whose eyes are not palled with their eternal contemplation. When the first gloom of evening "deepens the horror of the woods," it is finely impressive to thread their dark mazes, and greatly interesting when the night closes in to catch the glimmer of some settler's fire, and, as you approach, to see its rays streaming across your path from his cabin door.

During the summer nights, a log hut often presents a very singular appearance. It is not unusual, when the hot months set in, to clear away the mud which stops the interstices between the logs, as they are raised horizontally upon each other, so as to allow a free passage to the external air. In the darkness of the forest, the light streaming through these crevices gives to the cabin the appearance of being either illuminated or on fire. A painter might then often pause to consider the family group assembled in the little dwelling: the father resting after the day's fatigues, his prattling urchins round him, while the busy matron prepares the evening meal. Insensible were the heart that could pass without emotion this little scene of human industry and human happiness. The cotter's evening light is interesting everywhere, but doubly so when it shines in a world of solitude such as this.

LETTER XII.

Indian Village. Observations on the Indians. Conduct of the American Government Towards Them.

Geneseo, August 1819.

My Dear Friend,

Some days since we made two of a large party to the high banks of the Genesee, and in our return visited an Indian village. The huts were scattered wildly over a little hill jutting forward from the forest and commanding a magnificent prospect down the course of the river.

These Indians had more of the character of the lords of the wilderness than any I had yet seen, but even these are a wasting remnant that must soon disappear with the receding forest. Notwithstanding their frequent and friendly intercourse with their white neighbours, they keep their language pure, and their manners and habits with but little variation. The richness of the soil, or the beauty of the spot, seems to have attached them to the neighbourhood, as they refuse to sell their patrimony, though every year renders the game more shy and, consequently, the business of the hunter more doubtful and toilsome.

The falling greatness of this people, disappearing from the face of their native soil, at first strikes mournfully on the imagination, but such regrets are scarcely rational. The savage, with all his virtues, and he has some virtues, is still a savage, nobler, doubtless, than many who boast themselves civilized beings— nobler far than any race of slaves who hug their chains while they sit in proud contemplation of days of glory that have set in night—but still holding a lower place in creation than men who, to the proud spirit of independence, unite the softer feelings that spring only within the pale of civilized life. The increase and spread of the white population at the expense of the red is, as it were, the triumph of peace over violence; it is Minerva's olive bearing the palm from Neptune's steed.

Not that the aborigines of this fine country have never had to complain of wrong and violence, offered by the invaders of the soil. The Indian, as he looks mournfully upon the scattered remnant of his once powerful tribe, recounts a long list of injuries received by his ancestors from those strangers whom they

were at first willing to receive as friends and brothers. Though he should acknowledge that the right by which the early settlers were willing to hold a portion of their territory was that of purchase, he may justly complain that the sale
had little in it of fair reciprocity, which was often rather compelled than proposed. The first contracts, indeed, were peaceful, entered into with tolerable
fairness on the one side and with willingness on the other; but it was not in
human nature that the native inhabitants should long view without jealousy the
growing strength of newcomers, whose knowledge and cultivation of the peaceful arts secured a ratio of increase to their population so far beyond that of the
wild aborigines, and whose hardihood, scarce inferior to that of the savage,
marked them as such dangerous antagonists. Actuated by this jealousy, the
massacre of the various colonies, thinly scattered along the shores of the Atlantic, was often attempted, and had these savage measures been taken in concert by the different tribes and nations, the extermination of the obnoxious in-
truders must have been effected. Hostile feelings, so naturally aroused on the
one side, were soon as naturally aroused on the other. In these earlier acts of
aggression, were we to allow nothing to the jealous passions common to the
Indians as men and to the wild passions peculiar to them as savages, we might,
perhaps, find more cause to charge the natives with cruelty and treachery than
the European settlers with injustice.

In considering the sufferings of those hardy adventurers, we are filled with
astonishment, as well as pity and admiration. How powerful the charm of independence to reconcile man to such a course of hardship, to lead him forth
from the pale of civilized life to seek his subsistence among wolves, and bears,
and savages, now exposed to Siberian rigors and then to African heats, enduring
famine, and breathing unwholesome exhalations, lighting his nightly fire to
ward off the attack of the wild beast, and apprehending from every thicket the
winged arrow of the Indian! Well may we look to find a proud and vigorous
nation in the descendants of such hardy progenitors.

The attacks of the Indians usually ended to their disadvantage, weakened
their numbers, and forced them to make concessions. By each succeeding
treaty, the boundaries receded, and, as the new people gained in strength what
the natives lost, the latter became as much exposed to European rapacity as the
former had ever been to Indian cruelty. The contention for mastery between
the French and English, which, had the natives been united in their councils,
might possibly have afforded them the opportunity of crushing both, only
hurried forward their own ruin. The subsequent policy of the British government, so magnificently denounced by the generous Chatham, which, during
her struggle with the revolted colonies, raised the war whoop of their savage

neighbours, was the cause of additional ruin to the native tribes, whose numbers were always thinned, whatever might be the issue of their incursions.

After the establishment of American independence, the Indians soon felt the effect of the wise and humane system of policy adopted by the federal government. The treaties entered into with the natives have never been violated by her sanction or connivance, while she has frequently exerted her influence to preserve or to make peace between contending tribes. She has sought to protect them from the impositions of traders and land jobbers, and to lure them to the cultivation of the peaceful arts. Among the most useful of the government regulations are those which deprive individuals of the power of entering into land contracts with the Indians, and which exclude spirituous liquors and firearms from the bartering trade prosecuted on the western borders. It is to be wished that the Canada government would equally enforce the latter regulation. Intoxication has proved a yet worse scourge to the wild natives than the smallpox. It not only whets their ferocity, but hurries them into the worst vices, and consequently the worst diseases. While blankets, wearing apparel, implements of husbandry, peltry, &c. are the American articles of barter for the game and furs of the Indian hunters, those of the traders of the Northwest are chiefly spirituous liquors and firearms. This secures to them the preference in the Indian market, where more furs will be given for a keg of whiskey or a musket than for a whole bale of woollen goods. But this is a short-sighted policy. The northern tribes, armed with muskets and intoxicated with liquor, go to war with each other, or else with the more southern tribes, which last they have, in many cases, almost, if not altogether, exterminated. The intrigues of European traders and the species of goods exchanged by them with the savages have, of late years, done more towards the extermination of the aborigines, by war and disease, than has even the rapid spread and increase of the white population, by the felling of the forest and destruction of the game. The last cause operates only on the borders, but the others are felt to the Pacific and the icy barrier of the north. The Indians are now disappearing from the face of the earth by the silent but sure operation of corruption and misery: wherever the Canadian trader pierces, he carries poison with him and thus is at once working the destruction of the native hunters and of the rich trade which he prosecutes with them.

The Americans are the only people who can ultimately benefit by the destruction of the tribes, and therefore it is highly to the credit of their government to have placed the trade under such regulations as are calculated to promote the interests of the aborigines. The restrictive laws upon the Indian trade are carefully enforced. Government agents, with fixed salaries, are stationed in the line of forts protecting the western frontier, to whom appeals can always be made by the Indians. Under the eye of these agents, trading establishments are conducted, in which a fair and stated price is laid upon the American articles of barter. This has the effect of constraining the private traders to honesty, who, of course, will find no market if they do not sell on equal terms with the government establishments. The price fixed by the government places on the prime cost what is sufficient to defray the expenses of the establishment, which is conducted on the strictest principles of American economy.

The humane policy of the American government in this matter may be supposed to have had in view the protection of the white settlements on the frontier, as well as of the native tribes. The fact is, however, that the introduction of distilled spirits and firearms among the latter occasions them rather to make war upon each other than upon the distant whites. A quarrel in their feasts produces murder, and this is seldom expiated but by the blood of the aggressor and of his tribe. Some of the savage incursions on the western frontier have originated in disputes between a white and a red hunter, but such quarrels have easily been healed by the intervention of the federal government. The cruel Indian wars, which have occasionally desolated the frontier, massacring whole families of women, children, and infants at the breast, have been invariably produced by the machinations of Florida or Canadian traders, or of European emissaries. The policy of America upon these occasions has proved rather humane than interested. Her friendly Indians, more peaceful and less trained in the use of the musket, have proved feeble allies, and often, by drawing upon her for protection from their ferocious neighbours, have turned the tide of their enemies' fury upon her borders.

There are in many of the states some sorry remnants of the aborigines, settled down as cultivators of the soil, and yet this character can hardly be applied to them, so little skill or, what is the same thing, so little interest do they exhibit in pursuits so opposed to the habits of their ancestors.

In the sale of territory made at different times by the native tribes to the states and now to the national Congress, some reservations of particular tracts have been stipulated for by the original proprietors. As the white population flows up to these districts, the game, of course, takes flight, and the wilder hunters take flight with it. The Indians are then frequently disposed to move off in a phalanx and to make a final sale of their landed property. Frequently, however, by the humane intervention of the legislature or of philanthropic individuals, the more peaceful, which, with the savage, usually signifies the more lazy, are induced to remain and gradually to forego the occupation of the chase for that of husbandry. Thus it is that, in the vast field of the white population now stretched from the Atlantic to the Missouri, we find some little specks of the red Indian, scattered like the splinters of a wreck upon the surface of the ocean.

The issue of these experiments has invariably been such as to stamp them with benevolence rather than wisdom. It is, indeed, truly melancholy to see what slender success has hitherto attended all the attempts, whether on the part of the legislature, societies, or individuals, to improve the condition of these half-civilized natives. Filth and sloth are in their cabins, sometimes superstition, but very rarely knowledge, in their minds. With scarcely an exception, the Indian, on emerging from the savage state, sinks, instead of rising in the scale of being. There are two principal causes to which, perhaps, this may be attributed: first, that the nobler the spirit, the more attached is it to its race and to what it conceives to be the dignity of that race. Such fly the approach of civilization and bury themselves deeper in the forest, identifying happiness with liberty and liberty with the wide earth's range. Thus it is only the more tame and worthless who are submitted to the experiments of the humane or the curious.

But there is another cause which has operated generally to prevent the approach of the Indian habits to those of the whites: they have been each too violently opposed to the other. Had the red man been less savage or the white man less civilized, each would have yielded a little to the other, and the habits of the two people, and gradually the two people themselves have, in some measure, assimilated and amalgamated.* In the southern continent, we see that the haughty and cruel Spaniard often condescended to mix his blood with that of his conquered vassals, and it is probable that many of the early adventurers consulted their pride, as well as their interest, in uniting themselves to the daughters of tributary or slaughtered Incas. It is this mixed race, remarkable no less for their intelligence than their high spirit, who are now working out the deliverance of their country from the odious thraldom of Spain and who are destined, perhaps, in the course of a few generations, to rival in strength and civilization the proudest empires of the old hemisphere.

The marriage of Rolfe, a companion of the heroic father of Virginia, with the amiable Pocahontas is almost the only instance on record of a legal engagement contracted by the early settlers with the women of this county. From the

---

*It may seem strange after this to conjecture that, had the North American continent been colonized entirely by French, this would have happened. That people, though in a relish for many of the ornamental arts, seemingly further advanced in mental cultivation than their English neighbours, yet from their inferior acquaintance with the science of government, and from their being less practised in the exercise of steady industry, there has always been a less gap between them and the wild hunter, than between the latter and the English. The French have always lived on more friendly terms with the natives than either the English or the Anglo-American. Many wild Indians have a mixture of French blood in their veins, and in the miserable remains of the old French settlements in the western territory is found a mongrel population but little removed from the half-civilized savage.

moral habits and religious principles of the former, it is probable that illicit intercourse was very rarely indulged in; where this might occur, the offspring would, of necessity (as well as by the Indian customs), remain with the mother and become incorporated with her tribe. The aborigines having remained *in statu quo,* or, if anything, retrograded in the scale of being, while the new population has been making farther advances in civilization, it is little surprising that an instance is hardly to be found of a mixture between the two races.

To account for the untameable spirit of the wild Indian or the seemingly unimprovable dispositions of the half-domesticated Indian, it is not necessary that we should imagine any distinctions implanted by nature between the red man and the white. The savage is not brought within the pale of civilized life in a day, nor a year, nor a generation: ages are required to mould him by imperceptible degrees, as the water smooths the rock over which it flows. The hand of nature must work, not that of art; it is circumstance, not precept, that must operate on his mind and lead him, unknown to himself, to submit to constraints and to yield to the sway of feelings which his ancestors would have spurned. There is a charm in the hunter's life to which even the civilized man is not insensible; it speaks at once to the imagination, is felt in the nerves and the spirits, sets fate at defiance, cancels the list of the moral ills, and in the very increase of the physical braces the frame to bear and the spirit to mock at them. It would need wiser teachers than were easily found to uproot the associations that are fixed in his mind, to break the habits that form a part of his existence and that have given the bent to his character, but, even if such teachers could be found, they must go to the savage, not bring the savage to them. They must not place him in a world whose feelings and habits are as far removed from his, as the east from the west, whose virtues he cannot understand, but whose vices he will certainly imitate.

It has been remarked that there is no instance of any Indian youth, who has been educated in the colleges of these states, having risen to distinction or assumed a place in civilized society. We must bear in mind, first, that not one in a thousand of any race whatsoever is gifted by nature so as to become distinguished. Experiments of this kind have hitherto been few, and we must draw many blanks in a lottery before we can draw a prize. Secondly, it may be supposed that the prouder spirits, who are usually the stronger intellects, have been those who spurned the restraint imposed by habits and laws foreign to those of their race and who fled from the refinements of strangers to the savage woods and the savage ways of their fathers. Where is the young mind of vigor and enthusiasm that is not curious to trace the character of those who gave it being and is not prone to ascribe to it something noble and singularly excellent? They who have known the feelings of an orphan—when in a house and country foreign to his race, how he yearns to hear of those who nursed his infancy, but whose voice and features are lost to his memory, how he muses on them in solitude, calls upon their names in moments of distress, and idly fancies that fortune could never have wrung from him a tear had they lived to cherish and protect him—they whose fate it has been to know such feelings will easily conceive how the young Indian, alone among strangers, must look wistfully to the wilderness, where his tribe tread the haunts of their fathers, free as the winds and wild as the game they pursue. I know not if the circumstances of my own early life have tended to make me sympathize peculiarly with such a situation, but the position of the Indian youth, as an alien and an orphan, among his American guardians and playmates, strikes me as singularly affecting.[1]

If we look to those feeble remnants of the aborigines, who here and there have settled down in the states under protection of their laws, and marvel to see them dwindling away from the face of the soil, a prey to the pestilence of intemperance and sloth in spite of all the efforts to reclaim them, we may, perhaps, without calling in doubt the judiciousness of these efforts, perceive that they are counteracted by circumstances beyond the control either of the legislature or of individuals. It is invariably seen that the savage when removed into the centre of a civilized world acquires a taste for the coarser indulgences that he finds within his reach, before he can be taught to engage in irksome employments that promise only moderate and future good. Industry and temperance are virtues of calculation, and the savage is unused to calculate. When removed from the forest, the Indian has lost his accustomed incentives to exertion; those more hidden ones that surround him he does not see, or, if pointed out to him, does not feel. His old virtues are no longer in demand, and a length of years were requisite to lead him to adopt new ones. Ere this season comes, his slender and decreasing numbers will probably be reduced to a cypher. In passing lately through the Oneida settlement, we saw many cabins deserted and the inhabitants, who still haunted the remainder, dragging on a drowsy existence, painfully contrasted with the life and vigor of the white population that is flowing past them. In many parts of the old states, such settlements have totally disappeared, so gradually and silently that none can tell when or how.

I cannot help remarking, however, upon a circumstance which may be supposed to have considerably impeded the exertions of the humanizers of the Indian. Religion has been too generally employed as the first agent. A practical philosopher were the best tutor in this case. The more beautiful, not to say the more abstruse the religion, the more should the mind be prepared to receive it. The untutored ears of the Indians are assailed by teachers of all kinds. The

Friends and Moravians are undoubtedly the best, and their exertions are sometimes partially repaid, and even when unsuccessful, humanity is still their
debtor. But there are sects which this world shares in common with the old,
who, considered by themselves, are harmless and so far as intention goes virtuous, but attending to the effect they work upon others, the weak and the ignorant, are as mischievous members as a community can well be troubled with.

It is strange, in this nation of practical philosophers, to find, here and there,
a society of the wildest fanatics and a perambulating teacher, compared to
whom the wildest followers of Wesley or Whitefield were rational.[2] These
strange expounders of the simple lessons of Christ are ever most zealously employed in doubly confounding understandings already bewildered, in making
the ignorant foolish and the foolish insane. Their more frequent victims are the
poor blacks, who are sometimes seen assembled in crowds round one of these
teachers, groaning and gesticulating like Pythia on the tripod.[3] Their success
on the whole is but indifferent among the Indians. Where they fail to persuade,
they probably disgust or perhaps only astonish, and though these last are the
best of the three consequences, it were doubtless as well that they were secured
from all.

I suspect that the doctrines or, more properly, absurdities of these wild fanatics are what chiefly arrest the mental advance of the negro in these northern
states, and form one of the minor causes which prevent that of the savage.
Among the ignorant, one fool can work more harm than twenty wise men can
work good, though indeed with the Indian, it is doubtful whether the wise
men, if left to themselves, could work much. It seems that the fate of the aborigines of this magnificent country is governed by immutable laws, which no
efforts of man can turn aside. They appear destined to dwindle away with the
forests that shelter them, and soon to exist only in traditionary lore or in the
wild tale of some wild genius.

Though it is of necessity singularly difficult to obtain any accurate knowledge
of a people wholly unacquainted with the arts and possessed of no other means
of retailing the most important national revolutions than that of oral tradition,
yet the persevering labours of some American citizens and literary societies, as
well as of some eminent European travellers, have done much towards eluci-
dating the past as well as present condition of the native tribes. The Philosophical Society of Philadelphia has more particularly collected much valuable
information.*

* The observations of the amiable missionary John Heckewelder upon the history, manners,
and customs of the six nations, Delawares, Mohicans, &c., lately published at the request of that
society, are peculiarly interesting.[4] Perhaps he may be accounted somewhat partial to his wild

It is certainly greatly desirable that some just knowledge of the aborigines, so fast disappearing from the earth, should rapidly be obtained. Europeans in general may peruse with little curiosity the legends of a people with whom they or their ancestors were never placed in contact, but with Americans they must ever possess a national interest, the romance of which will gradually increase with their increasing antiquity.

I hope I do not send you in this letter too serious a dissertation. I sometimes fear lest I answer your questions and those of * * * * with too much detail, and at other times with too little. You must allow something occasionally to my more slender stock of information upon one subject than another, and something also to the humour of the moment. Farewell.

---

associates, but his statements are made with so much simplicity that it is impossible not to receive them as accurate. This distinguished missionary is attached to the Moravian establishment of Bethlehem in Pennsylvania. The Moravians have peculiarly distinguished themselves, not merely by their zeal in the religious conversion of the savages, but by their patient and judicious exertions to lead them to the cultivation of the peaceful arts.

LETTER XIII.

Niagara, September 1819.

My Dear Friend,

We left Geneseo on a lovely morning that breathed the first freshness of autumn, our conveyance one of those light waggons universal in these states. Many a kind parting glance we threw back upon the fair valley and on the roofs which sheltered so much worth and seemingly so much happiness.

Our route, after some miles, crossed the great western road and traced the course of the Genesee to within four miles of its discharge into Ontario. Here the river makes three considerable falls. At the head of the first stands the flourishing young town of Rochester, and at the head of the third one of minor fame, hight [1] Carthage.

A singular fate seems to pursue the latter colony. A farmer with whom I fell into conversation informed me that it had first assumed the more modest appellation of Clyde, from the resemblance that some travelled settler had discovered between the neighbouring fall of the Genesee and that of the Clyde at Stone Byres, which resemblance, by-the-bye, allowing for the superior dimensions of the American river, is striking enough. After some time the new occupants received information that there existed an older settlement of that name in the same county, and, to rectify the confusion that this occasioned in the post office, the Scots changed themselves into Punicians. But now, *delenda est Carthago:* it is discovered that there are two more infant Carthages, claiming the right of primogeniture.

There is, it must be confessed, the strangest confusion of names in the western counties of this state that ingenuity could well imagine. In one district you have all the poets from Homer to Pope, nay, for ought I know, they may come down to Byron; in another, you have a collection of Roman heroes; in a third, all the mighty cities of the world, from the great Assyrian empire downwards; and, scattered among this classic confusion, relics of the Indian vocabulary, which, I must observe, are often not the least elegant and are indisputably always the most appropriate.

For the Roman heroes, bad, good, and indifferent, who in one district are scattered so plentifully, the new population is indebted to a land surveyor and a classical dictionary. Being requested, in parcelling out the lots, to affix a name to them, the worthy citizen, more practised in mensuration than baptism, shortly found his ingenuity baffled, and in despair had recourse to the pages of Lempriere.[2]

There is something rather amusing in finding Cato or Regulus typified by a cluster of wooden houses, nor, perhaps, are the old worthies so much disgraced as some indignant scholars might imagine.

I met with one name on my route which somewhat surprised me and which struck me as yet more inappropriate than the sonorous titles of antiquity, nor was I ill pleased to learn that it had occasioned some demur among the settlers. I thought that I had left *Waterloo* on the other side of the Atlantic, in the streets, bridges, waltzes, ribands, hotels, and fly-coaches of Great Britain and Ireland. When objections were made to the founder of the little town flourishing under this appellation, the story goes that he called to his aid the stream of water whch turned the wheel of his mill, gravely affirming that he had that in his eye and not the battle in his thoughts when he christened the settlement. "The name speaks for itself," said he, with a humourous gravity peculiar to his native district of New England—"*Water*-loo." If the name did not speak for itself, it was impossible not to let him speak for it, and so his neighbours turned away laughing, and the title of Waterloo stands more undisputed than that of poor Carthage.

The falls of the Genesee are well worth going fifty miles out of your way to look at. The first is a noble cascade of ninety feet. Seen from the bottom (to get to which we had to traverse a marsh and a score of mill-streams), I have since thought it a sort of miniature of Niagara, but this is woefully comparing small things to great. It is, however, a lovely sheet of water, and truly grand when you have not seen the wonder of nature that is now roaring in my ears. I believe we should have enjoyed the scene more, if the swamp and the slime and the mud had not suggested rattlesnakes to the fancy of my companion. The apprehension was every way groundless; at least we saw no rattlesnakes, and these reptiles, when seen, I believe are seldom seen in mud but among rocks moist with clear water.

The second fall is inconsiderable compared to that either above or below. The third, though not upwards of eighty feet, is the most picturesque of the whole.

The effect is, at present, singularly heightened by a stupendous bridge, thrown across the chasm just below the basin of the fall in the manner of that over the Wear at Sunderland. The chord of the arch, as I was informed, is upwards of 300 feet, the perpendicular, from the centre to the river, 250. We were desirous of viewing it from the bottom of the chasm, but to do this it seemed necessary to go two miles farther down the river to seek a boat, which even then, we were assured, it would be but a chance if we found. To descend to this spot and wait this chance, daylight would hardly have served us. To see what we could, we scrambled a fourth of the way down, first by means of the woodwork of the bridge, and then by advancing cautiously along the shelving edge of the precipice, resting our weight on one hand until we reached an acute angle formed by the roots of a blasted pine, which afforded us a narrow footing while the broken stem yielded us support.

Having assumed this position, which had we duly considered we should perhaps not have ventured upon, we gazed up and down with a sensation of terror that I do not remember to have felt in an equal degree more than once in my life. Beneath us, on either hand, the precipice now shelved perpendicularly, or rather we were projected over it so that a pebble would have dropped into the gulf of water below. To the left, we looked upon the falling river; beneath us was the basin, broad, deep, and finely circular; opposite, the precipice answering to that we stood upon; on our right was the bridge, suspended as it were in mid-air. We were on a level with the spring of the arch, and I shuddered to observe that on the opposite side, projecting over the precipice, the beams which sustained it seemed to rest on a hair's breadth. Tracing also the semicircle with my eye, I perceived that it was considerably strained, about 20 feet on the same side from the centre. Afterwards, on crossing the bridge, we found several heavy logs placed over the spot to prevent the springing of the arch. You cannot conceive the horror with which we gazed upwards on its tremendous span. After a while it appeared as if in motion, and the impulse was irresistible which led us to shut our eyes and shrink as in expectation of being crushed beneath its weight. I cannot yet recall this moment without shuddering. Our sight swimming, our ears filled with the stunning roar of the river, the smoke of whose waters rose even to this dizzy height, while the thin coating of soil which covered the rock and had once afforded a scanty nourishment to the blasted tree which sustained us seemed to shake beneath our feet. At the time I judged this to be the work of busy fancy. To restore our confused senses and save ourselves from losing balance, which had been the loss of life, we grasped the old pine with considerable energy, and it was at last, with trembling knees and eyes steadily fixed upon our footsteps, neither daring to look up nor down, that we regained the height from which we had descended. Having regained it, I thought we never looked more like fools in our lives.

Crossing the bridge (which brought us down not quite to the level we had sought by a more perilous descent on the other side), we walked round upon a fine carpet of verdure, kept always fresh by the spray from the basin beneath, till we stood above the brink of the fall and nearly facing the arch. While making this circuit, we again shuddered, perceiving for the first time that the point we had descended to on the opposite side had a concealed peril more imminent than those which had so forcibly affected our imagination, the earth beneath the old pine being completely excavated and apparently only held together by one of its roots. A young man, who the next day became our fellow traveller, told me that he had seen us take this position with such alarm that his blood ran cold for many minutes after we left it, adding that he had observed the earth crumble beneath our weight and strike in the water below. I know not if his fancy had been as busy as ours in exaggerating our perils, but I will confess that they were sufficient to startle me from sleep twenty times during the ensuing night in all the horrors of tumbling down precipices and falling through bridges in the manner of the sons of men, as seen in the vision of Mirza.[3] I have heard it said that the art of swimming has lost more lives than it has saved; perhaps the art of clambering has done the same.

The flourishing town of Rochester, thus strikingly situated, is seven years old —that is to say, seven years ago the planks of which its neat white houses are built were growing in an unbroken forest. It now contains upwards of two hundred houses, well laid out in broad streets, shops, furnished with all the necessaries and with many that may be accounted the luxuries of life, several good inns, or taverns as they are universally styled in these states. We were very well and very civilly treated in one of them, but, indeed, I have never yet met with any incivility, though occasionally with that sort of indifference which foreigners, accustomed to the obsequiousness of European service, sometimes mistake for it.

In the country, especially, service, however well paid for, is a favour received. Every man is a farmer and a proprietor; few therefore can be procured to work for hire, and these must generally be brought from a distance. Country gentlemen complain much of this difficulty. Most things, however, have their good and their evil. I have remarked that the American gentry are possessed of much more personal activity than is common in other countries. They acquire, as children, the habit of doing for themselves what others require to be done for them, and are, besides, saved from the sin of insolence, which is often so early fixed in the young mind. Some foreigners will tell you that insolence here is with the poor. Each must speak from his own experience. I have never met with any, though I will confess that if I did it would offend me less than the insolence offered by the rich to the poor has done elsewhere. But insolence forms no characteristic of the American, whatever be his condition in life. I verily believe that you might travel from the Canada frontier to the Gulf of Mexico, or from the Atlantic to the Missouri and never receive from a *native-born citizen* a rude word, it being understood always that you never *give one.*

On arriving at a tavern in this country, you excite no kind of *sensation,* come how you will. The master of the house bids you good day, and you walk in. Breakfast, dinner, and supper are prepared at stated times, to which you must generally contrive to accommodate. There are seldom more hands than enough to dispatch the necessary work. You are not therefore beset by half-a-dozen menials, imagining your wants before you know them yourself; make them known, however, and, if they be rational, they are generally answered with tolerable readiness, and I have invariably found with perfect civility. One thing I must notice, that you are never anywhere charged for attendance. The servant is not yours but the innkeeper's; no demands are made upon you except by the latter. This saves much trouble, and indeed is absolutely necessary in a house where the servant's labour is commonly too valuable to be laid at the mercy of every whimsical traveller. But this arrangement originates in another cause— the republican habits and feelings of the community. I honor the pride which makes a man unwilling to sell his personal service to a fellow creature; to come and go at the beck of another—is it not natural that there should be some un-willingness to do this? It is the last trade to which an American, man or woman, has recourse; still some must be driven to it, particularly of the latter sex, but she always assumes with you the manner of an equal. I have never in this country hired the attendance of any but native Americans, and never have met with an uncivil word, but I could perceive that neither would one have been taken. Honest, trusty, and proud, such is the American in service; there is a character here which all who can appreciate it will respect.

At Rochester we dismissed our waggon, and the following morning, between three and four o'clock, once again seated in the regular stage, struck westward to the Niagara River. It was not, I assure you, without some silent alarm that, on leaving Rochester, we crossed by starlight the tremendous bridge, for the purpose of opening the mail at Carthage.

The mode in which the contents of the post bag are usually distributed through the less populous districts had often before amused me. I remember, when taking a crosscut in a queer sort of a caravan bound for some settlement on the southern shore of Lake Erie, observing, with no small surprise, the operations of our charioteer: a paper flung to the right hand, and anon a paper flung to the left, where no sight or sound bespoke the presence of human beings. I asked if the bears were curious of news, upon which I was informed that there was a settler in the neighbourhood, who ought to have been on the lookout, or some of his children for him. "But when I don't find them ready, I throw the paper under a tree; and I warrant you they'll look sharp enough to find it; they're always curious of news in these wild parts"; and curious enough they seemed, for not a cabin did we pass that a newspaper was not flung from the hand of this enlightener of the wilderness. Occasionally making a halt at some solitary dwelling, the post bag and its guardian descended together, when, if the assistance of the farmer who here acted as postmaster could be obtained, the whole contents of the mail were discharged upon the ground, and all hands and eyes being put in requisition, such letters as might be addressed to the surrounding district were scrambled out from the heap, which, being then again scrambled together, was once more shaken into the leathern receptacle and thrown into the waggon. But it sometimes happened that the settler was from home. On one occasion, I remember, neither man, woman, nor child was to be found. The stage driver whistled and hallooed, walked into the dwelling, and through the dwelling, sprang the fence, traversed the field of maize, and shouted into the wood, but all to no purpose. Having resumed his station and set his horses in motion, I enquired how the letters were to find their destination, seeing that we were carrying them along with us, heaven knew where. "Oh! they'll keep in the country anyhow; it is likely, indeed, they may go down the Ohio, and make a short tour of the states. This has happened sometimes, but it is a chance but they get to Washington at last, and then they'll commence a straight course anew, and be safe here again this day twelvemonth maybe, or two years at farthest."

At Carthage we found the postmaster, very naturally fast asleep; after much clatter against his door and wooden walls, he made his appearance with a candle, and according to custom the whole contents of the mail were discharged upon the floor. The poor Carthaginian rubbed his eyes, as he took up one letter after another from the heap before him, but his dreams seemed still upon him. "Not a letter can I see," he exclaimed, as he again rubbed his eyes, and snuffed his candle. "Friend, lend me your eyes, or you may just take the whole load away with you." "I am none of the best at decyphering handwriting," replied the driver. "Why then I must call my wife, for she is as sharp as a needle." The wife was called, and in gown and cap soon made her appearance. The candle and the papers placed in the middle, wife, husband,

and driver set about deciphering the hieroglyphics; but that the wife had the character of being as sharp as a needle, I should have augured ill of the labours of this triumvirate. Whether right or wrong, however, the selection was soon made, and the budget once again committed to the waggon.

The road between this and Lewiston is chiefly remarkable from its being, such as it is, the work of nature; a bed of gravel was discovered to run almost in a direct line, its breadth seldom greater than that of the road to the Niagara River, commencing four miles from the Genesee. Between Utica and the Lesser Falls of the Mohawk, the great western road strikes into a shorter ridge of the same description, but which there crosses a deep valley, while here it is scarce raised above the vegetable soil it traverses: for forty miles this natural highway, formerly the confining boundary of the waters of Ontario, remains unbroken, save now and then where it gives passage to some muddy creek, the sluggish drain of the vast swamps whose noxious exhalations breed fevers, intermitting and bilious, during the autumnal months, in the new and scanty population. Five years since there was but one log house between Rochester and Lewiston. A citizen who got into the stage during the morning for a dozen miles and who united the professions of doctor and farmer, and painter also, if I understood right, told me that he had five-and-thirty patients within the stretch of one mile. This may convey to you some idea at once of the rapid settling of the country, and the physical evils that the first occupiers of the soil have to encounter. We did not enter a house in which there were less than two of the family either in bed, or looking as if they ought to be there. The autumn is always the trying season, and the prolonged and extreme heats of the summer months have this year doubled its usual fatality. These evils, dreadful while they last, are, however, but temporary; as the axe and the drain advance into the forest, the *mal'aria* recedes. It would recede more rapidly, as well as more certainly, if the new settlers would contrive to do without, or at least with fewer, mills. The collection of the waters from the creeks and the swamps, soon brought by the action of a powerful sun to a state of putrefaction, increases tenfold the deadly air already spread by nature. I could not pass one of these reservoirs of disease without a sickness at the heart, and this was not a little increased when a young farmer was assisted by his father into the waggon, seemingly in the last stage of decline. As I placed the poor creature in the seat least uneasy of the comfortless vehicle, and arranged a buffalo skin with the addition of a great coat behind his back, he told me he was recovering from the intermitting fever and going to seek change of air at the house of a neighbour, twenty miles distant. The family had migrated from New England some two years since and had been perfectly healthy until the late erection of a mill in the close neighbourhood of their dwelling. After a stage of fifteen miles, he left us to be rattled over a causeway of logs that struck off into the forest at a right angle from the road, and which might have shattered limbs less feeble than those of this living spectre. "God help thee over it!" said I inwardly, as the poor youth was lifted half fainting into a waggon.

Forty miles from Lewiston, the ridge is broken for a considerable extent, and the log causeway, through a deep swamp that fills up the deficiency, is only to be crossed on foot. Fatigued and bruised as we by this time were, it was no easy matter to clamber over these cruel miles, which though few seemed eternal. We might have broken this heavy journey, for there were numerous dwellings which a sign, swinging upon a pole before the doors, designated as taverns, and occasionally, in the young settlements, which in the earlier section of our route already flourished under the name of towns and the appearance of villages, these "traveller's rests" were, all things considered, of very tolerable appearance. But we were anxious to relieve our eyes from the sight of squalid faces and our ears from the eternal sound of ague and fever, which we trusted to do on emerging from these shades.

For the first forty miles, the road was, with some intermissions, bordered by a line of cultivation, or, where the plough had not absolutely turned up the soil, the axe was waging war with the trees. To this succeeded a stretch of forest, relieved at long intervals by the settler's rugged patch, smoking with burning timber and encumbered with blackened logs.

A log road, or causeway, as it is denominated, is very grievous to the limbs, and when it traverses a dense and swampy forest is not very cheering to the eyes, nor always is the travelling greatly more agreeable when, in lieu of the trunks of trees, you are dragged over their roots and a soil scooped into holes. Storms had been busy here also; immense trees had been torn up from their beds, and the road, never in its best days oversmooth and delicate, cut and channelled into sevenfold ruggedness and deformity. And yet, had it been a healthier season, these heavy miles would not have been altogether without their interest. There was, indeed, neither rock, nor dale, nor hill, nor pleasant valley—nothing but the settler's cabin, and now and then a growing village, backed by the ragged forest. But had health here dwelt with industry, the eye might have found beauty even in this monotonous landscape. As it was, all seemed sad and cheerless in this young world: the stroke of the axe fell mournfully on the ear, when the hand that lifted it seemed unnerved by past or approaching sickness, the cabin told nothing of the stir of human life, one solitary figure was sometimes the only moving creature within its walls. I shall not soon forget the aspect of a young family who were scattered over a little knoll jutting forward from the forest into the waters of a creek that came sluggishly winding through the shades. A group of urchins, some sitting, some standing, were gathered, possibly to observe our approaching vehicle; the gaze of their lustreless eyes and the hue of their sallow cheeks haunted me for many hours afterwards.

The settlers' fires have now scared away the wolves and bears, who, not five years since, held undisputed dominion in these unbroken shades; as many more, and the noxious vapors may be dispersed also. It is possible, however, that the low tracts in the neighbourhood of the great northwestern waters may never be wholly free from autumnal sickness. We started twice or thrice in the forest a solitary deer, and once put a whole herd in motion. The wild creatures glanced at us from the covert, and, bounding over a little rivulet, were soon lost in the depths of the forest.

The moon was up ere the dull level which we had so long traversed was varied by the appearance of the ridge which is afterwards torn open by the Niagara. We ran along its base for some miles on a smooth and firm road, which would have relieved our tired limbs had they not now been too tired to be relieved by anything. The chills of an autumnal night succeeding to a day of summer heat had yet farther increased our discomfort, when we entered the frontier village of Lewiston.

Alighting at a little tavern, we found the only public apartment sufficiently occupied and accordingly made bold to enter a small room, which, by the cheering blaze of an oak fire, we discovered to be the kitchen and, for the time being, the peculiar residence of the family of the house. An unusual inundation of travellers had thrown all into confusion. The busy matron, nursing an infant with one arm and cooking with the other, seemed worked out of strength and almost out of temper. A tribe of young urchins, kept from their rest by the unusual stir, were lying half asleep, some on the floor and some upon a bed, which filled a third of the apartment. We were suffered to establish ourselves by the fire, and having relieved the troubled hostess from her chief incumbrance, she recovered good humour and presently prepared our supper. While rocking the infant, it was with pleasure that I observed its healthy cheeks and those of the drowsy imps scattered around. It was unnecessary to be told that we were now on healthy ground. There had, the mother said, been some fever in the neighbourhood, but the cases were few. The season probably will be a trying one everywhere.

In the night, when all was still, I heard the first rumbling of the cataract. Wakeful from overfatigue, rather than from any discomfort in the lodging,

I rose more than once to listen to a sound which the dullest ears could not catch for the first time without emotion. Opening the window, the low, hoarse thunder distinctly broke the silence of the night. When, at intervals, it swelled more full and deep, you will believe that I held my breath to listen; they were solemn moments.

This mighty cataract is no longer one of nature's secret mysteries; thousands now make their pilgrimage to it, not through

Lakes, fens, bogs, dens, and caves of death,

but over a broad highway, none of the smoothest, it is true, but quite bereft of all difficulty or danger. This in time may somewhat lessen the awe with which this scene of grandeur is approached, and even now we were not sorry to have opened upon it by a road rather more savage and less frequented than that usually chosen.

Next morning we set off in a little waggon, under a glorious sun and a refreshing breeze. Seven miles of a pleasant road, which ran up the ridge we had observed the preceding night, brought us to the cataract. In the way we alighted to look down from a broad platform of rock, on the edge of the precipice, at a fine bend of the river. From hence the blue expanse of Ontario bounded a third of the horizon, Fort Niagara on the American shore, Fort George on the Canadian, guarding the mouth of the river where it opens into the lake, the banks, rising as they approached us, finely wooded and winding, now hiding and now revealing the majestic waters of the channel. Never shall I forget the moment when, throwing down my eyes, I first beheld the deep, slow, solemn tide, clear as crystal and green as the ocean, sweeping through its channel of rocks with a sullen dignity of motion and sound, far beyond all that I had heard or could ever have conceived. You saw and *felt* immediately that it was no river you beheld, but an imprisoned sea, for such indeed are the lakes of these regions. The velocity of the waters, after the leap, until they issue from the chasm at Queenston, flowing over a rough and shelving bed, must actually be great, but from their vast depth they move with an apparent majesty that seems to temper their vehemence, rolling onwards in heavy volumes and with a hollow sound as if labouring and groaning with their own weight. I can convey to you no idea of the solemnity of this moving ocean. Our eyes followed its waves until they ached with gazing, and had not our little guide and waggoner startled us by hurling a fragment of rock from the precipice, I know not when we should have awakened from our dream.

A mile farther, we caught a first and partial glimpse of the cataract, on which the opposing sun flashed for a moment, as on a silvery screen that hung suspended in the sky. It disappeared again behind the forest, all save the white cloud that rose far up into the air and marked the spot from whence the thunder came. We now pressed forward with increasing impatience, and after a few miles reaching a small inn, we left our rude equipage and hastened in the direction that was pointed to us.

Two footbridges have latterly been thrown, by daring and dexterous hands, from island to island, across the American side of the channel, some hundred feet above the brink of the fall. Gaining in this manner the great island which divides the cataract into two unequal parts, we made its circuit at our leisure. From its lower point, we obtained partial and imperfect views of the falling river; from the higher, we commanded a fine prospect of the upper channel. Nothing here denotes the dreadful commotion so soon about to take place; the thunder, indeed, is behind you, and the rapids are rolling and dashing on either hand, but before, the vast river comes sweeping down its broad and smooth waters between banks low and gentle as those of the Thames. Returning, we again stood long on the bridges, gazing on the rapids that rolled above and beneath us, the waters of the deepest sea-green, crested with silver, shooting under our feet with the velocity of lightning, till, reaching the brink, the vast waves seemed to pause as if gathering their strength for the tremendous plunge. Formerly it was not unusual for the more adventurous traveller to drop down to the island in a well-manned and well-guided boat. This was done by keeping between the currents as they rush on either side of the island, thus leaving a narrow stream, which flows gently to its point and has to the eye, contrasted with the rapidity of the tide where to right and left the water is sucked to the falls, the appearance of a strong back current.

It is but an inconsiderable portion of this imprisoned sea which flows on the American side, but even this were sufficient to fix the eye in admiration. Descending the ladder (now easy steps) and approaching to the foot of this lesser fall, we were driven away blinded, breathless, and smarting, the wind being high and blowing right against us. A young gentleman, who incautiously ventured a few steps farther, was thrown upon his back, and I had some apprehension, from the nature of the ground upon which he fell, was seriously hurt; he escaped, however, from the blast, upon hands and knees, with a few slight bruises. Turning a corner of the rock (where, descending less precipitously, it is wooded to the bottom) to recover our breath and wring the water from our hair and clothes, we saw, on lifting our eyes, a corner of the summit of this graceful division of the cataract hanging above the projecting mass of trees, as it were in mid-air, like the snowy top of a mountain. Above, the dazzling white of the shivered water was thrown into contrast with the deep blue of the unspotted heavens; below, with the living green of the summer foliage, fresh and sparkling in the eternal shower of the rising and falling spray. The wind, which for the space of an hour blew with some fury, rushing down with the river flung showers of spray from the crest of the fall. The sun's rays glancing on these big drops, and sometimes on feathery streams thrown fantastically from the main body of the water, transformed them into silvery stars or beams of light, while the graceful rainbow, now arching over our heads and now circling in the vapor at our feet, still flew before us as we moved. The greater division of the cataract was here concealed from our sight by the dense volumes of vapor which the wind drove with fury across the immense basin directly towards us; sometimes indeed a veering gust parted for a moment the thick clouds and partially revealed the heavy columns that seemed more like fixed pillars of moving emerald than living sheets of water. Here, seating ourselves at the brink of this troubled ocean beneath the gaze of the sun, we had the full advantage of a vapor bath, the fervid rays drying our garments one moment and a blast from the basin drenching them the next. The wind at length having somewhat abated, and the ferryman being willing to attempt the passage, we here crossed in a little boat to the Canada side. The nervous arm of a single rower stemmed this heavy current, just below the basin of the falls, and yet in the whirl occasioned by them, the stormy northwest at this moment chafing the waters yet more. Blinded as we were by the columns of vapor which were driven upon us, we lost the panoramic view of the cataract, which, in calmer hours or with other winds, may be seen in this passage. The angry waters and the angry winds together drove us farther down the channel than was quite agreeable, seeing that a few roods more and our shallop must have been whirled into breakers, from which ten such arms as those of its skilful conductor could not have redeemed it.

Being landed two thirds of a mile below the cataract, a scramble, at first very intricate, through and over and under huge masses of rock, which occasionally seemed to deny all passage and among which our guide often disappeared from our wandering eyes, placed us at the foot of the ladder by which the traveller descends on the Canada side. From hence a rough walk along a shelving ledge of loose stones brought us to the cavern formed by the projection of the ledge over which the water rolls and which is known by the name of the Table Rock.

The gloom of this vast cavern, the whirlwind that ever plays in it, the deafening roar, the vast abyss of convulsed waters beneath you, the falling columns that hang over your head, all strike, not upon the ears and eyes only, but upon the heart. For the first few moments the sublime is wrought to the terrible. This position, indisputably the finest, is no longer one of safety. A part of the Table Rock fell last year, and in that still remaining the eye traces an alarming fissure, from the very summit of the projecting ledge over which the water rolls, so that the ceiling of this dark cavern seems rent from the precipice, and whatever be its hold it is evidently fast yielding to the pressure of the water. You cannot look up to this crevice and down upon the enormous masses which lately fell, with a shock mistaken by the neighbouring inhabitants for that of an earthquake, without shrinking at the dreadful possibility which might crush you beneath ruins yet more enormous than those which lie at your feet.

The cavern formed by the projection of this rock extends some feet behind the water, and, could you breathe, to stand behind the edge of the sheet were perfectly easy. I have seen those who have told me they have done so; for myself, when I descended within a few paces of this dark recess, I was obliged to hurry back some yards to draw breath. Mine to be sure are not the best of lungs, but theirs must be little short of miraculous that can play in the wind and foam that gush from the hidden depths of this watery cave. It is probable, however, that the late fracture of the rock has considerably narrowed this recess, and thus increased the force of the blast that meets the intruder.

From this spot (beneath the Table Rock) you *feel,* more than from any other, the height of the cataract and the weight of its waters. It seems a tumbling ocean, and you yourself what a helpless atom amid these vast and eternal workings of gigantic nature! The wind had now abated, and what was better, we were now under the lee and could admire its sport with the vapor, instead of being blinded by it. From the enormous basin into which the waters precipitate themselves in a clear leap of 140 feet, the clouds of smoke rose in white volumes, like the round-headed clouds you have sometimes seen in the evening horizon of a summer sky, and then shot up in pointed pinnacles, like the ice of mountain glaciers. Caught by the wind, it was now whirled in spiral columns far up into the air, then re-collecting its strength, the tremulous vapor again sought the upper air till, broken and dispersed in the blue serene, it spread against it the only silvery veil which spotted the pure azure. In the centre of the fall, where the water is the heaviest, it takes the leap in an unbroken mass of the deepest green, and in many places reaches the bottom in crystal columns of the same hue, till they meet the snow-white foam that heaves and rolls convulsedly in the enormous basin. But for the deafening roar, the darkness, and the stormy whirlwind in which we stood, I could have fancied these massy volumes the walls of some fairy palace—living emeralds chased in silver. Never surely did nature throw together so fantastically so much beauty with such terrific grandeur. Nor let me pass without notice the lovely rainbow that at this moment hung over the opposing division of the cataract as parted by the island, embracing the whole breadth in its span. Midway of this silvery screen of shivered water stretched a broad belt of blazing gold and crimson, into which the rainbow dropped its hues and seemed to have based its arch. Different from all other scenes of nature that have come under my observation, the cataract of Niagara is seen to most advantage under a powerful and opposing sun; the hues assumed by the vapor are then by far the most varied and brilliant, and of the beauty of these hues I can give you no idea. The gloom of the cavern (for I speak always as if under the Table Rock) needs no assistance from the shade of evening, and the terrible grandeur of the whole is not felt the less for being distinctly seen. We now ascended the precipice on the Canada side, and, having taken a long gaze from the Table Rock, sought dry clothes and refreshment at a neighbouring inn.

We have again visited this wonder of nature in our return from Lake Erie, and have now gazed upon it in all lights and at all hours—under the rising, meridian, and setting sun, and under the pale moon when

> riding in her highest noon.

The edge of the Table Rock is not approached without terror at the latter hour. The fairy hues are now all gone, excepting, indeed, the rainbow, which, the ghost of what it was, now spans a dark impervious abyss. The rays of the sweet planet but feebly pierce the chill dense vapor that clogs the atmosphere; they only kiss, and *coldly* kiss, the waters at the brink, and faintly show the upper half of the columns, now black as ebony, plunging into a storm-tossed sea of murky clouds, whose depth and boundaries are alike unseen. It is the storm of the elements in chaos. The shivering mortal stands on the brink, like the startled fiend

> on the bare outside of this world,
> Uncertain which, in ocean or in air.

> La buja campagna
> Tremò sì forte, che dello spavento
> La mente di sudore ancor mi bagna.[4]

LETTER XIV.

Lake Erie. Water Scenery of America. Massacre on the River Raisin. Naval Engagement on Lake Erie. Mr. Birkbeck.

Erie, September 1819.

My Dear Friend,

It is a pleasant drive from Ontario to Lake Erie along the banks of the magnificent Niagara. There is something truly sublime in the water scenery of America—her lakes, spreading into inland seas, their vast, deep, and pure waters reflecting back the azure of heavens, untainted with a cloud; her rivers, collecting the waters of hills and plains interminable, rolling their massy volumes for thousands of miles, now broken into cataracts to which the noblest cascades of the old hemisphere are those of rivulets, and then sweeping down their broad channels to the far-off ocean the treasures of a world. The lakes and rivers of this continent seem to despise all foreign auxiliaries of nature or art and trust to their own unassisted majesty to produce effect upon the eye and the mind; without alpine mountains or moss-grown ruins, they strike the spectator with awe. Extent, weight, depth—it is by these intrinsic qualities that they affect him. Their character is one of simple grandeur; you stand upon their brink, or traverse their bosom, or gaze upon their rolling rapids and tumbling cataracts, and acknowledge at once their power and immensity and your own insignificance and imbecility. Occasionally you meet with exceptions to this rule. I recall at this moment the beautiful shores of the Passaic, its graceful cascades, its walls of rock, shelving into a glassy peaceful flood, its wooded hills and rich and varied landscapes, all spread beneath a sky of glowing sapphires, a scene for Claude to gaze upon. These northwestern waters, however, have nothing of this character; you find them bedded in vast level plains, bordered only by sable forests, from which the stroke of the axe has but just startled the panther and the savage.

The Niagara and northwestern frontier still exhibit some faint traces of the war. The villages and towns have indeed sprung up like the Phœnix from her ashes; yet it is to be wished, for the sake of humanity, that their vigor and elasticity had not been so proved.

The burning of Newark, on the part of the Americans, was the act of an individual, disclaimed instantly on the part of the government and reprobated by the American public. The governor of Canada expressed himself satisfied with the explanation given, and it had been well if the system of warfare had been then changed.

It might have been conjectured that in the burning of Newark some blind vengeance was intended for the massacre at Frenchtown, had it not appeared that it originated in a mistake of orders and had it not been so honorably disclaimed by the government. General McClure was dismissed instantly from the service and covered with opprobrium by his fellow citizens, who refused to admit a mistake of orders as an apology for an act of inhumanity.[1]

The honor of a government may often be committed by officers acting under its name, yet contrary to its wishes and instructions. Enquiry and condemnation may then avert disgrace, but if, in lieu of these, favour and reward be accorded to the offenders, their employers are justly chargeable with all their crimes. These observations naturally occur to the traveller as he approaches the northwestern frontier.

We must turn our eyes from the River Raisin. Would to Heaven that we could find, not an excuse, for that were impossible, but some palliation of the horrors perpetrated on this spot![2] It were well to commit the tale to oblivion were it not for the warning that breathes from it and which must never be forgotten by the British people. Many of their most generous statesmen had reprobated the practice of associating the Indian tribes with the British soldiers. If there be yet in England an apologist for a military league between savage hordes and civilized nations, let him visit the shores of this river; the blood that here cries up from the earth, not of soldiers slain in battle, but of wounded prisoners surrendered upon terms and trusting in British faith, will convince him, though he should have heard unmoved the thunders of a Chatham.

A small detachment, composed of the choicest sons of Kentucky, many of them allied to the most distinguished families in the state, had advanced to the little village of Frenchtown, situated between the rapids and Detroit, on the strait which pours the waters of the great northwestern lakes into Erie. The object to be effected was to guard the inhabitants from an advanced party of the enemy, peculiarly dreaded because half composed of Indians. The attempt was one of difficulty and hazard. This little band of volunteers, however, with infinite bravery had dislodged and driven back the enemy, and being joined by General Winchester, from whose main body they had been detached, threw up a rude breastwork and entrenched, seven hundred and fifty strong, against fifteen hundred or upwards, headed by Colonel Proctor and two Indian warriors. After some furious sallies, in which General Winchester was made prisoner, the Americans were exhorted to surrender. They had lost nearly a third of their little number, when the flag of truce, which had been twice returned, was received with a message from Colonel Proctor that unless they immediately surrendered they and the village must be delivered to the fury of the savages. They at length capitulated upon honorable terms, securing the safety of the village, the care of the wounded, the burying of the dead, and the protection of the prisoners. How were these engagements fulfilled?—The British commander marched off his troops, gave his prisoners in charge to the savages, and left them, with the wounded and the dying, to be tomahawked and roasted at the stake.* Did not the thunders of the English government strike this English officer? Was he thanked *at home* as he was in *Montreal* for his bravery and *humanity?* I trust that the English government was not found so callous to the honor of a nation that has ever laid claim to the character of generosity, as to let pass without investigation the horrors of that day, still less to reward with promotion the officer under whose eye they were perpetrated! † However this may be, they did not altogether pass without punishment. The fate of war, at the opening of the next campaign, threw into

* I do not repeat all the atrocities of the scene to which I have alluded in the text, as they would be too shocking to the feelings both of the reader and the writer, but there is one circumstance which I will not omit. The American General Winchester, who had been taken prisoner in the sally, was made the betrayer of his own men. Being told by Colonel, now I believe General Proctor, that instant surrender could alone secure them from being given up to the savages and the village to the flames, he was induced to send himself a flag of truce, urging them to accede to the terms proposed. Who shall paint the feelings of that officer when he found himself rendered an accomplice in the complicated treachery and cruelty! There were some British officers who, on this occasion, felt and acted as they ought in the cause of humanity and the honor of their country; Major Muir, Captains Curtis and Aikens, the Reverend Mr. Parrow, and Dr. Bowen, though they may not have received any mark of public approbation from their government, are secure of the esteem of the English as they possess that of the American people. The virtuous McIntosh will ever live in the remembrance of the latter;[3] this gentleman spared no exertions to redeem the lives of the unfortunate and deserted captives; he tracked the Indians for miles through the forests, and purchased, at a high price, such of the naked and fainting Americans as the savages, weary of slaughter, had spared, to inflict on them more lingering tortures.

When this gentleman some time afterwards visited the United States, his benevolence was amply repaid; his entrance into Baltimore and New Orleans had the appearance of a triumph: the whole population crowded to gaze upon him, and every honor was rendered to him that enthusiasm could devise.

† A large portion of the Canadian community retrieved the honor of the colonial character, and expressed their amazement and indignation at the thanks bestowed by their governor, and the rewards conferred by the home authorities, upon the officer who had thus dared to disgrace his profession and his nation.

the hands of the friends and relatives of these unfortunate men the very enemies who had betrayed them. With a refinement of cruelty that must have tortured the inmost souls of their prisoners, they forbore even to upbraid them by a look and lodged them in their towns and private dwellings with the minutest and most fastidious attention to their convenience.* Lord Castlereagh, you may remember, in answer to some remarks made in the House of Commons upon the humanity of the Americans to their prisoners ascribed it to *fear*. It would be little surprising if that Irish nobleman felt himself interested in confounding the words "courage" and "cruelty." The English people, however, are not accustomed to account them synonymous, and should it be decreed that they and the Anglo-Americans, so formed by nature to be friends and brothers, are ever again to meet as enemies, may their voice be loudly heard and may it prevent the Indian tomahawk from being farther associated with the British sword. In Europe little is known of the horrors of Indian warfare. To hunt down a people with bloodhounds would be nothing to it. His war whoop is the yell of fiends; age, sex, infirmity—the savage knows no distinction; nor is it death alone, but death, aggravated by tortures and infernal horrors, that madden the wretched victim before dispatching him. The only excuse ever forged for Colonel Proctor was that he had it not in his power to interfere, that to have checked the ferocity of his savage allies had been to risk the loss of their friendship and future co-operation. Such an argument, without screening *him,* well exposes the atrocity of employing, in civilized warfare, such co-adjutors. Were it possible to enumerate the number of helpless individuals, of women and infants, who have expired in tortures under the hands of savages in league with European governments, it is not impossible but that their employers might shudder. Let us hope that the last of these outrages has been committed and that America, henceforward, is to find in her English brethren warm-hearted friends or high-minded foes.

I turn with pleasure from the dreadful recollections awakened by the name of Frenchtown. The broad inland sea, now spread before me, recalls an action of a very different character. The naval battle fought upon these fine waters was equally honorable to the combatants of either nation. It was the generous fighting the generous. The praise accorded by the English officer to

*Among those who expired at Frenchtown were gentlemen and senators of Kentucky, members of Congress, &c., for of such citizens were the volunteers of the western army composed. One individual was a near relative of the celebrated orator and statesman Mr. Clay, and almost all were allied to the most distinguished families in his state or in that of Ohio. The whole population of Kentucky went into mourning, and their weeds were scarcely thrown aside when they received their captive enemies into their houses.

the heroism of his adversary had as much of greatness in it as had his adversary's victory. War when thus conducted is stripped of half its horrors; nay, it has in it something noble when we find it calling forth the greatest energies with the best feelings of our nature.

Those who estimate the importance of a naval combat by the size of the ships engaged may pass over with little interest that of Lake Erie.[4] And yet the fleet that here met in desperate rencounter must be accounted of considerable force and size, when we remember that it floated upon a fresh-water sea. The ships on Lake Ontario were equal, and latterly superior, in size to the proudest frigates that ever floated on the Atlantic. The bed of those magnificent waters, deepening gradually to the centre like the crater of some exhausted volcano, admits of the freest navigation; that of Lake Erie, on the contrary, is broken by shallows, presenting an intricate chart, even to the fine steamboat which now navigates these waters.

Nine vessels mounting together fifty-four guns were here opposed by the Americans to six larger vessels, mounting in all sixty-three guns. You are possibly not acquainted with the circumstance which decided the engagement.

Commodore Perry (then Captain) having contended for two hours with two vessels of equal force and the wind preventing any of his squadron from making to his assistance, he determined to abandon the vessel which he could no longer manage. Rolling her flag round his arm, he sprang into her boat, and thus, standing upright and waving his sword triumphantly, while the balls rattled in showers round his head, passed through the midst of the enemy. The English commander is said to have uttered a shout of admiration as his young and proud adversary passed unhurt through his fire. Having gained the largest vessel of his little fleet, he bore down again upon the enemy, and cutting through their line for some minutes engaged four of their flotilla alone and simultaneously. The wind gradually enabling the rest of the squadron to support their commander, the struggle was decided, when, to this desperate contest, succeeded those kind and generous greetings which the brave know to exchange with the brave. The noble-minded Captain Barclay, a veteran sailor, who had lost an arm in the battle of Trafalgar, took pride in declaring publicly, "that the conduct of Commodore Perry towards himself, the other captive officers and men, had been alone sufficient to have immortalized him." I dwell on this splendid engagement with pleasure. It tended not to widen but to heal the breach between two nations who should never be at war, or if at war, should contend for mastery not by the mere exertion of brute force but by the display of all those more generous virtues which, as they can alone immortalize conquest, so can they also impart honor to defeat.*

In recalling the events of the border war between Canada and the United States, there is one singular fact which forces itself on the mind and which is fraught with an important lesson. When on the offensive, the Americans were usually defeated; when on the defensive, as usually successful. Herein lies the virtue of militia as opposed to regular troops, and it is this too which gives so peculiar an interest to both the wars in which the young America has been engaged. I know that in England, generally speaking, little attention was paid to the events of a contest which to her was a sort of byplay, while occupied in a deeper game upon which she had staked her all. It is probable, indeed, that one half of the nation scarce remembered that they were at war with their young rivals in the New World, until they found their ships, one by one, swept from the seas by a people they had scarce deigned to consider as holding the place of an independent nation. They then looked round and grew angry. This, if not very wise, was perhaps very natural, and those who mortified the pride of the most powerful of the then existing European empires may well excuse if they excited her indignation. But it is time that this jealousy should subside. The more thinking and the more generous will now consider, with much interest, the little history of that struggle which established America's independence, fixed and elevated her national character, and gave her an opportunity of displaying those energies and virtues which liberty had secretly nourished in the breasts of her people. She may justly be proud of the late contest; it did honor to her head and her heart. She fought a second time for independence and existence, and, as all must do who fight for these, she conquered.

Settlements are fast springing up on the forested shores of Lake Erie. The situation is wonderfully advantageous to the farmer. I have already spoken of the canal, so far in progress, which is about to open a free water carriage from these waters to the eastern Atlantic. Another of only a few miles extent is in contemplation, which, by connecting them with the Allegheny, one of the main sources of the Ohio, will perfect the line of communication with the Gulf of Mexico, an extent of 3,400 miles.

It is impossible to consider without admiration the inland navigation of this

---

* Commodore Perry, who appears to have united every quality that goes to the forming of a hero—bravery, magnanimity, ardent patriotism, disinterested generosity, unassuming modesty and gentleness—died at Angostura of the yellow fever about the period of the date of this letter.[5] He had sailed on a mission from his government to that of the patriots. When the tidings of his premature death reached Washington, the members of the two houses of Congress went into mourning, an honor that is never paid but to the most respected and distinguished sons of the republic. A provision also was voted to his widow, and his children taken under the national guardianship.

magnificent country. From this fine basin, north and west, you open into lakes and rivers which, not many years hence, will pour into it the produce of human labour from states now in embryo; to the northeast, these accumulated waters seek their way to the Atlantic, through the broad channel of the St. Lawrence; to the southeast, they are about to communicate with the same ocean by the magnificent Hudson; to the south and west, stretch the vast waters of the Mississippi with his million of tributaries. There is something unspeakably sublime in the vast extent of earthly domain that here opens to the mind's eye, and truly sublime is its contemplation when we consider the life and energy with which it is fast teeming. An industrious and enlightened people, laying in the wilderness the foundations of commonwealth after commonwealth, based on justice and the immutable rights of man! What heart so cold as to contemplate this unmoved!

The other morning, wandering from the little village which afforded us lodging, I had gained, by a swampy thicket, the beach of the lake. Admiring the first blaze of the sun, which flashed over the waters and tinged the crest of the waves that rippled its azure surface and broke on the pebbled beach, fresh and sounding as those of the ocean, I came suddenly upon a solitary figure, seated on a little rock that lay at the edge of the water—it was an Indian. His tomahawk rested upon his shoulder; his moccasins ornamented with the stained quills of the porcupine, and his hat grotesquely and tawdrily decked with feathers and strips of tin. The countenance had much in it of dignity and savage grandeur; the cheekbones were not so high, nor the face so flat as is usual with the Indian physiognomy, not that it was handsome; wind- and weather-beaten, its copper hue deepened by the gaze of some forty suns, a scar under the left eye, its character might rather have been denominated hideous. He suffered my gaze, as is usual with his race, without turning his head. I know not whether he was musing upon the fallen strength of his tribe and on the days when his fathers pursued their game through unbroken forests and desert prairies, where now are smiling hamlets and waving fields of grain. I could at the moment have mused on these for him, and sighed that even this conquest of the peaceful over the savage arts should have been made at the expense of his wild race. But, in fact, how singular, and, for the well-being of man, how glorious the change, which has turned these vast haunts of panthers, wolves, and savages, into the abode of industry and the sure asylum of the oppressed. What a noble edifice has here been raised for hunted Liberty to dwell in securely! It is impossible to tread the soil of America and not bless it, impossible to consider her growing wealth and strength without rejoicing.

We felt no small desire to strike south from Erie to Pittsburgh and view with our own eyes the growing wonders of the western territory, but our plans having been previously arranged for the descent of the St. Lawrence, we retrace our course to Ontario.

You have expressed in your late letters some curiosity regarding the condition of Mr. Birkbeck's settlement in the Illinois, adding that the report has prevailed that those spirited emigrants had been at first too sanguine and had too little foreseen the difficulties which the most fortunate settler must encounter. This report, I believe, to have originated with Mr. Cobbett, who thought proper to pronounce upon the condition of the farmer in the Illinois in his own dwelling upon Long Island.[6] Feeling an interest in the success of our countrymen in the West, I have been at some pains to inform myself as to their actual condition. The following statement is chiefly taken from the letters of two American gentlemen of our acquaintance who have just visited the settlement: they inform me that its situation possesses all those positive advantages stated by Mr. Birkbeck, that the worst difficulties have been surmounted, and that these have always been fewer than what are frequently encountered in a new country.

The village of Albion, the centre of the settlement, contains at present thirty habitations, in which are found a bricklayer, a carpenter, a wheelwright, a cooper, and a blacksmith, a well-supplied shop, a little library, an inn, a chapel, and a post office, where the mail regularly arrives twice a week. Being situated on a ridge between the Greater and Little Wabash, it is, from its elevated position and from its being some miles removed from the rivers, peculiarly dry and healthy. The prairie in which it stands is described as exquisitely beautiful: lawns of unchanging verdure, spreading over hills and dales, scattered with islands of luxuriant trees, dropped by the hand of nature with a taste that art could not rival—all this spread beneath a sky of glowing and unspotted sapphires. "The most beautiful parks of England," my friend observes, "would afford a most imperfect comparison." The soil is abundantly fruitful and, of course, has an advantage over the heavy-timbered lands, which can scarcely be cleared for less than from twelve to fifteen dollars per acre, while the Illinois farmer may in general clear his for less than five and then enter upon a much more convenient mode of tillage. The objection that is too frequently found to the beautiful prairies of the Illinois is the deficiency of springs and streams for mill seats. This is attended with inconvenience to the settler, though his health will find in it advantage. The nearest navigable river to Albion is the Wabash, eight miles distant; the nearest running stream that is not liable to fail at mid-summer, the Bonpaw, four miles distant. The stock water in ponds for cattle, our correspondent judged, was liable to run dry in a few weeks, and the settlement apprehended some temporary inconvenience from the circumstance. The finest water is everywhere to be raised from twenty to twenty-five or thirty feet from the surface; these wells never fail, but are of course troublesome to work in a new settlement.*

The settlement of Albion must undoubtedly possess some peculiar attractions for an English emigrant, promising him as it does the society of his own countrymen, an actual or ideal advantage to which he is seldom insensible. Generally speaking, however, it may ultimately be as well for him as for the community to which he attaches himself that he should become speedily incorporated with the people of the soil. It is not every man who is gifted with the vigorous intellect and liberal sentiments of Mr. Birkbeck; many emigrants bring with them prejudices and predilections which can only be rubbed away by a free intercourse with the natives of the country. By sitting down at once among them, they will more readily acquire an accurate knowledge of their political institutions and learn to estimate the high privileges which these impart to them, and thus, attaching themselves to their adopted country not from mere sordid motives of interest but also from feeling and principle, become not only *naturalized* but *nationalized*. I have met with but too many in this country who have not advanced beyond the former. I must observe also that the European farmer and mechanic are usually far behind the American in general and practical knowledge as well as enterprise. You find in the working farmer of these states a store of information, a dexterity in all the manual arts, and often a high tone of national feeling, to which you will hardly find a parallel among the same class elsewhere. His advice and assistance, always freely given to those who seek it, will be found of infinite service to a stranger. It will often save him from many rash speculations, at the same time that it will dispose him to see things in their true light and to open his eyes and heart to all the substantial advantages that surround him.

It is amusing to observe the self-importance with which the European emigrant often arrives in these states. The Frenchman imagines that he is to new-model the civic militia, or, at the least, the whole War Department in the city of Washington; the Englishman, that he is to effect a revolution in agriculture by introducing the cultivation of the turnip and the planting of hedgerows; the Scotchman, that he is to double the national produce by turning

---

* The same objection, "the want of fountains and running streams," is stated by Mr. Brackenridge as existing in the prairies of the Missouri, and, I have been informed, is generally applicable to all the prairie lands of the western territory, when removed from the immediate neighbourhood of the great water. Mr. Brackenridge states the depth of the wells in the Missouri at the same rate as that stated above for those of the Illinois.[7]

out the women to work in the fields; and even the poor German conceives that he is to give new sinews to the state, heighten the flavour of the Kentucky tobacco, and expand the souls of the citizens who smoke it.*

France and Ireland, the former from her political revolutions and the latter from her misfortunes, have sent, among the crowd of poorer emigrants, many accomplished and liberal-minded gentlemen, who have assumed a high place in this community, but, till very lately, federal America has seen few of our countrymen except the vulgar and the illiterate. The exceptions to this rule, however, are now multiplying yearly; this will consequently make this nation better known and therefore more esteemed in our island. A friend to the latter can perhaps hardly rejoice in this; to see England drained of her best citizens may justly excite the grief of her patriots, and the jealousy of her rulers. And yet what would the latter have? Should these Hampdens stay, it might be to "push" them "from their stools," as their fathers did their predecessors: they depart, and the mighty are left to sit in state until their "stools" shall break down beneath them. It is idle for travellers to deface this Hesperia; they may deceive the many ignorant, and a few wise, but what then? Are the poor made richer, and the dissatisfied more content? The farmer complains that he sows and reaps for others, that the clergy, the state, and the parish carry off the produce and leave him the gleanings. "It is not thus," he observes, "in America." He is answered that, in America, "he will not meet with even an approach to simplicity and honesty of mind"; that "a nonintercourse act seems to have passed against the sciences, morals, and literature"; that "in Philadelphia the colour of the young females is produced by art"; and that "every man in the United States thinks himself arrived at perfection." * Now were all this nonsense true, what answer were it to the observation of the farmer? He objects to tithes, taxes, and poor-rates, and he is told of sciences and morals, and paint upon ladies' faces. I laugh, but truly there is more cause to sigh. Are the English yeomen kept to their sacred hearths only by such gossiping as this?

* The German self-importance has lately been most amusingly set forth in the work of a M. Von Fürstenwärther, entitled *The German in America.* His observations, written after three months' residence in the United States, with scarcely a smattering of the English language, are truly entertaining. I cannot forbear quoting a sentence. "If the Americans are justly proud of their civil freedom, and of their freedom in thinking, printing, and speaking, and in the social life, they still know not that higher freedom of the soul which is to be found only in Europe;— and, I say it boldly, *most abundantly in Germany.*" I am indebted for all the acquaintance that I possess with this curious production to a paper in the *North American Review.* This work, conducted by Professor Everett, of the University of Cambridge, Boston, may be read with almost equal interest in either hemisphere. I pretend not to be able to appreciate all its merits, but those who are not qualified to do justice to its profound learning must still admire its just and candid criticism, delivered with gentlemanly forbearance, its elegant diction, liberal views, and sound philosophy.[8]

* See Fearon's *Sketches of America.*

Must they be frightened to stay at home with scarecrows that a child might laugh at? Truly the people who are thus cozened are more insulted than the people who are thus libelled. Could the graves yield up their dead, how would the sturdy patriots of England's better days look upon these things?

LETTER XV.

Upper Canada. Mr. Gourlay. Poor Emigrants. Lake Ontario. Descent of the St. Lawrence. Montreal and Lower Canada.

Montreal, September 1819.

My Dear Friend,

I shall send you few details respecting our route along the Canada frontier, both because I find little leisure for making notes and because I can impart little that is new.

I was surprised to find much discontent prevailing among the poorer settlers in Upper Canada. I could not always understand the grounds of their complaint, but they seemed to consider Mr. Gourlay as having well explained them. Mr. Gourlay, you would see, was prosecuted, and his pamphlets declared libels; not having read them, I cannot pronounce upon either their merits or demerits, but they certainly appear to have spoken the sentiments of the poorer settlers, whose cause he had abetted against the more powerful landholders, land surveyors, and government agents.[1] One ground of complaint, if just, should certainly be attended to, and might, one would think, without much difficulty—that the emigrants are often sent so far into the interior and at so great a distance one from another as to be exposed to insurmountable difficulties and labour. The case of one poor but intelligent settler, as stated to me by himself, moved in no small degree my compassion.

The sufferings from which these poor creatures fly—I will take for instance the starving paupers of Ireland, who throng here without a farthing in their hands and scarce a rag upon their backs—the sufferings of these poor creatures, humanity might hope were ended when thrown upon these shores, but too often they are increased tenfold. First come the horrors of the voyage: ill-fed, ill-clothed, and not unfrequently crowded together as if on board a prison ship, it is not uncommon for a fourth and even a third of the live cargo to be swept off by disease during this *mid-passage*. I have sometimes thought if the societies for the suppression of vice would employ some part of their funds in fitting out these poor creatures in clean and well-regulated ships, under the charge of honest and humane captains, and in furnishing them with the means of subsistence in these distant colonies until they can be settled upon the lands—I have thought that they would render more substantial service to their fellow creatures than the best they may have rendered at present. You will conceive the sufferings of a troop of half-clad paupers, turned adrift in this Siberia, as it often happens, at the close of autumn; the delays, perhaps unavoidable, which occur after their landing, before they are sent to their station in the howling wilderness, kill some and break the spirit of others. Many are humanely sheltered by Canadian proprietors; not a few find their way to the United States and are thrown upon the charity of the city of New York. After fearful hardships, some rear at last their cabin of logs in the savage forest; polar winds and snows, dreary solitudes, agues, and all the train of evils and privations which must be found in a Canadian desert—surely it needs not the art of man to increase the settler's troubles.

It is curious to see how patient men are of physical sufferings when endured voluntarily and when they have it not in their power to charge them upon their rulers. On the southern shores of Lake Ontario, heaven knows, we found sickness sufficient to have broken down the stoutest spirits, and yet there we never heard a complaint. On its northern shores, we found discontent everywhere. Perhaps it was often unjust, but it is in human nature to charge our calamities upon others whenever a pretext is afforded us. The only sure way to keep the peace, therefore, is to remove all pretext. This being done in the United States, a man shivers in the ague, swallows his remedies, recovers or dies, without having quarrelled with anyone save perhaps with his apothecary.

How strangely do statesmen employ money! Hundreds of thousands lodged in frigates larger than ever fought at Trafalgar, in naval and military stores, batteries, martello towers. Where? Upon the shores of the Canadian Siberia. To do what? To protect wolves and bears from a more speedy dislodgment from frozen deserts, which would little repay the trouble of invading, and some few thousands of a people, scattered along an endless line of forest, from the infection of republican principles. What a magnificent idea does this convey of the wealth of that country which could thus ship treasures across the Atlantic to be flung into the wilderness! How flourishing must be her condition! How full, to overflowing, her coffers! Surely her people must be princes; her merchants, kings; and her kings, the Incas of Peru! * But whereto tends all this?

---

* Lieutenant Hall states the disbursements at Kingston during the war at "£1,000 per diem"; the expense of the frigate *St. Lawrence* at £300,000.[2] I was informed by a gentleman long resident in Canada that the ships of war sent from England in frame to be employed on Lake Ontario were all supplied with *stills*. "Do the people of London take this lake for a strip of the ocean," exclaimed the Canadian, "that they send us a machine to freshen its waters?"

Will it answer the purpose, without asking whether the purpose be worth answering? "An army of opinions can pierce where an army of soldiers cannot." A people learn to grumble, and then what becomes of troops, frigates, batteries, and martello towers? The petty squabbles which agitate a colony are like those which split the ears in a country town. Let those who listen, understand. There are those, however, whose business it is to listen, and such might possibly find the prevention of abuses a surer, as well as a cheaper, way of securing their authority than the erection and maintenance of garrisons and all the *et ceteras* attached to them. If the Canadas are not the most expensive of the British colonies, are they not the most useless? One would think so to look at them.[3]

Two immense steamboats, from four to five hundred tons' burden, now navigate Ontario, in lieu of the mighty ships of war that sleep peacefully in their harbours on either shore. The American has every possible convenience, as is common with all these floating hotels found on the waters of the United States; the Canadian (probably from having been established for the transportation of soldiers, stores and goods of various kinds, rather than for the service of passengers) is dirty and ill attended. There is now also a fine steamboat, of a smaller size, plying between Kingston and Prescott, a flourishing village in the neighbourhood of the rapids, and another will soon be launched upon Lake St. Francis, when the navigation of the river will be yet farther facilitated.

We preferred to take our way with more leisure and less convenience than would have been afforded by a steamboat passage, a curiosity, perhaps, ill repaid at the expense of much fatigue and, for myself, with a slight fever, that, however, did not prove the *maladie du pays*. We found the intermitting or *lake* fever, as it is styled in the country, prevailing very generally, especially along the shores of the St. Lawrence. I cannot advise a traveller to choose the autumn for the descent of this river. The wintry chills and heavy fogs of the night, succeeding to the scorching heats of the day, and this in an open bateau, are what few constitutions can undergo with impunity. The varieties of climate endured in the space of twenty-four hours on these northern waters and in the uncleared districts in their neighbourhood during this season surpass all you can have an idea of and are what I certainly should not choose to experience a second time.

At Kingston we took to the water in a well-manned bateau, which brought us in four days and the better part of three nights (for we were seldom tempted by the nature of our accommodations to rest more than a few hours) to La Chine, seven miles above Montreal.

There is something impressive in the savage monotony of the Canadian frontier—the vast river, the black cedars which line its shores and crown its rocky islands, the settler's cabin peering out of the shades, and here and there a little village and a line of cultivation breaking upon the desert; add to this the profound silence, broken only by the discordant voices of your Canadian boatmen as they hail some distant solitary canoe or rise and fall in harsh cadence to the paddle and the oar. There is little in such scenery to talk or write about, yet it has its effect on the mind. Salvator [4] might sometimes find a subject, when the night closes upon these black solitudes and the Canadian boatman kindles his fire on the bare granite, while, below, the waters sleep in sullen calm, and above, the dark boughs of a scathed cedar flicker with the flame.

The rapids present a singular scene, especially when you are in the midst of them. The breakers dashing to right and left, the big green billows crested with foam tossing your bark at their mercy and driving it onwards with the speed of light. You here find the Niagara in all his grandeur.

It is a beautiful little drive from La Chine to Montreal, though you make it not in the most elegant, but that were a small matter, were it a more *secure* vehicle: the tackling (for it could not be called harness) of our steed gave way once, and a fellow traveller absolutely came to the ground twice; *"mais ce n'est pas toujours ainsi,"* as our charioteer assured us. But though it *should* be always the same, the traveller's neck is but little endangered, for though the tottering *calèche* is mounted sufficiently high, the Canadian steed moves sufficiently slow, so that if you fall far, you will fall gently.

It is a pleasant relief to the eye, tired with the contemplation of dreary forests and wide watery wastes, when the fair seigniory of Montreal suddenly opens before you: rich and undulating lands sprinkled with villas, and bounded on one hand by wooded heights and on the other by the grey city, its tin roofs and spires then blazing in the setting sun; the vast river, chafed by hidden rocks into sounding and foaming rapids, and anon spreading his waters into a broad sheet of molten gold, speckled with islands, bateaux and shipping; the distant shore, with its dark line of forest, broken by little villages, penciled on the glowing sky; and far off, two solitary mountains, raising their blue heads in the vermeil glories of the horizon, like sapphires chased in rubies. Along the road, French faces, with all the harshness of feature and good humour of expression peculiar to the national physiognomy, looked and gossiped from door and window, orchard and meadow, a passing salutation easily winning a smile and courteous obeisance. We were for some miles escorted on our way by the good-humoured and loquacious pilot, whose songs had for so many days measured time to the stroke of his paddle. I yet hear his reiterated parting benedictions and see the wild grimaces with which they were accompanied.

The population of Lower is strangely contrasted with that of Upper Canada, nor do they appear to know much concerning each other. In one thing only are they said to be agreed—in a thorough detestation of their republican neighbours. In Upper Canada, however, so far as my observations went, I did not find that this hostile feeling was much shared by the poorer settlers. In either colony where the hostility exists, it is very easily accounted for—in one, by the jealousy of the power and wealth of the republic, and in the other by the influence of the priests.

In ignorance and infatuated superstition, the Canadian remains *in statu quo,* as when he first migrated from his native France. Guarded from the earthquake by British protection, the shock of the Revolution was in no degree, however small, felt here; the priest continues to hoodwink and fleece the people, and the people to pamper and worship the priest, just as in the good old times. You may learn some curious particulars here concerning the policy of the London cabinet, as connected with that of Rome. Among other things, a request has lately been referred to the Pope that he will raise the bishopric of Quebec into an archbishopric, and the prelate of this Canadian diocese is now about to embark for Italy to receive from the hands of his Holiness this addition to his honors. The people, meanwhile, are exhorted to remember in their prayers the pious prince who, though ruling in a land of heretics, bears thus in remembrance the servants of the most High. The priests have in their hands some of the best lands in the country and claim, of course, some fruit offerings from their spiritual children. Conceiving the security of the tenure to lie in the ignorance of the people, they enforce every prohibition calculated to preserve it entire, such as marrying with heretics, reading any book without the permission of the confessor, and learning the English language. The proximity of the States and their growing power and, worse than all, their institutions civil and religious are naturally looked upon by these shepherds of the flock with suspicion and terror. As the union of Canada to the republic would of necessity pave the way to their downfall, interest binds fast their loyalty to the ruling powers; these again, equally jealous of the States and aware of the precariousness of the tenure by which they hold these colonies, pay much deference to the men who hold the keys of the people's minds. Thus goes the world! And yet with the Canadian peasant it would seem to go very happily: he eats his crust, or shares it with the passenger right cheerily; his loyalty, transferred from King Louis to King George, sits equally light on his light spirits. As to the government, if he shares it not, as little does he feel it. Too poor to be oppressed, too ignorant to be discontented, he invokes his saint, obeys his priest, smokes his pipe, and sings an old ballad, while shrewder heads and duller spirits enact laws which he never hears of and toil after gains which he contrives to do without.

There is said generally to be no very friendly understanding between the old French and the new English population, the latter being given to laugh at the superstition of the former, and resenting the supremacy of Catholic over Lutheran [5] episcopacy. The government, however, leaves "Protestant ascendancy" to make its way here as it can, which, unbacked by law, makes its way very slowly. These national and religious jealousies have occasionally produced bickerings and even political disturbances.

Before the breaking out of the late war, an attack was made in an English Quebec journal upon the political and religious tenets, habits, and manners of the Canadian population, which provoked hostility, not merely in a French opposition paper, under the name of *Le Canadien,* but a party under the name of *Democrat.* This last name was probably bestowed without being merited, as it has often been elsewhere. The parties, however, warmed in the dispute, until the governor and the House of Assembly made war on each other, as well as on the newspaper editors; vexatious measures were had recourse to, the opposition press was forcibly put down, arbitrary acts passed, and imprisonments, without reason assigned or trial following, inflicted by the executive on the more contumacious members of the assembly and others of the disaffected. The wealthier and more educated Canadians, who conducted this opposition, were guided, apparently, by political views and patriotic motives, but it never appeared that they were otherwise hostile to the English interest than as they conceived it to be unjustly opposed to that of their own people. This ferment was at its height under the administration of Sir James Craig, between the years 1808 and 1811. Upon the arrival of Sir George Prevost, a bill extraordinary "For the better preservation of His Majesty's Government" being defeated by the obstinate resistance of the House of Assembly, a milder course of administration was adopted.[6] The public mind being thus somewhat soothed, upon the opening of hostilities in the year following between the United States and Great Britain, no unwillingness appeared on the part of the legislature to meet the wishes of the executive, and as for the peasantry, the nation represented by their spiritual fathers as the enemies of God were the enemies of the Canadians. Perhaps the governor was more cautious of putting to the proof the fidelity of the colonists than was necessary. The peasants had never understood the quarrel of their representatives, and the latter, even supposing their views to have gone farther than appeared, were too conscious of their weakness to venture upon a disclosure of them. The war evidently soon became national, and the militia would willingly have done more than was demanded. Antipathy towards the heretical Americans was as powerful an incentive to loyalty as could have been a love to the British; this last it will never be easy to excite. Independent of national and religious prejudices, the presence of a haughty soldiery is not calculated to lull jealousies to sleep.

As respects the ignorance of the Canadians, with the peasantry it is probably with justice called absolute, but that the House of Assembly should, as is generally asserted by the anti-Canadian English, be composed of men who know neither to read nor write can hardly be received as a fair statement. Some such instances may occur, but a body of men who have frequently made a stand for important rights, and in the persons of some of its members endured arbitrary imprisonments for conscientious and constitutional opposition to the dictum of the governor and Legislative Council—that such men should invariably be a crowd of illiterate peasants is not easy of belief.

The government of the Canadas consists of a governor appointed by the crown; a Legislative Council, composed in Upper Canada of seven members, and in the Lower or French Canada of fifteen (these are appointed by the governor and nominated for life); a lower House of Assembly, whose members are chosen by the freeholders in either province, the elections occurring every four years. In Lower Canada the French forming the majority of the population are able to combat in the House of Assembly the power of the English executive and Legislative Council, which virtually forms a part of the former. It is easy to see with what candor this House will be judged of by the party it opposes. It is doubtful whether it would be more praised were it more enlightened.

You will ask, perhaps, whether some pains is not taken to amalgamate the old with the new population or to break down the strongest national distinction by the establishment of English schools. I have stated that the priests are in no way desirous of enlightening their communicants. To resist the authority of these spiritual pastors were not very politic on the part of the temporal powers, and perhaps it is considered as equally the interest of both to leave the Canadian to sing his song and tell his Ave Mary in the language of his fathers. It is curious to compare the stationary position of the French Canada with the progress of the French Louisiana. Not sixteen years since this vast territory was ceded to the United States, and already its people are *nationalized*. Not held as a military possession, but taken into the confederated republics as an independent state, it feels its existence and has learned to prize the importance that it enjoys. A population as simple and ignorant as that of French Canada has been transformed, in the course of one generation, into a people comparatively enlightened. Superstition is fast losing its hold on their minds; the rising youth are educated in village schools established throughout the country, even in the least populous districts; distinctions of manners, feelings, and language between the old and new population are gradually disappearing, and in the course of a few generations they will be mingled into one. Instead of expensive colonies, the acquisitions of America are thus turned into wealthy states, additions to her power and her riches. She quarters no soldiers to awe them into obedience, but imparts to them the right of self-government and *admits* them to her *alliance*. How strangely contrasted to this is the position of these provinces—expensive appendages to a distant empire, military depots, in short, into which England throws her armed legions to awe the peaceful population of the neighbouring republic.

Is there not some erroneous calculation here? By opposing an armed frontier to America, is she not constrained to nourish more or less of a military spirit? Remove it, and were she not deprived of all incentives to martial ardor? Would not her institutions, essentially peaceful, then operate more perfectly than at present, to prevent the exertion of her strength to the injury of other nations? Leave her alone, and she might go to sleep; as it is, she is forced to keep her eyes open, and though her sword be sheathed to wear it always at her side. Some say she is ambitious of conquest, and that her invasion of Canada, both during the Revolutionary and the late war, proves it. She was certainly ambitious of dislodging an armed enemy, and of turning hostile fortifications into inoffensive villages. Had she obtained possession of the Canadas—what then? She would have said to them as she said to Louisiana—*Govern yourselves.* Her own fortifications had then been removed, instead of being strengthened as they now are, to keep pace with those of her neighbours. For *her,* it may probably be as well that she has an enemy skirmishing at her doors. Peaceful as she is, it serves to keep alive her spirit, which might otherwise relax too much. It makes her weigh her strength and feel it; this may be useful, seeing that her institutions and the policy necessarily resulting from them prevent her exerting it without provocation. But this effect, it may be presumed, is not that intended by her enemies. They surely do not expend their treasures with an eye to her advantage. If their object were to increase her energy and keep alive her national feeling could they take surer means than by pointing cannon at her gates. *"Delenda est Carthago"* should not be the motto of the republic. The rivalship of hers with European power, on this Siberian frontier, is a wholesome and spiritualizing stimulus, corrective of the soporific otherwise administered by her security and prosperity. To interrupt these were now probably impossible, though the whole of Europe should league against them, but it is as well, perhaps, that America should not feel this, for, were she to feel it, might not her security and prosperity be then once more endangered?

I fear that I have written a dull letter, but perhaps I do this always. Should you, however, find me yet more dull than usual, consider the hard travelling that I have undergone and the drowsiness of convalescence, which still hangs about me; consider this, and be merciful in your judgment. A few excursions into the surrounding country have finished our Canadian travels. The icy winds of the equinox, and some remaining weakness, scolding me into prudence, we sacrifice our visit to Quebec and strike south for the States.

LETTER XVI.

Lake Champlain. Battle of Plattsburg. Burning of the Phœnix *Steamboat.*

Plattsburg, Lake Champlain, September 1819.

My Dear Friend,

The shores of this beautiful lake are classic ground to the American and perhaps to all those who love liberty and triumph in the struggles for it. For myself, I have listened with much interest to the various stories attached to the different villages and ruined forts that line these waters.

The Americans, rich and poor, gentlemen and mechanics, have all the particulars of their short but eventful history treasured in their minds, with an accuracy which, at first, cannot fail to surprise a foreigner. A citizen, chosen at random, may generally serve you for a cicerone anywhere and everywhere throughout these states; nor is he ever better pleased than when satisfying the curiosity of a stranger upon the subject of his country. He does this, too, with so much intelligence and good nature, and knows so well to discriminate between what is interesting and what is tiresome, that you usually come from the conference more awake than when you engaged in it.

The little town and pleasant bay of Plattsburg is pointed out with peculiar satisfaction to those who show a willingness to sympathize in the brave defence of an invaded people, fighting for all that life has of best and dearest—honor and liberty, property, and the domestic hearth.

At the commencement of hostilities, in the year 1812, the American policy had been to seek the enemy in his own garrisons. It was believed that the Canadas would have been willing to raise the flag of independence and join the federal Union, and rashly judged that raw militia or volunteer troops might be sufficient to drive veteran regulars from their posts. The attempt was daring and, if successful, would doubtless have best secured the country from invasion, and, by cutting off the enemy from communication with the Indians, have screened the scattered settlements on the western frontier from the cruel war with which they were threatened. That success, however, should have been calculated upon proves only that ignorance is always rash; and most profoundly ignorant of the science of war must the republic have been, after thirty years of profound peace, without owning either an army or a navy, or knowing more of military discipline than could be found in the organization and harmless exercise of a peaceful militia. The unsuccessful campaign in the Canadas was not altogether unproductive of advantage to the republic. It served to make apparent her weakness, while the subsequent campaigns equally made apparent her strength. In offensive land operations she first saw her citizens repulsed, when facing, on their own soil, the best-trained soldiers in the world; she afterwards saw them successful. There is a useful lesson here to her and to all other nations.

The stand made at Plattsburg was as spirited as it was important.[1] An army of veterans, from the school of the Duke of Wellington, having entered the St. Lawrence was suddenly marched by Sir George Prevost into the state of New York. Had this army succeeded in obtaining command of Lake Champlain and the line of forts running southward, a simultaneous attack was to be made from the sea on the city of New York, when, the command of the Hudson being secured, the eastern states would have been cut off from the rest of the Union. You will perceive the plan to be the same as that traced for General Burgoyne, but, perhaps, then with more chance of success than in the present instance. Much, however, seemed to favour the undertaking. In the first place, an attack from this quarter was at the time unexpected: for many miles beyond the frontier, the population was thinly scattered through forests and hills; the army was busily engaged in remote parts of the Union; and an attack upon the city of New York being apprehended, the militia of the state had been chiefly drawn towards the coast. Fifteen hundred regulars, principally composed of raw recruits and invalids, was the only force in readiness, when the British troops took possession of the little town of Champlain within the American frontier.

The scattered militia of the vicinity was instantly summoned, and all hands set to work to throw up fortifications and to prepare a fleet to engage that of the enemy. The exertions made during these anxious days are almost incredible: night and day the axe and the hammer were at work.

Let me remark here the peculiar fitness of the American population for such exertions. Every man, or nearly every man, in these states knows to handle the axe, the hammer, the plane, all the mechanic's tools in short, besides the musket, to the use of which he is not only regularly trained as a man but practised as a boy.

The enemy soon advanced up the shores of the lake to the little River Saranac, at the mouth of which stands the village of Plattsburg, backed and flanked by the forest, whose dark interminable line it sweetly breaks with its neat and cheerful dwellings, overlooking the silver bosom of a circular bay, which receives the waters of the river. Continual skirmishes now took place between the enemy and flying parties of militia, seven hundred of which soon collected from the surrounding forests. The state of Vermont, which lines the opposite shores of the lake, then poured forth her mountaineers. Scattered through a mountainous country, it might have been thought difficult to collect the scanty population, but the cry of invasion echoed from hill to hill, from village to village. Some caught their horses from the plough, others ran off on foot, leaving their herds in the pastures, and scarce exchanging a parting blessing with their wives and mothers as they handed to them their muskets.

> From the grey sire, whose trembling hand
> Could hardly buckle on his brand,
> To the raw boy, whose shaft and bow
> Were yet scarce terror to the crow,
> Each valley, each sequester'd glen,
> Muster'd his little horde of men,
> That met, as torrents from the height,
> In highland dale their streams unite;
> Still gathering as they pour along,
> A voice more loud, a tide more strong.

Their guns on their shoulders, a powder flask at their sides, sometimes a ration in their pockets, crowd after crowd poured into Burlington, and all, as a friend who had witnessed the scene described it to me, "came at a run, whether on their own legs or their horses."

The beautiful little town of Burlington covers the breast of a hill on the opposite shore and somewhat higher up the lake than Plattsburg. Here every boat and canoe was in requisition; troop after troop hurried to the shore, and as the scattered crowds poured into Plattsburg, they collected in lines on the Saranac to resist the passage of the enemy or struck into the woods with orders to harass their rear.

The fleet was now equipped, and, when that of the enemy appeared in sight, moored in line across the entrance of the bay. With such breathless alacrity had the Americans prepared to meet this encounter that one of the vessels which then entered into action had been built and equipped in the space of a fortnight; eighteen days previous to the engagement, the timber of which it was constructed had been actually growing in the forest upon the shores of the lake.

The British flotilla, under the command of Captain Downie, mounted ninety-five guns and upwards of a thousand men; the American, under Commodore

Macdonough, eighty-six guns and nearly eight hundred men. The first exchange of cannon between the fleets was the signal of the armies on land. A desperate contest ensued. The British, with daring bravery, twice attempted to force the bridges, and twice were driven back. Then, filing up the river, a detachment attempted to ford, but here a volley of musketry suddenly assailed them from the woods and forced them to retreat with loss.

The issue of the day was felt by both parties to depend upon the naval engagement then raging in the sight of both armies. Many an anxious glance was cast upon the waters by those stationed near the shore. For two hours the conflict remained doubtful. The vessels on either side were stript of their sails and rigging; staggering and reeling hulks, they still gave and received the shocks which threatened to submerge them. The vessel of the American commodore was twice on fire, her cannon dismounted and her sides leaking; the enemy was in the same condition. The battle for a moment seemed a drawn one, when both attempted a maneuver which was to decide the day. With infinite difficulty, the American ship veered about. The enemy attempted the same in vain; a fresh fire poured upon her, and she struck. A shout then awoke upon the shore, and, ringing along the American lines, swelled for a moment above the roar of the battle. For a short space, the British efforts relaxed, but then, as if nerved rather than dismayed by misfortune, the experienced veterans stood their ground and continued the fight until darkness constrained its suspension.

The little town of Burlington, during these busy hours, displayed a far different but not less interesting scene; all occupation was interrupted, the anxious inhabitants lining the heights and straining their eyes and ears to catch some signal that might speak the fate of a combat upon which so much depended. The distant firing and smoke told when the fleets were engaged. The minutes and the hours dragged on heavily, hopes and fears alternately prevailing, when, at length, the cannonading suddenly ceased. But still, with the help of the telescope, nothing could be distinguished across the vast waters, save that the last wreath of smoke had died away and that life, honor, and property were lost or saved.

Not a sound was heard; the citizens looked at each other without speaking. Women and children wandered along the beach, with many of the men of Vermont, who had continued to drop in during the day but found no means of crossing the lake. Every boat was on the other shore, and all were still too busy there to ferry over tidings of the naval combat. The evening fell, and still no moving speck appeared upon the waters. A dark night, heavy with fogs, closed in, and some with saddened hearts slowly sought their homes, while others still lingered, hearkening to every breath, pacing to and fro distractedly and wildly imagining all the probable and possible causes which might occasion this suspense. Were they defeated—some would have taken to the boats; were they successful—some would have burned to bring the tidings. At eleven at night a shout broke in the darkness from the waters. It was one of triumph. Was it from friends or enemies? Again it broke louder; it was recognized and re-echoed by the listeners on the beach, swelled up the hill, and "Victory! Victory!" rang through the village. I could not describe the scene as it was described to me, but you will suppose how the blood eddied from the heart, how young and old ran about frantic, how they laughed, wept, and sang, and wept again. In half an hour, the little town was in a blaze of light.

The brunt of the battle was now over, but it still remained doubtful whether the invaders would attempt to push forward, in despite of the loss of their fleet and of the opposing ranks of militia, now doubly inspired by patriotism and good fortune. At daybreak the next morning were found only the sick, the wounded, and the dead, with the military stores and munitions of war. The siege had been raised during the night, and the baggage and artillery having been sent back, the army were already some miles on their way towards the frontier. The skirmishing that harassed their retreat thinned their numbers less than the sudden desertion of five hundred men, who threw down their muskets and sprang into the woods. A few of these sons of Mars are now thriving farmers in the state of Vermont; others fared, with more or less success, according to their industry and morals.

Sir George Prevost was much blamed, both in Canada and at home, for this precipitate retreat. That he might have forced the American works is admitted by the Americans themselves; indeed, from their hasty and imperfect construction, it is wonderful how they were made to stand the siege as they did. But what advantage would have been gained by strewing the earth with dead to break down a breastwork of planks, to retire or surrender afterwards? Without the co-operation of a fleet, with exhausted and dispirited troops, to have forced a passage through woods and over roads of logs, contending for every step with thickening crowds—not of soldiers, but of fathers, husbands, citizens, standing on their own soil, and inspired with every feeling that can raise men above themselves—surely the commander judged wisely and humanely who preferred retreat to certain destruction. "It might have been a day later," was the observation of an American officer, "but the enemy must have retreated, or surrendered, or been cut to pieces by degrees."

There is in militia a moral force, which, in moments of great exigency, is more than a match for trained skill and hardy experience. Defeat, which dispirits the best veteran regulars fighting in a foreign land for the point of honor or the prospect of booty, invigorates national militia contending on their own soil for all that is dearest to the human heart. Contrast for a moment the exterior of the hostile bands who here engaged: a line of plain citizens, their dusky garments breathing of home, opposed to flaring uniforms speaking only of the trade of war—the heart acknowledges the difference between such armies.

It is customary in the more wealthy cities, and occasionally even elsewhere, for some of the militia companies to provide themselves with uniforms, and though this proves a generous spirit on the part of the citizens, I have never looked upon these well-clad regiments in exercise with the same interest with which I invariably regard those clad in the everyday garments of domestic life. You need to be told that the other are militia; nothing remains to be said here. I remember well observing, for the first time, a troop of citizens going through military exercise—the blacksmith from his forge, the mechanic, his coat marked with sawdust, the farmer with the soil yet upon his hands. "What think you of our soldiers?" said a friend smiling. Think!—I know not what I thought; but I know that I secretly brushed a tear from my eye.

I feel tempted to pass another idle half hour in detailing to you a story of a different character, and which, though it will never be placed on record, is not less worthy of being so than the victory of Macdonough.

One of the finest steamboats ever built in the United States lately ran upon this inland sea, and was destroyed, ten days since, by fire, in a manner truly terrible. The captain of the vessel had fallen sick and entrusted its management to his son, a young man just turned of one and twenty. Making for St. John's with upwards of forty passengers, they encountered the equinoctial gale, which blew with violence right ahead. The fine vessel, however, encountered it bravely and dashed onwards through the storm, until an hour after midnight she had gained the broadest part of the lake. Some careless mortal, who had been to seek his supper in the pantry, left a candle burning on a shelf, which, after some time, caught another which was ranged above.

The passengers were asleep, or at least quiet in their births, when a man at the engine perceived, in some dark recess of the vessel, an unusual light. Approaching the spot, he heard the crackling of fire and found the door of the pantry a glowing and tremulous wall of embers. He had scarcely time to turn himself ere he was enveloped in flames; rushing past them, he attempted to burst into the ladies' apartment by a small door which opened into the interior of the vessel. It was locked on the inside, and the noise of the storm seemed to drown all his cries and blows. Hurrying upon the deck, he gave the alarm to the captain, and flew to the women's cabin. Ere he leaped down the stairs, the flames had burst through the inner door, and had already seized upon the curtains of the bed next to it. You may conceive the scene which followed.

In the meantime the young captain roused his crew and his male passengers, warning the pilot to make for the nearest island. Summoning his men around him and stating to them that all the lives on board could not be saved in the boats, he asked their consent to save the passengers and to take death with him. All acquiesced unanimously, and hastened to let down the boats. While thus engaged, the flames burst through the decks and shrouded the pilot, the mast, and the chimney in a column of flames. The helmsman, however, held to the wheel, until his limbs were scorched and his clothes half consumed upon his back. The unusual heat round the boiler gave a redoubled impetus to the engine. The vessel dashed madly through the waters, until she was within a few roods of land. The boats were down, and the captain and his men held the shrieking women and children in their arms, when the helm gave way and the vessel, turning from the wind, flew backwards, whirling round and round from the shore. None could approach to stop the engine; its fury, however, soon spent itself, and left the flaming wreck to the mercy only of the winds and waves. With dreadful struggles, the naked passengers got into the boats and received the women and children from the hands of the captain and the crew, who, while the flames whirled over their heads, refused the solicitations to enter the overburdened barks and pushed them off from the fire which had nearly caught their sides. It was now discovered that one woman and a youth of sixteen had been forgotten. Hurrying them to the windward of the flames, the youth was bound to a plank, and a skilful swimmer of the crew leapt with him into the lake. The captain, holding the frantic woman in his arms, stood upon the edge of the scorching and crackling wreck, until he saw the last of his companions provided with a spar and committed to the waters; then, throwing from him with one arm a table which he had before secured for the purpose and with the other grasping his charge, he sprang into the waves. The poor woman, mad with terror, seized his throat as he placed and held her upon the table. Forced to disengage himself, she was borne away by the waves; he tried to follow and saw her, for the last time, clinging to a burning mass of the vessel. One last shriek and the poor creature was whelmed in flood and fire. Swimming round the blazing hulk, and calling aloud to such of his companions as might be within hearing to keep near it, he watched for the falling of a spar. He seized one while yet on fire, and, quenching it, continued to float round the wreck, deeming that the light might be a signal, should the boats be able to return. But these had to row, heavily laden, six miles through a mountainous sea. It was long before they could make the land and that, leaving their helpless freight naked on the shore of a desert island in the dark and tempestuous night, they turned to seek the drowning heroes.

The day broke while they were labouring against the roaring elements, seeking in vain the extinguished beacon that was to guide their search. At length a blackened atom appeared upon the top of a wave; stretched upon it was a human figure. It was, I rejoice to say, the young captain—senseless, but the generous soul not quite departed. He is alive and doing well. One other of these devoted men was picked up late in the morning and wonderously restored to life, after having been eight hours swimming and floating on the water. Seven perished.

The citizens of Bordentown hastened with clothing and provisions to the sufferers on the island, took them to their homes, and nursed them with affectionate solicitude.

The blackened wreck of the *Phœnix* is now lying, in the midst of the lake, upon a reef of rocks, to which it was drifted by the storm.

LETTER XVII.

Town of Burlington. Character and History of the State of Vermont.

Burlington, State of Vermont,
October 1819.

My Dear Friend,

Ascending the waters of Lake Champlain, the shores assume a wilder and more mountainous character. The site of the flourishing town of Burlington is one of singular beauty, the neatness and elegance of the white houses ascending rapidly from the shore, interspersed with trees, and arranged with that symmetry which characterizes the young villages of these states, the sweet bay, and, beyond, the open waters of the lake, bounded by a range of mountains, behind which, when our eyes first rested on them, the sun was sinking in golden splendour. It was a fairy scene, when his flaming disk, which might have dazzled eagles, dropt behind the purple screen, blazing on the still broad lake, on the windows and the white walls of the lovely village, and on the silver sails of the sloops and shipping, gliding noiselessly through the gleaming waters.

Not forty years since, and the ground now occupied by this beautiful town and a population of two thousand souls was a desert, frequented only by bears and panthers. The American verb to "progress" (though some of my friends in this country deny that it is an Americanism) is certainly not without its apology; even a foreigner must acknowledge that the new kind of advancement which greets his eye in this country seems to demand a new word to portray it.

The young town of Burlington is graced with a college, which was founded in the year 1791 and has lately received considerable additions. The state of Vermont, in which it stands, whose population may be somewhat less than 300,000, contrives to support two establishments of this description, and, perhaps, in no part of the Union is greater attention paid to the education of youth.

The territory passing under the name of Vermont is intersected, from north to south, by a range of mountains covered with evergreen forests, from which the name of the country. This Alpine ridge, rising occasionally to three and four thousand feet, nearly fills up the breadth of the state, but is everywhere scooped into glens and valleys, plentifully intersected with streams and rivers flowing, to the eastward, into the beautiful Connecticut and, to the west, into the magnificent Champlain. The gigantic forests of white pine, spruce, cedar, and other evergreens, which clothe to the top the billowy sides of the mountains, mingle occasionally their deep verdure with the oak, elm, beech, maple, &c. that shadow the valleys. This world of forest is intersected by tracts of open pasture, while the luxuriant lands that border the watercourses are fast exchanging their primeval woods for the treasures of agriculture. The most populous town in the state contains less than three thousand souls, the inhabitants, agricultural or grazing farmers, being scattered through the valleys and hills, or collected in small villages on the banks of the lakes and rivers.

In scrupulous regard to the education of her citizens, in the thorough democracy of her institutions, in her simple morals and hardy industry, Vermont is a characteristic daughter of New England. She stands conspicuous, however, among her sister states for her patriotic spirit; her services have always been rendered to the nation unsparingly, nor could she ever be charged with separating her interests from those of the confederacy.

During the Revolutionary struggle, her scanty population, thinly scattered along the borders of rivers and streams, in mountains and forests, were signally generous and disinterested. The short history of this spirited republic is not without a peculiar interest and is very highly honorable to the character of her people.

During her colonial existence, she was engaged in a dispute with the neighbouring provinces, involving all those great principles which afterwards formed the basis of the quarrel between the colonies and the mother country. Under the administration of Great Britain, in consequence of various contradictory acts passed at different periods and under different reigns, the Vermont lands were claimed by the two adjoining provinces of New Hampshire and New York. Most of the early settlers held their possessions under the patent granted to the former, when the latter asserted a prior claim and essayed to constrain the ejection of the proprietors. The proclamation of the royal governor of New York was answered by a proclamation of the royal governor of New Hampshire; the matter being referred to the home authority, a verdict was pronounced in favour of New York against the wishes and claims of the Vermontese, but this imperial verdict was as little respected by the hardy mountaineers as had been the proclamation of the governor. "The gods of the valleys," cried the spirited Ethan Allen, "are not gods of the hills." An opposition was instantly organized, and the New York claims and jurisdiction so set at defiance that a civil war had very nearly ensued. The ground assumed by this infant colony was the right of a people to self-government, and accordingly she established her own in defiance of the threats of New York and her governor. But a greater cause soon fixed the attention of this high-minded people. In the very heat of their contention with the New York claimants and legislature, the quarrel broke out between the British government and the American people. From this quarrel the mountaineers of Vermont might easily have excused themselves. Far removed from the sea, without commerce, untaxed and ungoverned, the arbitrary measures of the English ministry clashed with no immediate interests of theirs, and, heated as they were in other disputes, might have been supposed little calculated to excite their opposition by wounding their pride, but, superior to all selfish considerations, their own quarrel was lost in that of the community. The news of the Battle of Lexington had no sooner reached them than we find Ethan Allen, at the head of a troop of Vermont mountaineers, surprising the important post of Ticonderoga. Summoning the surrender of the fort in the dead of night, "In whose name?" said the astonished and irritated commander. "In the name of the great Jehovah and the Continental Congress," replied the patriot. This Continental Congress contained no representatives of the people of Vermont; it had not pronounced upon the justice or injustice of the claims preferred against them, nor acknowledged the independent jurisdiction which they had established. But it was an assembly gathered under the wings of freedom; it asserted for others those rights which the Vermontese had asserted for themselves. Without hesitation, therefore, without waiting to be solicited or essaying to make stipulations, voluntarily and unconditionally these champions of the rights of man forsook their ploughshares and their pruning hooks, recommended their women and their children to the protection of heaven, and went forth to fight the battles of their brethren.

After the Declaration of Independence, the Vermontese appealed to the Congress as to the supreme government, demanding to be admitted into the confederacy as an independent state. They grounded their plea upon the same great principles by which the other states had justified their resistance to Great Britain—the right of a people to institute their own government and the invalidity of all contracts uncemented by a mutual agreement between the parties. New York, on the other hand, could appeal only to royal grants and deeds legally rather than justly executed. The feelings of the Congress were well disposed towards the Vermont cause, but New York was too important an ally to be decided against rashly; judgment therefore was deferred until the two states should come to agreement between themselves, or until more peaceful days should bring leisure to the Congress to examine into all the bearings of the question. Thus thrown out of the pale of the Union, it was imagined by the enemy that Vermont might easily be won from the common cause. She was now promised high privileges and an individual existence as a royal province, but this generous republic was not to be so bought from honor: firm in her resistance to New York, she was as true to the cause of America. Her handful of freemen asserted their own rights and sustained those of their brethren throughout that trying contest. At its close and when the national independence was finally established, the dispute with her sister state was amicably adjusted, and she then voluntarily joined herself as a fourteenth state to the thirteen original confederated republics, whose cause she had so zealously and magnanimously made her own.

In consequence of her resistance to the jurisdiction of New York, Vermont had asserted and enjoyed an independent existence several years before the dismemberment of the colonial provinces from Great Britain, but the constitution, as it now stands, was not finally arranged until the year 1793.[1]

The plan of government is among the most simple of any to be found in the Union. The legislative department is composed of one house, whose members are chosen by the whole male population of the state. In this mountainous district, peopled by a race of simple agriculturists, the science of legislation may be supposed to present few questions of difficulty, nor has it been found necessary to impede the process of law-making by forcing a projected statute to pass through two ordeals. You find in the constitution of Vermont another peculiarity which marks a people Argus-eyed to their liberties. In the other republics, the people have thought it sufficient to preserve to themselves the power of summoning a convention to alter or amend their plan of government whenever they may judge it expedient. But the Vermontese, as if unwilling to trust to their own vigilance, have decreed the stated election of a Council of Censors, to be convened for one year at the end of every seven years, whose business it is to examine whether the constitution has been preserved inviolate—"whether the legislative or executive branches of government have performed their duty as guardians of the people, or assumed to themselves, or exercised other or greater powers than they are entitled to by the constitution"—to take in review, in short, every public act, with the whole course of administration pursued since the last meeting of the censors. If any acts appear to them to have been unconstitutional, their business is to refer them to the legislative assembly then sitting, stating the grounds of their objection and recommending a revisal of the same. They are farther empowered to judge of the propriety of revising the existing constitution, and, should any article appear defective or not clearly defined, to promulgate the articles objected to and the amendments proposed, which, being considered and approved by the people, other delegates are appointed to decree the same in convention, according to the instructions received from their constituents.

The assembly now meets in the little town of Montpelier, situated in a secluded valley in the centre of the state. Having gained the centre, the seat of government is now probably fixed. It is a strange novelty in the eyes of a European to find legislators assembled in a humble and lonely village to discuss affairs of state. How strangely has liberty been libelled! Behold her in the mountains of Vermont, animating a people, who, at the first sound of oppression, would rise like lions from their lair, but who, in the free exercise of undisputed rights and walking erect among their hills with a spirit untamed and thought unshackled, live on a life of peace and industry, unharming and unharmed, proud as the noble in feudal seigniory, and peaceful as the flocks which graze upon their mountains!

The men of Vermont are familiarly known by the name of "Green Mountain boys"; a name which they themselves are proud of and which, I have remarked, is spoken with much complacency, and not unfrequently with a tone of admiration or affection, by the citizens of the neighbouring states.

Before leaving Vermont, I would observe that the Scotch emigrant would probably find it peculiarly suited to his habits and constitution. A healthy climate, a hilly country, affording either pasture or arable land—the frugal, hardy, and industrious Scotch farmer might here find himself at home, or rather in a home somewhat improved. There are many valuable tracts unreclaimed in the lower valleys and much land of moderate value on the sides of the mountains. Our sons of the mist might here see their Grampians and Cheviots swelling out of a better soil and smiling under a purer heaven. They would find, too, a race of industry and intelligence equal or superior to their own and animated with a spirit of independence that they might imbibe with advantage.*

European emigrants are, perhaps, given to roam too far into the interior of this continent. The older states have still sufficient of vacant lands to settle down multitudes, and, as I have before remarked, men have usually many things to learn when they arrive in this country. The American enters the western wilderness skilled to vanquish all difficulties; and understanding to train his children in the love of their country, founded upon a knowledge of its history and an appreciation of its institutions, he is fitted to form the advanced guard of civilization; the foreigner, in general, will be better placed in the main body, where he may himself receive instructions and imbibe feelings suited to his newly assumed character as a citizen of a republic.

* There is one Scotch settlement in Vermont in a very flourishing condition, and, I believe, stragglers continue occasionally to join it.

LETTER XVIII.

Direction of American Genius. Founders of the American Republics. Establishment of the Federal Government.

Whitehouse, New Jersey, December 1819.

My Dear Friend,

I regret that the circumstances which constrained us to cut short our journey through the eastern states have also prevented me, for some time past, from writing with my usual punctuality.[1]

With this short summary, you must allow me to pass over the remainder of our tour and come at once to the subject of your letter, now before me. I will do my best to reply to * * * *'s enquiries, not pretending, however, to give a better solution of them than I apprehend others may have given before.

It has been common of late years to summon the literature of America to the European bar and to pass a verdict against American wit and American science. More liberal foreigners, in alluding to the paucity of standing American works in prose or rhyme, are wont to ascribe it to the infant state of society in this country; others read this explanation, I incline to think at least, without affixing a just meaning to the words. Is it not commonly received in England that the American nation is in a sort of middle state between barbarism and refinement? I remember that, on coming to this country, I had myself but a very confused notion of the people that I was to find in it. Sometimes they had been depicted to me as a tribe of wild colts, chewing the bit just put into their mouths and fretting under the curb of law, carelessly administered and yet too strict withal for their untamed spirits; at other times I understood them to be a race of shrewd artificers, speculating merchants, and plodding farmers, with just enough of manners to growl an answer when questioned and enough of learning to read a newspaper, drive a hard bargain, keep accounts, and reason phlegmatically upon the advantages of free trade and popular government. These portraits appeared to me to have few features of resemblance—the one seemed nearly to image out a Dutchman and the other a wild Arab. To conceive the two characters combined were not very possible; I looked at both and could make nothing of either.

The history of this people seemed to declare that they were brave, high-minded, and animated with the soul of liberty; their institutions, that they were enlightened; their laws, that they were humane; and their policy, that they were peaceful, and kept good faith. But I was told that they were none of these. Judge a man by his works, it is said, but to judge a nation by its works was no adage, and, I was taught, was quite ridiculous. To judge a nation by the reports of its enemies, however, seemed equally ridiculous, so I determined not to judge at all, but to land in the country without knowing anything about it and wait until it should speak for itself. The impressions that I have received, I have occasionally attempted to impart to you; they were such at first as greatly to surprise me, for it is scarcely possible to keep the mind unbiassed by current reports, however contradictory their nature and however intent we may be to let them pass unheeded.

There is little here that bespeaks the infancy of society in the sense that foreigners usually suppose it applicable. The simple morals, more equalized fortunes, and more domestic habits and attachments, generally found in this country as compared with Europe, doubtless bespeak a nation young in luxury, but do they bespeak a nation young in knowledge? It would say little for knowledge were this the case.

It is true that authorship is not yet a trade in this country. Perhaps for the poor it is a poor trade everywhere, and could men do better, they might seldom take to it as a profession. But, however this may be, many causes have operated hitherto, and some perhaps may always continue to operate, to prevent American genius from showing itself in works of imagination or of arduous literary labour. As yet, we must remember that the country itself is not half a century old. The generation is barely passed away whose energies were engrossed by a struggle for existence. To the harassing war of the Revolution succeeded the labors of establishing the national government and of re-organizing that of the several states, and it must be remembered that, in America, neither war nor legislation is the occupation of a body of men, but of the whole community; it occupies every head and every heart, rouses the whole energy, and absorbs the whole genius of the nation.

The establishment of the federal government was not the work of a day; even after its conception and adoption a thousand clashing opinions were to be combated. The war of the pen succeeded to that of the sword, and the shock of political parties to that of hostile armies; the struggle continued through the whole of that administration denominated *Federal*.[2] After the election of Mr. Jefferson, it revived for a moment with redoubled violence, and though this was but the flickering of the flame in the socket, it engaged the attention of the whole people and continued to do so until the breaking out of the second war, which, in its progress, cemented all parties and, in its issue, established the national independence and perfected the civil union. It is but four years, therefore, that the public mind has been at rest; nay, it is only so long that the United States can be said to have enjoyed an acknowledged national existence.

It was the last war, so little regarded in Europe but so all-important to America, that fixed the character of this country and raised it to the place which it now holds among the nations of the world. Am I mistaken in the belief that Europeans (and I speak here of the best informed) have hitherto paid but little attention to the internal history of the United States? When engaged in the Revolutionary struggle, they were regarded with a momentary sympathy; the fate of mankind hung upon the contest. It was Tyranny's armed legions opposed to Liberty's untrained but consecrated band, and the enlightened patriot of every clime felt that the issue was to decide the future destinies of the world. The battle being fought, this young and distant nation again seemed to shrink into insignificance. The whirlwind had now turned upon Europe, and all her thinking heads were employed in poising state against state, empire against empire, or one tyrant against another tyrant, while America, removed from the uproar, was binding up her wounds and arranging her disturbed household. The people of Europe had soon well nigh forgotten her existence, and their governors only occasionally remembered her, to tell her that she was not worth regarding. Her ships were robbed upon the seas and insulted in the ports, and from these at length shut out. She remonstrated to be laughed at; she resented the insults and at last challenged the aggressors, and was stared at. The ministry which had dared her to the quarrel drew carelessly a million from their treasury, dispatched some detachments from their fleets and armies, and sat down in quiet expectation that the American republics were once again to be transformed into British colonies. A few more generous politicians occasionally threw a glance across the ocean, curious to see how the Herculean infant would once again cope with the matured strength of a full-grown empire, and were perhaps scarcely less surprised than the cabinet of St. James's by the issue of the rencontre.

If * * * * will study the history of this country, he will find it *teeming with business*. America was not asleep during the thirty years that Europe had forgotten her. She was actively employed in her education, in framing and trying systems of government, in eradicating prejudices, in vanquishing internal enemies, in replenishing her treasury, in liquidating her debts, in amending her laws, in correcting her policy, in fitting herself to enjoy that liberty which she had purchased with her blood, in founding seminaries of learning, in facilitating the spread of knowledge—to say nothing of the revival of commerce, the reclaiming of wilderness after wilderness, the facilitating of internal navigation, the doubling and tripling of a population trained to exercise the rights of freemen, and to respect institutions adopted by the voice of their country. Such have been the occupations of America. She bears the works of her genius about her; we must not seek them in volumes piled on the shelves of a library. All her knowledge is put forth in action, lives in her institutions, in her laws, speaks in her senate, acts in her cabinet, breathes even from the walls of her cities and the sides of her ships. Look on all she has done, on that which she is; count the sum of her years, and then pronounce sentence on her genius. Her politicians are not ingenious theorists, but practical statesmen; her soldiers have not been conquerors, but patriots; her philosophers not wise reasoners, but wise legislators. Their country has been and is their field of action; every able head and nervous arm is pressed into its service. The foreign world hears nothing of their exploits and reads none of their lucubrations, but their country reaps the fruits of their wisdom and feels the aid of their service, and it is in the wealth, the strength, the peace, the prosperity, the good government, and the well-administered laws of that country that we must discover and admire their energy and genius.

In Europe we are apt to estimate the general cultivation of a people by the greater or less number of their literary characters. Even in that hemisphere, it is, perhaps, an unfair way of judging. No one would dispute that France is greatly advanced in knowledge since the era of the Revolution, and yet her literary fame from that period has been at a stand. The reason is obvious— that her genius was called from the closet into the senate and the field, her historians and poets were suddenly changed into soldiers and politicians, her peaceful men of letters became active citizens, known in their generation by their virtues or their crimes. Instead of tragedies, sonnets, and tomes of philosophy, they manufactured laws or martialled armies, opposed tyrants or fell their victims, or played the tyrant themselves. Engaged in the war of politics, a nation is little likely to be visited by the muses; they are loungers, who love quiet and sing in the shade. They come not upon the field until the battle is long over, and before they celebrate the actions of the dead, the moss has grown upon their graves. The battle is now over in America, but it is no more than over, and it is doubtful, perhaps, whether her popular government must not always have something too bustling in it for the "gentle nine." A youth, conscious of talents, here sees the broad way to distinction open before him; the highest honors of the republic seem to tempt his ambition, and the first wish of his heart is to be a statesman. This secures able servants to the commonwealth and quickens the energy and intelligence of the whole people, but it causes all their talent to be put forth in the business of the day, and thus rather tends to impart dignity to the country than to procure immortality to individuals. Those Americans who have been known in Europe as authors have been better known in their own country as active citizens of the republic, nor does my memory at this moment furnish me with more than two exceptions to this rule.* [3] The able political writers of the Revolution and of the busy years succeeding it were all soldiers or statesmen, who with difficulty snatched a moment from the active duties which their country devolved upon them to enlighten their fellow citizens upon points of vital national importance. Barlow, known only in England as the author of *The Columbiad,* was a diplomatist, and an able political writer.[4] The venerable Dwight was here held in honor, not as the author of *The Conquest of Canaan,* but as the patron of learning, the assiduous instructor of youth, and a popular and energetic writer of the day.[5] I could in the same way designate many living characters whose masterly abilities have been felt in the cabinets of Europe, and which here are felt in every department of the civil government and in all the civic professions. These men, who in other countries would have enlarged the field of the national literature, here quicken the pulse of the national prosperity; eloquent in the senate, able in the cabinet, they fill the highest offices of the republic, and are repaid for their arduous and unceasing labours by the esteem of their fellow citizens and the growing strength of their country.

No nation has, perhaps, ever produced in the same term of years more high-minded patriots and able statesmen than the American. Who laid the foundation of these republics? Not robbers and bandits, as some of our ministerial journals would persuade their readers, but the wisest citizens of the wisest country then existing on the globe. The father of Virginia was an English hero, who might adorn a tale of chivalry, a knight errant, who hunted honor through the world and came at last, in the pure love of liberty and daring adventure, to found a colony in the American wilderness.† The fathers of Maryland were sages and philanthropists, who placed freedom of conscience before the privileges of birth or the enjoyments of luxury—English noblemen, whose birth was their poorest distinction, who taught religious and political equality in an age when both were unknown and raised an asylum in this

---

* Brown, the author of the well-known novels, *Arthur Mervyn, the Ventriloquist,* &c., and Mr. Washington Irving. When the latter left his country to visit Europe, he was too young to have been known in any other character than that of an author. The elegant work of this gentleman, entitled *The Sketch Book,* is equally admired on both sides of the Atlantic.

† Captain John Smith.

distant world for the persecuted of every sect and every clime.* The fathers of New England were the Hampdens of Britain, who came to enjoy liberty and serve their austere God, among savage beasts and yet more savage men, bearing all things rather than the frowns of tyranny and the jurisdiction of hierarchs. Among them were men of erudition and of opinions before their age. The venerable Roger Williams (an advocate of religious as well as civil liberty) promulgated principles which were afterwards abetted by Milton and Locke.† Oglethorpe, the father of Georgia, united the characters of a soldier, a legislator, a statesman, and a philanthropist. In his youth, he learned the art of war from Prince Eugene; in his maturer years he supported, in the British Parliament, the interests of his country and the claims of humanity. He was the leader of

> the generous band,
> Who, touched with human woe, redressive searched
> Into the horrors of the gloomy jail.‡
>
> THOMSON's *Winter,* lines 359–361.

Pennsylvania wears the name of her sage. In fact there is not one of the colonies whose foundations were not laid by the hands of freemen and men wise in their generations. The political revolutions of England continued to throw into them many of her best and bravest citizens, many, too, of gentle birth and refined manners. The Edict of Nantes sent to them some of the most

---

* George and Cecilius Calvert, the Lords Baltimore, and Leonard Calvert, brother of Cecilius. This distinguished family was attached to the Church of Rome. While all the European nations and, more or less, the other American colonists were harassing each other for their differing opinions, a Roman Catholic promulgated the doctrine, not of religious toleration, but religious equality. The Puritans, under the reign of Cromwell, first disturbed the peace of the infant Maryland, but it was not till after the English revolution that her wise and philanthropic institutions were broken down by a royal decree. William the Third finally annihilated Catholic ascendancy in England and established Protestant ascendancy in Ireland and Maryland: 1688 was a happy year for only one portion of the British empire.

† A comparison between the Rhode Island charter and the constitution presented to Carolina by Locke would lead us to pronounce Roger Williams a more sapient legislator than his more distinguished disciple.

‡ In the forty-fifth year of his age, General Oglethorpe placed himself at the head of a crowd of poor sufferers and embarked for the American wilderness. Having, by his wisdom and valour, secured the first settlers from intestine commotions and foreign enemies, he returned to England. At the breaking out of the Revolutionary War, the command of the British army was tendered to him, as to the oldest officer in the service. "I will undertake the business without a man or ship of war," was the reply of the veteran to the minister, "provided you will authorize me to assure the colonists on my arrival among them that you will do them justice." The infant Georgia was animated with the soul of her founder; her handful of patriots (the whole population was within fifty thousand) joined the league and unfurled the standard of independence. The venerable Oglethorpe saw the colony that he had planted raised into a free republic, heard the independence of America acknowledged, and died at the advanced age of ninety-six.[6]

enlightened and virtuous sons of France; similar edicts, many of the noblest sons of Ireland. From the loins of such exiles proceeded the heroes of the Revolution. Until the very period of the quarrel which raised America to the rank of an independent nation, many of England's most distinguished families came to establish their penates in the New World, either from a spirit of adventure or attracted by the superior beauty of the climate and the frank and hospitable character of the people. We find, among others, the representative of the noble house of Fairfax foregoing the baronial honors of his native land for the liberty and simplicity of America, laying down his title and establishing himself in patriarchal magnificence in Virginia, abetting, in his old age, the cause of liberty, and wearing the simple and freely-bestowed dignities of a republic in lieu of the proud titles of an aristocracy.* [7]

But while America was thus sought by enlightened individuals, the Parliamentary speeches and pamphlets of the time show how little was known by the English community of the character and condition of the colonists. Because the government had chosen at one time to make Virginia a Botany Bay, an insult which tended not a little to prepare her for the Revolution, the country of Franklin, Washington, Patrick Henry, Jefferson, Schuyler, Gates, Greene, Allen, Dickinson, Laurens, Livingston, Hamilton, Jay, Rush, Adams, Rittenhouse, Madison, Monroe, and a thousand other high-minded gentlemen, soldiers, orators, sages, and statesmen, was accounted a hive of pickpockets and illiterate hinds! Never was a national revolution conducted by greater men, by men more magnanimous, more self-devoted, and more maturely wise. And these men, too, were not self-elected, nor raised by chance to pilot the vessel of the state; they were called by the free voices of their fellow citizens to fill the various posts most suited to their genius. The people were as discriminating as their servants were able—not an illiterate multitude, hurried by a few popular orators or generous heroes into actions above themselves. They were a well-informed and well-organized community, animated with the feeling of liberty, but understanding the duties of citizens and the nature and end of civil government.

As colonies, the American states had, for the most part, lived under constitutions as essentially democratic as those of the present day; the chief difference was that they were engaged in continual struggles to support them. In their

* See Wood's *Scotch Peerage* for a short but interesting account of Thomas, the sixth Lord Fairfax. The present representative of this noble house also prefers the character of an American citizen to that of an English nobleman. There might be as much calculation in this as philosophy, for after all, it is preferring a sceptre to a coronet. The American citizen has no superior and is one of a race of sovereigns; the European baron has many superiors and is one of a race of subjects.

first infancy, their future destiny was little foreseen. The patents, carelessly granted to the early settlers of New England, involved rights which the arbitrary monarchs who signed them had never dreamed of, but of this remissness they very speedily repented.

The colonial history of America would be alone sufficient to stamp the character of the Stuart kings: not content with torturing the consciences and outraging the rights of the English people in their own island, we find them hunting the patriots whom their tyranny had made exiles even in the howling wilderness of the New World, as if determined that a freeman should not live on the whole surface of the globe. One might pause to smile at the contradictory acts of Charles II, at once a thoughtless voluptuary and a rapacious tyrant, had they sported with matters of less value than the rights and happiness of mankind. This spoiled child of power carelessly set his hand to the noblest charters ever accorded by a king to a people, and then waged an eternal war with the peaceful and far-distant handful of freemen who determined to abide by them.* The hard contest in which the young colonies were unceasingly engaged with the successive monarchs and varying administrations of the mother country sharpened the wits of their people. Occasionally their charters were broken down by force, but never was a fraction of their liberties yielded up by themselves or stolen from them without their knowledge: they struggled and bled for every right which fell. "To die by the hands of others rather than by their own" was the early motto of this people, nor, perhaps, could one have been imagined more calculated to render them invincible.

What is most worthy of admiration in the history of America is not merely the spirit of liberty, which has ever animated her people, but their perfect acquaintance with the science of government, which has ever saved that spirit from preying on itself. The sages who laid the foundation of her greatness possessed at once the pride of freemen and *the knowledge of English freemen;* in building the edifice, they knew how to lay the foundation; in preserving untouched the rights of each individual, they knew how to prevent his attacking those of his neighbour. They brought with them the experience of the best governed nation then existing, and, having felt in their own persons the errors inherent in that constitution, which had enlightened but only partly protected them, they knew what to shun as well as what to imitate in the new models which they here cast, leisurely and sagely, in a new and remote world. Thus possessed from the beginning of free institutions or else continually occupied in procuring or defending them, the colonies were well prepared to

* The present of a curious ring from Winthrop, the enlightened father of Massachusetts, is said to have won the royal signature to the democratic charter of Connecticut.

assume the character of independent states. There was less of an experiment in this than their enemies supposed.* Nothing, indeed, can explain the obstinacy of the English ministry at the commencement of the Revolutionary struggle but the supposition that they were wholly ignorant of the history of the people to whom they were opposed. May I be forgiven the observation that the enquiries of * * * * have led me into the belief that some candid and well-informed English gentlemen of the present day have almost as little acquaintance with it as had Lord North.

Respecting the Revolution itself, the interest of its military history is such as to fix the attention of the most thoughtless readers, but in this, foreigners sometimes appear to imagine, was expended the whole virtue of America. That a country who could put forth so much energy, magnanimity, and wisdom, as appeared in that struggle, should suddenly lose a claim to all these qualities, would be no less surprising than humiliating. If we glance at the civil history of these republics since the era of their independence, do we find no traces of the same character? Were we to consider only the national institutions, the mild and impartial laws, the full establishment of the rights of conscience, the multiplication of schools and colleges to an extent unknown in any other country of the world, and all those improvements in every branch of internal policy which have placed this people in their present state of peace and unrivalled prosperity, we must allow them to be not only wise to their interests but alive to the pleas of humanity. But there are not wanting instances of a yet more liberal policy.

How seldom is it that history affords us the example of a voluntary sacrifice on the part of separate communities to further the common good! It appears to me that the short history of America furnishes us with more examples of this kind than that of any other nation, ancient or modern. Throughout the War of the Revolution, and for some years preceding it, the public feeling may be said to have been unusually excited. At such times, men and societies of men are equal to actions beyond the strength of their virtue at cooler moments. Passing on, therefore, to the Peace of 1783, we find a number of independent republics gradually reconciling their separate and clashing interests, each yielding something to promote the advantage of all, and sinking the pride of

---

* Mr. Burke, who seems to have possessed a more thorough acquaintance with the institutions and character of the colonists than any other British statesman, insisted much on "the form of their provincial legislative assemblies," when tracing the consequences likely to result from the oppressive acts of the Parliament. "Their governments," observed this orator, "are popular in a high degree: some are merely popular; in all, the popular representative is the most weighty; and this share of the people in their ordinary government, never fails to inspire them with lofty sentiments, and with a strong aversion from whatever tends to deprive them of their chief importance." [8]

individual sovereignty in that of the united whole. The remarks made by Ramsay on the adoption of the federal Constitution are so apposite that I cannot resist quoting them.

"The adoption of this Constitution was a triumph of virtue and good sense over the vices and follies of human nature; in some respects, the merit of it is greater than that of the Declaration of Independence. The worst of men can be urged on to make a spirited resistance to invasions of their rights; but higher grades of virtue are requisite to induce freemen, in the possession of a limited sovereignty, voluntarily to surrender a portion of their natural liberties; to impose on themselves those restraints of good government which bridle the ferocity of man, compel him to respect the claims of others, and to submit his rights and his wrongs to be decided upon by the voices of his fellow citizens. The instances of nations which have vindicated their liberty by the sword are many; of those which have made a good use of their liberty when acquired, are comparatively few." [9]

Nor did the liberality of these republics evince itself only in the adoption of the general government; we find some making voluntary concessions of vast territories that they might be devoted to national purposes, others releasing part of their own people from existing engagements and leaving them to consult their wishes and convenience by forming themselves into new communities.

Should we contrast this policy with that employed by other nations, we might hastily pronounce this people to be singularly free from the ordinary passions of humanity. But, no; they are only singularly enlightened in the art of government: they have learned that there is no strength without union, no union without good fellowship, and no good fellowship without fair dealing. And having learned this, they are only singularly fortunate in being able to reduce their knowledge to practice.

With these loose observations, I must conclude this letter. When leisure permits me, I will endeavour to reply to your enquiries upon the present state of parties and tone of the public feeling. To make this intelligible, it may be necessary to take a hasty review of the national administration since the establishment of the federal government.

LETTER XIX.

On the Federal Administrations. Mr. Jefferson. Causes of the Last War. Regulations of the Navy and Merchantmen. Effects of These on the Sailor's Character. Anecdote. Defence of the Country. How Conducted by the People. Army of the West. Policy of the New England States. Effect of the War on the National Character.

New York, January 1820.

My Dear Friend,

The history of the Federal Party,[1] which, after a short reign and a struggle of some years, drew its last breath in the Hartford Convention, is now chiefly worth recalling as an evidence of the ease with which the machinery of this government is moved. A complete revolution of parties, effected by the quiet exertion of a free elective franchise, is a novelty in the history of nations. That extreme of liberty from which so much mischief had been foretold by those who, in argument, were wont to confound the American with the Greek democracies (two forms of government having as much in common as those of China and England) was here proved to be the safeguard of the public peace. What temptation have men to employ the sword who can effect what they want by a word? There must be a power to resist ere violence can be attempted; this power is wanting in America.

Party names are seldom significant of party principles, but perhaps no names were ever less so than those of "Federal" and "Antifederal," as once known in this country. The absurdity of the latter was soon tacitly acknowledged even by their opponents, and with this tacit acknowledgement ended their own power. When the Federal stood opposed to the Democrat, it was the government opposed to the people—the shadow against the substance.

It is not my intention to enter into a dull exposition of parties now extinct; I would only remark that, in the gradual decay of the Federal opposition, we may trace the gradual formation of a national character. I remember an observation you once repeated to me as having been made by one of the enlightened veterans of the Revolution. "I want our people to be neither French

172

nor English, Federals nor Democrats; *I want them to be Americans.*" And Americans they now are. The present generation have grown up under their own national institutions; these are now sacred in their eyes, not from the mere beauty of those principles of abstract justice upon which they are founded, but from the tried experience of their wisdom. They now understand all the movements of the sublime but simple machinery of their government. They have learned not to fear either its strength or its weakness; both have been proved. If danger threatens the state, it can rouse the whole energy of the nation; if it encroaches on the liberties of that nation, it is stopped with a touch.

The establishment of the federal Constitution was an era in the history of man. It was an experiment never before made, and one upon which the liberties of a nation, perhaps of a world, depended. It was natural, therefore, that all should regard it with anxiety and some be doubtful of its results. While the people were yet apprehensive lest they might have delegated too much power to the new government, it was most singularly fortunate that the man existed whose integrity was no less tried than his name was popular. How various soever the clashing interests and opinions of the day, the name of the first President was always a rallying point of union—even those most inimical to the administration bore testimony to the virtues of Washington—and perhaps nothing speaks better for the hearts and heads of the American people, than the unanimous re-election of that venerable patriot, at the same time that the ranks of the opposition to the measures of the government were daily thickening.

This opposition, as you may remember, was mainly pointed at the system of finance introduced by the secretary Hamilton. The measures of that able statesman restored the credit of the nation, revived commerce, invigorated agriculture, and created a revenue. Some thought, however, that they did too much, tending so to strengthen the government as to make it approximate in some measure to that of England. However idle these fears may now seem, they were natural at the time; having just set the engine of government at work, the people were startled at its power and could scarcely believe that their breath, which had set it in motion, could check it as instantaneously.

It is possible that some desire existed on the part of the earlier administrations to strain to the utmost the powers delegated to them; there seemed even to be a necessity for this. The political machine had been so shaken during the protracted War of the Revolution that it demanded nervous as well as skilful hands to arrange all its parts and set all its wheels in play. The vigor of Hamilton and the prudence of Washington seemed well to balance each other; they established an efficient government at home and commanded respect from abroad. Whatever might be the political opinions of the former, whether purely republican or leaning, as was suspected, towards aristocracy, it was soon universally acknowledged that his *measures* had promoted the prosperity and lasting interests of his country. We may observe, indeed, that there is one peculiar excellence in the American Constitution—that while an able statesman has it in his power to promote the public good, he must ever find it difficult to work public mischief. He cannot work for himself, or for a part of the community; he must work for the whole, or give up working at all. This was made apparent at the ejection of the Federal Party under the administration of Mr. Adams.

The Federal, or, to speak more properly, the high government party, comprised many pure patriots and able statesmen. Their errors were those of judgment, we may say of education. They were born under a different system of things from that which arose out of the Revolution which they had assisted to guide. Some lingering prejudices might naturally cling to the minds and influence the feelings of men who, in their youth, had looked with admiration to the political experience, as well as the science, of Europe. It needed to be a philosopher as well as a statesman to foresee how, out of the simple elements of a fair representative government, order might grow out of chaos, and a people guide themselves, evenly and calmly, without the check of any controlling power, other than that administered by the collision of their own interests balanced against each other.

To these leading statesmen, whose public services had been such as to ensure the respect and consequently the voices of their fellow citizens, even while their opinions were understood to be in some things at variance with those of the majority, a party gradually attached themselves, by no means inconsiderable in numbers and possessing the influence of superior wealth. This influence, however, was more apparent than real, and probably effected the ruin of the party which admitted its support.

The American Revolution, though conducted with an unanimity unexampled in the history of nations, was not wholly without enemies, declared as well as secret. The state of New York, particularly, was encumbered with a powerful band of Tories, who, enjoying under the British government high patronage and places of trust and emolument, and in many cases possessing hereditary property, were little disposed to transfer their loyalty from George III to their fellow citizens until circumstances should render it necessary. These circumstances occurred, and to make the best of a bad case they forthwith attached themselves to the existing powers, and ranging themselves on the side of the new *administration* declared themselves sworn friends of the new *Constitution*. This reminds me of the game played in England, and indeed of the game played by the Tories everywhere: they are at all times and in all places the exclusively loyal, and their opposers, enemies, not to the measures of government, but to government itself. The game here, however, was innocent enough; it was the rattling of the dice while no stake could be betted on the throw. In the quiet exercise of their powers, the sovereign people set all things to rights. The majority *without doors* is here always the majority *within*. The Democratic Party gained the ascendant, and Mr. Jefferson, the framer of the Declaration of Independence, the friend and disciple of Franklin, the able statesman and warm patriot, the enlightened philosopher and generous friend of the human race, stood the chief magistrate of the republic.

Mr. Jefferson affords a splendid elucidation of a remark contained in my last letter—that the literary strength of America is absorbed in the business of the state. In early life, we find this distinguished philosopher and elegant scholar called from his library into the senate, and from that moment engaged in the service and finally charged with the highest offices of the common-wealth. Had he been born in Europe, he would have added new treasures to the store of science and bequeathed to posterity the researches and generous conceptions of his well-stored and original mind, not in hasty "notes," but in tomes compiled at ease and framed with that nerve and classic simplicity which mark the "Declaration" of his country's "independence." Born in America,

The post of honor is a *public* station;

to this therefore was he called, and from it he retires, covered with years and honors, to reflect upon a life well spent and on the happiness of a people whose prosperity he did so much to promote. The fruits of his wisdom are in the laws of his country, and that country itself will be his monument.

The elections which raised Mr. Jefferson to the chief magistracy brought with them a change both of men and measures. The most rigid economy was carried into every department of government, some useless offices were done away, the slender army was farther reduced, obnoxious acts, passed by the former Congress, repealed, and the American Constitution administered in all its simplicity and purity.

Of course so complete a revolution of parties could not take place without some commotion. The anger of the fallen minority vented itself in a paper war: some sounded the tocsin to the religious, declaring the President a Deist; others, to the friends of good government, declaring him an anarchist. This truly wise statesman turned a deaf ear to the clamour, aware that a government, whose every act is done in the light of day, whose members dwell among their fellow citizens, in whose ears all their words are spoken, and in whose sight all their measures are conducted, has nothing to fear save from its own misconduct.

It is curious to see the governments of Europe encircled with armed legions and yet trembling at every squib cast upon them by an unarmed multitude, while that of America, standing naked in the midst of an armed nation, counts the breath of slander like the whisper of the wind, and seeks no other way of refuting it than by steadily pursuing the path of duty and consulting, in all its measures, the vital interests of the community.

The policy of Mr. Jefferson and that of his venerable successor, Mr. Madison, was so truly enlightened and magnanimous as to form an era in the history of their country. The violence of the fallen party vented itself in the most scurrilous abuse that ever disgraced the free press of a free country. It did more—it essayed even to raise the standard of open rebellion to that government of which it had professed itself the peculiar friend and stay.* The former administration had had recourse to libel laws and legal prosecutions to repress the vehemence of political hostility, but these chief magistrates, with a dignity becoming their character and station, passed unheeded every opprobrium cast upon them, leaving it to the good sense of the nation, whose unbought voices had placed them at its head, to blunt the steel of calumny and defeat the machinations of disappointed politicians and ambitious incendiaries. This policy was in the true spirit of the American Constitution, and the result proved that it was in the true spirit of philosophy and good sense.

The unrestrained clamours of the slender minority, which waxed louder in proportion as it waxed weaker, betrayed the foreign enemy into a belief that the pillars of the Union were shaken. If they were so, it undoubtedly took the best method of refixing them in their places, when it offered assistance in the work of pulling them asunder. The foreign enemies of America have often done more than her internal friends to school her into reason. The obstinacy of one English ministry forced her into independence; the intrigues of another forced her into union. One taught her to look to her rights; another to her interests, and her wounded honor. Both together have made her a nation.

---

* Can anything expose better the absurdity of party names than the hostility of the Federalists to Mr. Madison and the nation who declared him its President? Mr. Madison, who had been the chief assistant in the establishment of the federal Constitution, who first moved for the convention which digested it, and was himself one of the sages who laboured in its formation! Thus is it in England; the Whigs, who procured the constitution of their country and whose whole efforts have been put forth for its protection, are branded as its enemies.

This republic has also been fortunate in having excited the hostility of all the European governments generally. Had France continued to favour her as steadily as England to maltreat her, she might have admitted idle predilections into her councils and perhaps have taken part in the mad warfare that has so lately ceased to devastate Europe from one end to the other.

The neutrality, so wisely maintained by Washington, with the contending powers of Europe, had at first met with a vehement opposition in every part of the Union. France, Fayette, and Liberty were names that spoke to the heart of every American, and had not the Gallican republic been so soon disgraced by crimes and follies, even the influence of Washington might have proved insufficient to prevent his country from taking part with a people who had so lately bled in their cause. The subsequent policy of France rendered her nearly as obnoxious as her adversary. Between the British orders in council and the French imperial decrees, there was little to choose. America was bandied to and fro, like a shuttlecock between the contending empires, and if one struck less hard than the other, it was not that her intentions were less hostile but that her hand was less vigorous.

There was, however, an insult offered by one of the parties which turned the balance against her yet more decidedly than the forcible interruption of American trade. It was the impressment of American seamen. In considering the long forbearance of this government, we scarcely know whether to admire or to smile at it—to admire, if we look at its good faith, its good cause, and its just and firm arguments, and to smile, if we consider these as pleaded in European cabinets. May this republic never barter her simplicity for the cunning policy of older states!

It were painful to review the circumstance which provoked the young America to throw down the gauntlet a second time to the most powerful empire in the world. When she did so, the odds seemed scarcely less against her than when she first ranged herself under the standard of Liberty; if she had increased in strength, so had her enemy. Her progress, too, had been all in the arts of peace, while that of her enemy had been all in the science of war. The veterans of the Revolution slept with their fathers, or were disabled by years. An immense territory, its former extent more than doubled, its coasts and lines unfortified, and harbouring in its population some secret enemies and many lukewarm friends,* was suddenly laid open to the incursions of veteran troops and tribes of savage Indians, and the descent of fleets

---

* During the war, the liberality of the republic seemed to recoil upon herself; strangers and in some cases naturalized citizens received the enemy's gold and spied out the weakness of the land that sheltered them.

which had hitherto ruled the ocean without a rival. All that she could oppose to these was an infant navy, whose bravery and skill had been proved in a short but desperate conflict with the pirates of the Mediterranean, a good cause, and a good spirit—"free trade and sailors' rights." It was a war of defence, not of aggression, a war entered into by a nation whose citizens had been torn from under their flag, and that flag insulted on every sea and in every port.

The aggressions which roused the republic were such as singularly to fire the spirit of her seamen. I have the authority of many of her distinguished citizens for stating that there was scarcely a vessel in her navy which did not contain one or more men who had escaped to their country with infinite perils, after constrained service of two, four, and even seven years' duration on board British ships of war. To this union of personal or professional with national wrongs, I have commonly heard ascribed the superhuman bravery which animated their crews.*

There are, however, other causes to be found in the regulations of American vessels, alone sufficient to account for the spirit of the navy. Not a man walks the decks but with a free will. The sailor's here is a voluntary engagement, which binds him only for three years, and which, in removing him from the shores of his country, does not remove him from the shield of its laws. On board a United States ship, no offender can be punished at the mere option of a superior officer. For small offences, the sailor may be subjected to a slight punishment by the watch present at the time of the offence; for greater misdemeanors, he cannot be so much as tried on board the vessel in which they are committed; his trial must stand over until an impartial court can be found, either in the United States territories, or a United States ship. His commander can then only put him upon trial, and his companions become witnesses for or against him. It requires little acquaintance with our nature to see how the exemption from arbitrary law and corporal punishments, which, in this country, are in no case allowed, whether in the army, navy, or elsewhere, must tend to elevate the character. Assertion, which so often usurps the place of argument, tells us in Europe, that brutal coercion is necessary to produce naval discipline. The navy of America affords to this a simple confutation. A case of mutiny in it is unknown, desertion as little. The ships evince the perfection of cleanliness, discipline, activity, and valour. Their crews, it is true, are formed of a higher class than are found in the vessels of any other nation; men of decent parentage

---

* A friend of the author's saw, not long since, the American Scævola in his own country, who, after the declaration of war on the part of the republic, struck off his hand with a hatchet, and presenting it to the British commander, into whose vessel he had been pressed some months before, told him that if that was deemed insufficient to disable him from the service of his country's enemies and to purchase his liberty, *he had a hand still to strike off a foot.*[2]

and education, free and proud citizens of a country, at whose expense, if poor, they have been taught to read her history and understand her laws, with all the rights that these impart to them. These crews, also, are furnished by volunteers from merchantmen placed under regulations unknown, I believe, to the merchantmen of any other nation, and which afford an easy explanation of that intelligence, dexterity, and good order, which astonish all foreigners who tread for the first time the deck of an American trader.

Before a vessel can clear out of port, a list is taken by certain officers, salaried for the purpose, of every living creature on board of her, passengers and men. The name, age, &c. of the latter are preserved, and the captain is held responsible for every life thus registered. However long the vessel may be absent, at whatever country or countries she may touch, her captain is bound for the support of his men on sea and land, and on his return must either produce them or bring with him vouchers, attested by the American consul stationed in the foreign port to which he has traded, that those not produced are dead or absent by their own will. Should the captain break his engagements or treat any man with capricious severity, he can be placed on trial by the aggrieved party in the first American port the vessel enters, all those on board of the vessel being summoned as witnesses.* These regulations, enforced with the utmost strictness, place the men, as it were, under the tutelage of the captain, obliging him at the same time to be a fair and gentle guardian. While in foreign ports, an American captain hedges in his crew like a schoolmaster entrusted with the charge of other men's children, well knowing that if any secret mischief should befall them, the republic will not rest satisfied unless it be made apparent how and when it occurred.† In this manner, an unusual security is given for the lives and

---

* Among the minor regulations are those which provide the quantity and quality of the ship stores and apportion the rations of the men. The captain is farther required to have on board a box of approved medicines and to understand, in ordinary cases, to administer them.

† An American captain, well known to the author as a man of singular intelligence, integrity, and humanity, once lost, off the shores of Lima, his black cook, who suddenly fell down dead while handing to his master a cup of coffee when alone writing in the cabin. A young sailor boy, who had entered with the cook and then passed into an adjoining cabin, heard the fall and ran to the spot at the call of his master. The latter summoning his men, after trying in vain all the remedies that occurred to him, noted the death on the logbook, with a clear statement of the manner in which it had occurred, giving the same statement to his men, corroborated so far as was possible by the testimony of the boy. There was at the time no trade between the republic and Lima, and the vessel in question had only put in to water. There being, therefore, no consul to appeal to, the captain, with some trouble and expense, procured and brought on board a Spanish doctor. Showing him the dead, the American requested him, in the best Spanish he could command (a language he had learned in his youth during a short residence in South America), to open the body and note down in the logbook, in the presence of the ship's crew, of what the negro had died. Sangrado stared, shook his head, and gravely pronounced that the body before him was dead. No explanations or entreaties could draw forth any other answer. Had the Spaniard possessed more surgery and penmanship, it is doubtful whether he

morals of the sailor, and a dignity imparted to the profession which often allures the sons of the most respectable citizens to serve before the mast. It is not uncommon even for naval officers to make their first apprenticeship as sailor boys in merchantmen, and, from what I have stated, you will perceive that this may here be done without degradation.

This discipline practised on board the merchantmen, and not, as was supposed in England, the desertion of British sailors, was the magic spell which called into being the spirited navy of the republic. A British deserter was never (knowingly at least) employed throughout the war. It was absolutely forbidden by law, as well from motives of humanity, as to avoid disputes with the enemy. An anecdote occurs to me which well evinces the strict and even fastidious regard that was had to this rule.[3]

The frigate *President* (Commodore Decatur) had received damage in clearing out of port and was in a leaking state, when she captured one of the enemy's squadron. The capture was left a wreck, and the prisoners taken on board the *President* not in a much better condition. The enemy's squadron in pursuit and the ship foundering, one of two evils was in the option of the Americans; of course they preferred the drowning and determined to make what sail they could for their country. It seemed hard, however, to condemn those whose honor was not engaged in the affair to drown with them. Delay was dangerous, but British ground not being far off, the commodore determined first to make for it and put out the prisoners.

There chanced among the strangers to be an Irishman, a thorough Paddy in everything. Captain Rodgers, the sailing master, hearing a noise before the mast, went to enquire into the cause, and found the Irishman drunk and quarrelling with his companions. The captain took him by the shoulders and locked him up below. An hour or two afterwards, he went to seek his prisoner and, finding him sobered, restored him to liberty, warning him, in future, to abstain from whiskey and swearing. The good promises of Paddy were not put to a long trial. The ship neared the shore of Nova Scotia, and the prisoners were put off in the boats, with provisions, and directions to make their way along the beach to a

---

could have been made to understand the case before him, or brought to comply with the requisitions. As it was, he ran away. The captain then had recourse to a convent of priests, and, by a bribe of fifty dollars, got them to bury his cook, after the Romish fashion, in his presence, and to attest in writing that they had done so. Returning to New York, he stated the matter and produced his logbook and attestations of the Spanish priests. But, though a known and respected citizen with good connexions in the city, his word was not taken as sufficient. All the ship's crew were examined separately and the depositions compared with each other, before the captain was absolved. The captain, in conversation with the author, gave her part of this story to elucidate the ignorance of the old Spaniards in South America, but as it struck her as curious on other accounts, she drew from him the particulars here given.

neighbouring town. Captain Rodgers, perambulating the deck while the boats were making for the land, descried a figure shunning his eye, and dodging him behind the masts. "Why, Paddy!" cried the captain, "is that you?" "Ay, if it plase your honor, just to let me drown with you." The captain explained that this termination was more inevitable than he was, perhaps, aware of, and ordered him kindly into the return boat. The Irishman was obstinate. If the ship was leaky, he argued, more need of hands to work the pumps, and if the enemy should overtake them, still the more hands the better, and, as for himself, he pledged his word to fight like the devil. "Yes, and then be hanged to the yard-arm, Paddy, when you're taken prisoner; no, my good fellow, you must e'en to the shore." He was forced by the men into the boat. A few minutes afterwards, a shout from the water attracted the attention of the captain. Paddy was in the sea, swimming back to the ship, and the boat rowing after him. "My heart never so smote me in my life," said Captain Rodgers, when he told me the story, "as it did when I refused him admittance, and saw him forcibly carried to the shore. I, for one, would have let him drown with us, but the enemy was in our rear, his tongue would have declared him a deserter, and at any rate we should have broken through our laws." *

To return from these digressions. A vigorous navy was soon formed; an army was not so easy. The first difficulty was the sudden defalcation of the revenue, which, for many years past, had been wholly dependent upon a prosperous commerce. Internal taxation is seldom popular anywhere, but least of all in a democracy, and here its rulers appear to have been unwilling to have had recourse to measures which might have checked the enthusiasm of the nation. They have been blamed for this, but, perhaps, unwisely. In considering the constituent elements of this singular republic, one is led to think that there was more foresight than rashness in leaving her to rouse herself pretty much after her own manner.

When hostilities commenced, the American navy comprised ten frigates and a hundred and odd gunboats, and the army thirty-five thousand men, hastily organized and officered with few exceptions by men knowing about as much of military science as those they were appointed to command. It was natural that careless observers should smile or tremble, according to their humour, at such an outset. But those acquainted with the character and hidden resources of the republic could well foresee how one would draw forth the other. A few months and the trees of her forests floated on the ocean, manned with hearts of

* The *President* was overtaken by the squadron and captured. It is probable that this must have happened at all events, but the generosity of the chivalrous Decatur, in landing his prisoners, ensured the catastrophe.

flame worthy of their cause and their English ancestry. The exertions of the great maritime cities, as well as of individuals, greatly assisted those of the government. As the war advanced, privateers, matchless as sailors and manned with spirited citizens, who forsook their usual occupations and civic professions, swarmed in every sea. These privateers, though private property, were ranked in the national navy and placed under the same regulations.

In the land service, the people had to serve a longer apprenticeship. To fill the ranks of a regular army was found impracticable. Although the citizen was asked only to enlist for two years, and this with high pay, it was scarcely possible to fill up a regiment. Volunteers were to be had in multitudes and militia was ready everywhere, but to fight for hire is here held in a contempt and abhorrence, which no inducements can vanquish. The government doubled the pay—still with no better success. It was necessary, therefore, to trust the defence of the country pretty much to the citizens themselves. They conducted it, as might be expected, with a great deal of folly, a great deal of rashness, and a great deal of heroism.

A raw militia makes a curious army—sometimes brave to desperation, sometimes cowardly as a flock of geese, and in both cases wilful as a troop of schoolboys. It is impossible to help smiling at some of the occurrences in the first campaign. An unpleasing order from the general, a popular officer superseded in the command, a march of unusual fatigue, and—*every man to his tents, Oh Israel!* At one time we find the general going one way and the troops, or more properly the multitude, absolutely going the other. Orders, entreaties—all alike in vain; the horsemen wheeling rightabout in the wilderness and trotting away home, with their angry officer, no longer at their head but their heels, bringing up the rear.* At another time, we find troops and general at a sudden stand for want of the common munitions of war, their swords and pistols being still in Philadelphia, while they themselves were at the northern frontier.

But with all this deficiency of discipline, conduct, and skill, even the first opening of the war affords instances of spirited and successful bravery. Indeed the fault usually lay more in want of skill than want of valour, and it is truly wonderful to consider how rapidly the high-spirited and wilful multitude were tamed, or rather tamed themselves, into subordination.

Throughout the contest, the young states of the West furnished the most generous assistance to the confederacy. Nursed under the wings of republican

---

* During a harassing warfare with the Indians, in the Indiana and Illinois wilderness, General Harrison could presume no farther than to make *propositions* to his Kentucky volunteers, and closed the expedition with a polite request that he might be permitted to dictate their course to them *just for one day.*

liberty, removed from the luxuries of cities, and exposed to continual harassment from their savage neighbours, the aborigines, their character is very peculiarly marked for ardor, disinterested patriotism, determined courage, and a certain chivalric spirit of enterprise and generosity, which perhaps has not its equal on the globe. The indignities offered to the nation had roused the pride of this people for some years previous to the declaration of war. Kentucky particularly had organized ten regiments of volunteers, comprising upwards of five thousand men, and at the first opening of hostilities the enthusiasm of this commonwealth was wrought so high that the authority of the executive seemed necessary to prevent the whole male population of the state from turning out as soldiers. The women shared the patriotism of the men, vying with each other in repressing their tears and actually buckling on the swords and cartridges and arming the hands of their sons and husbands. The neighbouring state of Ohio, the infant territory (now state) of Indiana, and indeed the whole western region was animated with the same spirit. To the more organized regiments, furnished by these states, the wanderers of the frontier joined themselves almost to a man. Trained from their infancy to the use of the rifle and all the perils of a hunter's life—marksmen who, in hitting a bird on the wing, can say with the adventurous bowman to Philip of Macedon, "To the right eye"; horsemen who can ride untired through swamp and forest, swimming rivers and leaping bogs, like the old mosstroopers of the Scotch borders—the inhabitants of the western frontier were peculiarly fitted to carry through with spirit the harassing war with which their country was threatened.

To the west of the Alleghenies, to draft the militia had been a work of supererogation; all the demands of the republic were answered and more than answered by volunteers. In fearlessness and enterprise this army of patriots was unrivalled, but discipline was only to be learned in the school of adversity. It is doubtful, indeed, whether they ever completely acquired it, in the sense understood by military men. It was rather a sympathy of feeling than submission to authority that produced concert of action; it was enthusiasm supplying the place of skill, or intuitive genius that of experience. We find a handful of youths, whose leader had numbered but twenty years, putting to flight a band of veteran troops and practised Indian warriors, flushed with victory and tenfold the number of their stripling adversaries. But they had pledged their lives to redeem the honor of the republic, tarnished in the preceding campaign, and moreover to avenge the death of their friends and relatives, slaughtered by the savage allies of their opponents.* It is worthy of notice that the employment of

* This young hero, no less distinguished for his tender humanity than his romantic valour, had been entrusted with the defence of a fort, commanding one of the rivers that fall into Lake

Indians in the British service has always had a different effect from that intended. It does not strike terror, but rather whets the valour of those opposed to
such relentless adversaries. After the massacre at the River Raisin, noticed in a
former letter, the tide of victory turned in favour of the Americans.

The spirit of the southern and middle states was little less ardent than that
of the West, but had it been otherwise, the descents made on their shores by the
enemies' ships, the sack of villages, which, scattered along a coast of two thousand miles extent, it was often impossible to guard, and finally the burning of
the infant capital had been sufficient to rouse the energy displayed at Baltimore
and New Orleans.

However mortifying at the moment, the conflagration of the seat of government was, perhaps, productive of more lasting benefit to the republic than any
one of its most splendid victories. There was one quarter of this great confederacy which had hitherto exhibited a lamentable deficiency of patriotism.

The conduct of some of the New England states at the opening of the contest is not very easy to explain. That Massachusetts, who thirty years before
had led the van in the army of patriots, whose cause too it was that her sister
states so generously advocated, that she should suddenly so forget her former
self as to stand by a sullen spectator of a conflict which involved the honor and
national existence of the great republic, of which till now she had formed so
distinguished a member, seems at once the most extraordinary and lamentable
dereliction of principle to be found in the annals of nations! She appears to have
been made the dupe of a party whose name, until this time, had been respected
even by the nation from whom it stood aloof, and then to have been angry because others saw this and laughed at her gullibility.

Among the first Federals, there were men no less respectable for their virtues
than their talents, but these had gradually fallen off from the minority to mingle
themselves with the bulk of the nation, leaving only the old Tories and some
disappointed politicians to disgrace a title which patriots had worn and under
its specious mask to attempt the ruin of their country. In this, fortunately, they

Erie. His general, receiving intimation that a strong party of the enemy was about to invest
it, dispatched orders to the little garrison to destroy the works and make good a retreat. Young
Croghan, knowing the importance of the post he occupied and recalling with his companions
their sacred engagement, determined to disobey orders and wait the enemy. A more desperate
stand was, perhaps, never made. The solemn obligation which bound these devoted youths, and
the steady composure with which they took their measures, preserves them from the charge of
rashness. Provided as they were with no other weapons than their muskets and one piece of
ordnance and surrounded on all sides by gunboats, veteran soldiers, and yelling savages, their
victory seems little less than miraculous; it was, however, complete, and led the way in that
train of successes which followed on the western and northern frontier ending in the Battle of
Plattsburg.[4]

failed, but may the lesson prove a warning not to Massachusetts only, but to each and all of these confederated states!

I have already had occasion to observe upon the change wrought by the last war in the condition of the republic; it not only settled its place among the nations, but cemented its internal union. Even those who from party ill humour had refused their concurrence with the measures of government and their sympathy in the feelings of their fellow citizens were gradually warmed by the enthusiasm that surrounded them or by the pressure of common danger forced to make common cause. At the close of the contest, one general feeling pervaded the whole great Union. The name of a party once respectable, but now disgraced by iself, became universally odious, and its members, to rise from the contempt into which they had fallen, found it advisable to declare their own conversion to the principles of popular government and federal union.

It may now be said, that the party once misnamed Federal has ceased to exist. There is indeed a difference of political character, or, what will express it better, a varying intensity of republican feeling discernible in the different component parts of this great Union, but all are now equally devoted to the national institutions and in all difference of opinion admit the necessity of the minority yielding to the majority. And, what is yet more important, these differences of opinion do not hinge upon the merits or demerits of foreign nations, French or English, Dutch or Portuguese. The wish of your venerable friend is now realized— his countrymen are *Americans*. Genêt may now make the tour of the states, and Henry of New England, with infinite safety to the peace of their citizens, and even Massachusetts herself would now blush at the name of the Hartford Convention.*

---

* Genêt is, or was at least when the author was last in Albany, a peaceable and obscure citizen of the state of New York. It is curious in a democracy to see how soon the factious sink into insignificance. Aaron Burr was pointed out to me in the mayor's court at New York, an old man whom none cast an eye upon except an idle stranger.[5] In Europe, the bustling demagogue is sent to prison or to the scaffold, and metamorphosed into a martyr; in America, he is left to walk at large and soon no one thinks about him.

LETTER XX.

Unanimity of Sentiment Throughout the Nation. National Government. Federal Constitution.

New York, January 1820.

My Dear Friend,

There is at present no appearance of any regular and standing minority in the nation, or consequently in the house of Congress. It is no longer a dispute how the nation is to be governed; the sovereignty is avowedly and practically with the people, who have agreed to exercise that sovereignty in no other way than by representatives, bound to obey the instructions of their electors. If they do not obey their instructions, they are thrown aside and others put in their place. An opposition on the part of the governors to the governed would here only be absurd; they are the servants of the people, not their masters, vested with just as much power as their employers see good to charge them with, and constrained to exercise that power, not after their own fancy, but after that of the nation.*

The government of the United States has been denominated weak, but that only by those who are accustomed to consider a government as arrayed against a people. It is quite another thing here: the government acts with the people, is part of the people, is in short the people themselves. It is easy to see that such a

---

* The representative will, of course, sometimes find a struggle within him between his own conviction and the expressed wishes of his electors, and sometimes conscientiously abide by the former. I remember the case of a distinguished member from the west of Pennsylvania (Mr. Baldwin), who once voted in decided opposition to his received instructions.[1] At his return home, he was summoned to give an explanation or apology, under risk of being thrown out. The member replied that at the time of his vote he had expressed his regret that his opinion differed from that of his electors, but that he should be unworthy of the distinguished office he held, and of the public confidence which he had for so many years enjoyed, if he could apologize for having voted according to the decision of his judgment; that his fellow citizens were perfectly right to transfer their voices to the man who might more thoroughly agree with them in sentiment than in this case he had done; that for himself he could only promise to consider every question attentively and candidly, to weigh duly the wishes of his constituents, but never to vote in decided opposition to his own opinion. His fellow citizens received his declaration with applause, and, as his whole political life had been in unison with their sentiments, they took this one instance of dissent as an additional proof of his integrity and unanimously re-elected him.

government must be the strongest in the world for all the purposes for which governments are ostensibly organized. The advocates of arbitrary power tell us that men are bad and therefore unfit to govern themselves, but if they are bad, it is clear that they are still more unfit to govern each other. When rulers are gifted with the perfection of goodness and infallibility of judgment, it may be rational to leave the interests of men at their mercy. Here it is supposed that rulers are swayed by all the vulgar passions of humanity; care is therefore taken to bridle them, or rather it is contrived that they shall be made to work for the advantage instead of the mischief of the community. If a man be ambitious, he can only rise to importance by advocating the interests of others. The moment that he ostensibly opposes his own to those of his fellow citizens, he must throw up the game.

It is not very apparent that public virtue is peculiarly requisite for the preservation of political equality; envy might suffice for this: *You shall not be greater than I.* Political equality is, perhaps, yet more indispensable to preserve public virtue than public virtue to preserve it; wherever an exclusive principle is admitted, baleful passions are excited. Divide a community into classes, and insolence is entailed upon the higher, servility or envy, and often both united, upon the lower.

In all other republics, ancient or modern, there has been a leaven of aristocracy. America fortunately had, in her first youth, virtue sufficient to repel the introduction of hereditary honors. This was virtue as well as knowledge, when she had to resist not only the example of all the nations of the earth but the persuasions and even the authority of her acknowledged sovereigns. Had she received this taint in her infancy, it is probable that no subsequent exertions could have wiped it away; her republics would at this moment have been provinces of the British empire, or if not this, her citizens would have been caballing among themselves like the patricians and plebeians of ancient Rome, or those of more modern Florence.*

"Le gravi e naturali inimizie che sono tra gli' uomini popolari e nobili, causate dal voler questi comandare, e quelli non ubbidire, sono cagioni di tutti i mali che nascono nelle città."[2] If the disturbances of the Florentine republic warranted this assertion of its philosophic historian, the peace of the American republic tends to confirm it. Liberty is here secure, because it is equally the portion

---

*The Stuart kings were peculiarly anxious to break down the democratic spirit of New England by the creation of a nobility; temptations were held out to the wealthier proprietors by the royal governors to assume to themselves the style of barons. The grants of land *in tail male*, frequent in the southern colonies and in New York, had probably the same end in view. These hereditary proprietors were the Tories of the Revolution; among them, of course, there were signal and magnanimous exceptions.

of all. The state is liable to no convulsions, because there is nowhere any usur-
pations to maintain, while every individual has an equal sovereignty to lose.* [3]
No king will voluntarily lay down his sceptre, and in a democracy all men are
kings.

It is singular to look round upon a country where the dreams of sages, smiled
at as utopian, seem distinctly realized, a people voluntarily submitting to laws of
their own imposing, with arms in their hands respecting the voice of a government which their breath created and which their breath could in a moment
destroy! There is something truly grand in this moral restraint, freely imposed
by a community on itself.

I do not wonder that Europeans refuse credence to those who report truly of
the condition of these commonwealths. That a nation of independent sovereigns
should be a nation of all others the most orderly and the most united, may well
pass the understandings of men accustomed to the rule of the sword. It may be
questioned whether the institutions of America could with propriety be trans-
planted to Europe. The attempt failed in France, and the same causes may produce the same failure elsewhere, but surely it is proposed to force the same
attempt elsewhere. I laid down my pen to look through a file of London papers.
I need not say with what feelings I threw them aside, when I state that their
columns record the history of the sixteenth of August. The English people trampled and cut down by a soldiery! Savile, Whitbread, and Romilly are well in
their graves.[4]

Back a government with an army, and the liberties left with a people are no
longer held of right but held as a matter of grace and favour. Here this is not
only understood in theory, but in practice. The people keep the sword in their
own hands and leave their rulers without any; they are thus the guardians of
their own rights and the enforcers of their own laws.†

I suppose you tolerably familiar with the Constitution of the United States,
and * * * * also, though he seems somewhat to miscalculate the strength of the
bond it imposes upon the Union. The Articles of Confederation, hastily adopted

---

* A grievous exception to this rule is found in the black slavery of the commonwealths of
the South. May the wisdom of the masters preserve them from that "revolution of the wheel
of fortune" contemplated by their venerable philanthropist Mr. Jefferson as "among possible
events," or "probable by supernatural interference!" The heart of the bystander will acknowledge
with him that "the Almighty has no attribute that can take side with them in such a contest."

† There was once (I do not recollect the time) an attempt of the felons in the Philadelphia
gaol to break prison. They had succeeded in gaining the outer court before the alarm was given.
The citizens of the neighbourhood seized their muskets, and ran to the spot; some dexterously
gained the top of the wall surrounding the court in which the conspirators were at war with
their gaolers and their prison gates. The muskets pointed at their lives, of course the first
summons produced order, and sent back the obstreperous convicts to their cells. Are not such
citizens as good keepers of the peace as a troop of horse?

at the Revolution, did in truth only act upon the *states,* not upon *individuals.* Under those, the general Congress (which then consisted of only one house) could neither raise men nor levy taxes but through the medium of the legislatures of the different republics. The people of each state regulated their trade by their own government instead of that of the united confederacy, collected their quota of the army or the revenue in whatever manner they thought proper, and pronounced even upon the propriety of the quota demanded. This was productive of much confusion in time of war, and yet more in time of peace. When the federal Constitution superseded these articles, the people parted with no new powers, but transferred some of those before delegated to their representatives in their own houses of assembly to their representatives in the general Congress.

The general government was now without appeal and was exercised not upon the legislatures of the different states but upon the people themselves, who were then first gathered into one great family, legislating in Congress without regard to their sectional position, at the same time that the landmarks of their different republics remained unmoved. The central or national government regulates commerce, imposes and levies taxes, coins money, establishes post offices and post roads, declares war, may raise armies, maintain a navy, call forth the militia, direct its discipline, and exercise authority over it when called into the service of the United States. Its powers in short extend to all matters connected with the common defence and general welfare of the confederacy, and these powers being clearly defined, it may make laws necessary and proper for rendering them effective. For the just administration of these powers, it is directly responsible to the people, so that while it is incalculably stronger than it was formerly, it may be said in some ways also to be weaker. The Articles of Confederation seemed to leave a possibility to the government assembled under them of exerting undue influence over the nation through the legislatures of the different states. It is now possessed singly of direct power; to exert influence is impracticable.

The two houses of legislature in which these great powers are vested represent, in one, the population of the whole Union; in the other, the different republics into which the Union is divided. Perhaps the hall of the Representatives may be said to speak the feelings of the nation, and the Senate to balance the local interests of the different sections of its vast territory: a member in the former house represents forty thousand souls; two members in the latter represent a state, whatever be its size or population. It follows, therefore, that no law can be enacted without a majority of the states, as well as of the people, which must always secure a very large majority of the nation to every measure. In a country where the people govern themselves, this is highly important.

But this representation of the people by their local position as well as their number has yet other salutary effects. It balances duly the different interests into which all civilized communities must more or less be divided, but which, in a territory so vast as that of America, may perhaps be arranged more geographically, if I may use the expression, than can be the case in less extensive countries. The western states, fast growing in wealth and strength, will soon have an exclusive and powerful interest to support in agriculture and manufactures. Should the sum of their population outweigh that of the Atlantic states, the commercial interest might be overlooked in the national assembly, and at present the population of these states, exceeding that of the younger section of the Union, its interests might be forgotten, so as to generate ill will in those rising republics. The mode of representation adopted in the Senate seems to obviate this danger, and the advantage resulting from it will probably be more and more apparent, according as the inland states become more and more vigorous.

Perhaps the English and the Anglo-Americans are the only nations who know how to draw an accurate line between the legislative, executive, and judicial departments of government. In the former, the distinctions are thoroughly understood; in the latter, perfectly reduced to practice. In England, the legislative and executive are nominally separate but actually conjoined when a majority of the house of legislature is within purchase of the crown, and the cabinet ministers have a direct voice upon every question in debate. Here, not only is the President himself positively excluded from both houses of Congress, but every person holding an office or in any manner employed under the authority of the government.* I had occasion to observe in a former letter that this distinction between the different departments of government is equally preserved by the constitutions of the states, as by that of the United States, "to the end," as it is expressed in the Massachusetts Declaration of Rights, "that it may be a government of laws, and not of men."

The election of the President is managed with some ingenuity, so as to unite the two modes of representation found in the Senate and the Representatives. It was necessary to guard, first against the too great influence of a state more popu-

---

* The President of the United States is never seen within the walls of the Capitol, except on the day of his inauguration. Should he ever be present at any debate, it could only be as a citizen among the audience, but even this would be considered an impropriety, and of course never occurs. I do not remember to have been questioned by any individual, since my return to England, upon the subject of the American Constitution and officers of government, who has not confounded the President of the United States with the president of the Senate. This has sometimes recalled to me the mistake of a well-known political economist in London, who (as I was told in Washington) once addressed a letter, apparently intended for Mr. Madison, "To the President of Congress." I understand that a similar error is to be found in a published work of Mr. Jeremy Bentham.

lous than her neighbours, who might have commanded the choice of the chief magistrate, had his nomination been left solely to the mass of the population without regard to its position; and secondly, against a junction of states more peculiarly united by interests or near neighbourhood, which might have enabled one portion of the Union to command an equally unfair advantage, were the point decided by the vote of the states. How far the union of these two modes of representation is effected or how far it is possible to effect it, I am not adequate to judge.*

The powers of the President are great, but are always under the check of the legislature. He appoints ambassadors, consuls, judges of the Supreme Court, and other officers of the United States, but this only with the approbation of the Senate, unless both houses of Congress shall see good, in times which may demand peculiar dispatch and decision, to vest him with discretionary power. He can make treaties, but only with the advice and concurrence of *two thirds* of the Senate. His signature renders valid an act of the legislature, but, if refused, a majority of *two thirds* of both houses gives to it the effect of a law without his concurrence. He may convene the Congress during its adjournment, upon extraordinary emergencies, but cannot disperse it any time; only, should the two houses dispute as to the time of adjournment, he is the arbiter between them. He is commander in chief of the army and navy and of the militia, when called into the service of the nation by law of Congress, in which case the authority of the President supersedes that of the governors of the different states, who are commanders in chief of their militia.

The powers lodged with the President have been by some judged too great, and by some too little, but at present, I believe, few think them either one or the other. A chief magistrate whose reign is only for four years and who stands liable to impeachment for malversation might, perhaps, be trusted with the gift of public offices held only upon good behaviour, without much risk of the prerogative being abused. By making his will, however, subservient to a branch of the legislature, a double security is given for the impartiality of appointments, much petty wrangling for public offices prevented, and the President relieved from painful responsibility.

The judicial power of the United States is vested in a Supreme Court held at

* Some amendments in the presidential elections have been made by subsequent conventions since the first establishment of the federal Constitution, but directed (I believe *solely*) to enforce the necessity of voting distinctly for a Vice President as well as a President. The inferior office fell originally to the second candidate on the list. Upon one occasion, the votes being equal, it was thought proper to avoid all confusion in future, by specifying the person voted for as Vice President from the person voted for as President.[5]

Some more important amendments have lately been proposed and I believe submitted to the people.

Washington. This court of law is, perhaps, not the least beautiful contrivance in the singular frame of this government. It holds together the links of the federal Union, keeps the peace between republic and republic, and again between all these different component parts and the great centre to which they are all bound. It settles all controversies between the different states, or between the citizens of one state and the government or citizens of another; also all controversies between individuals and the general government, and between the citizens of the United States, and "foreign states, citizens, or subjects." In fine, its powers "extend to all cases in law and equity" arising under the federal Constitution, or the laws passed by the government acting under that Constitution, to all treaties made by the national government, "to all cases of admiralty and maritime jurisdiction," and "to all cases affecting ambassadors, other public ministers and consuls."

We find, in the writings and speeches of some of the early federal statesmen, frequent parallels drawn between the American and the English government. The parallels are necessarily very loose. What the one is in practice, the other is partly in theory, and here ends the comparison. The Constitution of the United States is formed upon the model of those of the different states of which the United States is composed, but furnishes its administrators with other and more extended powers, not clashing with or superseding those exercised by the state governments, but directed to different ends. Like the motions of the planetary system, each republic revolves upon her own axis but moves in unison with the others, exerting her own centrifugal force and yielding to the power which holds her in the magic circle of the confederacy.

The singular position of this government as the centre of a mass of republics, strengthening and multiplying every lustre that rolls by, gives to it a character of its own and one as wonderful as it is grand. I cannot speak the effect that its minute consideration produces on the mind: it is such as the spectator feels when he contemplates for the first time a steam engine of the great Watt—its powers, as simple as they are sublime, playing evenly, and noiselessly, and irresistibly, and then, when the mind is startled at the consideration of its energy and the vast world which it regulates and pervades, comes the reflection that the hand of the workman can check it in a moment of time!

I must again direct your attention to that feature in American government which distinguishes it so peculiarly from that of all other countries: it can neither add nor take away from its own powers, and yet it can always be so moulded as to reflect the image of the public mind. In Europe, a constitution is often a vague word: one says it is this, another says it is that, and a third searches for it and declares it is nowhere. A constitution means sometimes ancient customs, sometimes ancient charters, sometimes the acts of government themselves, framed in accordance, or in open contradiction to those charters; sometimes it means things as they are, at another time things as they were. Every man talks of it, understands it in his own manner, and perhaps can explain it in no manner at all. Here the Constitution is in the hands of all the people: they give it to their representatives, and say, "There is your guide. We judge of its fitness to direct your proceedings, as we do of your fitness to legislate by it. If upon trial you conceive it to be defective, state your objections, and we shall decide upon their reasonableness." The representative here can neither alter the manner of his election nor enlarge his powers when elected. The people do not petition for rights, but bestow authority upon their rulers. Experience shows how much authority will suffice; if more than sufficient has been imparted, the overplus is retracted; if less than sufficient, what the exigency demands is bestowed. Proposals for alterations or additions to the Constitution originate in Congress, a vote of two thirds of both houses being requisite for the same. The amendments thus proposed are submitted to the people, who, if they approve, summon conventions in their different states. The assent of *three fourths* of these conventions then carries the proposition and affixes it as a new article to the Constitution.

I have, at your request, touched upon a subject much beyond my powers to do justice to. The most ordinary mind is attracted to the consideration of the political machine that is here in play: the simplicity and sublimity of its movements impress it solemnly; it reverts with admiration to the genius that conceived it, and considers with delight the peace that it secures and the happiness that it distributes.

LETTER XXI.

Character and Interests of the Different Sections of the Confederacy, and Their Influence on the Floor of Congress. New England. Final Extinction of the Federal Party. Central States. New York and Pennsylvania. Southern States. Policy and Influence of Virginia. Western States. Manufactures. Powers of Congress Respecting Black Slavery. Formation and Government of Territories. Generous Policy of the Western States. Character of the First Settlers. Shepherds and Hunters of the Border. Anecdote of Laffite. Various Ties Which Cement the Union of the States.

New York, February 1820.

My Dear Friend,

Looking to the general plan of the central government, it will be seen with what extreme nicety the different interests of the multitudinous parts of this great confederacy are balanced, or employed as checks one upon the other. In the course of years these interests may be somewhat more distinctly marked than they are at present; some have even thought that they may be more strongly opposed. This appears more than doubtful. But even admitting the supposition, we cannot calculate the probable effects of this without counting for something the gradual strengthening of the national Union by the mixture of the people, the marriages and friendships contracted between the inhabitants of the different states, the tide of emigration, which shifts the population of one to the other, the course of prosperity enjoyed under a government more and more endeared as time more and more tries its wisdom and imparts sanctity to its name. The time was when none or but a few of these sacred bonds existed, and still a friendly sympathy was not wanting among the different and uncemented communities scattered along the shores of the Atlantic.

During their colonial existence, the inhabitants of these states had but little intercourse with each other. Vast forests separated often the scanty population of the infant provinces. Varying climate and religion influenced also their cus-

toms and character; but still, however parted by trackless wastes, how little connected soever by the ties of private friendship, they had always two things in
common—language and a fierce spirit of liberty, which sufficed to bind with a
sure though invisible chain all the members of the scattered American family.
The strength of this chain has seldom been fully appreciated by the enemies of
America. They expected to break it even during the War of the Revolution, and
were certain that it would of itself give way when the high-toned sentiment kept
alive by a struggle for independence should subside, or when the pressure of
common danger being removed, the necessity of cordial co-operation should not
be equally apparent. Experience has hitherto happily disproved these calculations. The advantages of a vigorous and the blessings of a beneficent government, directing the energies and presiding over the welfare of the great whole,
have been more and more felt and understood, while the influence of just laws,
and still more the improved intercourse of the states one with another, have
broken down prejudices and, in a great measure, obliterated distinctions of
character among the different quarters of the republic.

The portion of the Union that has most generally preserved her ancient moral
distinction is New England. The reason may be found in the rigidity of her
early religious creed and in the greater separation of her people from the rest of
the nation. Strictly moral, well-educated, industrious, and intelligent, but
shrewd, cautious, and, as their neighbours say, at least, peculiarly long-sighted
to their interests, the citizens of New England are the Scotch of America. Like
them, they are inhabitants of a comparatively poor country and send forth
legions of hardy adventurers to push their fortunes in richer climes. There is
this difference, however, that the Scotchman traverses the world and gathers
stores to spend them afterwards in his own barren hills, while the New Eng-
lander carries his penates with him and plants a colony on the shores of the
Ohio, with no less satisfaction than he would have done on those of the Connecticut.

The nursery of backwoodsmen, New England, sends forth thousands and of
course takes in few, so that her citizens are less exposed to the visitation of foreigners, and even to mixture with the people of other states, than is usual with
their more southern neighbours. This has, perhaps, its advantages and disadvantages: it preserves to them all the virtues of a simple state of society, but with
these also some of its prejudices; it serves to entrench them against luxury, but
imparts to them something of a provincial character. Zealously attached to their
own institutions, they have sometimes coldly espoused those of the nation. The
Federal opposition chiefly proceeded from this quarter of the Union.

The political conduct of New England subsequent to the establishment of the federal government sunk her a little for some years in the esteem of the nation. The narrowness of her policy was charged to some peculiar selfishness of character in her people, but their conduct during the Revolutionary struggle redeems them from this charge and leads us to ascribe their errors to defect of judgment rather than to obliquity of principle. Since the war the liberal party, ever numerous, has gained the ascendant, and consequently the eastern states are resuming that place in the national councils which they originally held. It is difficult now to find a *Federalist,* absolutely so called. A certain soreness upon some political topics, a coldness of manner in pronouncing the name of Jefferson, and, I have observed, of *Franklin,* is what may sometimes enable you to detect a *ci-devant* member of the fallen party.*

New York and Pennsylvania may perhaps be considered as the most *influential* states of the Union. The elegant expression lately employed by Mr. Clay, in rendering his tribute to the important services of the latter, may with propriety be applied to both. They are "the key-stones of the federal arch." Their rich and extensive territories seem to comprise all the interests into which the Union is divided. Commerce, agriculture, and manufactures are all powerfully represented by them on the floor of Congress. Their western division has much in common with the Mississippi states, and their eastern with those of the Atlantic. Their population stands conspicuous for national enterprise and enlightened policy, whether as regards the internal arrangement of their own republics or their share in the federal councils. These powerful states return no less than fifty members to Congress, being more than a fourth of the whole body.† In proportion as the western states increase, this preponderance will be taken from them; in the meantime, however, it is in no case exerted to the prejudice of the general interests of the Union.

Whether it be from their wealth, or their more central position affording them the advantage of a free intercourse with the citizens of all the states of the Union, as well as foreigners from all parts of the world, the people of Pennsylvania and New York, but more particularly of the latter, have acquired a liberality of sentiment which imparts dignity to their public measures. They raise extensive funds, not only for the general education of their citizens (which is equally the case elsewhere), the founding of libraries, and seminaries of learn-

---

* The secret hostility borne by some of the Federal Party towards the departed Franklin is rather amusing. This benign sage, whose last efforts were spent in fixing the wheels of the federal government, and who sunk beneath the weight of years and honors before the struggle of the two parties commenced, might be supposed to have had it little in his power to give umbrage to either. The reverence in which his name was ever held by the Democratic Party, who were the children of his school, explains the enigma.

† There are at present in the hall of the Representatives 195 members and three or four delegates. The delegates are sent by territories and have no vote.

ing, but in the clearing of rivers, making roads and canals, and promoting other works of extensive utility, which might do honor to the richest empires of Europe. The progress of the New York state during the last thirty years is truly astonishing. Within this period, her population has more than quadrupled, and the value of property more than doubled. She has subdued the forest from Hudson to Erie and the Canadian frontier, and is now perfecting the navigation of all her great waters and connecting them with each other.

The national revenue, being chiefly drawn from the customs, is greatly dependent upon the commercial spirit of New York. Her great seaport has sometimes furnished one fourth of the revenue of the United States. The late war of necessity fell very heavily upon her maritime capital. But while her commerce was ruined, she showed no disposition to injure the common cause by separating her interests from those of the confederacy. Her opposition in Congress was greatly in the minority to her national support, and, war being once declared, the opposition passed over to the side of the majority. The conduct of Mr. Rufus King, the venerable leader of the Federal Party in the Senate, is worthy of being recorded in the annals of his country.[1] He had opposed the declaration of war simply from an apprehension that the republic was unequal to cope with her adversary, but finding her determined to brave all hazards rather than submit to degradation, he instantly seceded from his party, pronouncing it to be the duty of every patriot to assist his country with heart and hand in weathering the storm, and volunteered to throw into the treasury part of his private fortune, which he stated to be greater than his necessities.*

No state in the Union can point to a longer line of public services than Virginia: she rung the first alarm of the Revolution by the mouth of her Patrick Henry; she led the army of patriots in the person of her Washington; she issued the Declaration of Independence from the pen of her Jefferson; she bound the first link of the federal Union by the hand of her Madison—she has given to the republic four of the purest patriots and wisest statesmen that ever steered the vessel of a state.

The policy of this mother of the Union has always been peculiarly magnanimous. She set the example to her sister states in those cessions of territory which have so richly endowed the general government and out of which have arisen such a host of young republics. The cession made by Virginia comprises the present states of Ohio, Indiana, and Illinois, with the territory of Michigan. For

---

* I had this anecdote from a senator of Congress, one, too, I must observe, usually opposed to Mr. King in politics, who is still ranked among the least democratic party in the Senate. Such a patriot is a true relic of the veteran federal band of the Revolution, and may well command the respect of those who differ, as well as of those who agree with him in opinion.

the thousandth part of such an empire as was here bestowed in free gift, men have deluged the earth with blood. We find the liberality of Virginia yet farther evinced in her conduct towards a neighbouring state, first peopled by her citizens and subject to her laws. The manner in which she released Kentucky from her jurisdiction, pointing out the inconveniencies arising to her people from their remoteness from the Virginia capital and encouraging her to erect an independent government, affords a beautiful example of national generosity.

The public spirit of Virginia has invariably been felt in the national councils, and consequently has procured to her a weight of influence more than proportionate to the numerical strength of her representation in Congress. There has latterly been a partial hue and cry in the northern division of the Union on the subject of *the Virginia influence*. I can only say, in the words of a Vermont farmer, who accidentally closed in conversation with me upon *affairs of state,* "Whatever be the influence of Virginia, she seems to use it well, for we surely go on very thrivingly; besides that, I see no way in which she could exercise it but by coinciding with the feelings of the majority." The words "Virginia influence," you will perceive to mean (so far as they mean anything) the accident which has drawn from her commonwealth four out of the five presidents who have guided the councils of federal America.*

I know nothing which places the national character in a fairer point of view than the issue of the presidential elections. We find local prejudices and even party feelings laid aside, and the people of this multitude of commonwealths fixing their eyes on the most distinguished servant of the state and rendering the noblest tribute to his virtues that a patriot can receive or a country can bestow. All the chief magistrates of the republic have been veterans of the Revolution and distinguished no less for their private virtues than their public services. It was thought that, as Virginia had already given three presidents to the republic, a strong opposition would have been made to Colonel Monroe. So far from this being the case, no president (Washington excepted) was ever more unanimously chosen, and his name is spoken with respect, and even affection, from Maine to Missouri.

The dignified position taken by Virginia in the national councils has placed her at the head of the republics of the South, whose policy, it may be remarked, has uniformly been liberal and patriotic and, on all essential points, in accordance with that of the central and western states. Whatever be the effect of black slavery upon the moral character of the southern population—and that upon

* The late unanimous re-election of Colonel Monroe proves that the good farmer of Vermont, quoted in the text, spoke the sentiments of his nation.[2]

the mass it must be deadly mischievous there can be no question—it has never been felt in the national Senate. Perhaps the arrangement has been prudent, or at least fortunate, which has somewhat tempered the democracy of American government in the south Atlantic states. By the existing constitution of Virginia and the states south of her, the qualifications required of a representative throw the legislative power into the hands of the more wealthy planters, a race of men no less distinguished for the polish of their manners and education than for liberal sentiments and general philanthropy. They are usually well-travelled in their own country and in Europe, possess enough wealth to be hospitable and seldom sufficient to be luxurious, and are thus, by education and condition, raised above the degrading influence which the possession of arbitrary power has on the human mind and the human heart. To the slight leaven of aristocracy, therefore, thrown into the institutions of Virginia and the Carolinas, we may, perhaps, attribute, in part, their generous and amiable bearing in the national councils. We must not omit, however, the ameliorating effect produced by the spread of education and the effect of liberal institutions on the white population generally. Even before the close of the Revolutionary War, Mr. Jefferson thought "a change already perceptible"; and we have a substantial proof that the change traced by that philosopher in the character of his fellow citizens was not imaginary, the first act of the Virginia legislature being the abolition of the slave trade. May she now set an example to her neighbouring states, as she then did to the world, by combating steadfastly the difficulties which her own fears or selfish interests may throw in the way of emancipation!

But the quarter of the republic to which the eye of a stranger turns with most curiosity is the vast region to the west of the Alleghenies. The character of these republics is necessarily as unique as their position, and their influence is already powerful upon the floor of Congress.

In glancing at their geographical position, the foreigner might hastily be led to consider them as growing rivals rather than friendly supporters of the Atlantic states. It will be found, however, that they are at present powerful cementers of the Union, and that the feelings and interests are such as to draw together the north and south divisions of the confederacy.

The new canals will probably draw off the produce of the western counties of New York to the Atlantic; still, however, a portion will find its way down the western waters, as their navigation shall be perfected from Erie to New Orleans. At all events, this route will continue to be preferred by the western counties of Pennsylvania, shortly destined to be the seat, if they are not so already, of flourishing manufactures. The advance made in this branch of industry during the last war and for some years previously has received some checks since the peace, but appears likely soon to proceed with redoubled energy.

It may be worth observing that there is something in the character of the American population, as well as in the diverse products of the soil, which seems favourable to the growth of manufactures. I do not allude merely to their mechanical ingenuity, which has shown itself in so many important inventions and improvements in shipbuilding, bridges, steamboat-navigation, implements of husbandry and machinery of all kinds, but to that proud feeling of independence, which disinclines them from many species of labour resorted to by Europeans. There are some farther peculiarities in the condition and character of the scattered population of the West, which rendered the birth of manufactures simultaneous with that of agriculture. In planting himself in the bosom of the wilderness, the settler is often entirely dependent upon his own industry for every article of food and raiment. While he wields the axe and turns up the soil, his wife plies the needle and the spinning wheel, and his children draw sugar from the maple and work at the loom. The finely watered state of Ohio affords so easy an egress for its internal produce that could a sure market have been found, it seems little likely that it would have attempted for many years any great establishments of domestic manufactures. But the policy of foreign countries threw so many checks in the way of the agriculturist and so completely suspended commerce that the new stimulus given to human industry was felt in the most remote corners of the Union.

The instantaneous effect produced by the commercial regulations of Europe, it seems almost impossible to credit; cotton mills and fulling mills, distilleries, and manufactories of every description, sprung, as it were, out of the earth, in city, town, village, and even on the forested shores of the western waters. The young Ohio, for instance, which had existed but eight years, in 1811 poured down the western waters woollen, flaxen, and cotton goods, of admirable but coarse texture, spirituous liquors, sugars, &c., to the value of two millions of dollars.

The wonderful aptitude of the Americans for labour of every species, however removed, seemingly, from their accustomed habits, is easily explained, if we consider, first, the mental energy inspired by their free institutions, and, secondly, their general and practical education. An American youth is usually trained to hit a mark with the certainty of an old English crossbowman, to swim with that dexterity which procured for the young Franklin in London the name of the "American aquatic," to handle a musket like a soldier, the mechanic's tools like a carpenter, the husbandman's like a farmer, and, not very unfrequently, the needle and scissors like a village taylor. I have taken Ohio as an instance, but the people of the western region universally were in the habit of making in their own families the cotton and woollen garments in which they were clad. This prepared them for that new direction of national industry which the policy of foreign countries rendered indispensable.

The ports being again thrown open by the peace, many of the young manufactures began to decline; many, however, have kept their place from their intrinsic excellence (more especially the coarse cotton and woollen fabrics), in spite of the imprudent trade which has glutted the market with foreign goods and ended by ruining half the fortunes of the great commercial cities. Things seem now to be finding their level, and the citizens are discovering that mercantile speculation is a ruinous game, when the raw produce of the country is not taken in kind for the wrought fabrics of Europe. Perhaps Europe may find this a losing game, too, but of this I am not learned enough to speak.

The inhabitants of the West have seen with peculiar dissatisfaction the decay of their manufacturing establishments. It is not only that they have been driven back upon agriculture, without finding a sufficient market for their produce, but (what you may perhaps smile at) those simple but proud republicans are by no means pleased to see their good homespun forsaken by their daughters for the muslin and silks of France and the Indies. Many make a positive resistance to so unbecoming a dereliction of principle and good taste and hold staunchly to the practice of clothing every member of their family in articles of domestic manufacture. Many gentlemen of property are in the habit of making, on their own estates, every single article of clothing and household furniture. Young women of cultivated education and elegant accomplishments are found dressed in plain cotton garments, and men presiding in the senate house of their country in woollen clothes, woven and fashioned by the hands of their own domestics, or even by those of their children.

The reviving ascendancy of the manufacturing over the commercial interest creates a strong community of feeling between the northern and western sections of the Union.* Pittsburgh, the young Manchester of the United States, must always have the character of a western city, and its maritime port be New Orleans. Corinth was not more truly the eye of Greece than is Pittsburgh of America. Pennsylvania, in which it stands, uniting perfectly the characters of an Atlantic and a western state, is truly the keystone of the federal arch.

---

* The author some weeks subsequent to the date of this letter heard the *whole* representation of New York, as well as of Pennsylvania and Jersey, advocate upon the floor of Congress the manufacturing as opposed to the trading interest.

But if the new states are thus linked with the North, they have also some feelings in common with the South, and thus, drawing two ways, seem to consolidate that confederacy which Europeans have sometimes prophesied they would break. In the first place, Kentucky and Tennessee, the oldest members of this young family, have not only been peopled from Virginia and the Carolinas, but originally made part of those states. Generously released from their jurisdiction, they still retain a marked affection for their parents, and have, too, a community of evil with them, as well as of origin, in the form of black slavery. It is not unlikely that the mixture of slaveholding and non-slaveholding states to the west of the Alleghenies helps to balance the interests between the northern and southern sections of the Union on the floor of Congress.

I must here refute a strange assertion, which I have seen in I know not how many foreign journals, namely, that the United States government is chargeable with the diffusion of black slavery.* Every act that this government has ever passed regarding it has tended to its suppression, but the extent and nature of its jurisdiction are probably misunderstood by those who charge upon it the black slavery of Kentucky or Louisiana, and they must be ignorant of its acts who omit to ascribe to it the merit of having saved from this curse every republic which has grown up under its jurisdiction.

When first torn from the British empire, we have seen that every corner of the then peopled America was smitten with this plague. Now not one half is, although by the acquisition of Louisiana an immense foreign addition has been made to the evil. It was not until the adoption of the federal Constitution that the Congress possessed any power to legislate upon the subject of the slave trade. The abolition laws passed before that period were passed by the states in their individual capacity and could not be enforced beyond their own respective territories. The powers vested by the new Constitution in the gen-

---

* One of the most extravagant blunders of this kind I lately found in MacKenzie's *History of America,* a work comprising much valuable topographical and statistical information upon the subject of the United States, but containing a compilation of the most contradictory and positively ludicrous portraits of their moral character (to those at least who have any personal acquaintance with it) that has yet come under my eye. The passage I allude to is the following: "Negro slavery has spread its baleful effects over a great part of the Union. Some writers, particularly Englishmen, who would wish to represent the states as a second Arcadia, have offered an apology for this detestable practice, by contending that it formed *a part of the policy of the colonial system:* but this excuse does not apply to the *new* states; for the Congress has resigned the inhabitants of these vast regions to its demoralizing effects." [3] Now were this all that stood between the United States and a second Arcadia, they would be much nearer a terrestrial paradise than I had imagined. Not a single one of the new states that has grown up under the jurisdiction of the Congress but has been positively and absolutely saved by its laws from slavery in any shape or form whatsoever. It would save some mistakes if authors would read the laws of foreign countries before they write about them.

eral government enabled it to enforce the cessation of the trade throughout the Union, but gave it no control over the domestic slavery wherever existing. The emancipation already effected in eight of the thirteen original states has been effected in each by the acts of its own legislature.

There are at present twenty-two republics in the confederacy; of these, twelve have been rendered free to black and white; the remaining ten continue to be more or less defaced by negro slavery. Of these five are old states, and the other five either parted from these or formed out of the acquired territory of French Louisiana. Thus—Kentucky was raised into an independent state by mutual agreement between herself and Virginia, of which she originally formed a part. Tennessee, by mutual agreement between herself and Carolina, to which she was originally attached. Mississippi was surrendered to the general government by Georgia, to be raised when old enough into an independent state, but with a stipulation that to the citizens of Georgia should be continued the privilege of migrating into it with their slaves. Louisiana proper, formed out of a small portion of the vast territory ceded under that name, came into the possession of the United States with the united evils of black slavery in its most hideous form and the slave trade prosecuted with relentless barbarity. The latter crime was instantly arrested, and, under the improving influence of mild laws and mental instruction, the horrors of slavery have been greatly alleviated.*

In all these cases the federal government has been powerless to effect the eradication of slavery. It has, however, been all powerful to prevent its introduction in such territories as have been placed under its control.

Ohio was the first state formed from the commencement upon American principles. It was planted by the hand of Congress, in the vast region ceded by Virginia to the northwest of the river Ohio. In the formation of a new state out of the national wastelands, its government is entrusted to the Congress of

---

* Travellers afflicted with the anti-American mania are fond of drawing their portrait of the national character in New Orleans. This is much the same as if we should draw that of the English in Guadaloupe or St. Lucia. Such tourists may now have an opportunity of sketching the American character among the Spaniards of Florida.

The Missouri question, which so greatly agitated the nation and the Senate last winter, turned solely upon what were the powers of Congress to legislate for the territory in question. Missouri was colonized by slaveholding French when the territory was ceded to the United States by a treaty securing to the inhabitants their property, including slaves. Emancipation, therefore, was not within the power of Congress. The question was whether it possessed the right of preventing the citizens of other states from migrating into Missouri *with their slaves*. The error seems to have been the having omitted to pass this prohibitory law before the period when Missouri assumed the place of a state. Congress, after months of anxious deliberation, came to a compromise which seemed the only one in their power. A law was passed preventing the possibility of the formation of any other slaveholding state in the French Louisianian territory, and the slavery of Missouri was placed under every restriction, which the previous treaty and the Constitution would permit.[4]

the United States, who mark its boundaries, nominate its public officers, and defray the expenses of its government, until its population amounts to sixty thousand souls, when it is entitled to summon a convention, establish its own constitution, enter upon the administration and expenses of its own government, and take its place in the confederacy as an independent republic.*

In 1787, the Congress passed an act establishing a temporary government for the infant population settled on the lands of Ohio, and the government then established has served as the model of that of all the territories that have since been formed in the vacant wilderness. The act then passed contained a clause which operated upon the whole national territory to the northwest of the Ohio. By this, "slavery and involuntary servitude" was positively excluded from this region, by a law of the general government. Ohio, Indiana, Illinois, and Michigan have already sprung up in the bosom of this desert, the three first independent states, and the latter about to pass from her days of tutelage to assume the same character.[5]

It is deserving of observation that for the passing of this law a unanimous vote of the states was necessary, according to the old Articles of Confederation then in force. By a unanimous vote it *was* passed, not a dissentient voice being raised by Virginia, who had ceded the territory in question, nor by the other states of the South, who thus voluntarily deprived their slaveholding citizens of the right of migrating into it.†

Thus saved from the disgraceful and ruinous contagion of African servitude, this young family of republics have started in their career with a vigor and a purity of character that has not an equal in the history of the world. Ohio, which twenty-five years since was a vacant wilderness, now contains half a million of inhabitants and returns six representatives to the national Congress. In the other and younger members of the western family, the ratio of increase is similar. It is curious to consider that the adventurous settler is yet alive who felled the first tree to the west of the Alleghenies. The log hut of Daniel Boone

* Several territories have passed to the condition of states before they comprised the population demanded by law. Illinois, for instance, having preferred a request to Congress that she might be permitted to assume the reins of her own government, was allowed to join the confederacy with a population of less than 40,000.

† In observing upon the policy of the southern states generally, it would be ungenerous to pass without notice that their representatives in Congress have been among the most strenuous enforcers of the last penalties of the law against those convicted of the surreptitious introduction of slaves into the southern ports. The close neighbourhood of Cuba and the Spanish Floridas affords great facilities for this atrocious smuggling. The navy of the United States is actively employed in intercepting this stolen traffic, not only on the American but the African coasts, and agents are stationed in Africa to receive the stolen negroes, returned in the safekeeping of the republic to their native country. In all these measures, the members from the South have not only invariably concurred, but some of the most important have originated with them.

is now on the wild shores of the Missouri, a host of firmly established republics stretching betwixt him and the habitation of his boyhood.

It is plain that in the course of a few generations the most populous and powerful division of the American family will be watered by the Mississippi, not the Atlantic. From the character of their infancy we may prophesy that the growing preponderance of the western republics will redound to the national honor and will draw more closely the social league, which binds together the great American family.

Bred up under the eye and fostered by the care of the federal government, they have attached themselves to the national institutions with a devotion of feeling unknown in the older parts of the republic. Their patriotism has all the ardor and their policy all the ingenuousness of youth. I have already had occasion to observe upon the enthusiasm with which they asserted the liberties and honor of their country during the last war. Their spirit throughout that contest was truly chivalrous. The anecdotes recorded not only of the valour, but of the romantic generosity of the western army of volunteers, might grace the noblest page of the Revolutionary history. Nor have the people of the West shown themselves less generous in the Senate than the field. In the hall of the Representatives, they are invariably on the side of what is most honorable and high-minded. Even should they err, you feel that you would rather err with them than be wise with more long-headed or more cold-hearted politicians.

In considering America generally, one finds a character in her foreign to Europe—something which there would be accounted visionary: a liberality of sentiment and a nationality of feeling, not founded upon the mere accident of birth, but upon the appreciation of that civil liberty to which she owes all her greatness and happiness. It is to be expected, however, that in the democracies of the West, these distinctions will be yet more peculiarly marked.

It seems to be a vulgar belief in Europe that the American wilderness is usually settled by the worst members of the community. The friend I write to is well aware that it is generally by the best. The love of liberty, which the emigrant bears with him from the shores of the Connecticut, the Hudson, or Potomac, is exalted and refined in the calm and seclusion of nature's primeval woods and boundless prairies. Some reckless spirits, spurning all law and social order, must doubtless mingle with the more virtuous crowd, but these rarely settle down as farmers. They start ahead of the advanced guard of civilization, and form a wandering troop of hunters, approximating in life and, sometimes, in character to the Indians, their associates. At other times they assume the occupation of shepherds, driving on their cattle from pasture to pasture, according as fancy leads them on from one fair prairie to another still fairer, or according as the approaching tide of population threatens to encroach upon their solitude and their wild dominion.

You may, however, find among these borderers many rare characters, who, like their veteran leader Daniel Boone, depose none of the social virtues in their Arab life. "The frontier," observes Mr. Brackenridge, a gentleman who has an intimate acquaintance with the people of whom he writes, "the frontier is certainly the refuge of many worthless and abandoned characters, but it is also the choice of many of the noblest souls. It seems wisely ordered, that in the part which is weakest, where the force of laws is scarcely felt, there should be found the greatest sum of real courage, and of disinterested virtue. Few young men who have migrated to the frontier are without merit. From the firm conviction of its future importance, generous and enterprising youth, the virtuous, unfortunate, and those of moderate patrimony, repair to it, that they may grow up with the country, and form establishments for themselves and families. Hence in this territory there are many sterling characters. Among others I mention, with pleasure, that brave and adventurous North Carolinian, who makes so distinguished a figure in the history of Kentucky, the venerable Col. Boone. This respectable old man, in the eighty-fifth year of his age, resides on Salt River, up the Missouri. He is surrounded by about forty families, who respect him as a father, and who live under a kind of patriarchal government, ruled by his advice and example. They are not necessitous persons, who have fled for their crimes or misfortunes, like those that gathered unto David in the cave of Adullam: they all live well, and possess the necessaries and comforts of life as they could wish. They retired through choice. Perhaps they acted wisely in placing themselves at a distance from the deceit and turbulence of the world. They enjoy an uninterrupted quiet, and a real comfort in their little society, beyond the sphere of that larger society where government is necessary. Here they are truly free; exempt from the vexing duties and impositions even of the best governments, they are neither assailed by the madness of ambition, nor tortured by the poison of party spirit. Is not this one of the most powerful incentives which impels the Anglo-American to bury himself in the midst of the wilderness?" * 6

---

* The lord of the wilderness, Daniel Boone, though his eye is now somewhat dimmed and his limbs enfeebled by a long life of adventure, can still hit the wild fowl on the wing with that dexterity which in his earlier years excited the envy of Indian hunters, and he now looks upon the "famous river" Missouri with feelings scarce less ardent than when he surveyed with clearer vision "the famous river Ohio." The grave of this worshipper of nature, wild adventure, and unrestrained liberty will be visited by the feebler children of future generations with such awe as the Greeks might regard those of their earlier demigods. The mind of this singular man seems best portrayed by his own simple words: "No populous city, with all the varieties of commerce and stately structure, could afford so much pleasure to my mind as the beauties of nature that I find here."

The borderers universally took an active part in the war and were eminently useful in repelling the incursions of the Indians. Not even the most lawless but was found ready to pour his lifeblood for the republic.

A curious instance of the strange mixture of magnanimity and ferocity often found even among the demisavages of the borders was afforded, during that contest, by the Louisianian Laffite. Some years previous to the war, this desperado had placed himself at the head of a band of outlaws from all nations under heaven, and fixed his abode upon the top of an impregnable rock, to the southwest of the mouth of the Mississippi. Under the colours of the South American patriots, they pirated at pleasure every vessel that came in their way and smuggled their booty up the secret creeks of the Mississippi with a dexterity that baffled all the limbs of the law. The depredations of these outlaws, or, as they styled themselves, "Baratarians" (from Barata, their island), becoming at length intolerable, the United States government dispatched an armed force against their little Tripoli. The establishment was broken up, and the pirates dispersed. No sooner, however, had the fleet fairly disappeared, than Laffite again collected his outlaws and took possession of his rock. The attention of the Congress being now diverted by the war, he scoured the gulf at his pleasure and so tormented the coasting traders that Governor Claiborne of Louisiana set a price on his head.

This daring outlaw, thus confronted with the American government, appeared likely to promote the designs of its enemies. He was known to possess the clue to all the secret windings and entrances of the many-mouthed Mississippi, and in the projected attack upon New Orleans it was deemed expedient to secure his assistance.

The British officer then heading the forces landed at Pensacola for the invasion of Louisiana, opened a treaty with the Baratarian, to whom he offered such rewards as were best calculated to tempt his cupidity and flatter his ambition. The outlaw affected to relish the proposal, but, having artfully drawn from Colonel N——— the plan of his intended attack, he spurned his offers with the most contemptuous disdain, and instantly dispatched one of his most trusty corsairs to the governor who had proscribed his life, advising him of the intentions of the enemy and volunteering the aid of his little band, on the single condition that an amnesty should be granted for their past offences. Governor Claiborne, though touched by this proof of magnanimity, hesitated to close with the offer. The corsair kept himself in readiness for the expected summons and continued to spy and report the motions of the enemy. As danger became more urgent and the steady generosity of the outlaw more assured, Governor Claiborne granted to him and his followers life and pardon, and called them to the defence of the city. They obeyed with alacrity and served with a valour, fidelity, and good conduct, not surpassed by the best volunteers of the republic.* [7]

I have given but a rude sketch of the great divisions of this republic; a subject of this kind admits not of much precision, or, at any rate, my pencil is not skilled enough to handle it ably. I wish you to observe, however, that the birth of the new states has tended to consolidate the Union, and that their growing importance is likely to be felt in the same manner, contrary to the calculations of long-sighted politicians, who foretold that as the integral parts of this great political structure should strengthen and multiply, the cement which held them together would crumble away, and that as the interests of the extended community should become more various, it would be distracted with more party animosities.

The fact is that every sapient prophecy with regard to America has been disproved. We were forewarned that she was too free, and her liberty has proved her security; too peaceable, and she has been found sufficient for her defence; too large, and her size has ensured her union. These numerous republics, scattered through so wide a range of territory, embracing all the climates and containing all the various products of the earth, seem destined, in the course of years, to form a world within themselves, independent alike of the treasures and the industry of all the other sections of the globe. Each year they are learning, more and more, to look to each other for all the various articles of food and raiment, while the third great human necessity, defence, they have been from infancy practised to furnish in common. The bonds of union, indeed, are more numerous and intimate than can be easily conceived by foreigners. A people who have bled together for liberty, who equally appreciate and equally enjoy that liberty which their own blood or that of their fathers has purchased, who feel, too, that the liberty which they love has found her last asylum on their shores—such a people are bound together by ties of amity and citizenship far beyond what is usual in national communities.

---

* The restless Laffite again hoisted the flag of Carthagena, to follow, however, a more regular mode of warfare than that with which he commenced his career. I believe he has rendered some signal services to the patriot cause.

LETTER XXII.

Unrestrained Liberty of the Press. Elections. Effect of Political Writings. Newspapers. Congressional Debates. Deportment of the Members in Congress.

New York, February 1820.

My Dear Friend,

The Americans are certainly a calm, rational, civil, and well-behaved people, not given to quarrel or to call each other names, and yet if you were to look at their newspapers you would think them a parcel of Hessian soldiers. An unrestricted press appears to be the safety valve of their free Constitution, and they seem to understand this, for they no more regard all the noise and sputter that it occasions than the roaring of the vapor on board their steamboats.

Were a foreigner, immediately upon landing, to take up a newspaper (especially if he should chance to land just before an election), he might suppose that the whole political machine was about to fall to pieces and that he had just come in time to be crushed in its ruins. But if he should *not* look at a newspaper, he might walk through the streets on the very day of election and never find out that it was going on, unless, indeed, it should happen to him, as it happened to me, to see a crowd collected round a pole surmounted by a cap of liberty, and men walking in at one door of a house and walking out at another. Should he then ask a friend hurrying past him, "What is going on there?" he may receive for answer, "The election of representatives. Walk on—I am just going to give in my vote, and I will overtake you."

It might seem strange that the sovereign people should judge proper to exercise the right of abusing the rulers of their choice (a right which they certainly do exercise without mercy), but when we consider that in this democracy there is generally a yielding of a minority to a majority, the case seems quite easy of explanation. Besides, after a man has assisted in the choice of his representative, he may take offence at him. It of course then follows that he will tell him so, and that he will tell his fellow citizens the same, and that he will endeavour to eke out his philippic with the aid of all the epithets

209

in the dictionary. Now, though this practice of vilifying the freely chosen officers of the republic is not very reputable to the community, it evidently brings its own cure with it. Public opinion, after all, is the best and, indeed, the only efficient censor of the press: in this country it is found all-sufficient, while in other countries fines, imprisonments, and executions are had recourse to in vain.

The public prints were never more outrageous than after the discomfiture of the Federal Party in 1805, and never did the shafts of slander fall more harmless than on those wise rulers to whom the people had transferred their confidence. The speech of Mr. Jefferson after his second inauguration contains some observations of so general an application that I am tempted to direct your attention to them:

"During this course of administration, and in order to disturb it, the artillery of the press has been levelled against us, charged with whatever its licentiousness could devise or dare. These abuses of an institution, so important to freedom and science, are deeply to be regretted, inasmuch as they tend to lessen its usefulness, and to sap its safety. They might, perhaps, have been corrected by the wholesome punishments reserved to and provided by the laws of the several states against falsehood and defamation; but public duties more urgent press on the time of the servants of the public, and the offenders have therefore been left to find their punishment in the public indignation.

"Nor was it uninteresting to the world, that an experiment should be fairly and fully made whether freedom of discussion, unaided by power, is not sufficient for the propagation and protection of truth; whether a government, conducting itself in the true spirit of its constitution, with zeal and purity, and doing no act which it would be unwilling the whole world should witness, can be written down by falsehood and defamation. The experiment has been made: you have witnessed the result. Our fellow citizens have looked on cool and collected. They saw the latent source from which these outrages proceeded. They gathered around their public functionaries; and when the constitution called them to the decision by suffrage, they pronounced their verdict, honorable to those who had served them, and consolatory to the friends of man, who believe that he may and ought to be trusted with the control of his own affairs. No inference is here intended that the laws provided by the states, against false and defamatory publications, should not be enforced. He who has leisure renders service to the public morals, and public tranquillity, in reforming these abuses by the salutary coercions of the law. But the experiment is noted to prove, that, since truth and reason have maintained their ground, against false opinions in league with false facts, the press calls for few legal restraints. The public judgment will correct false reasoning and opinion, upon a full hearing of all parties, and no other definite line can be drawn between the inestimable liberty of the press, and its demoralizing licentiousness." [1]

Never was there a country in which a demagogue had less in his power than in this. The citizen here learns to think for himself. His very pride as a sovereign revolts from a blind surrender of his judgment to those who may be willing to set up as his teachers. He looks to facts, considers the conduct of his public functionaries, and pronounces accordingly. Sedition here may safely ring her alarm; no man regards it. The eyes of the people are fixed upon the wheel of government, and so long as it moves fairly and steadily, the servants that guide it are supported by the national suffrage.

But if the declamation of the press passes unregarded, its sound reasoning, supported by facts, exerts a sway beyond all that is known in Europe. Here there is no *mob*. An orator or a writer must make his way to the feelings of the American people through their reason. They must think with him before they will feel with him, but, when once they do both, there is nothing to prevent their acting with him. It was thus that the effect of *Common Sense* on the public mind produced an effect upon the public councils. It unfurled the standard of independence. Prior to this the eloquent Patrick Henry had roused the soul of Virginia and put arms in her hand; Dickinson, by the most admirable train of reasoning, had led the people to calculate the inevitable results of the acts of the British Parliament, and strengthened them in that spirit of resistance which redeemed the liberties of mankind.[2] Throughout the Revolutionary struggle not a pamphlet, not a fable, not a ballad, but had its influence on the feelings, and thus on the affairs of the nation.

The writings of the great and good Franklin, the Socrates of modern times, the father of independent America, and the oracle of those philosophic statesmen whom the public voice has fixed at the helm since the first election of Mr. Jefferson, exert to this day their holy influence on the national character and, consequently, on the national councils. You cannot enter the house of a farmer or the log hut of a settler that you will not find the writings of this sage upon the shelf. His apophthegms and parables are graven upon the memory of childhood; "his life written by himself" is the pocket manual of the youth when he enters into the world; his divine precepts (for such they truly are) of justice, humanity, forbearance, industry, economy, simplicity, philanthropy, and liberty regulate the administration of many a patriotic statesman and the life of many a virtuous citizen.

The nervous and classical papers of *The Federalist* greatly furthered the adoption and peaceable establishment of the federal Constitution; many other writings had a similar tendency. The resolutions passed by the legislature of Virginia, in 1798, framed by Mr. Jefferson and Mr. Madison, declaring the Congress to have exceeded the powers delegated to it, fixed the attention of the whole nation, and for this reason: that the declaration was supported by facts which had already occupied the public mind, and which proved the truth of the charge.[3] *The Olive Branch: or, Faults on both Sides,* the work of Mr. Carey, a respectable bookseller and patriotic citizen in Philadelphia, is said to have produced the greatest sensation of any political treatise since the appearance of *Common Sense.* Its ostensible object was to cement the two old parties, Democratic and Federal, but its enumeration of their mutual faults made out so much heavier a catalogue against the latter, as was little calculated to subdue it by kindness. The work rather assisted the destruction of the malcontents by covering them with confusion, perhaps, too, by provoking them to acts of greater intemperance and thus forcing them to work out their own ruin. However this may be, the ability and utility of *The Olive Branch* were acknowledged and felt by the nation: it ran through thirteen large editions with the speed of light and was in the hands of every citizen of the republic.[4]

It would be impossible for a country to be more completely deluged with newspapers than is this; they are to be had not only in the English but in the French and Dutch languages, and some will probably soon appear in the Spanish. It is here not the amusement but the duty of every man to know what his public functionaries are doing: he has first to look after the conduct of the general government and, secondly, after that of his own state legislature. But besides this, he must also know what is passing in all the different states of the Union: as the number of these states has now multiplied to twenty two, besides others in embryo, there is abundance of home politics to swell the pages of a newspaper. Then come the politics of Europe, which, by-the-bye, are, I think, often better understood here than on your side of the Atlantic. Another and a more interesting subject to Americans is found in the affairs of their brethren of the south. Many generous citizens of this republic have embarked their lives and fortunes in a cause which bears so strong a parallel to that for which they or their fathers bled on their own soil. Several friendly missions have been dispatched from this government to those of the southern republics, the account of which you will, I think, read with much interest.*

* The English reader will find a most able and interesting account of the Buenos Aires republic in a work entitled *Voyage to South America, performed by Order of the American Government, in the Years 1817 and 1818, in the Frigate Congress. By H. M. Brackenridge, Esq., Secretary to the Mission* [Baltimore, 1819]. A highly interesting account of the affairs of Mexico will be found in the work of William Davis Robinson of Philadelphia, entitled *Memoirs of the Mexican Revolution, including a Narrative of the Expedition of General Xavier Mina* [Philadelphia, 1820].

But, independent of politics, these multitudinous gazettes and journals are made to contain a wonderous miscellany of information. There is not a conceivable topic in the whole range of human knowledge that they do not treat of in some way or other, not unfrequently, I must observe, with considerable ability, while the facts that they contain and the general principles that they advocate are often highly serviceable to the community. The party rancor which occasionally defaces their columns appears, as I have said, to be more ludicrous than mischievous; at any rate, it is clearly an evil which comes in the train of liberty, and which, for the sake of the good company it keeps, the republic may well be content to bear with.

As you will have remarked in the Congressional debates, this scurrility never finds its way into the senate. The language of the representatives of the nation, however warm be the argument, is invariably decorous and gentlemanly. Even during the hottest period of that political strife which agitated the nation and the senate during the struggles of the Democratic and Federal parties, there is but one instance on record where the decorum of the House was openly violated. It was, to be sure, an outrageous exception: one member gave another the lie, upon which he was felled by his adversary to the ground, and both were expelled.[5]

The tone assumed in the debates of Congress has for many years been worthy of the Roman senate in its best days, nor is the oratory and sound reasoning displayed in them less remarkable than the temper which is invariably preserved. I believe this moderation, so different from what is found in the English House of Commons, may be explained by considering that here there are no regular majorities and minorities. It is a fair combat of opinions, not principle standing opposed to power. As those who differ from each other today may be found in the same majority tomorrow, it is seldom that personal animosity is mingled with political opposition. The broad principles, too, of justice and the rights of man, which are so eternally appealed to in the hall of the Representatives, are calculated to impart dignity to the national politics. The vessel of the state has to be navigated through the broad ocean of liberty, not through the tortuous canal of political expediency. The soul of the statesman expands over the vast prospect before him; the generous principles which form his weapons of attack or defence dispose him to wage an honorable and chivalrous combat with his adversary. He presses him home, indeed, attacks him on all sides, and occasionally thunders down his blows with all the fever of impatient enthusiasm, but he does not permit himself to seek any unfair advantage by attempting to vilify his adversary, which could only injure his own cause or mar the honor of his triumph.

We may further observe that personal invective is not likely to be tolerated in an assembly composed of men all equally proud and equally free. The political institutions doubtless give the key to this peculiarity, which so often excites the surprise of foreigners, accustomed in Europe to look for noise and confusion in the courts of liberty.

LETTER XXIII.

Education. New England. Public Seminaries. Discipline of Schools. Condition of Women.

New York, March 1820.

My Dear Friend,

The education of youth, which may be said to form the basis of American government, is in every state of the Union made a national concern. Upon this subject, therefore, the observations that apply to one may be considered as, more or less, applying to all. The portion of this widespread community that paid the earliest and most anxious attention to the instruction of its citizens was New England. This probably originated in the greater democracy of her colonial institutions. Liberty and knowledge ever go hand in hand.

If the national policy of some of the New England states has been occasionally censurable, the internal arrangement of all amply redeems her character. There is not a more truly virtuous community in the world than that found in the democracies of the East. The beauty of their villages, the neatness and cleanliness of their houses, the simplicity of their manners, the sincerity of their religion, despoiled in a great measure of its former Calvinistic austerity, their domestic habits, pure morals, and well-administered laws must command the admiration and respect of every stranger. I was forcibly struck in Connecticut with the appearance of the children, neatly dressed, with their satchels on their arms and their faces blooming with health and cheerfulness, dropping their courtesy to the passenger as they trooped to school. The obeisance thus made is not rendered to station but to age. Like the young Spartans, the youth are taught to salute respectfully their superiors in years, and the artlessness and modesty with which the intelligent young creatures reply to the stranger's queries might give pleasure to Lycurgus himself.

The state of Connecticut has appropriated a fund of a million and a half of dollars to the support of public schools. In Vermont, a certain portion of land has been laid off in every township, whose proceeds are devoted to the same purpose. In the other states, every township taxes itself to such amount as is necessary to defray the expense of schools, which teach reading, writing,

215

and arithmetic to the whole population. In larger towns these schools teach geography and the rudiments of Latin. These establishments, supported at the common expense, are open to the whole youth, male and female, of the country. Other seminaries of a higher order are also maintained in the more populous districts, half the expense being discharged by appropriated funds and the remainder by a small charge laid on the scholar. The instruction here given fits the youth for the state colleges, of which there is one or more in every state. The university of Cambridge, in Massachusetts, is the oldest and, I believe, the most distinguished establishment of the kind existing in the Union.

Perhaps the number of colleges founded in this widespread family of republics may not, in general, be favourable to the growth of distinguished universities. It best answers, however, the object intended, which is not to raise a few very learned citizens but a well-informed and liberal-minded community.

It is unnecessary that I should enter into a particular detail of the internal regulations of all the different states relative to the national instruction. The child of every citizen, male or female, white or black, is entitled by right to a plain education, and funds sufficient to defray the expense of his instruction are raised either from public lands appropriated to the purpose, or by taxes sometimes imposed by the legislature and sometimes by the different townships. But, notwithstanding the universality of these regulations, it must sometimes happen, from the more scattered population of the new states, and in the central states from the occasional patches of a foreign population, that knowledge is more unequally spread. The Germans of Pennsylvania and the Dutch of New York are here and there in full possession of the temple of ignorance, and three or four generations have, in some cases, proved insufficient to root out their predilection for the leaden deity so long worshipped within its walls. German schools have, however, done much towards the overthrow of the idol, and it may be anticipated that even German obstinacy will at last be brought to exchange the Dutch alphabet for that of the country. There is something inexplicable in national character, everywhere so distinctly marked. A dozen years, and the French of Louisiana are cementing themselves with their new fellow citizens and rearing up their children, more or less, in the language of the nation, while the Dutch of Communipaw,[1] on the shores of the New York Bay, have taken a century to learn half a dozen English words and to acquire the fifth part of a new idea.

If we must seek the explanation of national manners in national institutions and early education, all the characteristics of the American admit of an easy explanation. The foreigner is at first surprised to find in the ordinary citizen that intelligence and those sentiments which he had been accustomed to seek in the writings of philosophers and the conversation of the most enlightened. The better half of our education in the Old World consists of unlearning: we have to unlearn when we come from the nursery, to unlearn again when we come from the school, and often to continue unlearning through life, and to quit the scene at last without having rid ourselves of half the false notions which had been implanted in our young minds. All this trouble is saved here. The impressions received in childhood are few and simple, as are all the elements of just knowledge. Whatever ideas may be acquired are learned from the page of truth and embrace principles often unknown to the most finished scholar of Europe. Nor is the *manner* in which education is here conducted without its influence in forming the character. I feel disposed at least to ascribe to it that mild friendliness of demeanor which distinguishes the American. It is violence that begets violence, and gentleness, gentleness. I have frequently heard it stated by West Indians that a slave invariably makes the hardest slave driver. In English schools it is well known that the worst-used *fag* becomes, in his turn, the most cruel tyrant, and in a British ship of war it will often be found that the merciless disciplinarian has learned his harshness in the school of suffering. The American, in his infancy, manhood, or age, never feels the hand of oppression. Violence is positively forbidden in the schools, in the prisons, on shipboard, in the army; everywhere, in short, where authority is exercised, it must be exercised without appeal to the argument of a blow.

Not long since a master was dismissed from a public school, in a neighbouring state, for having struck a boy. The little fellow was transformed in a moment from a culprit to an accuser. "Do you dare to strike me? You are my teacher, but not my tyrant." The schoolroom made common cause in a moment, the fact was enquired into, and the master dismissed. No apology for the punishment was sought in the nature of the offence which might have provoked it. As my informer observed, "It was thought that the man who could not master his own passions was unfit to control the passions of others; besides, that he had infringed the rules of the school and forfeited the respect of his scholars." By this early exemption from arbitrary power, the boy acquires feelings and habits which abide with him through life. He feels his own importance as a human and a thinking being, and learns to regard violence as equally degrading to him who exercises it and to him who submits to it. You will perceive how the seeds of pride and gentleness are thus likely to spring up together in the same mind. In the proper union and tempering of these two qualities were, perhaps, found the perfection of national as well as of individual character.

In the education of women, New England seems hitherto to have been peculiarly liberal. The ladies of the eastern states are frequently possessed of the most solid acquirements, the modern and even the dead languages, and a wide scope of reading; the consequence is that their manners have the character of being more composed than those of my gay young friends in this quarter. I have already stated, in one of my earlier letters, that the public attention is now everywhere turned to the improvement of female education. In some states, colleges for girls are established under the eye of the legislature, in which are taught all those important branches of knowledge that your friend Dr. Rush conceived to be so requisite.

In other countries it may seem of little consequence to inculcate upon the female mind "the principles of government, and the obligations of patriotism," but it was wisely foreseen by that venerable apostle of liberty that in a country where a mother is charged with the formation of an infant mind that is to be called in future to judge of the laws and support the liberties of a republic, the mother herself should well understand those laws and estimate those liberties. Personal accomplishments and the more ornamental branches of knowledge should certainly in America be made subordinate to solid information. This is perfectly the case with respect to the men; as yet the women have been educated too much after the European manner. French, Italian, dancing, drawing engage the hours of the one sex (and this but too commonly in a lax and careless way), while the more appropriate studies of the other are philosophy, history, political economy, and the exact sciences. It follows, consequently, that after the spirits of youth have somewhat subsided, the two sexes have less in common in their pursuits and turn of thinking than is desirable. A woman of a powerful intellect will of course seize upon the new topics presented to her by the conversation of her husband. The less vigorous or the more thoughtless mind is not easily brought to forego trifling pursuits for those which occupy the stronger reason of its companion.

I must remark that in no particular is the liberal philosophy of the Americans more honorably evinced than in the place which is awarded to women. The prejudices still to be found in Europe, though now indeed somewhat antiquated, which would confine the female library to romances, poetry, and belles-lettres, and female conversation to the last new publication, new bonnet, and *pas seul,* are entirely unknown here. The women are assuming their place as thinking beings, not in despite of the men, but chiefly in consequence of their enlarged views and exertions as fathers and legislators.

I may seem to be swerving a little from my subject, but as I have adverted to the place accorded to women in one particular, I may as well now reply to your question regarding their general condition. It strikes me that it would be impossible for women to stand in higher estimation than they do here. The deference that is paid to them at all times and in all places has often occasioned me as much surprise as pleasure.

In domestic life there is a tenderness on the part of the husband to his weaker helpmate, and this in all situations of life that I believe in no country is surpassed and in few equalled. No *cavaliere servente* of a lady of fashion, no sighing lover, who has just penned a sonnet to his "mistress's eyebrow," ever rendered more delicate attentions to the idol of his fancy than I have seen rendered by an American farmer or mechanic, not to say gentleman, to the companion of his life. The wife and daughters of the labouring citizen are always found neatly dressed and occupied at home in household concerns; no field labour is ever imposed upon a woman, and I believe that it would outrage the feelings of an American, whatever be his station, should he see her engaged in any toil seemingly unsuited to her strength. In travelling, I have myself often met with a refinement of civility from men, whose exterior promised only the roughness of the mechanic or working farmer, that I should only have looked for from the polished gentleman.

Perhaps the condition of women affords, in all countries, the best criterion by which to judge of the character of men. Where we find the weaker sex burdened with hard labour, we may ascribe to the stronger something of the savage, and where we see the former deprived of free agency, we shall find in the latter much of the sensualist. I know not a circumstance which more clearly marks in England the retrograde movement of the national morals than the shackles now forged for the rising generation of women. Perhaps these are as yet more exclusively laid upon what are termed the highest class, but I apprehend that thousands of our countrywomen in the middle ranks, whose mothers, or certainly whose grandmothers, could ride unattended from the Land's End to the border and walk abroad alone or with an unmarried friend of the other sex armed with all the unsuspecting virtue of Eve before her fall —I apprehend that the children and grandchildren of these matrons are now condemned to walk in leading strings from the cradle to the altar, if not to the grave, taught to see in the other sex a race of seducers rather than protectors and of masters rather than companions. Alas for the morals of a country when female dignity is confounded with helplessness and the guardianship of a woman's virtue transferred from herself to others! If any should doubt the effect produced by the infringement of female liberty upon the female mind, let them consider the dress of the present generation of English women. This will sufficiently settle the question without a reference to the pages of the daily journals. Of the two extremes it is better to see a woman, as in Scotland, bent over the glebe, mingling the sweat of her brow with that of her churlish husband or more churlish son, than to see her gradually sinking into the childish dependence of a Spanish *donna*.

The liberty here enjoyed by the young women often occasions some surprise to foreigners, who, contrasting it with the constraint imposed on the female youth of Paris or London, are at a loss to reconcile the freedom of the national manners with the purity of the national morals; but confidence and innocence are twin sisters, and should the American women ever resign the guardianship of their own virtue, the lawyers of these democracies will probably find as good occupation in prosecuting suits for divorce as those of any of the monarchies of Europe.*

I often lament that in the rearing of women so little attention should be commonly paid to the exercise of the bodily organs; to invigorate the body is to invigorate the mind, and Heaven knows that the weaker sex have much cause to be rendered strong in both. In the happiest country their condition is sufficiently hard. Have they talents? It is difficult to turn them to account. Ambition? The road to honorable distinction is shut against them. A vigorous intellect? It is broken down by sufferings, bodily and mental. The lords of creation receive innumerable, incalculable advantages from the hand of nature, and it must be admitted that they everywhere take sufficient care to foster the advantages with which they are endowed. There is something so flattering to human vanity in the consciousness of superiority that it is little surprising if men husband with jealousy that which nature has enabled them to usurp over the daughters of Eve. Love of power more frequently originates in vanity than pride (two qualities, by the way, which are often confounded) and is, consequently, yet more peculiarly the sin of little than of great minds. Now an overwhelming proportion of human minds appertain to the former class and must be content to soothe their self-love by considering the weakness of others rather than their own strength. You will say this is severe; is it not true? In what consists the greatness of a despot? In his own intrinsic merits? No, in the degradation of the multitude who surround him. What feeds the

---

* The law of divorce is one so little referred to in America that it never occurred to me to hear or enquire how it stood. In the state of Rhode Island, however, there is a very singular regulation. As it was explained to me: if a married couple shall give in to the civil magistrate a mutual declaration that they are desirous of separating from (as the French would express it) *incompatibilité*, and shall then live entirely apart, but within the precincts of the state, for two full years, conducting themselves with propriety during that period, they may obtain, upon application, a disannulment of the marriage contract. I was surprised to hear that few had ever sought *the benefit of the act*, and that of those who had applied for it, some had broken the exacted stipulations before the expiration of the two years. Might it not tend to cement rather than weaken the marriage tie throughout the world if every country had a Rhode Island?

vanity of a patrician? The consciousness of any virtue that he inherits with his blood? The list of his senseless progenitors would probably soon cease to command his respect if it did not enable him to command that of his fellow creatures. "But what," I hear you ask, "has this to do with the condition of women? Do you mean to compare men collectively to the despot and the patrician?" Why not? The vanity of the despot and the patrician is fed by the folly of their fellow men, and so is that of their sex collectively soothed by the dependence of women: it pleases them better to find in their companion a fragile vine, clinging to their firm trunk for support, than a vigorous tree with whose branches they may mingle theirs. I believe they sometimes repent of their choice when the vine has weighed the oak to the ground. It is difficult, in walking through the world, not to laugh at the consequences which, sooner or later, overtake men's follies, but when these are visited upon women I feel more disposed to sigh. Born to endure the worst afflictions of fortune, they are enervated in soul and body lest the storm should not visit them sufficiently rudely. Instead of essaying to counteract the unequal law of nature, it seems the object of man to visit it upon his weaker helpmate more harshly. It is well, however, that his folly recoils upon his own head, and that the fate of the sexes is so entwined that the dignity of the one must rise or fall with that of the other.

In America much certainly is done to ameliorate the condition of women, and as their education shall become, more and more, the concern of the state, their character may aspire in each succeeding generation to a higher standard. The republic, I am persuaded, will be amply repaid for any trouble or expense that may be thus bestowed. In her struggles for liberty much of her virtue emanated from the wives and daughters of her senators and soldiers, and to preserve to her sons the energy of freemen and patriots she must strengthen that energy in her daughters.*

To invigorate the character, however, it is not sufficient to cultivate the mind. The body also must be trained to wholesome exercise, and the nerves braced to bear those extremes of climate which here threaten to enervate the more weakly frame. It is the union of bodily and mental vigor in the male population of America which imparts to it that peculiar energy of character which in its first infancy drew forth so splendid a panegyric from the British orator: "What in the world is equal to it?" exclaimed Mr. Burke. "Whilst we follow them (the colonists) among the tumbling mountains of ice, and behold them pene-

---

* In the Revolutionary War the enthusiasm of the women is acknowledged to have greatly assisted that of the men. In all successful struggles for liberty I believe the same co-operation of the sexes will be found to have existed.

trating into the deepest frozen recesses of Hudson's Bay and Davis' Straits, whilst we are looking for them beneath the Arctic Circle, we hear that they have pierced into the opposite region of polar cold, that they are at the antipodes, and engaged under the frozen serpent of the South. Falkland Island, which seemed too remote and romantic an object for the grasp of national ambition, is but a stage and resting place in the progress of their victorious industry; nor is the equinoctial heat more discouraging to them than the accumulated winter of both the poles. We know that while some of them draw the line and strike the harpoon on the coast of Africa, others run the longitude, and pursue their gigantic game along the coast of Brazil. No sea but what is vexed by their fisheries; no climate that is not witness to their toils." *

Now, though it is by no means requisite that the American women should emulate the men in the pursuit of the whale, the felling of the forest, or the shooting of wild turkeys, they might, with advantage, be taught in early youth to excel in the race, to hit a mark, to swim, and in short to use every exercise which could impart vigor to their frames and independence to their minds. But I have dwelt enough upon this subject, and you will, perhaps, apprehend that I am about to subjoin a Utopian plan of national education: no, I leave this to the republic herself, and, wishing all success to her endeavours, I bid you farewell.

* [Edmund Burke], "Speech on Conciliation with America" [March 22, 1775].

LETTER XXIV.

Religion. Temper of the Different Sects. Anecdotes.

New York, March 1820.

My Dear Friend,

Yes, it is somewhat curious to see how travellers contradict each other. One says things are white, and another that they are black; some write that the Americans have no religion, and others that they are a race of fanatics. One traveller tells us that they are so immersed in the affairs of the republic as not to have a word to throw at a stranger, and another, that they never think about politics at all and talk nonsense eternally.*

* * * * may well ask what he is to believe, but he flatters me too much if he be willing to refer the matter to my decision. He may argue thus, however, for himself: if the Americans had no religion, it is to be presumed that they would have no churches, and if they were a race of fanatics, it is equally to be presumed that they would force people to go into them. We know that they *have* churches and do *not* force people to go into them, nor force people to *pay for them,* and yet they *are* paid for and filled.

It is impossible to apply any general rule to so widespread a community as this. Perhaps Selden's were the best: "Religion is like the fashion. One man wears his doublet slashed, another laced, another plain, but every man has a doublet. So every man has his religion. They differ about trimming." But we cannot subjoin another axiom of the same philosopher: "Every religion is a

---

* Compare Mr. Fearon and Lieutenant Hall upon this subject. It appears to me, however, that both are equally far from the truth. That the Americans never trouble themselves about the affairs of the nation, which is the assertion of the former, seems scarcely to merit refutation. That they are so immersed in them as to be "habitually serious and silent," surely found its way into the pages of the latter after an evening passed with some citizen, of whom nature had made "an original." But if this observation, as applied to the men, appears strange, when applied to the women it appears absolutely incomprehensible. I think this intelligent officer was looking at the Marquis de Chastellux,[1] instead of the young women of New York and Philadelphia, when he drew his portrait of them—or, perhaps, it was *that they mistook him for the Marquis.* The licentious pen of the French nobleman knew how to traduce those who gave way to the innocent gaiety of their hearts in his presence, as well as to ridicule those who had awed him by their reserve.† Perhaps the young women of America are now somewhat too suspicious of European cavaliers. I have often perceived that the entrance of a foreign traveller into a party has damped the hilarity of the evening.

† See the travels of Brissot de Warville.[2]

getting religion." [3] It gets nothing, and so, whatever it be, it is sincere and harmless.

Some contend that liberality is only indifference; perhaps, as a general rule, it may be so. Persecution undoubtedly fans zeal, but such zeal as it is usually better to be without. I do not perceive any want of religion in America. There are sections of the country where some might think there is too much, at least that its temper is too stern and dogmatical. This has long been said of New England, and, undoubtedly, the Puritan ancestry of her citizens is still discernible as well in the coldness of their manners as in the rigidity of their creed. But it is wonderful how fast these distinctions are disappearing. An officer of the American navy, a native of New England, told me that when a boy he had sooner dared to pick a neighbour's pocket on a Saturday than to have smiled on a Sunday. "I have since travelled through all parts of the Union, and over a great part of the world, and have learned, consequently, that there are all ways of thinking; and I find now that my fellow countrymen are learning the same."

You will conceive how great is the change wrought in the religious temper of the eastern states, when I mention that the Unitarian faith has been latterly introduced and, in some parts, has made such rapid progress as promises, ere long, to supersede the doctrines of Calvin.[4] There were, of course, some vehement pulpit fulminations in Massachusetts when these mild teachers of morals and simple Christianity first made their appearance. But, fortunately, Calvin could no longer burn Servetus, however much he might scold at him, and, having scolded till he was tired, he laid down the "drum ecclesiastic" and left his gentle adversary to lead his flock to heaven after his own way. This affords, I believe, the only instance of war waged by American theologians since the days of the Revolution. Polemics, indeed, is not a science at all in fashion, nor ever likely to be so. Where no law says what is orthodoxy, no man is entitled to say what is heresy, or, if he should assume to himself the right, it is clear that he will only be laughed at. It required, however, some years to satisfy the whole American community of this fact. Although few cared to contend for the doctrine of the Trinity with the vehemence of the Calvinists of Massachusetts, the Unitarians had still some prejudices to encounter in other parts of the Union. Philadelphia and even New York had their zealots as well as Boston. In the latter city they were few, but perhaps more noisy on that very account. It is some years since a Calvinistic preacher here exclaimed to the nonelect of his congregation, "Ha! ha! you think to get through the gates of heaven, by laying hold of my coat; but I'll take care to hold up the skirts." Such an intimation, we may suppose, not much calculated to conciliate the vacillating heretics. The teacher who points the way to heaven through paths of peace, and by the candor and gentleness of his judgments leads us to worship with him a God of love and mercy, may easily draw into his fold the children of such a merciless fanatic.

American religion, of whatever sect (and it includes all the sects under heaven), is of a quiet and unassuming character, no way disputatious, even when more doctrinal than the majority may think wise. I do not include the strolling Methodists and Shaking Quakers, and sects with unutterable names and deranged imaginations, who are found in some odd corners of this wide world, beating time to the hymns of Mother Ann and working out the millennium by abstaining from marriage.* [5]

The perfect cordiality of all the various religious fraternities might sometimes lead a stranger to consider their members as more indifferent to the faith they so quietly profess than they really are. There is undoubtedly a considerable body scattered through the community who are attached to no establishment, but as they never trouble their neighbours with their opinions, neither do their neighbours trouble them with theirs. The extent to which this liberality is carried, even by the most dogmatical of the churches, is now well evinced in New England. In one or two of her theological colleges, the practice continued, till within some years, of inculcating one creed exclusively under the protection of the legislature, but the legislature have now left teachers and students to themselves, and even Connecticut has finally done away the last shadow of the privileges of her Congregationalists. It really does seem possible for fanaticism, or something very like it, and liberality to go together. It is not long since, in some of the New England states, there was an edict in force that no man should travel on a Sunday, and this, while all men were eligible to the highest honors of the state, let them believe or disbelieve as little or as much as they might.† [6]

Alluding to this edict recalls to me the adventure of a Pennsylvania farmer, which, as it may elucidate the good humour with which this people yield to the whims of each other, I will repeat to you.

The good farmer was bound on his way to Boston and found himself within the precincts of Connecticut on a Sunday morning. Aware of the law of Calvin, but still being in haste to proceed, our traveller thought of shifting himself from

---

* The *Shakers,* as they are called, emigrated to America some forty years ago. Ann Lee, or Mother Ann, their spiritual leader, was a niece of the celebrated General Lee, who took so active a part in the War of the Revolution. She became deranged, as it is said, from family misfortunes, fancied herself a second Virgin Mary, and found followers, as Joanna Southcott and Jemima Wilkinson did after her.

† The constitutions of two or three of the states require that the chief officers shall be Christians, or, at least, believe in a God; but, as no religious test is enforced, the law is, in fact, a dead letter. By the constitution of every state in the Union, an affirmation is equal to an oath; it is at the option of the asseverator either to invoke the name of God or to affirm, under the pains and penalties of the law, in cases of breach of faith.

the back of his steed into the mail which chanced to overtake him and which, appertaining to the United States, was not under the law of Connecticut. The driver advised him to attach his steed to the back of the vehicle, thinking that when they should have passed through a certain town which lay before them, the honest farmer might remount in safety. But, as ill luck would have it, the citizens were just stepping forth from their doors on their way to church, when the graceless horse, with a saddle on his back, passed before them. Stopping at the inn, a citizen made up to the side of the vehicle and civilly demanded if the horse was his, and if he was aware that the Sabbath was a day of rest, not only by the law of God, but by the law of Connecticut. The Pennsylvanian as civilly replied that the horse *was* his, begged to return thanks in his name for the care shown to his ease and his morals, and offered to surrender the keeping of both, until his return, to the individual who addressed him. "I will most willingly lodge the horse in my stable and his master in my house," returned the other; "but the people will not see with pleasure the beast keeping the commandments and the man breaking them." "Well, friend, then beast and man shall keep them together. I will eat your dinner, and he shall eat your hay; and, to begin things properly, you shall show him to the stable and his master to the church." The compact was fulfilled to the satisfaction of all parties, the Pennsylvanian only allowing himself, through the day, gently to animadvert upon this abridgement of the liberties of the citizens of the United States, by the decree of the citizens of Connecticut, which might not always be as agreeable to them as, in this case, it was to him; and departed the next morning, assuring his host that he should be happy to repay his hospitality to him or his friends, whenever either might choose to travel his way on a Sunday, or a Saturday, or any day of the seven.

Some years afterwards, standing one Sunday morning at the gate of his own farm in Pennsylvania, he perceived a man riding along the road and driving before him a small flock of sheep. As he approached, our farmer recognized him for a neighbour of his *ci-devant* host in Connecticut. "Ah, friend! that's an odd occupation you are following on a Sunday!" "True," replied the man of New England, "and so I have chosen a byroad, that I may not offend the scrupulous." "Yes, friend, but supposing you offend me? And supposing, too, that the Pennsylvania legislature should have passed a law which comes in force this day that neither man nor beast shall travel on a Sunday?" "Oh!" replied the other, "I have no intention to disobey your laws; if that be the case, I will put up at the next town." "No, no, you may just put up here. I will show your sheep to the stable, and, if you be willing, yourself to the church." This was done accordingly, and the next morning the Pennsylvanian, shaking hands with his Connecticut friend, begged him to inform his old acquaintance, when he should return home, that the traveller and his horse had not forgotten their Sabbath day's rest in his dwelling, and that, unbacked by a law of the legislature, they had equally enforced the law of God upon his neighbour and his neighbour's sheep.

There is a curious spirit of opposition in the human mind. I see your papers full of anathemas against blasphemous pamphlets. We have no such things here; and why? Because every man is free to write them, and because every man enjoys his own opinion, without any arguing about the matter. Where religion never arms the hand of power, she is never obnoxious; where she is seated modestly at the domestic hearth, whispering peace and immortal hope to infancy and age, she is always respected, even by those who may not themselves feel the force of her arguments. This is truly the case here, and the world has my wish, and, I am sure, yours also, that it may be the case everywhere.

LETTER XXV.

Account of Colonel Huger. Observations on the Climate, &c.

New Jersey, April 1820.

My Dear Friend,

I am happy to have it in my power to reply to the question contained in the letter now before me, and this without any trouble as I am so fortunate as to be intimately acquainted with some near relatives of the individual about whom you enquire.

Colonel Huger is a native of South Carolina and the member of a family remarkable (so far at least as my acquaintance with it extends) for ardor of character and distinguished talents.[1] He passed to London in his youth to complete his medical studies, and was thus engaged when the news reached him of the seizure and imprisonment of General Lafayette, whom he had learned from his infancy to respect as the companion in arms of his father and the champion of his country's liberties. He instantly conceived the project of devoting his time and, if it should be necessary, his life to effect the rescue of the illustrious captive. Having digested his scheme and finding that a coadjutor would be necessary, he took into his confidence a young German, a companion of his studies, and embarked with him for Holland. The story of the attempted rescue, as commonly told, is pretty accurate; the best that I remember to have seen, was in a number of the *Annual Register*. I suppose you are acquainted with the incidents which defeated the scheme and gave back the rescued Lafayette to his prison, and made his generous deliverer also an inhabitant of the gloomy dungeons of Olmütz. The sufferings of the young American, after the failure of the attempt, were cruelly severe: alone, in a dank and stony cell, apprehensive for the safety, even for life of Lafayette, uncertain as to the fate of his friend, now cursing his own rashness, which had perhaps doubled the sufferings of him he came to rescue, and now the untoward chances which had defeated his attempt when so near success. This fever of the spirit soon fell on the blood, and, for three weeks, delirium rendered him insensible to the horrors of his dungeon. Without assistance of any kind that he can recollect, how the fever left him, he knows not; the damps and confinement ill forwarded the recovery of his strength. Stretched on the stones, he sought to divert his mind by laying plans for his future life, if his prison doors should ever be opened but for his corpse. What is singular, he has followed out the mode of life he then amused himself with scheming.

The first human sound that reached him was the cry of a child (for the keeper who supplied him with bread and water made neither query nor reply). "A child! then there must be a woman, and where there is a woman, there may be compassion." So saying, he crawled towards the wall, at the top of which was the grate that admitted light, air, and all the inclemencies of the seasons. Often he listened, watched, and called, till at last a woman's face was stooped towards the grate; he tried French, which fortunately she could reply to. "You are a mother": such was the manner of his address, to remove her scruples. "I have a mother; for her sake have pity on her son!" After a good deal of pathetic entreaty, she promised to bring him back an answer to his enquiries and to procure for him a German grammar. He learned that his friend was in a dungeon in the same fortress, and that Lafayette was in tolerable health but in stricter confinement than ever. The grammar was squeezed through the bars, another book was afterwards procured, and thus he acquired a tolerable knowledge of German. After some time he told his visitor that his grammar had afforded him so much amusement that if she could discover the grate of his friend's prison, he wished she would convey it to him. Having in vain tried to make intelligible marks upon the paper, he made some with a piece of mortar, scraped from the wall, upon a black silk handkerchief that he took from his neck and in which he folded the grammar; this, with a good deal of trouble, was squeezed again through the bars, and in a few days was returned, some words of English in reply having been scraped by his friend upon the cover, satisfying Huger as to his health. The grammar was his only amusement through the remaining months of his imprisonment, which were in all eight. The representations of Washington procured his release, after a trial where he pleaded his own cause in French: it was short and simply but eloquently stated that he and his friend had no accomplices and no motives but those supplied by their own enthusiasm, that he had not sought to rescue a state prisoner, but the friend of his father, of his country, and of mankind, to procure whose release he would then willingly return to his dungeon, and to save whose life he would joyfully give his own. Having concluded, the judge (whose German title I forget) ordered him to leave the place within so many hours and to be out of Germany within so many days, and then, leaving his seat and approaching him, he said, "Young man, you are chargeable with singular rashness, but I tell you that, had I to search the world for a friend, from what I have heard this day, I would seek him in America."

I may mention that the young prisoner came from his dungeon almost entirely bald, and that though the strength of his constitution soon removed all the other effects of his unwholesome confinement, he never recovered his hair; this, contrasted with the youth and animation of his countenance, gave him for many years a very singular appearance. Returning to his country, misfortune seemed to follow him. Entering the house of his brother, a bow window from the upper story fell on his head; for thirteen days he lay insensible, attended by his brother with agonized affection. What struck me as a fine instance of greatness of mind, when the surgeon, perceiving the skull to be injured, proposed trepanning, which he thought might save life, though without the hope of preserving the reason. "No," said his brother. "Never shall he live to be so different from what he was. I know his soul, and choose for him in preferring death." He repaid his cares, however, by a perfect recovery, when his brother, who was possessed of a large property, entreated him to share his fortune; this, however, he strenuously refused and settled in Charleston as a physician. Some time afterwards, he became attached to a young woman of a respectable family in that city. Though rising into eminence in his profession, his income was as yet small, and she had nothing. In this state of things, he determined not to venture on marriage, until his increasing practice should enable him to support a family. These circumstances coming to the knowledge of his brother, he instantly bestowed a fortune on the young woman, and an obligation thus delicately conferred could not be objected to by her lover. They married, and Colonel Huger then determined to carry into effect the dreams which had amused his prison. He took his wife to a farm beyond the mountains, where he settled, and was soon the father of a fine boy. The child, when two years old, sickened, and his knowledge of physic satisfied him that he could not recover; he reasoned like a philosopher with the doting mother, prepared her by degrees for her loss, represented the duty she owed to him, which should strengthen her to struggle with her grief and submit to an irremediable evil. She listened and had sufficient strength of mind to feel the weight of his words. She herself wrote the news of her loss to her father. "My husband has exhorted me to bear it as became your daughter and his wife, and he has imparted strength to me to do so; but, oh! what calamity is there for which his affection ought not to console me!" They were afterwards more fortunate parents. Colonel Huger has been the tutor of his children, who obey his words as the young Spartans those of Lycurgus. Trained to hardiness and independence, inspired by their father with sentiments of patriotism, and clad in garments woven by their own domestics, they exhibit, in their manners and character, that simplicity and ardor which form the true characteristics of the sons and daughters of a republic. Nor is it only when excited by feelings of peculiar enthusiasm, or when called upon to perform the duties of a husband, a father, and a citizen, that this distinguished individual has evinced the beauty of his character. He had an only sister, who, some years after his marriage, fell into a pitiable state of health; change of air and travelling were recommended as the last remedies. His brother found it impossible to move at the time, and there was no other friend or relative on whom could be devolved the care of the invalid. Colonel Huger left his farm, came to Charleston, deposited his wife and infant children with his father-in-law, became the travelling companion and physician of his sister, and nearly a year after brought her back in a state of recovery, joined his family, and returned to his estate.

During the war, when a descent of the enemy was expected on some of the great cities of the South, and then on Savannah rather than New Orleans, Colonel Huger repaired to the former. Assembling his children around him in the presence of their mother, he explained the duty which called him from them. "My country and your country calls me to its defence. I go with a willing heart, commending you and your mother to it and to heaven. Let me see that you, on your side, yield your father with willing hearts. Now embrace me, all of you, without a tear." He mounted his horse, and not a murmur was heard; even the youngest tried to smile as their beloved parent rode away; another proudly brushed the tear from his eye, and wished that he was old enough to defend his country. Are you not with the old Romans?

The winter has now finally disappeared, though indeed we had pronounced the same in March, and the grass and I were lifting up our heads together—for we seem to be pretty equally dependent on the warm sun—when the demon of frost threw his iron sleets into the lap of the spring, or I should rather write *summer,* for nature here steps at once from the "formless wild" to

> Brightening fields of ether, fair disclos'd.

This is a climate of extremes; you are here always in heat or frost. The former you know I never object to, and as I equally dislike the latter, I should perhaps be an unfair reporter of both. The summer is glorious: the resplendent sun "shining on, shining on," for days and weeks successively, an air so pure, so light, and to me so genial, that I awake as it were to a new existence. I have seen those around me, however, often drooping beneath fervors which have given me life. By the month of August, the pale cheeks and slow movements of the American women, and even occasionally of the men, seem to demand the invigorating breezes of the Siberian winter to brace the nerves and quicken the current of the blood. The severe cold, which succeeds to this extreme of heat, appears to have this effect and seldom to produce, excepting upon such as may be affected with constitutional weakness of the lungs, any effect that is not decidedly beneficial. Most people will pronounce the autumn to be the pride of the American year. It is indeed fraught with beauty to all the senses: the brilliant hues then assumed by nature, from the dwarf sumac with his berries and leaves of vivid crimson, up to the towering trees of the forest, twisting their branches in extreme and whimsical contrast of gold, red, green, orange, russet, through all their varieties of shade; the orchards too, then laden with treasures, and the fields heavy with the ripened maize; the skies bright with all the summer's splendour, yet tempered with refreshing breezes; the sun sinking to rest in crimsons, whose depth and warmth of hue the painter would not dare to imitate. This glorious season is, however, not the most wholesome, especially in the uncleared districts, as you know from my last year's letters.

The winter—those whom it likes, may like it. The season has its beauty and its pleasures. Sparkling skies shining down upon sparkling snows, over which the light "sleighs," peopled with the young and the gay, bound along to the chime of bells, which the horses seem to bear well pleased. In country and city this is the time of amusement. The young people will run twenty miles, through the biting air, to the house of a friend, where all in a moment is set astir, carpets up, music playing, and youths and maidens laughing and mingling in the mazy dance, the happiest creatures beneath the moon. Is it the bright climate or the liberty that reigns everywhere, or is it the absence of poverty and the equal absence of extreme wealth, or is it all these things together that make this people so cheerful and gay-hearted? Whatever be the cause, ill befall the callous heart that could see their happiness without sympathy, though it should be unable to share it!

The spring—there is properly *no* spring; there is a short struggle between winter and summer, who sometimes fight for the mastery with a good deal of obstinacy. We have lately seen a fierce combat between these two great sovereigns of the year. In the latter days of March, summer suddenly alighted on the snows in the full flush of July heat; every window and door were flung open to welcome the stranger, and the trees were just bursting into leaf, when angry winter returned to the field and poured down one of the most singular showers of sleet I ever witnessed. The water, freezing as it fell, cased every branch and twig in crystal of an inch thick, so transparent that each bud appeared distinctly through it; in some places, large trees gave way beneath the unusual burden, their heads absolutely touching the ground until their trunks snapped in twain. Fortunately, there was no wind, or the devastation would have been dreadful;

it has been cruel enough as it is, boughs and branches everywhere strewing the ground and stems shattered as if by lightning.

I am not sure if, even in our island, the spring does not appear to more advantage in description than in reality. There are, indeed, some lovely days in England, when the lark carols, unseen, at the gates of heaven, and primroses and cowslips are just bursting out of the green sward, the April sun peeping sweetly forth from a flying cloud, the earth and heaven all breathing freshness, and fragrance, and mild vernal airs. The beautiful valleys of Devonshire see many such days, but the island generally sees but few, or at least there are so many fogs and biting winds which intervene betwixt them that I, for one, have always been well pleased when

the turning spring
Averts her blushful face.

The close of the winter—for one may not term it the spring—is here decidedly the least agreeable season of the year. Siberian winds today, and Indian heats tomorrow, and then driving sleet the next day, and so on, from heat to cold and cold to heat, until the last finally prevails and all nature bursts into sudden life, as by the spell of a magician. The first flush of the summer is truly delightful; the instantaneous spring of vegetation, the multitude of blossoms, clothing orchard and forest, and the chirp and song of birds, all breaking forth at once, have an unspeakably cheering effect. The birds here are less numerous than in our island but will, of course, multiply as cultivation encroaches more and more on the forest. I do not think there is any songster that may compare with our lark, whose note breathes more of the upper spheres than any of earth's creatures. With this exception, the note of the American songsters may, I think, vie with ours. The Virginia nightingale, his feathers all crimson with fine black marks on his head, has a singularly melodious song. The robin is more like our thrush, both as to size and note and even colour, except that he has a red breast, from which, and perhaps also from his familiar habits, it is probable that he obtained his name. The mockingbird, who, besides imitating all others, bad, good, and indifferent, has a powerful and exquisite note of his own. The bluebird, the red-headed woodpecker, a small yellow bird resembling the canary are the others that occur to me as the most frequent. The hummingbird, that fairy creature, half butterfly, half bird, does not make his appearance until midsummer.

The observations that I can make upon the climate apply of course but to a small portion of this vast world, which comprises all the climates of the earth, with the exception perhaps of one—the gloomy. The Atlantic border of New England is indeed liable, in the spring months, to fogs blown from off the Newfoundland Bank, but these temporary visitors do not despoil the atmosphere of the general character of brilliancy which, summer and winter, it may be said more or less to possess from Maine to Missouri. The vividness of the light, which is at first painful to English and even European eyes of whatever country, I could imagine had wrought an effect on the national physiognomy. The Americans in general are remarkable for even brows, much projected over the eyes, which, small and piercing, usually glance from beneath them with singular intelligence and quickness of observation. The climate of this continent, except where influenced by local causes, seems to be peculiarly healthy and highly favourable to the growth of the human figure. Other circumstances doubtless assist its effect; a population free from poverty, and in consequence comparatively of vice, might perhaps attain to nature's full standard in an atmosphere less pure. The diseases of the country appear to be few and violent—fevers and other inflammatory disorders, common during the first autumnal months; the temperate habits of the people, however, preserve them in a great measure from these attacks or moderate their violence. I imagine there are more instances of extraordinary longevity in these states than you could find in any part of Europe.

The western states seem destined to be the paradise of America. The beauty of their climate is probably unrivalled, unless it be by that of some of the elevated plains of the southern continent. The influence of the mild breezes from the Mexican gulf, which blow with the steadiness of a trade wind up the great valley of the Mississippi, is felt even to the southern shore of Lake Erie, and affects the climate of some of the northwestern counties of New York. The explanation given by Volney of this phenomenon is, in the highest degree, ingenious and more than plausible, as it seems to be confirmed by the subsequent observations of other philosophers and to be borne out by every fact that has been adduced.*

Have I written enough about wind and weather? Forgive me for handling so dull a subject, and this too so superficially. The American climate has so

---

* The facts adduced by Volney tend to demonstrate "that the southwest wind of the United States is nothing but the trade wind of the tropics turned out of its direction and modified, and that consequently the air of the western country is the same as that of the Gulf of Mexico, and previously of the West Indies, conveyed to Kentucky. From this datum, flows a simple and natural solution of the problem, which at first must have appeared perplexing, why the temperature of the western country is hotter by three degrees of latitude than that of the Atlantic coast, though only separated from it by the Allegheny mountains." ² Volney's *View of the Climate and Soil of the United States of America.* If the southwest wind tempers, in the western country, the cold of the winter, it also tempers the heat of the summer. This does not seem to be clearly admitted by Volney, but I have never questioned any individual, familiar with the western territory, who did not concur in the statement.

many peculiarities that to trace them to their causes would afford a curious and interesting subject; for this, however, I am totally inadequate.

I send you a very careless reply to your last letter. A few weeks' patience, my dear friend, and I will answer your questions, to the best of my power at least, in person. Receive it as no small proof of anxious affection, that we lay aside all thoughts of crossing the Alleghenies, and that, closing, for the present, our American travels with a visit to Washington, we shall embark in May for England. Does this look like return, and do you now believe that we shall keep good faith with you? Farewell.

LETTER XXVI.

Philadelphia Market. Deportment of the Citizens. Mode of Guiding and Breaking Horses. Hints to an Emigrant. Consequences of Bringing Foreign Servants to America. German Redemptioners. Manner in Which the Importation of the Peasants of the European Continent is Conducted. Reply to the Quarterly Review. *Descent of the Delaware. Letter of Count Survilliers (Joseph Bonaparte). Rencontre with English Travellers.*

Philadelphia, April 1820.

My Dear Friend,

Thus far on our own way to Washington, having just left the Trenton steamboat for one bound to Baltimore, and now lying at the wharf at the foot of Market Street, surrounded by sloops and boats, filled with shad, a fine fish between our salmon and mackerel, just come into season and which are now selling for a cent apiece.

How strangely quiet is this Quaker city! I am writing in this cabin scarce disturbed by a sound, except the tread of two men on the deck, and yet the great market of the city, and the largest, perhaps, of any city in the states, is now holding not two hundred yards distant from this spot. We took a turn through it just now, and surely never was a crowd so orderly and quiet! I know not if the fishwomen be all Quakers, but they certainly are few of them Billingsgates. And here I will observe what has struck me, not in Philadelphia only, over which the peaceable spirit of Penn may be supposed to hover, but in all the towns and cities of these republics that I have chanced to visit—the orderly behaviour of the citizens. You not only see no riots in the streets, but no brawls—none of that wrangling, enforced by oath and fist, which some might hold as proofs of brutish ignorance, though a Windham might see in them the tongue and soul of valour.[1] The absence of noise does not argue the absence of activity, any more than the absence of inhumanity argues that of courage. If any man doubt either position, let him visit these republics and

236

consider the character and habits of this people, together with their short but interesting history.

I observed in the carts and waggons standing in and around the market place the same well-fed, well-rubbed, healthy looking horses that have so often attracted my attention throughout this country. Truly, I do not remember to have seen a starved horse since I landed. The animals seem to share the influence of wholesome laws with their masters, their influence reaching them through that which they exert more immediately upon the character, as well as the circumstances, of the proud lords of the creation. I say character as well as circumstances, for though, when a man feeds his horse well, it may only argue that he has wherewithal to procure provender, when he uses him gently and guides him with the voice instead of the whip, it shows that he has good sense or humanity—good sense, if he consider his own ease, and humanity, if he consider that of the animal. It is a pretty thing to see a horse broke in this country; it is done entirely by gentleness. A skilful rider, after much previous coaxing and leading, mounts the wild creature without whip or spur, and soothes him with the hand and the voice, or allows him to spend himself in the race, and brings him at last to obey the check of the rein, or the note of the voice, with the readiness of the steed of a Bedouin. The lesson, thus learned, is never forgotten; a word or a whistle sets the horse to his full speed, whether in the carriage, the dearborn, or the stage. In travelling, I remember but once to have seen a driver who ever did more than crack his whip in the air. This exception too was a European.

If * * * *'s friends do finally determine upon passing to this country, let them by all means be advised against bringing servants with them. Foreign servants are here, without doubt, the worst; they neither understand the work which the climate renders necessary, nor are willing to do the work which they did elsewhere. A few weeks—nay, not unfrequently, a few days—and they either become a useless charge to their employers, or, by making inordinate demands and assuming airs of ridiculous importance, force their employers to dismiss them. You will easily conceive how an uneducated mind is likely to misconstrue the nature of that equality which a democracy imparts to all men. Those bred up under it can perceive and acknowledge the distinctions which education and condition place between the gentleman and the labourer, but those just released from the aristocracies of Europe, finding themselves in a country where all men are placed by the laws on an exact level, conceive, naturally enough, that they are transformed from the servants of their employer into his companions, and at one and the same moment lay aside obsequiousness and array themselves in insolence. I am not, however, prepared to say that the complaints which I have heard from my countrymen and countrywomen have been altogether just. It is probable that in these household quarrels there are often faults on both sides, the master and mistress preserving a tone which might be tolerated in Europe, but which their squires and hand-maidens have here learned to resent, and the servants, on the other hand, being too prone to exaggerate the offence offered, or too eager to seize the opportunity of paying off old scores by returning impertinence in kind. If * * * *'s friends are quite sure of the dispositions of their domestics and quite sure of their own, they may, perhaps, bring over their household with them without much hazard. I believe the plan seldom answers, but there are exceptions to all rules. One thing they must come prepared for. The day after their arrival, they will be styled Mr. and Mrs. * * * *. If they take no notice of this, things may go on smoothly, but if they ask why the epithets master and mistress are dropped, ten to one but they will receive for answer that there are no masters and no servants in America, that this is a free country, that all men are equal, &c., &c., the whole concluding with a toss of the head and a sudden whisk out of the room. I have witnessed several amusing scenes of this description, and some of my American friends have witnessed many more.

The * * * *s are perhaps curious to know what servants they will find here. In the first place, they will find in the Atlantic cities, where servants must generally be sought, many Irish and some British. These are, for the most part, stragglers from the crowd of emigrants poured into the St. Lawrence; with some exceptions, the former are poor, dirty, and ignorant, the latter, dis-contented and insolent. These, however, after a year or two, will sometimes recover their good humour and good manners and become civil, though never again servile domestics. There is something about the Irishman that everywhere seems to attract sympathy. Notwithstanding his thoughtless improvidence, his simplicity and warmheartedness make him friends, even among this industrious nation. The many distinguished Irish characters settled in these states, of course, interest themselves more peculiarly in the condition of their poor countrymen. The Hibernian societies of New York and Philadelphia provide some with work and support others. These emigrants sometimes make tolerable journeymen and outdoor labourers, but usually very indifferent household servants.

On the Atlantic border, to which, in the northern states, the black population is chiefly confined, negroes are much employed in domestic service. Their faults are indolence and an occasional tendency to intemperance and petty dishonesty. Those who employ negroes generally find it better to employ them exclusively. The native American, when he can be obtained, makes a valuable domestic. Household service, as I have observed in a former letter, is not an employment that the citizens are fond of, but the very qualities which disincline them from it make them the more trusty when engaged in it. The foreigner, however, must be careful not to rub their pride. No American will receive an insulting word. A common mode of resenting an imperious order is to quit the house without waiting or even asking for a reckoning. The sensitiveness of the American pride is sometimes not a little curious and amusing. Some months since, we were surprised in New York by a visit from a woman who had been our domestic the year before. We had parted with her, having no farther occasion for her service, and had seen her provided with another place before we left the city. It was not without pleasure that I recognized our old acquaintance as she entered neatly dressed, with a smiling countenance, which seemed also full of meaning. After some prefatory salutations, I began to enquire into her history since we parted. How had she liked her new situation? "They were foreigners, Madam, that I went to after leaving you." "Well, Mary." "They had some strange ways, Madam." "The short is, Mary, that you did not like them." "Why no, Madam. I left them the next morning." "That was somewhat hasty. They must have used you very ill." "They doubted my honesty," and she drew her head somewhat higher as she spoke. "Indeed!" "Yes; the lady herself locked away the plate and even the silver spoons." I believe I smiled as I asked, "Was that all, Mary?" "All!" A slight flush crossed her face, as she repeated the word; then, hesitating a moment, she added in a quiet tone, "I am afraid you think I behaved oddly; but I was not used to the sort of thing. The lady told me it was her practice. 'Why then, Madam,' said I, 'I think we are not assorted. I could not stay in a house where a doubt seemed to be cast on my honesty; and so I believe we had better part now.'" "And you did part?" "Yes, Madam, I went away directly." I was glad to learn that the pride of the honest creature was never likely to be tried again. After a few circumlocutions and awkward looks, she told me that she was married to a kind husband and an industrious man.

You will perceive that a character of this description requires some management. Indeed the same may be said of servants in this country generally. A master or mistress of an imperious temper will be served very ill. It is a chance, indeed, if they will be served at all, and certainly by none but the most worthless, either of the blacks or of the poorest foreign emigrants, who may think it worth while to make a compromise between their pride and their cupidity, and who will probably revenge affronts by picking their masters' pockets. There is one mistake which foreigners are very apt to fall into: that the blacks constitute a *second état,* possessing fewer privileges and, consequently, less pride than the white community, and who may, therefore, be treated *de haut en bas* with impunity. It is not occasionally without feelings of high resentment that Europeans are made sensible of their error, and that they find the privileges of an American negro often surpassing their's in their own country, and his pride equalling their's in its most towering mood. This, indeed, is not a country for the imperious or the vain. The man who can respect the pride of a fellow creature, in whatever condition of life fortune may have thrown him, and who does not feel his consequence to depend upon the cap-in-hand service of inferiors, but rather finds his own dignity, as one of the human species, raised by the dignity assumed by others—such a man may live here easily and comfortably, well-attended, well-esteemed, and civilly treated.

There is another race of servants who are highly useful to the farmer and country gentleman; these are the poor German and Swiss peasants, thrown into this country from Holland, chiefly by the port of Philadelphia. Pennsylvania has been in great part peopled from Germany (perhaps one third of the population are of German descent); it is natural, therefore, that the stream of emigration from the banks of the Rhine should continue to pour into the same quarter. The regulations under which merchant vessels are placed in New York seem, indeed, to shut that port against it. Every captain who there lands a foreigner is held responsible that he or she shall not be thrown as a charge upon the commonwealth. Should he be found in the character of a vagrant within the date of three years after his arrival, the captain who has landed him becomes chargeable with his sustenance and must pay a high fine to the state, to be appropriated to that purpose.

The more wealthy Germans and other philanthropic citizens of this state (Pennsylvania), in keeping the port of Philadelphia open to the suffering poor of the European continent, have exerted themselves to place the trade (for their exportation is absolutely made a subject of trade in Holland) under such regulations as shall save this community from an inundation of paupers, and the poor emigrants themselves from breach of faith in the traders to whom they entrust their lives and liberties. The ships chiefly employed in this trade are Dutch, but the depressed state of commerce has thrown into it vessels of all nations, British, American, and others, from the ports of the Baltic. It was, of course, found somewhat difficult to bring foreign ships under the jurisdiction of the state laws. The first regulations were, in some cases, so shamefully evaded that the national government took the subject under consideration and passed a law which extended to every port in the Union and has been found thoroughly effective.[2] At present, therefore, the trade is placed under the jurisdiction of the American Congress, while the Pennsylvania legislature appoint officers to see that the contracts between the emigrants and the ship captains are faithfully fulfilled. A ship, of whatever nation, arriving in port peopled beyond a rate prescribed by law, is forfeited to the national government. The captain of every ship is bound to support his emigrants, or *redemptioners* as they are styled, for one month after the date of their arrival in port, after which he may add the charge of their support, as determined by law, to the debt of their passage. This debt, which is contracted in Holland, is paid according to the means of the emigrant. If he has money to defray his passage and that of his family, he devotes it to this purpose, but this is rarely the case. Sometimes he pays half or a third part of the debt, and becomes bound to the captain for a term of service equivalent to the remainder, who is empowered to sell this indentureship to a resident citizen in Pennsylvania; more frequently he discharges the whole of the debt by the surrender of his liberty. Upon his arrival here, however, the laws effectually screen him from the results which might accrue from his own ignorance or rashness. He, or rather the captain for him, cannot, under any circumstances, indent his person for a term longer than four years, nor can he be taken without his consent beyond the limits of the state of Pennsylvania. An officer is appointed and salaried by the Pennsylvania government, who inspects the redemptioners on their arrival and witnesses and reports the agreement made between the captain and those who purchase their service. The purchasers must take the whole family, man, wife, and children, unless the redemptioners themselves shall agree to the contrary, the masters being also bound by the law to provide the children with schooling and clothing. There are some minor regulations with which I am not accurately acquainted. This service, you will perceive, is liable to be not a little expensive to the employers. It is attended, however, with fewer risks than might be expected, the Swiss and German peasants being, for the most part, simple, honest, and industrious, and excellent servants in the farm and the dairy. This mode of indenture is so serviceable to these emigrants that those who may have been able to defray their passage in money usually bind themselves to some American family for a couple of years, where they may be initiated in the language and habits of their new country. I have met with instances of this kind in Pennsylvania, and even in New York and Jersey, into which states the emigrants had consented to pass. After the expiration of the term, the redemptioners are often retained by their masters upon wages, when, if they are frugal and ambitious, they may, in the course of time, lay up sufficient to purchase a few acres and enter on their own farm.

It certainly cannot be expected that the American nation will submit to have their country turned into a lazar house for the suffering poor of Europe, who, with poverty, but too often bring its accompaniments, indolence and vice. Those states, probably, act wisely who, by such regulations as I have mentioned as adopted by New York, shut the door against them. That state, by-the-bye, receives, as it is, more than she finds agreeable, by the way of Canada, and her community are put to no small inconvenience and expense for their provision. It is a common belief in Europe that her surplus population will be as great an advantage for America to gain as for her to lose. The argument would have some plausibility were not the surplus population of all countries generally the vicious population. There is not, however, the same objections to that of the middle parts of the old Continent as to that which has sometimes flowed from France and the British islands. The starving emigrants of Switzerland and Germany are simple agriculturists and ignorant peasants, who here quietly devote themselves to the pursuits from which they have been driven in Europe and instantly become harmless and industrious citizens. Their prejudices, whatever they may be, are perfectly innocent, and of absolute vices they usually have none. The poor British but too often bring with them all the assumption and all the corruption of manufacturing towns and crowded seaports, too ignorant to be able to appreciate justly the advantages which this country affords, and too knowing to be willing to learn.* Nor even supposing them to have good habits, which is seldom the case, are they fitted for the work they can obtain here. An Englishman, in general, can do but one thing, and an Irishman, but too frequently, can do nothing. I know many instances of their being employed from pure charity, their wives and children supported in out-houses for weeks and even months together, a charge upon the benevolence of an American farmer or gentleman. But benevolence must have bounds, and the rulers of Europe can with little reason complain if the republic lays an embargo upon the importation of their obstreperous mob and onerous paupers. The fact is that those only are an acquisition to this continent who are a loss to the other, and melancholy is the truth that every ship which enters these ports brings some emigrants of this character. The heart of the English patriot may well sink within him when he reflects upon this. Where will be the strength of his nation when it shall consist only of the over-rich and the starving poor? Pharaoh's fat and lean kine, who ate up each other, is a true allegory.

Before quitting the subject of the German emigration, I must, in justice to the benevolent community of Philadelphia, advert to a writer who has been

---

* The Welsh form an exception to this rule: their habits are found to bear much resemblance to those of the German peasantry, and, consequently, their service is equally valued in Pennsylvania. Cargoes of Welsh redemptioners frequently enter the Delaware.

raised into consideration by the importance of his commentators. It was perhaps not possible that the authors of a much-read English journal should be able to detect the false statements of the English traveller they reviewed, but before they confirmed them by a farther assertion of their own, it was natural to suppose that they had accurately investigated the subject upon which they wrote. There is something painful in seeing the virtues of a community perverted into a source of reproach and calumny. That Philadelphia, who has been amiable enough to keep her ports open to the starving sufferers of Europe, when other states have closed theirs, should have been fixed upon as an object of peculiar obloquy, is, perhaps, no less singular than revolting.*

Mr. Fearon has given an account of a vessel in this port, calculated, from the seeming minuteness of its details, to gain implicit credit. The ship *Bubona,* which he says he boarded and describes as being overloaded with wretched Germans, he informs the English public was an American, commanded by an American, and belonging to Americans.[3] The *Bubona,* I regret to say, was a British brig, from the port of Sunderland, navigated and commanded by our countrymen and having British owners. She was, moreover, one of the foreign vessels which, the state laws of Pennsylvania being incompetent to control, occasioned the subject to be brought before the national Congress and procured the passing of those effective laws to which I have before alluded. I request you to communicate these particulars to your friend * * * *, who will judge from this specimen how far the *Sketches* of Mr. Fearon have been drawn by an accurate pencil. The ships employed in this trade (which, so far from meriting the term "infamous" bestowed upon it by the reviewer, is in its principle and its results essentially humane) are, as I have before remarked, principally Dutch, not English, as the instance of the *Bubona,* if it had been fairly stated by Mr. Fearon, might have led the British reader to suppose, nor American, as stated by the reviewer. The slightest acquaintance with the strict regulations laid upon American vessels and their captains would have prevented many of the misstatements which have appeared in English journals and travels. These regulations, carefully enforced, have raised the character of the American traders throughout Europe, and rendered the law passed by the national Congress less necessary on account of their own vessels than those of other nations.†

---

* The port of Baltimore is also resorted to by redemptioners. I believe the regulations under which the trade is there placed differ in little from those of Philadelphia.

† The particulars given in the text were first received by the author from an English gentleman, long resident in Philadelphia, and were afterwards confirmed to her from many other sources equally authentic. The reader will find the same detailed more minutely in the eighteenth article of the twenty-seventh number, and the first article of the twenty-eighth number of the *North*

Enquiring concerning Joseph Bonaparte in our way here, I learn that he is about to purchase or lease a house upon the Delaware, about ten miles below the ruins of his former residence. This neighbourhood has been endeared to him by the friendly behaviour of the people upon the occasion of his late misfortune. You will probably have seen in the papers, though I should not have written it to you, that the mansion in which we saw him last summer was some months since burned to the ground. His Canovas were mostly saved, all indeed except three, but they were among the most valued; his pictures also and many of his books; still, however, the loss was considerable, and if it be true that this included some family papers of importance, perhaps irreparable. He entered his gates, returning from Philadelphia, just as the roof fell in. All the neighbourhood was collected, and men and women striving, at the hazard of their lives, to save his property from the flames, he had himself to call them, and even to force them from the walls. The count seems to have been somewhat amazed by the honesty of his republican neighbours, and they, I am told, were no less amazed at his amazement. Possibly his letter of thanks appeared in your papers; if not, I throw it into this packet.

*Translation of a letter of the Comte de Survilliers (Joseph Bonaparte) on the sub-
ject of the loss of his house by fire, to William Snowden, Esq., Judge and Justice
of the Peace, Bordentown.*

Point Breeze, Jan. 8th, 1820.
"Sir,

"You have shown so much interest for me since I have been in this country, and especially since the event of the 4th instant, that I cannot doubt it will afford you pleasure to make known to your fellow citizens how much I feel all that they have done for me on that occasion. Absent myself from my house, they collected by a spontaneous impulse on the first appearance of the fire, which

---

American Review. That the English reviewer to whom the author has adverted in the text may be fully satisfied of the accuracy of her statement, she extracts from the Boston journal the attesta-tion of a German nobleman, dispatched by the minister plenipotentiary of the king of the Nether-lands, in the German diet, to America, for the purpose of procuring farther encouragement for the reception of the poor Germans in Pennsylvania and of examining into their condition in that coun-try. In the very year and month that Mr. Fearon wrote his account of the ships engaged in this trade, this German ambassador wrote the following:
"It is usually Dutch, but occasionally also American, Swedish, Russian, and English vessels which transport the emigrants to America. The ships made use of in this service are commonly of the worst quality, old and unseaworthy, and the commanders sent in them ignorant, inexperienced, and brutal characters. The American ships are the best, and deserve the preference before the others: they sail quicker, the treatment is better, *and the responsibility of the captains is greater.*" [4] This will explain how the law, passed by the Congress, was directed more against foreign than Ameri-can vessels.

they combated with united courage and perseverance, and, when they found it was impossible to extinguish it, exerted themselves to save all that the flames had not destroyed before their arrival and mine.

"All the furniture, statues, pictures, money, plate, gold, jewels, linen, books, and in short everything that was not consumed, has been most scrupulously delivered into the hands of the people of my house. In the night of the fire and during the next day, there were brought to me, by labouring men, drawers in which I have found the proper quantity of pieces of money, and medals of gold, and valuable jewels, which might have been taken with impunity. This event has proved to me how much the inhabitants of Bordentown appreciate the interest I have always felt for them, and shows that men in general are good when they are not perverted in their youth by a bad education, when they maintain their dignity as men and feel that true greatness is in the soul, and depends upon ourselves.

"I cannot omit on this occasion to repeat what I have said so often, that the Americans are the most happy people I have known; still more happy, if they understand well their happiness.

"I pray you not to doubt of my sincere regard.

Yours, &c.

Joseph, Comte de Survilliers."

While I have been writing, our vessel has made its way many miles down the Delaware; pitch and toss, pitch and toss! The wind has risen very suddenly and now blows a hurricane. We are likely to have a rough passage. I must seek the deck and see who and what are our fellow passengers. A face peeped into the cabin just now that looked very English, and a sentence with the Lancashire accent, now sounding on the stairs, seems to sanction my reading of the physiognomy. There is a grey duffle cloak, too, that seems not in the fashion of this country. Apropos to this cloak, I must express my concern for the too frequent deficit of such an article in the wardrobe of an American lady. Truly my teeth have chattered when I have seen in the streets of New York in the month of January, when the mercury stood but few degrees above zero, troops of young women in such attire as might have suited Euphrosynes[5] in the sweet days of May: no furs, no boots, no woollen hose, no, nor even woollen garb wore the delicate creatures, but silks, and feathers, and slippers, as gay as the sparkling skies that shone above them, or the glistering snows they trod upon. But here is too serious trifling with youth and health, and the prevalence of consumption proves the danger and the folly of this sacrifice of comfort to appearance. It is, doubtless, a cruel thing to bury a pretty ankle in a fur-lined boot or a stocking of worsted, and a well-turned throat and delicate waist in a coat with triple capes, but I would fain put it to the good sense of my fair friends in this country, if it is not more cruel to be cramped with rheumatism, or tortured with toothache, or sent out of the world in the very springtime of youth by a painful and lingering disease. I would that Franklin were alive to read them a lesson upon the folly of sacrificing health and life upon the altar of fashion: he would say more to them in a pleasant fable of ten lines than a wordy moralist or learned physician in a lecture of a thousand pages. But would they listen to an old sage any more than they would to me? Youth must buy its own experience, and the wisdom of our fathers usually lies on the shelf till we have split on all the rocks from which it would have warned us.

LETTER XXVII.

Baltimore. Yellow Fever at Fells Point. Appearance of the City. Miscellaneous.

Baltimore, April 1820.

My Dear Friend,

We pushed alongside of the wharf between two and three in the morning, and so gently that, but for the sudden pause of the machinery, we slumbering passengers should have received no intimation of the circumstance. Ascending to the deck before sunrise, we encountered the last drops of a spring shower, the loud pattering of which we had heard for some time over our heads, and had apprehended in consequence a comfortless termination to our journey; but "fiercer war, sooner peace" says a vulgar proverb, which, perhaps, you will call me vulgar for quoting, and a cloud which in our misty island takes a week or a month to dissolve itself will perform the operation here in a few minutes. I have seen rain in this country and taken it on my shoulders like the breaking of a waterspout; great on such occasions is the bustle and hurry of the forlorn wights exposed to the elements. You will hear a horseman whistle to his steed, who, on his part, seems scarcely to wait the hint of his master, and see a saunterer collect his limbs and set them to their full speed as though Death were behind him. I have often in fancy contrasted such a scene with that which a street or highway presents in England when the heavens are weeping from sunrise to sunset. The quiescent traveller, with slouched hat, close-buttoned coat, and dripping umbrella, holding on his way with measured steps and a face composed to patient endurance, neither expecting compassion from the elements nor seeking it from his fellow creatures.

This city is singularly neat and pretty, I will even say beautiful. It is possible that in the first gaze I threw upon it, it owed something to the hour, the season, and the just fallen shower of sweet spring rain, but what is there in life that owes not to time and circumstance the essence of its evil or its good? We looked forth from our cabin in the still grey dawn and paced awhile up and down the spacious deck of the lordly steamboat to enjoy the scene and the hour, to which the scene owed much. All yet was silent in the city—silent as the unpierced

247

forests of the West—not a foot trod the quays or was heard upon the pavements of the streets that branched from them, not a figure was seen on the decks or in the shrouds of the vessels that lay around us, the very air was sleeping, and the shipping reposed on the waters of the little bay (formed here by an inlet of the Patapsco), which lay motionless as the thin wreaths of vapor which hung above them. There is something strangely impressive in such a death of sound and motion in the very heart and centre of the haunts of men. A condensed population of thousands thus hushed to repose, all their hopes, and fears, and sorrows, and ambitions, steeped in forgetfulness, unconscious and unapprehensive of the checks and the crosses, and the pains and the weariness, which the big eventful day is to bring forth. If there is an hour in the twenty four that disposes one more than another to moralize upon the fate and condition of man, it is that which follows upon the first peep of dawn. The silence of the earth and skies is yet more profound than at night's mid-noon, while the mind more forcibly contrasts it with the busy hum and stir of life that is so instantly about to succeed. Even in the dead solitudes of the American wilderness, I have felt the impressive stillness of this hour: the black forests have stood more still, the vast waters have slept more profoundly, the mists lay more dense and unbroken, the work of nature seemed interrupted, her maternal eye closed and her pulse stopped.

The projecting point, whose curve forms one side of the little harbour in which we were moored, lined with wharfs and quays, was the seat of the pestilence of which such fearful and exaggerated accounts were spread last autumn, but the evil here, if less than report made it, was sufficiently alarming. The malignant nature of the disease, the silent enlargement of the seat of its contagion, the suddenness of its seizure, the rapidity of its progress, and the loathsomeness of its last stage, which renders the wretched object sinking beneath its virulence a sight of disgust even to the eye of affection, and the uncertainty which has hitherto existed (excepting in the unwholesome districts of the south Atlantic states, where its abode being more or less continual, its nature is better understood, the imagination more familiarized with its terrors, and the constitution more proof against its poison), the uncertainty which, excepting in these districts, has existed regarding the cause of its appearance and the manner in which its progress might be arrested—all this well explains the terror which its very name excites in those cities, which have only been subjected to the visitation at long intervals, and where tradition hands down the tale of its former ravages and the horrors with which they were fraught.

In this city, though the seat of contagion was of much greater extent than in that of New York, yet its limits were equally defined. A line might have been drawn across the streets, on the verge of which you might stand with impunity and beyond which it was death to pass. Had this line been drawn, and drawn too at the first appearance of the disease before time had been afforded it for the enlargement of its precincts (for the infected atmosphere slowly eating its way onwards, where it may be safe for you to breathe today, you may inhale poison tomorrow), and had the inhabitants, both the sick and the well, been removed from the seat of contagion, as was done in New York, and as I wrote you with perfect success, the fever would have died in the birth, instead of rankling and spreading as it did until it was killed by the winter's frost. The mistaken notion which here, as in Boston, prevailed, that the poison had been brought in a vessel from the south, prevented this precaution and prevented also any remedy being applied to the real cause of the evil—a cause so apparent that nothing but the obstinacy incident to the adherence to a favourite system could have blinded the people to its existence.* The nest of the fever here, as in New York, lay in the stagnant waters of the wharfs, into which the neighbouring inhabitants are in the habit of throwing vegetables and other refuse. The intense and unusually prolonged heats of the summer could not fail to render them so many reservoirs of putrefaction. These wharfs, too, and many of the houses adjoining have been raised upon forced ground, into which the water oozing, prepares against the hot months a rank bed, fatally propitious to the nurture of disease, if not sufficient for its conception. It is to be hoped that the possibility of inbred infection is now sufficiently established to leave no doubt upon the minds of the inhabitants of the northern cities of the imperative necessity of rigid cleanliness, which can alone prevent the appearance of yellow fever, in the event of a season of unusual and prolonged heat. That which, in a temperate climate, might be accounted as finical nicety, may barely suffice to keep the atmosphere untainted in the low and more populous quarters of cities lying under a sun whose fervors will often raise the mercury to ninety and upwards for days successively. While the infected air was gradually spreading along Fells Point and the low streets in its immediate vicinity, the higher parts of the town were perfectly healthy, and, though the sick were removed into it, no infection was there received, nor, after the first wild alarm had subsided, was it so much as apprehended.

We have met the summer in this city. In New York, though the grass had hastily spread its first carpet, we left no appearance of leaves, except that on the earlier trees the buds were ready to burst. In Philadelphia I remarked some green specks on the branches, but here it seemed like stepping into fairyland, when, leaving the vessel, we turned into a clean broad street, lined with balsam

* See No. 27th of the *North American Review* for some curious particulars of the malignant fever which appeared in Boston, New York, and Baltimore, during the autumn of the year 1819.

poplars, the fragrance of whose young leaves, glistering with raindrops, perfumed the air. We proceeded with our new friends—but you know not who they are. I will go through the ceremony of introduction. I wrote in my last letter of an English face and duffle cloak. These might not seem to promise much; and, as to the first, let alone the one in question and some others whom I shall name, and some others of whom you are aware, though they, indeed, have ta'en so long the burning gaze of America's sun, as to have well nigh lost their native character—but let alone these, and I must confess, however the confession might displease my countrymen, that an English face has seldom been a sight that has caused me much satisfaction on this side the Atlantic. Voltaire describes a travelling *Milord;* the picture might suit here many a travelling Mr., and some lords too, for a few noble faces have at odd times been seen in this land of plain citizens, and all were not like the unassuming, gentlemanly, enlightened Selkirk. Were I disposed to play upon words, I might say that the English people are as ill *represented* here as they are at home. The ordinary travellers who honor this republican earth with the touch of their feet are stragglers from Canada, who, besides coming and going from and to Europe by the way of New York as a more convenient port than Montreal or Quebec, will sometimes condescend so far as to yawn away a summer month or two, in spying out a few corners of the great nest of presumptuous democrats stretching south of them; and who, running through a few of their towns and cities, sometimes without looking to the right hand or the left, and sometimes entering the open door and seizing the open hand of America's kind citizen that they may afterwards, at their leisure, with better opportunity, jeer at the manners and traduce the character of the people whose hospitality they have shared. How is it that men can breathe the winds that have blown over the land of liberty, whose sacred shores even are within their sight, without inhaling something of the spirit of independence? And how can they see that land and contemplate the joyful scene of its prosperity—its towns and cities springing as it were out of the earth at the touch of a magician, its active and industrious population, spreading over regions boundless in extent and inexhaustible in fertility, carrying into the desert, before untrodden save by the foot of the savage or the beast of prey, the arts of peace, the lights of knowledge, and all the wealth and blessings of civilization—how can they contemplate this, a sight as novel as it is beautiful, without feeling their hearts expand with joyful, and proud, and generous sympathy? And yet our countrymen will often travel from the Dan to the Beersheba of this republic and contrive to shut their hearts from every generous feeling and their understandings from every conviction, finding, and so giving, nothing but vexation of spirit, and returning to the land of their fathers to traduce, in the name of the United States of America, the name of liberty, and, in that of their people, the names of public virtue and of private happiness. But what a strange exordium this to the English face and the duffle cloak! I know of nought that they have in common with the travellers to whom I have alluded. Things, however, are as often associated in our heads by contrast as by resemblance, and so in this case has it been with the English face and cloak, to which you shall now be introduced without farther digression or pre-amble. The owner of the face was—Who think you? A dozen guesses, and you have him not. Remember you, now some six-and-twenty years ago, to have seen in your house at ————— a young man of the name of Taylor? I little ex-pected in the vigorous and fresh-looking stranger, who carried his years so lightly that I hesitated to write him under the head of fifty, an old acquaintance of my dearest friend. It was not till after much conversation with him and his companions that I made this discovery, which you may suppose did not weaken the bond that similarity of sentiment upon the subjects on which we had pre-viously conversed had made between us. It will please you to hear that this your old friend wears on through his manhood the honorable feelings of his youth—no small, at least no common merit in old Europe, whose rulers so rarely fail to prove that the patriot has his price. His companions are a lady and gentle-man from Lincolnshire, whose acquaintance is a source of so much pleasure to us as to make us deeply regret that fortune was not kind enough to throw us earlier together. During our descent of the Delaware, we were too much tor-mented by the wind, which blew a heavy gale in our faces, to have any disposi-tion for conversation, but when, towards sunset, we exchanged water for land carriage and found ourselves shut into the same vehicle with three English travellers, we began to examine their faces, and, liking their language and they perhaps not disliking that of ours, dialogue commenced.

There are few accidents in life more agreeable than those which, in a foreign land, bring together wanderers from the same native soil, that is, when they are not of the class of Matthew Bramble, or Smelfungus, or ＊＊＊＊, &c.[1] Reaching the Elk River, the winds had hushed to sleep, and the hour and our long jour-ney might have seemed to warn us to follow the example, but once more on board of a steamboat, upon whose deck we could now keep our feet without holding a fight for the privilege with the enraged household of Æolus, we felt no disposition to separate until we had compared our sentiments and exchanged much of our information regarding the country in which we all met as wan-derers. In Baltimore we felt no disposition to part, and they being also bound to Washington, where they had passed the greater part of the winter, we made our arrangements for the day together and first (to go back a few pages) we proceeded in company to take a hasty view of the city.

Baltimore is not the least wonderful evidence of the amazing and almost inconceivable growth of this country. At the time of the Revolution, but forty-five years since, this city, which now contains a population of sixty-five thousands and has all the appearance of an opulent and beautiful metropolis, comprised some thirty houses of painted or unpainted frame, with perhaps as many of logs scattered in their vicinity. If this does not confound your understanding, it has well nigh confounded mine. Dutchmen or their descendants were not the surveyors here as in New York, where it is thought proper, when a street is planned, to shave the earth of every inequality, as though it were intended to preserve to the city the appearance of having been transported ready-made from Holland, in the manner of the house at Loretto, from Jerusalem. Baltimore, on the contrary, is spread over three gentle hills; the streets, without sharing the fatiguing regularity and unvarying similarity of those of Philadelphia, are equally clean, cheerful, and pleasingly ornamented with trees. The poplar, which in the country is offensive, not merely to the eye but to the understanding, being there destitute alike of beauty and utility, has a singularly pleasing effect in a city where its architectural form is in unison with the regularity and neatness which should everywhere prevail. I mean not, however, to prefer it to nobler trees, which, independent of superior beauty, have the farther advantage of healthy longevity and are not afflicted with the troublesome blight that frequently renders the poplar alive with caterpillars, which sometimes despoil the branches in midsummer and rain in offensive multitudes on the shoulders of passengers. To remove this inconvenience, the citizens of New York have removed their poplars, but I own that, notwithstanding my objection to the caterpillars, I never saw one of the guilty poplars fall without regret, the more so, because I saw no preparations made for supplying the vacancies with forest trees. I could wish that the householders in American towns would, on this matter as on all others, remember the advice of Franklin, whose wise mind, embracing the infinitely little as well as the infinitely great, considered no trifle below its notice that was connected with the comfort and well-being of man.

You see here, as in Philadelphia, the same neat houses of well-made and well-painted brick, the same delicately white doors, with their shining knockers and handles, and their steps of clean white marble, and windows with their green Venetian shutters. Considerable attention and expense have also been bestowed upon the public edifices, which, however, are chiefly remarkable for neatness and convenience, seldom making pretentions to architectural beauty. Some buildings of a different character are now erecting, in a style which does honor to the taste and public spirit of the community. I have heard, indeed, the citizens of Baltimore charged in this particular with undue extravagance. However this may be, we felt ourselves much indebted to them, when, heated with fatigue and want of rest, we suddenly came upon a spacious fountain, where the clear, cold water, gushing fresh from the spring, ran gurgling over a channelled floor of marble. In a neighbouring square, a clustered column of simple and pure architecture is raising to the memory of those who fell in the gallant defence of the city at the close of the late war; on the pedestal of the column is a blank stone, on which are simply engraved the names of the dead who are interred beneath. The thoughtless military leader and the calculating politician might smile at this enumeration of some hundred names. We cannot better contrast the feelings of such men than with an anecdote which recurs to me at the moment. During the war, when a body of American militia had repulsed a party of invaders and were pursuing them to their ships, the commanding officer suddenly called them from the pursuit. A citizen, surprised and irritated at the order, seeing the possibility of cutting off the retreat of the enemy, reproachfully observed that ere they could gain their boats, two thirds might be dead or prisoners. "True," calmly replied the other, having first enforced the order for retreat, "we might possibly, with the loss of a dozen men, have deprived the enemy of some hundreds, but what would have been the dozen?—sons, husbands, fathers, and useful citizens. And what would have been the hundreds? —men fighting for hire. Which loss in the balance had weighed the heavier?"

When we read of the fall of the three hundred at Thermopylæ, we feel something more than when we read of that of the legions of Varus in the wilds of Germany, and I own that I looked with deeper interest upon this memorial to a few private citizens, who fell in the defence of their domestic hearths and whose corpses were washed by the tears of bereaved mothers, widows, and orphans, than I ever did upon the proudest monument erected to the thousands sacrificed to kingly ambition. And I doubt if, in this sentiment, I am peculiar; I doubt, I mean, if the costly monuments that adorn the empires of Europe are regarded with the same deep and lasting interest by their people, as is this simple record by the citizens of America's republic. There, too often, the glory is monopolized and the honor awarded to the individual whose personal ambition, or whose talent, submitted to the ambition of a master, leads unnumbered and unknown thousands to the field of slaughter, and there places on his single brow the laurels steeped in the sweat and blood of the unheeded myriads, dead and dying, who surround him. And is it to be believed that, when the first mad frenzy of the multitude has subsided, they will see in the proud trophies, marked with the name of a Napoleon or a Wellington, much to rouse their sympathy or even their pride? The hero who lives in the hearts of a people is not he who has achieved the most numerous and imposing conquests, who has wrought the most daring exploits and seen the most costly memorials raised to his name; it is he who has struggled for the existence or defence of his country, whose patience and energy were exerted not so much to destroy its foes as to shield its sons; he it is, whose cause being that of his nation, so also is his dignity and his fame. The chariots of the Cæsars were followed by acclaiming multitudes, and their achievements live in the annals of their empire, but their names lived not in the hearts of the Romans, as did those of the Camillus and the Fabius, whose sword and whose shield were the saviours of the infant republic. We have seen the eagles of Napoleon overthrown, and have heard his name die on the lips of his people, but the memorials of Washington are beyond the reach of fortune as of time: seated in the hearts of America's citizens, their number increases with every child that is born to the republic, and will be lasting as the nation whose independence he assisted to establish. And thus, in like manner, is it that this simple commemoration of a few private individuals excites more interest in the mind of the spectator than the proudest trophies raised to unknown thousands who fell, they knew not wherefore, in a foreign land.

It would be difficult to imagine a more interesting scene than was here exhibited during the engagement which this monument is raised to commemorate. If the burning of Washington excited the whole continent, it more peculiarly called forth the spirit as well as the fears of Baltimore, from whose heights was distinctly descried the glow diffused through the atmosphere by the flames of the Capitol. An instantaneous attack was apprehended, but of the short interval which unexpectedly elapsed before the enemy ascended the Chesapeake, not a moment was lost. The whole population of Baltimore laboured on the entrenchments and in throwing up fortifications; troops of volunteers poured in from the neighbouring states of Pennsylvania and Virginia, and the most distinguished citizens of Maryland were found in the ranks of the battalions collected round the city. The city itself, on the day and night of the engagement, was peopled only by women and infants. Every man, from the decrepid veteran to the boy whose arm could scarcely steady the musket, was without the walls, in the character of a soldier. The death of General Ross is ascribed to a beardless youth, for whose hand the rifle which he pointed with unerring certainty was almost too heavy.[2] War in this country assumes a character so different from that which it wears in Europe that it is impossible to regard it with the same feelings. Who can consider without interest an army of citizens just summoned from their domestic hearths? the farmer, the lawyer, the merchant, the statesman, the private gentleman, converted into soldiers at the threshold of their own habitations for the defence of all that is most dear to men. Conceive, too, the position of this deserted city; the hearts which here beat with agony during the day and night that the cannon roared in the very harbour, each thunder of which seemed to sound the knell of a father and a husband. It was an affecting scene, as described by those who witnessed it, when the enemy withdrew and the citizens returned to their anxious homes, bearing with them the silent few whose hearts were now cold amid the impatience and joy that surrounded them. The soldier falls unregarded on a foreign soil, his remains left, perhaps, to the bleaching elements or thrown into a hasty grave by his weary and reckless comrades, or it may be by the very strangers whose lands he has invaded, whose laws he has trampled on, and whose brethren he has slain. Not so the citizen who falls on his native soil, amid his friends and relatives, by the hand of the invader raised against his country and himself. Here borne on the shoulders of his brethren, the father was brought to the house of his children, the son to that of his parent. The tears of agony bedewed the corpse, the hand of affection straightened the limbs, and performed the last duties to the dead, and when at length the sacred dust was consigned to its element, the assembled citizens formed the long line of the funeral procession, moving through silent streets, where the tumult of joy was hushed into the deep solemnity of mourning.

War is styled a necessary evil. Most truly it is so in countries burthened with standing armies, for if not employed in making war upon each other abroad, some late occurrences in England show us that they will attack their fellow citizens at home; but could a miracle destroy all the regular troops of Europe, where then were "Othello's occupation?"

> Curse on the crimson'd plumes, the banners flouting,
> The stirring clarion, the leader's shouting,
> The fair caparisons, the war-horse champing,
> The array'd legions pressing, rushing, tramping,
> The blazing falchions, crests that toss afar,
> The bold emprise, the spirit-rousing jar,
> The swelling pæans, thundering acclaim
> The death of glory, and the living fame,
> The sculptor's monument, the people's bays,
> The historian's narrative, the poet's lays;
> Oh! curse on all the splendour and the show,
> Which veileth o'er the fiendish hell below!
>
> *Thoughts of a Recluse.*

Threading the streets until we reached their extremity, we found ourselves at the foot of a little hill, sprinkled with trees, upon whose top is a noble column, raised to Washington, of similar form but of larger dimensions than that mentioned above. Ascending to it, we saw this beautiful little city spread at our feet, its roofs and intermingling trees shining in the morning sun, the shipping riding in the basin and crowded round the point, while, in the distance, the vast waters of the Chesapeake, and more near those of its tributary rivers, gleamed in broad lines of silver through the dark extent of forested plains that stretched beyond the more cultivated precincts of the young city. We made our return by a church that has been recently built by an extensive Unitarian congregation, and, being now fairly spent with fatigue, we rested on its steps, while one of our party ran to obtain the key of the clergyman, who was of his acquaintance. I do assure you at that moment I marvelled at his activity; what with a long walk, superadded to a long journey and two sleepless nights, I felt amazingly disposed to make a pillow of the marble. And here I recall an anecdote, told by himself of our friend * * * *. At the close of a tour through Europe, he asked of his host in some German town, what was to be seen. "Nothing," replied the host. "Thank God!" exclaimed the traveller. I was probably too dull to have this or anything else in my head at the moment, but I doubt not that would anyone have obligingly told me that there was nothing to be seen in that chapel, I should in like manner have returned thanks. I did, however, open my eyes upon entering it, and have seldom seen anything more simply elegant than the style of its interior. This beautiful church is close adjoining to that of a congregation of Roman Catholics, a circumstance that well exemplifies the liberality and Christian charity which is diffused among Christians of all persuasions throughout these democracies and which has been bred and fostered by that perfect liberty of action and opinion and those just laws, which, imparting equal rights and protection to the members of every church, teach the citizens that as they are all equal in the sight of earthly justice, so are they also in that of heaven.

It is not without a feeling of respect that the eye turns upon the Roman Catholic Church of Maryland, which may be truly regarded as the most venerable in the world. Those who denounce Christians of the Romish persuasion as bigoted persecutors surely forget that they gave the first example to the world of religious liberty. So true is it that illiberality or its opposite must be ascribed rather to the character of the age or of the individual than to the tenets of any particular church.

I regret that we have not more time to bestow on this city, which is interesting not only from the amazing rapidity of its growth, its neatness and beauty, but from the character of its citizens—peculiarly marked for courtesy, as well as for high spirit and daring enterprise. To these last qualities, indeed, must be attributed all the wonderful creations of the place. It is thought, however, that

Baltimore, like a promising child, has somewhat outgrown her strength. The ratio of her increase diminishes greatly, and it may perhaps be doubted whether, in the fallen state of commerce, she will extend her present limits for many years. By-the-bye, I see it is common on your side of the Atlantic to confound the wealth of America with that of her merchants; perhaps the depressed state of commerce should rather be considered as an evidence of the growing prosperity of this people, the fact being that they now make at home what they before received from abroad.* As the revenue is here drawn from the customs, the treasury affords no standard by which to judge of the internal resources of the country. The wealth of this young republic is not locked up in her seaports, but is spread through a community to whom want and oppression are unknown. The broken fortunes of her merchants may dim the splendour of her cities, but can subtract little from the aggregate of her strength, while the check that is thus given to luxury and extravagance can only produce beneficial effects on the national character. It is thought that a new mode of taxation must shortly be adopted; perhaps a well-regulated tax upon property may supersede the present system. A very slight one would suffice to defray the expenses of this economical government and have the advantage of yielding a certain return, whereas, at present, the revenue is continually fluctuating and always threatens to leave the government aground in the very moment of extreme exigency. The danger and utter inefficiency of the present system was fully proved in the late war; as it was not destroyed then, it will now in all probability find its own euthanasia, unless indeed Europe should correct her policy, of which I suppose there is little likelihood. It seems, however, that this sovereign people are determined to see their present system of finance die a natural death before they will have recourse to another. The Americans, it must be confessed, have some

---

* I believe it is not generally known in this country how completely some of the home fabrics have superseded the foreign in the American market. It is here supposed by many that the higher price of labour must prevent competition with the manufactures of Europe, but this drawback is balanced by other advantages: provisions are cheap, the raw material of first-rate quality is found in the country, and there are no taxes. The blankets and broadcloths, woven of the Merino wool, are not only in the average of superior quality, but can often undersell in the market those of Europe. The same is the case with the coarse cotton goods. I have seen cotton cloth, woven in New York, at a cent per yard, and in strength of fabric that of Europe will bear no comparison with it. The object here is to put as little of the raw material into the yard as possible; there is not the same temptation to this in America. It may be observed also that, the employment of machinery now enabling women to perform work which formerly demanded the agency of men, there is much less difference in the price of labour employed in some of the manufactories, in Britain and America, than is here supposed. American woman universally prefer employment in a cotton mill to domestic service, which they always feel to be a degradation. In accounting for any fact which, in America, strikes the foreigner as singular, he must always seek part of its explanation in the national character, which, influenced by the political institutions, is there probably more peculiarly marked than in any other country.

whims which seem peculiar to themselves; of these, not the least singular is an inherent innate antipathy to taxgatherers. Our good-natured islanders will support legions of these itinerant gentlemen and consent to surrender at their request the very coat off their backs and the bread out of their mouths, but our transatlantic brethren will not so much as part with a shred of the one or a crumb of the other. They will pay no taxes at all. What would the chancellor of the British Exchequer say to such obstinacy? How would his collectors of the revenue look around them in a country where their talents were in no request, and where even their right to existence was called in question!

LETTER XXVIII.

Washington. The Capitol. Hall of the Representatives. Senate Chamber. The President. Virginia Slavery. Conclusion.

Washington, April 1820.

My Dear Friend,

I am this evening fairly exhausted with heat and fatigue and in consequence have been forced to decline an invitation to a party which promised us much pleasure, from the individuals whom I understand to have been assembled. I could not take the liberty with them that I shall with you of being as dull as inclination or infirmity may dispose me, and here I only assume the privilege, which others have assumed before me, namely, of showing to a familiar friend a face that I might be ashamed to show to an indifferent world.

The road from Baltimore hither, about forty miles, leads through an uninteresting and, for the most part, barren district. On losing sight of the city, the traveller might think that he had lost sight of all the beauty and all the wealth of the state; there are, however, in Maryland, districts of great fertility, especially in the neighbourhood of the eastern waters. We observed some farms in good order and good cultivation and here, on the 19th of April, we saw rye full in the ear. We noticed also some hedgerows, which make a far more comfortable appearance than wooden fences. But these more interesting objects were unfrequent, and, tired of considering stunted trees or wastes of exhausted land (exhausted by the noxious weed tobacco, and left to be reclaimed by a more needy generation), we began to contemplate our fellow travellers. Added to our party was an old veteran, who seemed to have passed the written age of man, and a younger native, who appeared to be cheerfully entering upon the world which the other was about to quit. We had proceeded some miles before either of our new companions addressed himself to any of our party; from our conversation, they perceived us to be foreigners and waited to judge from the same to what class we belonged. I have observed that when the American stumbles upon a foreigner, he is wont, during a few minutes, to take a quiet perusal of his physiognomy, and, if opportunity permits, to remain the silent auditor of his remarks and comments and thus to satisfy himself of the temper of the man, before he evinces any disposition to make him his companion. If he likes his temper, he will then enter at once into the most easy and friendly intercourse, readily imparting his own information and gratefully receiving that of the stranger in return. And then I have frequently admired the deference with which he listens to his opinions, however they may differ from his own, or militate against the institutions of his country, the good temper with which he receives his strictures upon the national character, and the candor with which he points out errors and flaws which may have escaped the observation of the foreigner. If he like *not* his temper, he will entrench himself in the most careless and quiet indifference, apparently regardless of all that passes around him. It is only for an observing eye to detect, in the unruffled countenance of the mute republican, the suppressed smile which forms his humourous, though unsuspected commentary, upon the conversation of his uncourteous companions. An anecdote here recurs to me, as illustrative of this trait in the American character.

In a public conveyance in this country, an English traveller was drawing comparisons between America and his native island. The houses were barns, compared to what they were in England, the public conveyances were waggons, compared to an English coach, and so on, with all the conveniences and necessaries of life, the beef and the mutton, fish, flesh, and fowl. While he was speaking, a sudden storm gathered and a loud peal of the awful thunder, which, in this fervid clime, so nobly shakes the concave, cracked over the zenith and split the thread of the traveller's harangue. An American, who had hitherto sat silent and unnoticed in a corner of the vehicle, then leaned forwards, and gravely addressing the foreigner, "Sir, have you any better thunder than that in England?" I do not say that all the citizens can turn aside the wrath of man by such a reply as our venerable friend * * * *, who once, in travelling, finding it necessary to expostulate with the keeper of a turnpike and being in consequence greeted by the appellation of rascal, pleasantly retorted, "Your hand, friend! There are a pair of us." But the species of humour which framed this reply is here certainly a national characteristic, and I doubt not is of considerable service in keeping the peace among this proud community.

We did not care to put to the test the philosophy of our fellow travellers, who soon joined in our conversation. The old veteran fought over again the battles of the Revolution and gave us many interesting anecdotes of that period. We learned that he was bound, for the first and last time, on a pilgrimage to the infant capital, being desirous, he said, to see the city that bore the name of his old general and to look upon the seat of government once before he died. The morning after our arrival, while ascending the steps of the Capitol with several members of Congress, we perceived the old soldier at an angle of this fine building, leaning on his staff and looking down upon the young Rome, for whose liberties he had bled.

Those who, in visiting Washington, expect to find a city will be somewhat surprised when they first enter its precincts and look round in vain for the appearance of a house.

The plan marked out for this metropolis of the empire is gigantic, and the public buildings, whether in progress or design, bear all the stamp of grandeur. How many centuries shall pass away ere the clusters of little villages, now scattered over this plain, shall assume the form and magnificence of an imperial city? Were the heart to form a prayer for this republic, would it not be that the term of her youth might be long protracted? Which of her patriots can anticipate, without anxiety, the period when the road to the senate house shall lead through streets adorned with temples and palaces? and when the rulers of the republic, who now take their way on foot to the council chamber, in the fresh hour of morning, shall roll in chariots at midnoon, or perhaps midnight, through a sumptuous metropolis, rich in arts and bankrupt in virtue? Is such to be the destiny of this new-born empire? Heaven avert it! and I do more than hope that it is to be averted. At all events, you and I, my dear friend, shall long have been in our graves, ere the flush of youth and pride of liberty can forsake this favoured democracy.

I envy not the man who can enter without emotion the noble, though still unfinished, structure of the American Capitol. Never shall I forget the feelings with which I first looked down from the gallery of the hall upon the assembled representatives of a free and sovereign nation. Is there, in the whole range of this peopled earth, a sight more sublime? When the English friends who accompanied us first visited the Congress, some months since, the words that struck their ear, as they entered the gallery, formed part of the prayer with which the business of the day opens: "May the rod of tyranny be broken in every nation of the earth!" Mrs. ****, her husband told me, burst into tears. Were I curious to try the soul of a European, I should wish to see him enter the house of the American Congress. I defy a native of that Continent who has a soul not to find it at that moment. Yes, my dear friend, while this edifice stands, liberty has an anchorage from which the congress of European autocrats cannot unmoor her. Truly I am grateful to this nation; the study of their history and institutions, and the consideration of the peace and happiness which they enjoy, has thawed my heart and filled it with hopes which I had not thought it could know again. After all, we are fortunately constituted:

when we cease to feel for ourselves, we can better feel for others, and the pleasure of sympathy, if it be not as intense, is perhaps more pure than that of enjoyment.

We of course considered with much interest some of the more distinguished members, with whom we were previously only acquainted by report or the public prints, and waited with some curiosity until they should take their turn in the debate. It happened to be one of peculiar animation, and occupied the House for ten successive days: the subject was supplied by the proposed alterations in the tariff. And what may seem singular, they found not a single opposer from the state, or even the city of New York. The opposition to the bill seemed to proceed entirely from the southern planters and some members from New England. The representations from the central and western states were united to a man in flouting poor fallen commerce, whom they seemed to consider as no better than a professional gambler, who had fleeced the citizens of their morals as well as their money. Indeed, it would seem that men can seldom lose the one without the other, and perhaps it is little surprising that the more ardent of this republican race should rejoice in the fall of a deity who, of late years, has reclined one arm on Plutus and the other on bankruptcy; her ruin, however, seems sufficiently complete without any *fulminations from the Capitol*. It is possible, however, that the proposed duties may act as a very fair tax upon wealth, for as the more homely and essential manufactures can now stand their ground in the face of those introduced from abroad, the increase of the customs are chiefly calculated to raise the price of luxuries. I must say that I for one should not be sorry to see foreign silks give place to homespun cottons in the wardrobes of the young women of the Atlantic cities; perhaps, when they are sold half a dollar a yard dearer, this change in the fashions may be effected.

The bill was introduced by Mr. Baldwin, of Pennsylvania, a man of vigorous intellect, with a rough but energetic delivery.[1] The number of able speakers exceeded my expectation, though I had been prepared to find it considerable; they struck me as generally remarkable for close and lucid reasoning, and a plain, but gentlemanly and impressive diction. When Mr. Clay rose, I believe that some apprehension was mingled with our curiosity, for who has not learned from experience that when expectation is much raised, it is usually disappointed? The first words uttered by the Speaker of the House satisfied us that no defect of manner was to break the charm of his eloquence. This distinguished statesman has, for many successive years, been called to preside in the House by an almost unanimous vote, and it is said that no individual ever exercised in it a more powerful influence.[2] He seems, indeed, to unite all the qualities essential to an orator: animation, energy, high moral feeling, ardent patriotism, a sublimed love of liberty, a rapid flow of ideas and of language, a happy vein of irony, an action at once vehement and dignified, and a voice full, sonorous, distinct, and flexible, exquisitely adapted to all the varieties of passion or argument—without exception the most masterly voice that I ever remember to have heard. It filled the large and magnificent hall without any apparent effort on the part of the orator. In conversation he is no less eloquent than in debate, and no sooner does he kindle with his subject than his voice and action betray the orator of the hall; yet so unpremeditated is his language that even in a drawing room, the orator never appears misplaced. From the perusal of his speeches, you may have formed some idea of the ardor of feeling and expression which characterize this statesman but you must have heard one delivered to understand their effect in the national senate.

The influence of a masterly orator in the American Congress would somewhat surprise the invulnerable and immoveable majorities of the British House of Commons. The check to this influence remains with the nation, whose wishes, upon important questions, must, of course, more or less affect the decision of their representatives. But the voice of the sovereign people is not altogether absolute and by no means undisputed. If the people be proud, so also are their agents in Congress, and few are found who will passively surrender their right of judgment to their employers. Besides, the probability is that their employers will often differ among themselves, a circumstance which must leave their agents pretty much to the direction of their own reason. The power of an orator, therefore, if checked, is not destroyed by the responsibility of the members, as the sway exercised by the great western statesman appears sufficiently to demonstrate.

Mr. Clay has been understood to head a powerful opposition to some measures of the existing executive, an opposition chiefly, if not exclusively, directed against the policy pursued towards the rising democracies of the southern continent. It has been the aim of this ardent statesman to extort a public acknowledgment of the independence and national existence of these infant republics during their struggle for liberty. The thunders of his eloquence never sounded with more sublimity than on this occasion, and, could their influence have extended to the Senate, might have triumphed over the cold neutrality so obstinately preserved by the American government. Perhaps the policy pursued by the government has been the most wise, certainly the most prudent, but it is difficult not to feel with the orator, who, spurning all calculations of interest or state policy, draws his arguments from the lips of generosity and liberty. It may be doubted whether the neutrality assumed by the government has not in reality been impugned, as well by the supplies furnished to the patriots from some of the wealthy seaports, as by the friendly intercourse carried on privately between the first official characters of Washington and Angostura. But the idea may well suggest itself to an American that the vigorous navy of the republic could never have been more honorably employed than in asserting the liberties of the southern continent, and the unceasing importunity of the illustrious Speaker of the House to extort an open avowal of friendship for the patriots must command the admiration of every generous mind.*

Leaving the city to make a little excursion in Virginia, we missed the speeches of several distinguished members. We returned, however, to attend the close of the debate, which afforded us the opportunity of hearing Mr. Lowndes of Carolina.[3] The close and deductive reasoning of this gentleman forms a striking contrast to the fervid oratory of Mr. Clay. They were opposed in the debate, and each possessed a manner most appropriate to his argument. Mr. Lowndes is singularly correct in his selection of language and turn of the phrase; yet the syllables flow from his lips in an uninterrupted stream, the best word always falling into the right place, not merely without effort but seemingly without the consciousness of the speaker.

We were surprised at the readiness with which even the youngest members took their share in the discussion. The error of these, indeed, seems that of speaking too much, to which may be added another—that of coining new words when old ones do not occur to them. The patience of the House with the more inexperienced or less gifted speakers is truly admirable, and I must observe that, in spite of some inelegance and much prolixity, they appear seldom unworthy of attention, since sound reasoning, liberal philosophy, and generous feeling may generally be discovered through the mass of awkward words supplied by their vehemence.

I have sometimes amused myself in the hall by imagining how one of the marshalled troops of the British minister would look upon an assembly whose members, until the actual counting of the votes, are often ignorant of the issue of the most important questions. At one time, a member told me he expected the bill to be thrown out; a few hours afterwards, his hopes were that it would be carried; again he despaired, again he hoped, and at last listened to the ayes and noes with as much incertitude as myself. During the division, the curiosity of the assembly seemed wrought to the highest pitch of impatience;

---

* At the close of the session, in 1820, Mr. Clay had the satisfaction of seeing his favourite measure carried through both houses, and accredited ministers appointed to the republics of Colombia and Buenos Aires.

the seats were abandoned, and a humming and agitated crowd pressed round the chair, threatening with suffocation both the clerk and the speaker. The sonorous voice of the latter, however, quelled the tempest instantaneously and produced a silence so profound that the drop of a pin might have been heard upon the floor. Mr. Clay afterwards told me that since he had presided in the House, he had never but once seen it equally agitated.

The Senate being occupied in ordinary business, we had no opportunity of judging of its oratory, but being politely admitted on the floor, we admired the elegance of the chamber and made ourselves acquainted with the persons of the senators and the proceedings of the house. The debates of the chamber, as I am informed by some of its members, are conducted with less popular vehemence than those of the hall. I know not if it be the more advanced age of the senators, or the smaller size of the assembly, which imparts to the deliberations their character of senatorial gravity. The age fixed by law for a member of the Senate is thirty-five years, and though one or two gentle-men in the chamber seem to have numbered little more than the lustres demanded, the majority of the assembly have the air of veteran statesmen, some of whom have occupied a seat in the house from its first organization.* [4]

The Congress have met this session in the Capitol for the first time since the conflagration.[5] The two wings of the building (the one occupied by the hall of the Representatives and the other by the Senate chamber and judiciary court) are restored to more than their original grandeur. The centre of the building is still incomplete, though proceeding rapidly. Here is to be the inauguration hall, where the Presidents will be installed and the Congress assemble whenever circumstances may require a meeting of the two houses, also the national library, which a native of England now feels awkward at finding bestowed in a few small apartments; at present it comprises little more than the collection supplied by Mr. Jefferson, but a stated sum being ap-propriated annually to its enlargement, the spoliations of the war will soon, I trust, be effaced. These volumes, however, marked with the name of America's President and philosopher, will always constitute the most interesting portion of the national library. Beneath the central dome of the building are to be entombed the remains of Washington; the statue of the venerable patriot now engages the chisel of Canova.[6]

This skeleton city affords few of the amusements of a metropolis. It seems however to possess the advantage of very choice society. The resident families

---

* The hall of the Representatives also contains some grey-haired veterans. One gentleman was pointed out to me who had sat in the Continental Congress and been regularly returned by his fellow citizens until the present day.

are of course few, but the unceasing influx and reflux of strangers from all parts of the country affords an ample supply of new faces to the evening drawing rooms. To this continual intermixture with strangers and foreigners is perhaps to be ascribed the peculiar courtesy and easy politeness which characterize the manners of the city.

Although now sufficiently familiarized with the simple habits of this republican community, I still find myself occasionally wondering at the world which here surrounds us, and not unfrequently recall the words of an English correspondent addressed to me from this city: "I think it was Bonaparte who observed that from the sublime to the ridiculous, it was but one step. I have fully discovered the truth of this remark in America. When I first came here, I really found myself puzzled to decide as to many things whether they were sublime or ridiculous. The simplicity of manners among the truly great people of this country might at first, by a casual observer, fresh from the glare and frippery of Europe, be termed *ridiculous;* but I have now outlived this feeling and can appreciate it as truly *sublime."* I perfectly acknowledged the influence of that moral sublime, so candidly admitted by my friend, when first addressed by the President of the United States. I meant to rise, or, rather, I afterwards felt that I ought to have risen, but when suddenly introduced to me by a senator, and that with the simple air of a private gentleman and the calmness of a sage, he opened conversation, my recollection for a moment left me, and I fixed my eyes upon the venerable character before me with a silent emotion which he, quietly continuing his discourse, seemed unconscious of having excited, and thus relieved me from the awkwardness of framing an apology for my absence.

Colonel Monroe enjoys the felicity of having witnessed at his election the union of all parties, and of conciliating, during his administration, the esteem and confidence of the whole American nation. His illustrious predecessors having been placed in active political opposition to a strong, and once, a ruling party, of which they effected the overthrow and destruction, were exposed throughout their public career to the enmity of a discomfited minority, an enmity which, though their candor knew how to forgive, their virtues and high-minded forbearance were unable wholly to appease. The existing President came into office at a moment of all others the most fortunate—when the republic had just shaken hands with her foreign and internal enemies—and it had been difficult to find a statesman more fitted, by the benevolence of his character and mild urbanity of his manners, to cement the civil concord than he who was elected.*

---

* I feel tempted to quote a passage from the letter of an American friend, who, after some observations upon the happy spirit of union pervading the United States, subjoins, "All unite in

Would it not mortify some European diplomatists to find the mighty engine of government exposed to every eye as it is here—to behold the rulers of a nation legislating without mystery, and commanding respect by their talents and character and the name of their office? How would the courtiers of C*rlt*n H**s* [7] look upon the chief magistrate of a country who stands only as a man among men, who walks forth without attendants, lives without state, greets his fellow citizens with open hand as his companions and equals, seeks his relaxation from the labours of the cabinet at the domestic hearth, snatches a moment from the hurry of public affairs to superintend the business of his farm, and defrays all the expenses of his high office *with a stipend of £6,000 a year!* Or how would they regard a secretary of state, who, with an income of little more than £1,000, toils from sunrise to sunset, conspicuous only among his fellow citizens for abilities and science and a modesty of character and simplicity of manners and habits which might lead the fancy to recur to the early sages of Sparta or Rome!

And now, my dear friend, I approach the conclusion of the voluminous correspondence which I have addressed to you from this country. You contrive to persuade me that the information I have collected has often possessed for you the merit of novelty. I have, however, to regret that my personal observation has been confined to a portion of this vast country, the whole of whose surface merits the study of a more discerning traveller than myself. I own that as regards the southern states I have ever felt a secret reluctance to visit their territory. The sight of slavery is revolting everywhere, but to inhale the impure breath of its pestilence in the free winds of America is odious beyond all that the imagination can conceive. I do not mean to indulge in idle declamation either against the injustice of the masters or upon the degradation of the slave. This is a subject upon which it is difficult to reason, because it is so easy to feel. The difficulties that stand in the way of emancipation, I can perceive to be numerous; but should the masters content themselves with idly deploring the evil, instead of "setting their shoulder to the wheel" and actively working

---

approving of Monroe's mild and prudent guidance. When he lately travelled through our vast extent of country, the marks of respect which he received from all parties and classes must have been grateful to his heart. When he passed through our little town (and the same feeling prevailed everywhere), each person was anxious to speak to "the good President." The old men, who, like himself, had served in the Revolutionary War, took pains to make themselves known to him as old soldiers. To them, he showed peculiar attention and seemed to speak with pleasure, and even emotion, of the battles they had fought and the anxieties they had felt in common. His arrival having been expected, many little preparations had been made; those who had gardens had carefully preserved their finest fruit. But these things will read idly in Europe. It is, perhaps, only to those who have been trained up in a republic that such simple sacrifices of the heart speak more than wealth can buy, or power command."

out its remedy, neither their courtesy in the drawing room, their virtues in domestic life, nor even their public services in the senate and the field will preserve the southern planters from the reprobation of their northern brethren, and the scorn of mankind. The Virginians are said to pride themselves upon the peculiar tenderness with which they visit the sceptre of authority upon their African vassals. As all those acquainted with the character of the Virginia planters, whether Americans or foreigners, appear to concur in bearing testimony to their humanity, it is probable that they are entitled to the praise which they claim. But in their position, justice should be held superior to humanity; to break the chains would be more generous than to gild them, and, whether we consider the interests of the master or the slave, decidedly more useful. It is true that this neither can nor ought to be done too hastily. To give liberty to a slave before he understands its value is, perhaps, rather to impose a penalty than to bestow a blessing; but it is not clear to me that the southern planters are duly exerting themselves to prepare the way for that change in the condition of their black population which they profess to think not only desirable but inevitable. From the conversation of some distinguished Virginians, I cannot but apprehend that they suffer themselves to be disheartened by the slender success which has hitherto attended the exertions of those philanthropists who have made the character and condition of the negro their study and care. "Look into the cabins of our free negroes," said an eminent individual, a native of Virginia, in conversing with me lately upon this subject; "you will find there little to encourage the idea that to impart the rights of freemen to our black population is to ameliorate their condition, or to elevate their character." It is undoubtedly true that the free negroes of Maryland and Virginia form the most wretched and consequently the most vicious portion of the black population. The most casual observation is sufficient to satisfy a stranger of the truth of this statement. I have not seen a miserable half-clad negro in either state whom I have not found, upon enquiry, to be in possession of liberty. But what argument is to be adduced from this? That to emancipate the African race would be to smite the land with a worse plague than that which defaces it already? The history of the negro in the northern states will save us from so revolting a conclusion. To argue that he constitutes, even there, the least valuable portion of the population, will not affect the question. If his character be there *improving,* a fact which none will deny, we have sufficient data upon which to ground the belief that he may, in time, be rendered a useful member of society, and that the vice and wretchedness which here dwell in the cabins of the emancipated negroes may be traced, in part, to the mixture of freedmen and slaves now observed in the black population. Were the whole race emancipated, their education would necessarily become a national object, the white population would be constrained to hire their service, and they themselves be under the necessity of selling it. At present, when restored by some generous planter to their birthright of liberty, the sons of Africa forfeit the protection of a master without securing the guardianship of the law. To their untutored minds, the gift of freedom is only a release from labour. Poor, ignorant, and lazy, it is impossible that they should not soon be vicious. To exonerate herself from the increasing weight of black pauperism, Virginia has imposed a restriction upon the benevolence of her citizens by a law which exacts of the citizen who emancipates his vassals that he shall remove them without the precincts of the state. In obedience to this law, Mr. Coles, a native of Virginia, and for some years secretary to Mr. Jefferson, lately removed a black colony into the state of Illinois.[8] On the death of his father, this gentleman found himself in possession of seventeen slaves, valued at from eight to nine thousand dollars. His property was small, but he hesitated not a moment to relinquish his claims upon his negro vassals. He purchased a tract of land near the settlement of Edwardsville, in Illinois, where he supplies his former bondsmen with employment, encouraging them to lay up their earnings until they shall have realized sufficient to enter upon their own farms. * * * * spent some time at Edwardsville last summer and often visited Mr. Coles' settlement. The liberated blacks spoke of their former master with tears of gratitude and affection, and two of them, who were hired as servants by the family with whom * * * * resided, never omitted to pay a daily visit to Mr. Coles, anxiously enquiring if there was nothing they could do for him. I envy more the feelings of the man who hears that question than those of Cæsar in the capitol.

But why should this work of benevolence be left to the philanthropy of individuals? The virtue of a Coles, however beautiful in its nature and wholesome in its effects upon the little circle within the sphere of its influence, can do little or nothing for the community. Why does not Virginia recur to the plan marked out by herself in the first year of her independence? Has she not virtue to execute what she had wisdom to conceive? She has made so many noble sacrifices to humanity and patriotism, her history records so many acts of heroism and disinterested generosity, that I am willing to persuade myself she is equal to this also. Nor can she be so blind to the future as not to perceive the consequences with which she is threatened, should she not take some active measures to eradicate the Egyptian plague which covers her soil. A servile war is the least of the evils which could befall her; the ruin of her moral character, the decay of her strength, the loss of her political importance, vice, indolence, degradation—these are the evils that will overtake her. The Helots will sink into worse corruption, and *the Spartans become Helots themselves.*

But I shall weary you with my commentaries upon an evil that is so far removed from your sight. Had you studied with me the history and character of the American republic, did you see in her so many seeds of excellence, so bright a dawning of national glory, so fair a promise of a brilliant meridian day, as your friend imagines that she can discern, you would share all that regret, impatience, and anxiety, with which she regards every stain that rests upon her morals, every danger that threatens her peace. An awful responsibility has devolved on the American nation; the liberties of mankind are entrusted to their guardianship; the honor of freedom is identified with the honor of their republic; the agents of tyranny are active in one hemisphere; may the children of liberty be equally active in the other! May they return with fresh ardor to the glorious work which they formerly encountered with so much success—in one word, may they realize the conviction lately expressed to me by their venerable President that "the day is not very far distant when a slave will not be found in America!"

NOTES

INTRODUCTION

1. William R. Waterman, *Frances Wright* (New York, 1924), p. 13. This is the basic study of Frances Wright. A popular biography, which includes more of the Wright correspondence, is A. J. G. Perkins and Theresa Wolfson, *Frances Wright: Free Enquirer* (New York, 1939).

2. Frances Wright, *Course of Popular Lectures, as Delivered by Frances Wright . . . with Three Addresses on Various Public Occasions* (New York, 1829), p. 7.

3. Frances Wright, *Biography, Notes, and Political Letters of Frances Wright D'Arusmont,* part I (New York, 1844), p. 11.

4. Wright, *Biography,* part I, p. 15.

5. Wright, *Biography,* part I, p. 14.

6. Wright, *Course of Popular Lectures,* pp. 7–8.

7. See Allan Nevins, *America Through British Eyes,* rev. ed. (New York, 1948). Nevins has dubbed the years from 1789 to 1825 the period of "utilitarian inquiry" for British travelers in America, as contrasted with the subsequent period of "Tory condescension," extending almost to the mid-point of the century. During this first period British travelers visited the United States principally in order to satisfy their curiosity about the radical new national experiment and also to discover what trade and investment possibilities there were in America. In reporting their impressions they helped both to dispel British misconceptions about America and to prepare the ever-increasing numbers of emigrants for what they might expect to find overseas. In the second quarter of the nineteenth century the British travelers, often upper and professional class visitors, were characteristically disturbed by the new manifestations of widespread democracy, and their responses frequently condemned the novelties of American life. British descriptions of the United States later on in the second half of the century were more balanced, and later travelers even came to deplore the earlier attacks. See also Jane L. Mesick, *The English Traveler in America, 1785–1835* (New York, 1922).

8. Jefferson to Wright, Monticello, May 20, 1820, in Worthington Chauncey Ford, ed., *Thomas Jefferson Correspondence* (Boston, 1916), p. 254.

9. Wright, *Course of Popular Lectures,* p. 7.

10. Wright, *Biography,* part I, p. 15.

11. *North American Review,* XIV (January 1822), 19; see also the review in *The Port Folio,* XII (July–December 1821), 207–228.

12. Waterman, *Frances Wright,* pp. 61, 73.

13. Wright to Bentham, September 12, 1821, in Jeremy Bentham, *Works* (Edinburgh, 1842), X, 526.

14. Lafayette to Wright, April 26, 1824, quoted in Waterman, *Frances Wright,* p. 79.

15. Wright, *Course of Popular Lectures,* p. 8.

16. *Fanny Wright Unmasked by Her Own Pen. Explanatory Notes, Respecting the Nature and Objects of the Institutions of Nashoba, and of the Principles Upon Which It Is Founded* (New York, 1830), p. 8.

17. Waterman, *Frances Wright,* pp. 117–119.

18. Frances M. Trollope, *Domestic Manners of the Americans* (London, 1832), I, 38.

19. Quoted in Waterman, *Frances Wright*, p. 135.

20. Trollope, *Domestic Manners*, I, 100.

21. Frances Wright, *Address to the Industrious Classes: A Sketch of a System of National Education* (New York, 1830), p. 5.

22. Frances Wright, *Address on the State of the Public Mind, and the Measures Which it Calls For* (New York, 1829), p. 6.

23. Robert Dale Owen, "An Earnest Sowing of Wild Oats," *Atlantic Monthly*, XXXIV (July 1874), 75.

24. Orestes A. Brownson, *The Convert; or, Leaves from My Experience* (New York, 1857), p. 127.

DEDICATION

1. Soon after their arrival in New York in 1818, Fanny and Camilla Wright became acquainted with Charles Wilkes, who introduced the two young visitors to New York society. Born in London in 1764, the son of an elder brother of the famous John Wilkes, Charles Wilkes had come to the United States at the close of the Revolutionary War, later becoming cashier and president of the Bank of New York. To him the Wright sisters entrusted care of their finances. In 1829 when Fanny Wright moved to New York as a popular lecturer in the rationalist cause, Wilkes broke off the friendship and resigned the direction of their financial affairs.

LETTER I

1. The "friend" to whom these letters are addressed was Mrs. Rabina Craig Millar. The two sisters, Fanny and Camilla Wright, had lived for a time with Mrs. Millar in Whitburn, after their return from England to Scotland. Mrs. Millar had undoubtedly helped develop Fanny's interest in the United States, for the older woman had lived there for a short time when she and her husband, a political refugee, had been obliged to flee England in 1794 at the time of repressive countermeasures directed against the principles of the French Revolution. Until almost the time for their departure, the two sisters had told no one except Mrs. Millar of their plans for a visit to the United States.

2. In Greek mythology, one of the Titans, the sea-goddess.

LETTER III

1. Fanny Wright arrived in the United States toward the end of the so-called "Era of Good Feelings." By this time the old Federalist Party had largely died out, and the Jeffersonian Republicans had not yet split into well-defined factions. On his re-election in 1820, Monroe received every electoral vote but one. Nonetheless, below the surface, the period remained one of local factionalism and sectional wrangles.

LETTER IV

1. These and subsequent remarks foreshadow Fanny Wright's important later concern for women's rights.

2. Benjamin Rush (1745-1813), probably the foremost physician and medical teacher of the late eighteenth century in America and a signer of the Declaration of Independence, wrote widely not only on medical topics but on social issues as well. His considerations of educational theory and practice are especially important and help give him a secure place as one of the leading thinkers of the American Enlightenment. The quotation, with insignificant changes, comes from an essay in *Essays, Literary, Moral, and Philosophical* (Philadelphia, 1798), p. 19.

3. John Wells (c.1770-1823) and Thomas Addis Emmet (1764-1827) were the leading New York lawyers at this time. The latter, Irish-born and trained in both medicine and law, was arrested in Ireland for his political activity and subsequently banished from the British empire. Eventually he came to New York City, was admitted to the bar by a special act of the New York legislature, and quickly moved to the forefront of his profession. Both were associated with the famous interstate commerce case of *Gibbons* v. *Ogden:* as counsel for Gibbons in the lower courts, Wells lost his case against the New York law granting a shipping monopoly to Ogden, but his arguments were later presented to the Supreme Court to gain a reversal; Emmet unsuccessfully argued for the New York law before the Supreme Court.

4. Dr. William James MacNeven (1763-1841), like his friend Thomas Emmet, was trained as a physician and was arrested in Ireland for his political activity. He too came to New York, joining the faculty of the College of Physicians and Surgeons, where he concerned himself mostly with researches in chemistry. Dr. MacNeven was noted for his aid to Irish immigrants.

5. Simon Bernard (1779-1839), after a distinguished career as a military engineer under Napoleon, was recommended by Lafayette to the United States Congress, which named him a brigadier general and placed him on the committee in charge of coastal defenses. Bernard took the lead in this work, designing forts, roads, and canals. After the accession of Louis Philippe, Bernard returned to France and served as aide-de-camp to the king, as inspector general of engineers, and as minister of war.

6. Henry Bradshaw Fearon (b. c.1770) had published his *Sketches of America: A Narrative of a Journey of Five Thousand Miles* the previous year, 1818. Fearon had been sent to the United States in 1817 by a group of English families to see if a suitable place for their relocation could be found. His frequently critical though not unfriendly account of America and its people was fresh in Fanny Wright's memory as she made her own observations, and she refers several times to Fearon's work, with which she takes issue.

LETTER V

1. The first of these quotations is taken from Penn's Preface to the *Frame of Government of Pennsylvania* (April 25, 1682): "We have (with reverence to God, and good conscience to men) to the best of our skill, contrived and composed the *frame* and *laws* of this government, to the great end of all government, viz: *To support power in reverence with the people, and to secure the people from the abuse of power;* that they may be free by their just obedience, and the magistrates honourable, for their administration: for liberty without obedience is confusion, and obedience without liberty is slavery." The second quotation is taken from Article XXXV of Penn's *Laws Agreed Upon in England* (May 5, 1682): "That all persons living in this province, who confess and acknowledge the one Almighty and eternal God, to be the Creator, Upholder and Ruler of the world; and that hold themselves obliged in conscience to live peaceably and justly in civil society, shall, in no ways, be molested or prejudiced for their religious persuasion, or practice, in matters of faith and worship, nor shall they be compelled, at any time, to frequent or maintain

any religious worship, place or ministry whatever." F. N. Thorpe, *The Federal and State Constitutions* (Washington, 1909), V, 3054, 3063.

2. In reference to the Lutherans and subsequently to Lutheranism the author apparently meant the Anglicans and Anglicanism.

3. William Bradford (1755-1795), a prominent Pennsylvania jurist who succeeded Edmund Randolph in 1794 as the second attorney general of the United States, was influential in the revision of the criminal code of Pennsylvania, leading to the abolition of the death penalty except for first-degree murder. To Bradford's *Enquiry How Far the Punishment of Death is Necessary in Pennsylvania* (Philadelphia, 1793) was added *An Account of the Gaol and Penitentiary House of Philadelphia* by Caleb Lownes of Philadelphia.

4. See "An Enquiry into the Consistency of the Punishment of Murder by Death, with Reason and Revelation," in *Essays, Literary, Moral, and Philosophical*, pp. 164-182.

5. John Philip Kemble (1757-1823), a member of a famous British acting family, played a variety of roles during his career, including many from Shakespeare's plays. His final public appearance in 1817 was as Coriolanus, perhaps his best-known role.

6. The Virginia House of Burgesses in 1772 petitioned the king for his help "in averting a calamity of a most alarming nature"—the flow of slaves into the colonies might well endanger the very existence of the American dominions. The petition stressed that this traffic had retarded the settlement by more useful inhabitants, and it urged the king to remove those restraints on the governor that prevented him from assenting to laws which might check the influx. Despite this appeal, provincial anti-slavery measures continued to be vetoed, though Virginia like the other provinces did succeed in placing some duties on imported slaves.

7. A Virginia act of 1778, revived in 1785, prohibited the slave trade to that state. Delaware, Connecticut, Rhode Island, and Pennsylvania, as well as Vermont, had already restricted or prohibited traffic in slaves by the time of the original Virginia law. By 1778 the importation of slaves had largely ceased in the New England and middle states.

8. Fanny Wright apparently refers here to a law of 1794, the first national act against the slave trade, by which the slave trade from the United States to a foreign place or country or the fitting out of slavers for a foreign country were forbidden. But this law was only a mild restraint and did not greatly impair the still existing traffic. The basic prohibitions of the slave trade of both the United States and Great Britain came in acts of 1807, by which the traffic was forbidden commencing the following year.

9. The author's remarks on slavery and the Negro foreshadow her later interests in emancipation and colonization.

10. Henry Meigs (1782-1861) served as a representative in Congress from New York City from 1819 to 1821.

LETTER VI

1. Fearon, *Sketches of America*, p. 172. The italics and punctuation are the author's.

2. Lieutenant Francis Hall (d. 1833) visited the New World in 1816 and 1817, traveling extensively through Canada and the middle American states and going as far south as Charleston, S.C., before returning to England. His view of the United States was generally favorable, though he attacked the American spirit of speculation and the institution of slavery. The account of his travels was published in London and Boston in 1818.

3. Washington had died in 1799, Hamilton was killed in 1804, Horatio Gates had died in 1806, and Rush in 1813.

4. Harrisburg, located on the east bank rather than branch of the Susquehanna River,

had already been the capital of Pennsylvania since 1812; previously, from 1799 to 1812, the capital had been located in Lancaster, and before 1799 in Philadelphia.

5. Benjamin Latrobe designed the Bank of Pennsylvania in 1798 in the Greek revival style, with Greek Ionic porticos and a low and graceful dome.

6. Friedrich Rehberg (1758–1835), a German painter of portraits and historical events, was a member of the Berlin Academy. Washington Allston (1779–1843), one of the leading American romantic painters, after study with Benjamin West in London, traveled extensively on the Continent and spent several years in Italy. Later, following a short stay in the United States, he returned to England with his young pupil Samuel F. B. Morse, and during these years abroad did his best work. Returning to Boston in 1818, Allston devoted himself to a large canvas of *Belshazzar's Feast,* which remained unfinished at his death. Failing to fulfill his early promise, Allston later became a symbol to many critics of the plight of the artist in America. The Pennsylvania Academy of Fine Arts was founded in 1805 and opened in 1807.

7. Benjamin West (1738–1820), the first American artist to visit Europe, settled in England in 1763 and became one of the most influential artists of his time as a teacher and president of the Royal Academy. Charles R. Leslie (1794–1859) did genre and historical paintings as well as portraits. John Singleton Copley (1738–1815), the most talented early American painter, began his career as a professional portraitist while still a youth, making his own way into the aristocratic society of Boston. His best pictures come from the years before 1774, when he left the colonies to spend the rest of his career in England. John Trumbull (1756–1843) is best known for his representations of scenes of the American Revolution.

8. Toward the end of the eighteenth century, Charles Willson Peale (1741–1827) established the first important gallery of paintings and museum of natural history in America. In 1802, Peale was granted free use of the upper floor of Independence Hall for his collection.

9. This first allusion is actually to the Declaration of Causes of Taking Up Arms (July 6, 1775).

10. Fanny Wright's views here of the unquestioned rectitude of the members of the Continental Congress and her later remarks on the unanimity of sentiment and the unswerving patriotism of the American people during the Revolution are distorted by her overwhelming enthusiasm for the United States. During the war rumors often circulated that members of Congress were making use of inside information for private gain, and a few such instances have come to light. Samuel Chase of Maryland, for one, speculated on flour on the basis of inside information. And many merchants accumulated large fortunes, as patriotism lagged behind profiteering.

11. David Ramsay, *History of the United States* (Philadelphia, 1818), II, 408–409, with minor inaccuracies. Ramsay (1749–1815), who was trained as a physician, served as a delegate to the Continental Congress and in the South Carolina legislature and wrote several volumes on history, biography, and medicine.

12. Ramsay, *History of the United States,* I, 422–423, with minor inaccuracies.

13. From the so-called "Olive Branch Petition" sent by the Second Continental Congress to King George III in 1775. The original passage reads as follows: "We beg leave further to assure your Majesty, that notwithstanding the sufferings of your loyal colonists during the course of the present controversy, our breasts retain too tender a regard for the kingdom from which we derive our origin, to request such a reconciliation, as might in any manner be inconsistent with her dignity or her welfare."

14. Fanny Wright wrote this poem, under the influence of Byron's *Childe Harold,* before her first visit to America. Extracts are scattered through these letters and elsewhere in her published works.

15. Ramsay, *History of the United States,* I, 409, with insignificant punctuation changes.
16. Gen. Anthony Wayne (1745-1796).
17. Though hardships due to shortages of clothing and rations were basic causes for this mutiny, the immediate trouble in January 1781 arose over the soldiers' terms of enlistment. The Pennsylvania mutineers marched from Morristown to Princeton in New Jersey and threatened to move on Philadelphia. Joseph Reed (1741-1785), president of the Supreme Executive Council of Pennsylvania, was sent to negotiate with them, but the mutineers refused to disperse. Eventually the authorities were forced to capitulate. About half the mutineers were discharged and the others were furloughed; none was forced to serve to the end of the war. During the revolt, the mutineers turned over to Pennsylvania authorities two agents sent by Sir Henry Clinton; the agents were hanged.
18. In 1778, through an intermediary on behalf of George Johnstone, a member of the Carlisle Commission seeking peace with the colonists, Joseph Reed, then Congressional delegate from Pennsylvania, was offered a bribe of £10,000 and a high government post to further reunion between the two countries. His scornful reply was recorded in the Journals of the Continental Congress (August 11, 1778).
19. Henry Laurens (1724-1792) was the leading merchant of Charleston, S.C., at the outbreak of the Revolution. He became a member of the first and second provincial congresses of South Carolina and in 1777 was elected to the Continental Congress of which he served as president in 1777-1778.
20. From Penn's Preface to the *Frame of Government of Pennsylvania* (April 25, 1682).
21. Georgia in 1789 and Pennsylvania in 1790 changed to the bicameral system.
22. With the formation of the new state governments the old council of the colonial governor was split into the upper legislative house and an executive council, the members of the latter being elected either by the legislature or by popular vote. At the beginning of the nineteenth century, six states still retained the governor's council.
23. "Those republics which, if they do not have perfect order, have made a good beginning and are capable of improvement, may become perfect, should something occur which provides the opportunity." Niccolò Machiavelli, *Discourses on the First Ten Books of Titus Livy* (1531), Book I, chap. ii.
24. Paraphrase taken from a letter of Franklin to Barbeu Dubourg (1773), in Benjamin Franklin, *Works,* ed. John Bigelow (New York, 1904), VI, 111.

LETTER VII

1. "What does 'Yankee' mean?" "I should tell you, sir, that it means a man of perfect wisdom, of considerable ability, enjoying the blessings of fortune and of public esteem." "In a word, a wise and eminent man." "Exactly." "But, sir, how rich your republic is in wise and eminent men!" "These gentlemen do us the honor of believing so."
2. This theory of the derivation of the word "Yankee," first advanced by the Rev. John Heckewelder (1743-1823) in 1819, has been disputed by many authorities. The origins of the term have not been positively established.
3. Abbé José Francisco Correa da Serra (1750-1823), Portuguese botanist and diplomat, came to the United States in 1813 to pursue his scientific studies and in 1816 was named Portuguese minister to Washington. Jefferson considered him "learned beyond any one I had before met with" (letter to Dupont de Nemours, November 29, 1813).
4. In the dedication to *Views of Louisiana* (Baltimore, 1817), quoted here with slight inaccuracies, Henry Marie Brackenridge also praised Correa da Serra for his capacious mind and his extensive critical knowledge of the United States. Brackenridge (1786-1871), the son of the author Hugh Henry Brackenridge, practiced law in Missouri and Louisiana,

served on a diplomatic mission to Latin America, and wrote works on history and politics.

5. Patrick Brydone (1741?–1818) visited Sicily in 1770 and wrote *A Tour through Sicily and Malta* (London, 1773).

6. Robert Melville (1527–1621), first Lord Melville.

7. John Bernard (1756–1828), English comedian and stage manager, came to the United States in 1797 to join a Philadelphia company and later spent some years in Boston and with companies touring Canada and the United States. Portions of his autobiography concerning his years in America were issued as *Retrospections of America, 1797–1811* (New York, 1887). John Garnett (d. 1820), an English scientist who like Bernard shared Fanny Wright's enthusiasm for America, lived on a large estate on the banks of the Raritan River in New Jersey. In later years Miss Wright came to know Garnett's wife and daughters intimately in France. Thomas Ashe (1770–1835), an English visitor, published *Travels to America Performed in 1806* (London, 1808); this critical and unreliable work was unusual in its emphasis on American Indians and archaeology. Fearon, amid much practical information for the British immigrant in *Sketches of America,* expressed the belief that American theory was far in advance of American practice.

8. Probably Diethelm Lavater (1780–1827), Swiss painter.

LETTER VIII

1. Joseph Bonaparte (1768–1844), eldest brother of Napoleon, was proclaimed king of Naples in 1806 and king of Spain in 1808. When Napoleon surrendered after the Hundred Days, Joseph fled to the United States, where he assumed the title of Comte de Survilliers and settled on an estate near Bordentown, N.J. In 1832 he returned to Europe to live in England and after 1841 in Italy, where he died.

2. Henry Dearborn (1751–1829), an officer during the American Revolution and secretary of war under Jefferson, was named commanding general of the northern frontier from the Niagara River to the Atlantic at the start of the War of 1812 but was relieved the next year for incompetence. He apparently rode in such a light carriage in some of his campaigns.

3. Names omitted in the original edition are indicated in this manner.

4. Jean Victor Marie Moreau (1763–1813), a general of the French Revolutionary armies, aided Napoleon in the *coup d'état* of the Eighteenth Brumaire. Later involved with a group conspiring against Napoleon, he was banished and lived for some years in Morrisville, Pa.; he returned to Europe to advise the allies fighting Napoleon and was killed at the Battle of Dresden.

5. Antonio Canova (1757–1822), an Italian sculptor, who was ranked by his contemporaries with the greatest of the ancients, led and dominated the early movement of the neoclassical revival in European sculpture.

6. Jacques Louis David (1748–1825) founded the neoclassical school of painting. His portrait of Napoleon crossing the Alps to Italy before the Battle of Marengo (1800), done in four versions, is one of his more famous works.

7. In Greek mythology, a wooded island off the mouth of the Ister (Danube) River, the refuge of souls.

LETTER IX

1. Jonathan Williams (1750–1815) was named inspector of fortifications and the head of the West Point school for engineers in 1801; the following year he was appointed

chief of army engineers and superintendent of the new military academy. He served as superintendent until 1803 and again from 1805 to 1812.

2. The Royal Military Academy (founded 1741) at Woolwich, England, provided training for the artillery and engineers; the École Polytechnique (founded 1794) gave training in civil and military engineering.

3. Joseph Gardner Swift (1783–1865) was one of two men who comprised the first graduating class of West Point (1802). He constructed fortifications at New York during the War of 1812, and served as chief engineer of the army and superintendent of the West Point Academy in 1816–1818.

4. Although the ostensible reasons for the declaration of the War of 1812—declared by the United States on Great Britain—were the accumulation of intolerable offenses against American ships, commerce, and citizens, an important aspect of this declaration was the mood of the western Americans, who looked to expansion into Canada and Florida. Though the British enemy did invade the United States, the Americans also invaded Canada, and it can be questioned whether this war, only a few years past at the time of Fanny Wright's visit, was purely defensive.

5. Benedict Arnold began his negotiations with the British in May 1779; he met Major André on September 22, 1780, to arrange the details of the surrender of West Point and went over to the British lines three days later.

6. Ramsay, *History of the United States,* II, 386–387. The author changes only Ramsay's phrase "high trusts, exclusively, on men of clean hands."

7. Ramsay, *History of the United States,* II, 377.

8. "One never argues about virtue, because it comes from God; one only quarrels with the opinions that come from men."

LETTER X

1. Work began on the Erie Canal in 1817, and by the fall of 1825 the project was completed. Connecting Lake Erie to the Hudson River, the canal was some 363 miles in length and cost some $7,000,000 to construct. It opened up western New York state, provided a link to the Old Northwest, and was largely responsible for the phenomenal growth of New York City as the gateway to the interior of the country.

2. Gibbon attributes this saying to Hormisdas, a fugitive prince of Persia, who observed concerning Rome "that one thing only had *displeased* him, to find that men died at Rome as well as elsewhere." Gibbon discusses Hormisdas in connection with the visit to Rome in 357 of Constantius II, the son of Constantine. Edward Gibbon, *History of the Decline and Fall of the Roman Empire,* ed. J. B. Bury (London, 1925), II, 261.

LETTER XI

1. James Wadsworth (1768–1844), a land agent and large landholder in the Genesee River area, played an important role in the development of this part of upstate New York. He was particularly noted for his work with the school system of New York state, especially the establishment of school district libraries.

2. Lieut. Francis Hall, *Travels in Canada and the United States in 1816 and 1817* (London, 1818), p. 332.

LETTER XII

1. Fanny Wright was left an orphan when she was two and one-half years old.
2. John Wesley (1703-1791), founder of Methodism, and George Whitefield (1714-1770), Methodist evangelist.
3. The priestess of Apollo at Delphi.
4. John Gottlieb Ernestus Heckewelder (1743-1823) spent nearly a quarter century as a missionary of the Moravian Church to the Indians of Ohio and passed his last years recording some of his knowledge of Indian life. His "Account of the History, Manners, and Customs of the Indian Nations, Who Once Inhabited Pennsylvania and the Neighboring States" was published by the American Philosophical Society in 1819.

LETTER XIII

1. "called."
2. The classical dictionary of John Lemprière (1765?-1824), a popular authority for ancient history and mythology.
3. In the allegorical "Vision of Mirza," published in the *Spectator* (September 1, 1711), Joseph Addison conceived of life as a great bridge with many trap doors through which humanity fell.
4. "The gloomy countryside trembled so violently that the very memory of that terror bathes me again with sweat." Dante Alighieri, *The Divine Comedy*, "Inferno," canto III, ll. 130-132.

LETTER XIV

1. Once the capital of Upper Canada, Newark was destroyed on December 10, 1813, by order of Gen. George McClure (c.1770-1851), an incompetent officer of the New York militia, who had been placed in command of nearby Fort George. This fort on the Canadian side of the Niagara River had been taken by the American forces in May 1813. As the term of enlistment of his volunteer troops expired, General McClure's position at Fort George became precarious, and he decided to evacuate and destroy the fort and burn the village of Newark to prevent its use by British troops. Previously McClure had been instructed by the secretary of war to destroy the village only if the defense of Fort George required it. A few days after the destruction of Newark, British troops in retaliation captured Fort Niagara and the town of Lewiston, which their Indian allies ravaged and burned. The English continued to advance, destroying dwellings and villages and soon took Buffalo, which was also put to the torch. The following month McClure's act was officially disavowed, and public opinion was harshly critical of what he had done.
2. At Frenchtown (now Monroe, Michigan) on January 22, 1813, an American force, mostly consisting of Kentucky militiamen, under Gen. James Winchester (1752-1826) was defeated by British troops under Col. Henry Proctor (1763-1859). Winchester, who had fought in the Revolution and had been speaker of the senate of Tennessee just after that state was admitted to the Union, was taken prisoner at Frenchtown and held for over a year before being exchanged. As Fanny Wright points out, many of the Americans surrendered at Frenchtown under the promise of protection from the Indians

allied to the English, but the pledge was not adhered to and many were massacred in cold blood. Colonel Proctor, then in charge of Fort Detroit and of the captured Michigan Territory, was promoted to brigadier general for his victory at Frenchtown. Later, after abandoning Detroit following Perry's victory on Lake Erie, Proctor was overtaken as he was marching eastward toward Lake Erie by Gen. William Henry Harrison (1773–1841), who soundly defeated him at the Battle of the Thames River (October 5, 1813). Proctor escaped, but was subsequently court-martialed and temporarily suspended from rank and pay.

3. Fanny Wright seems to be in error about McIntosh. Duncan McIntosh, a Scottish-born naturalized American, was a merchant in Haiti, who at the time of the Negro insurrection (1802) at Cap Français (Cap Haytien) assisted the whites, rescuing some and ransoming others from their captors. On his return to the United States he was received with great public acclaim in New Orleans and Philadelphia. See "Memoir of Mr. Duncan McIntosh," *The Port Folio,* I (April 1809), 285–287.

4. Oliver Hazard Perry's victory over Capt. Robert H. Barclay in the Battle of Lake Erie took place on September 10, 1813. It was one of the few significant American victories in the War of 1812, and brought Lake Erie under American control.

5. Perry died at Angostura, Venezuela, on August 23, 1819.

6. In two letters addressed to Morris Birkbeck (1764–1825), published in *Cobbett's Political Register,* vol. XXXIV, February 6–13, 1819, and reprinted in his *Year's Residence in the United States of America* (London, 1818–1819), pp. 603–666, William Cobbett (1763–1835) had vigorously opposed Birkbeck's views that the western prairies were suitable for colonization by groups of Englishmen, stressing as well the need for considerable amounts of capital to make a start in America. Birkbeck had published his views in 1818 in *Notes on a Journey in America* and in *Letters from Illinois.* Cobbett had not himself visited Albion, Illinois, the community of English settlers which Birkbeck and George Flower had established in 1817–1818, but based his criticisms on his own general acquaintance with the country and on the journal of his friend Thomas Hulme, who had stopped at Albion. On her second trip to the United States, in March 1825, Fanny Wright visited Albion and Harmonie, where she became acquainted with George Flower, who later helped her set up her Nashoba project and contributed ideas on Negro emancipation.

7. Brackenridge, *Views of Louisiana,* p. 199.

8. Fürstenwärther's *Der Deutsche in Nord Amerika* (*The German in North America*) (Stuttgart and Tubingen, 1818) was reviewed in the *North American Review,* XI (July 1820), 1–19. Edward Everett (1794–1865) edited the journal while professor of Greek at Harvard College. The author here changes slightly the original italics and punctuation.

LETTER XV

1. Robert Gourlay (1778–1862), a Scotsman, immigrated in 1817 to Upper Canada, where he worked to promote settlement and investment. While preparing a statistical account of the province, he discovered that great quantities of land had been granted or sold to speculators. He soon uncovered much official incompetence and corruption, and did not hesitate to speak out and publish what he had found and what he felt had brought on the impoverishment of the settlers. At York in 1818 he called a convention of provincial delegates, which passed resolutions attacking the government. After a libel suit against him failed, Gourlay was subjected to imprisonment and persecution, and in 1819 he was banished from the province. Gourlay is significant for his role in developing reform agitation in Canada.

2. Hall, *Travels in Canada, and the United States, in 1816 and 1817*, p. 162. The Kingston navy yard at this time employed some 1,200 men and cost some £25,000 annually to maintain.

3. By the Rush-Bagot Agreement, which was concluded in 1817 and approved by the Senate in 1818, the United States and Great Britain agreed each to limit their naval forces to one vessel of not more than 100 tons and armed with one eighteen-pound cannon on Lake Ontario and on Lake Champlain and two such vessels on the upper Great Lakes. This agreement has been important as a model for effective border disarmament.

4. Salvator Rosa (1615–1673), Italian painter of landscapes and historical events, especially noted for his depictions of the wild, mountainous landscapes of the southern Apennines.

5. Anglican.

6. Sir James Henry Craig (1748–1812) was appointed governor general of Canada in 1807 and served to 1811. Sir George Prevost (1767–1816) served as governor of Lower Canada and governor general of British North America from 1811 to his death.

LETTER XVI

1. The Battle of Plattsburg took place on September 11, 1814. Hoping to detach New England from the rest of the country, Sir George Prevost, governor general of British North America, moved south into New York, supported on Lake Champlain by a small flotilla under Capt. George Downie. In his attack on Capt. Thomas Macdonough's squadron, then well positioned in Plattsburg Bay, Downie was killed and his ships were taken. Without naval support, the British land forces could not overcome the American troops at Plattsburg, under Gen. Alexander Macomb, and were forced to retreat northward. This American victory ended the threat of British invasion by way of Lake Champlain.

LETTER XVII

1. The Vermont constitution of 1777 was revised in 1793, two years after the state had been admitted to the Union. The unicameral legislature was retained until 1836 and the Council of Censors until 1869.

LETTER XVIII

1. The author indicated here that a part of her own original letter had been deleted.

2. Federalist.

3. Charles Brockden Brown (1771–1810), the first professional American author, published *Arthur Mervyn*, a psychological novel, in 1799–1800. Washington Irving's *Sketch Book of Geoffrey Crayon, Gent.* (1819–1820) was a great success and made his international literary reputation.

4. Joel Barlow (1754–1812) published his lengthy, ponderous epic poem *The Columbiad* in 1807. Barlow spent many years in Europe as an American land agent, a merchant, consul to Algiers, and minister to France.

5. Timothy Dwight (1752–1817) published *The Conquest of Canaan,* an epic on the settlement of the New World, in 1785. Unlike the liberal Barlow, Dwight, a Federalist

and Calvinist, stood squarely opposed to the rising American democracy. Chosen president of Yale in 1795, Dwight was perhaps the best-known figure in New England at the beginning of the nineteenth century.

6. James Edward Oglethorpe (1696–1785) founded Georgia in 1733 as a refuge for unemployed debtors and to provide a buffer state for Carolina. He first went to Georgia in his thirty-sixth year and died in his eighty-eighth year.

7. Thomas, the sixth Lord Fairfax (1693–1781), proprietor of the Northern Neck of Virginia, first visited his American estates in 1735–1737. He returned to Virginia in 1747 and later settled in a Shenandoah Valley hunting lodge, where he lived simply as the only resident peer remaining in America during the Revolutionary War.

8. Edmund Burke, "Speech on Conciliation with America" (March 22, 1775).

9. Ramsay, *History of the United States,* III, 53, quoted with insignificant changes.

LETTER XIX

1. Federalist Party.

2. The reference to Scaevola is to a Roman legend concerning a young man, Gaius Mucius, who attempted to free Rome from the Etruscan siege of Lars Porsena by murdering the invader. When he mistakenly killed the king's secretary, Mucius was seized and threatened with torture. To show his indifference to pain he thrust his right hand into an altar fire and held it there without flinching. The amazed king freed Mucius, who was subsequently known as Scaevola (the left-handed one).

3. The authenticity of the following anecdote must be questioned. In actuality, Capt. John Rodgers (1773–1838) had commanded the *President* from 1810 to 1814 when the ship was turned over to Stephen Decatur (1779–1820). On January 14, 1815, as the *President* slipped out of New York Bay, she grounded on a sand bar, where she remained for several hours and suffered considerable damage. Putting to the open sea the next day, the *President* encountered four British men-of-war which at once gave chase. One of these, the *Endymion,* soon approached the *President,* and the two ships engaged each other; the *Endymion* took a severe beating and fell astern, but by this time the other vessels had come up, and Decatur surrendered his ship, which was sent as a prize to Bermuda. The engagement and capture occurred off the south shore of Long Island.

4. Maj. George Croghan (1791–1849), in command of Fort Stephenson in northern Ohio, on August 1–2, 1813, successfully repelled an attack on his outpost by a far larger force of British and Indians under Col. Henry Proctor. The engagement had little military significance but stood out from the inept actions and defeats of the year.

5. Edmond Charles "Citizen" Genêt (1763–1834), first minister of the French Republic who became a storm center of American politics in 1793, refused to return to France when his recall was asked and spent his final years living quietly in New York, married to a daughter of Gov. George Clinton. Aaron Burr (1756–1836), too, spent his latter years in New York, retired from public life and engaged in the practice of law.

LETTER XX

1. Henry Baldwin (1780–1844), a Federalist, served in Congress from 1817 to 1822. In 1830, Jackson named him an associate justice of the Supreme Court.

2. "Those serious, though natural enmities, which occur between the popular classes and the nobility, arising from the desire of the latter to command, and the disinclination

of the former to obey, are the causes of most of the troubles which take place in cities."
Niccolò Machiavelli, *The History of Florence* (1532), Book III, ll. 1–5.

3. The quotation in Fanny Wright's footnote comment is from Query XVIII of Jefferson's *Notes on the State of Virginia* (Philadelphia, 1788), p. 173: "Indeed I tremble for my country when I reflect that God is just: that his justice cannot sleep for ever: that considering numbers, nature and natural means only, a revolution of the wheel of fortune, an exchange of situation, is among possible events: that it may become probable by supernatural interference! The Almighty has no attribute which can take side with us in such a contest."

4. At a great meeting held on August 16, 1819, in St. Peter's Fields on the outskirts of Manchester, England, to petition for Parliamentary reform and for repeal of the Corn Laws, the crowd was fired upon by cavalry troops under official orders. Several were killed and hundreds wounded in what came to be known as the "Peterloo Massacre." Sir George Savile (1726–1784), Samuel Whitbread (1758–1815), and Sir Samuel Romilly (1757–1818) were all prominent members of Parliament and noted for their interest in liberal reform measures.

5. The Twelfth Amendment, ratified in 1804, provided that the presidential electors should make a separate designation in their choice for president and vice-president. The amendment resulted from the controversy in the election of 1800 in which Jefferson and Burr, on the same ticket, were tied for the presidency.

LETTER XXI

1. Rufus King (1755–1827), who had been a delegate to the Continental Congress and to the Constitutional Convention, served for many years as senator from New York and as minister to England. He was the Federalist candidate for vice-president in 1804 and 1808 and the candidate of that party for president in 1816. Though originally opposed to the War of 1812, he later gave it his support and approved its vigorous prosecution.

2. As Fanny Wright indicates in the next paragraph, the re-election of Monroe in 1820 was not unanimous, one vote being cast against him in the Electoral College.

3. Eneas MacKenzie, *An Historical, Topographical, and Descriptive View of the United States of America, and of Upper and Lower Canada* (Newcastle-upon-Tyne, 1819; 2d ed.: London, 1830), p. 364. The original passage differed only in italicization of the first phrase, "Negro slavery."

4. The Missouri Compromise temporarily settled the question of the balance of political power in the United States Senate. By this compromise of 1820, Missouri was admitted to the Union with no restrictions on slavery and Maine was admitted as a free state. Slavery was to be prohibited in all territory acquired from France north of 36° 30′ except Missouri; nothing was said about slavery in the remainder of that territory, thus implicitly recognizing it there. The compromise was repealed with the Kansas-Nebraska Act of 1854.

5. Ohio was admitted to the Union in 1803; Indiana, in 1816; Illinois, in 1818; and Michigan, organized as a territory in 1805, became a state in 1837.

6. Brackenridge, *Views of Louisiana*, pp. 214–215, quoted with trifling changes.

7. Jean Laffite later set up again as a smuggler and freebooter, with headquarters at Galveston on Spanish territory. In 1821 his establishment was broken up by American authorities, and Laffite subsequently disappeared from public view. William Charles Coles Claiborne (1775–1817) had been named governor of the newly acquired Louisiana Territory in 1803.

LETTER XXII

1. Thomas Jefferson, "Second Inaugural Address" (March 4, 1805), in *Writings,* ed. Andrew A. Lipscomb (Washington, D.C., 1903), III, 380–382. Fanny Wright misquotes Jefferson significantly when in her fourth and second sentences from the end of the passage, she substitutes "states" for "State," and "press calls for few legal restraints" for "press, confined to truth, needs no other legal restraint." Other changes are trifling.

2. John Dickinson (1732–1808) published his *Letters from a Farmer in Pennsylvania to the Inhabitants of the British Colonies* in 1767–1768. Conciliatory in tone, the *Letters* set forth legal arguments against the Townshend Acts, denying the right of Parliament to levy internal or external taxes in the colonies but conceding to Parliament the right to collect duties incidental to the regulation of trade. The *Letters* were probably the most significant work to crystallize American public opinion before the publication of Thomas Paine's *Common Sense* (1776).

3. Conceived as a protest to the Alien and Sedition Acts, the Virginia and Kentucky Resolutions stressed the Constitutional limitations on the federal government, with its delegated powers. The Virginia Resolutions (December 24, 1798) were written by James Madison. The Kentucky Resolutions (November 16, 1798, and November 22, 1799) were the work of Thomas Jefferson; the second Kentucky Resolution added the idea of state nullification of unauthorized federal acts. In subsequent decades the Resolutions were used to support arguments for states' rights.

4. *The Olive Branch: or, Faults on Both Sides, Federal and Democratic* (Philadelphia, 1814) by Mathew Carey (1760–1839) treated internal dissensions during the War of 1812; as a plea for national unity and resistance to the British, the work helped arouse the country to its common dangers.

5. The author is somewhat in error here. The most famous of the early altercations in Congress involved Matthew Lyon (1750–1822) of Vermont, a Jeffersonian Republican, and Roger Griswold (1762–1812) of Connecticut, a Federalist. During a brief recess in the House on January 30, 1798, Lyon responded to a provocative question of Griswold by spitting in his face. On February 15, 1798, Griswold entered the chamber just before the House was called to order, and going up to Lyon proceeded to beat him severely with his walking stick. For some minutes the fight continued before the astonished members, Lyon taking up fire tongs to defend himself and the antagonists grappling on the floor. The two representatives were not expelled from the House, but they had to agree to a resolution promising they would not engage in any further personal contests during the session. Lyon later was indicted and jailed under the infamous Sedition Act. See *Annals of the Congress of the United States.* Fifth Congress, 1st Session, pp. 955ff.

LETTER XXIII

1. In Washington Irving's *Knickerbocker's History of New York* (1809), Communipaw was the village on the Jersey shore of New York Bay where the Dutch first settled in America and thus the mother settlement of New York City. Irving saw it as a place where the old way of life had long continued.

LETTER XXIV

1. Marquis de Chastellux (1734–1788), *Voyages de M. le Marquis de Chastellux dans l'Amérique Septentrionale dans les Années 1780, 1781, & 1782*, 2 vols. (Paris, 1786), tr. as *Travels in North-America in the Years 1780, 1781, and 1782*, 2 vols. (London, 1787).

2. The relevant works of Jacques Pierre Brissot de Warville (1754–1793) are *Examen Critique des Voyages dans l'Amérique Septentrionale, de M. le Marquis de Chatellux* (London, 1786), tr. as *A Critical Examination of the Marquis de Chatellux's Travels in North America* (Philadelphia, 1788), and *Nouveau Voyage dans les États-Unis de l'Amérique Septentrionale, fait en 1788*, 3 vols. (Paris, 1791), tr. as *New Travels in the United States of America. Performed in 1788* (London, 1792).

3. John Selden, *Table-Talk* (1st ed.: London, 1689).

4. The new liberal Unitarian views had already been making great headway in New England for some years. In 1785, Episcopalian King's Chapel in Boston had turned Unitarian, and the doctrine had become entrenched at Harvard with the appointment in 1805 of Henry Ware as Hollis professor of theology. The classic statement of Unitarian belief had come just the year before, in 1819, in William Ellery Channing's sermon for the ordination of Jared Sparks in Baltimore.

5. The American Shakers had their origins in a small group of English Quakers, who in 1774 followed their leader, Ann Lee (1736–1784), to America. Accepting the doctrines of open confession of sins and a dual deity, whose second appearance was Mother Ann herself, and practicing celibacy, separation from the world, communal property ownership, industry, and frugality, the Shakers established communities in New England and elsewhere. Fanny Wright is mistaken in her footnote comment that Mother Ann was the niece of Gen. Charles Lee. Joanna Southcott (1750–1814), an English religious fanatic, attracted large numbers of followers, especially when she declared she was soon to be delivered of the second messiah. Jemima Wilkinson (1752–1819), an American religious fanatic, who called herself the "Public Universal Friend," and believed that the "Spirit of Life" had inhabited her body, founded a colony in western New York state.

6. Connecticut disestablished the Congregational Church in 1818; disestablishment of the Congregational Church in Massachusetts was not carried out until 1833. As late as 1792, the Massachusetts legislature gave local authorities the power to deter those traveling on Sunday, and during the first quarter of the nineteenth century a lively dispute went on over the opening of post offices for Sunday mail delivery.

LETTER XXV

1. Francis Kinlock Huger (1773–1855).

2. Constantin F. Volney, *View of the Climate and Soil of the United States of America,* Eng. tr. (London, 1804), pp. 209–210.

LETTER XXVI

1. Probably William Windham (1750–1810), for many years a prominent member of Parliament.

2. The first federal law to protect immigrants from the worst conditions of transatlantic

travel was passed in 1819, the same year that a systematic enumeration of immigrant arrivals was first kept.

3. Fearon, *Sketches of America*, pp. 149–151.

4. Quoted in review of *"Der Deutsche in Nord Amerika"* in *North American Review*, XI (July 1820), 8.

5. One of the three Graces, Mirth or Joy.

LETTER XXVII

1. Two travelers: Matthew Bramble, a kindly but irascible figure in Tobias Smollett's *Humphry Clinker* (1771), and Smelfungus, a splenetic character in Laurence Sterne's *Sentimental Journey through France and Italy* (1768).

2. Maj. Gen. Robert Ross (1766–1814) led the British expeditionary forces to the American coast in the War of 1812. After his victory at Bladensburg he took Washington, D.C., burning many of the public buildings; on his march to Baltimore he was killed at North Point, Maryland.

LETTER XXVIII

1. Henry Baldwin (1780–1844), a protectionist, was chairman of the House Committee on Domestic Manufactures.

2. Henry Clay (1777–1852) was a member of the House of Representatives during the years 1811–1814, 1815–1821, and 1823–1825, and served as speaker the same years except 1821.

3. William Lowndes (1782–1822), from South Carolina, had been one of the "War Hawks" elected to Congress in 1810; he later served as chairman of the House Committees on Ways and Means and Foreign Affairs.

4. The minimum age for a senator set by the Constitution is thirty years.

5. In retaliation for the burning of York, the capital of Upper Canada, British troops burned the Capitol and the White House in 1814. Rebuilding was begun in 1815.

6. Washington remained buried at Mount Vernon. The statue of Washington, on which Canova was working at this time in Italy, was for the North Carolina state capitol, not for the United States Capitol. This classical statue of Washington, in the act of penning a message (in Italian) to the people of the United States, was shipped from Italy in 1821 and destroyed by fire in 1831.

7. The residence of George IV when prince of Wales.

8. Edward Coles (1786–1868) had served six years as private secretary to President Madison, rather than to Jefferson, though he had corresponded with Jefferson concerning slavery. Coles was subsequently elected governor of Illinois.

INDEX

THE JOHN HARVARD LIBRARY

*The intent of
Waldron Phoenix Belknap, Jr.,
as expressed in an early will, was for
Harvard College to use the income from a
permanent trust fund he set up, for "editing and
publishing rare, inaccessible, or hitherto unpublished
source material of interest in connection with the
history, literature, art (including minor and useful
art), commerce, customs, and manners or way of
life of the Colonial and Federal Periods of the United
States . . . In all cases the emphasis shall be on the
presentation of the basic material." A later testament
broadened this statement, but Mr. Belknap's interests remained constant until his death.*

*In linking the name of the first benefactor of
Harvard College with the purpose of this later,
generous-minded believer in American culture the
John Harvard Library seeks to emphasize the importance of Mr. Belknap's purpose. The John Harvard
Library of the Belknap Press of Harvard University
Press exists to make books and documents
about the American past more readily
available to scholars and the
general reader.*